American Jewish Women and the Zionist Enterprise

American Jewish Women and the Zionist Enterprise

Edited by

Shulamit Reinharz and Mark A. Raider

BRANDEIS UNIVERSITY PRESS
Waltham, Massachusetts

PUBLISHED BY UNIVERSITY PRESS OF NEW ENGLAND
HANOVER AND LONDON

BRANDEIS UNIVERSITY PRESS

Published by University Press of New England,
One Court Street, Lebanon, NH 03766
www.upne.com
© 2005 by Brandeis University Press
Printed in the United States of America

5 4 3 2 1

Library of Congress Cataloguing-in-Publication Data

American Jewish women and the Zionist enterprise / edited by Shulamit Reinharz and Mark A. Raider.
   p.   cm. — (Brandeis series on Jewish women) (Brandeis series in American Jewish history, culture, and life)
Includes bibliographical references and index.
ISBN 1-58465-438-4 (cloth : alk. paper) — ISBN 1-58465-439-2 (pbk. : alk. paper)
1. Jewish women—United States—Biography. 2. Zionists—United States—Biography.
3. Jewish women—United States—Societies and clubs. 4. Zionism—United States—Societies, etc. 5. Jews, American—Palestine—Biography. 6. Jewish women—Palestine—Biography. 7. Jews, American—Israel—Biography. 8. Jewish women—Israel—Biography. I. Reinharz, Shulamit. II. Raider, Mark A. III. Series. IV. Series: Brandeis series in American Jewish history, culture, and life
E184.36.W64A52 2004
320.54'095694—dc22   2004020265

Brandeis Series on Jewish Women

Shulamit Reinharz, General Editor

Joyce Antler, Associate Editor

Sylvia Barack Fishman, Associate Editor

The Brandeis Series on Jewish Women is an innovative book series created by The Hadassah-Brandeis Institute. BSJW publishes a wide range of books by and about Jewish women in diverse contexts and time periods, of interest to scholars, and for the educated public. The series fills a major gap in Jewish learning by focusing on the lives of Jewish women and Jewish gender studies.

Marjorie Agosín, *Uncertain Travelers: Conversations with Jewish Women Immigrants to America,* 1999

Rahel R. Wasserfall, editor, *Women and Water: Menstruation in Jewish Life and Law,* 1999

Susan Starr Sered, *What Makes Women Sick? Militarism, Maternity, and Modesty in Israeli Society,* 2000

Pamela S. Nadell and Jonathan D. Sarna, editors, *Women and American Judaism: Historical Perspectives,* 2001

Ludmila Shtern, *Leaving Leningrad: The True Adventures of a Soviet Émigré,* 2001

Jael Silliman, *Jewish Portraits, Indian Frames: Women's Narratives from a Diaspora of Hope,* 2001

Judith R. Baskin, *Midrashic Women: Formations of the Feminine in Rabbinic Literature,* 2002

ChaeRan Y. Freeze, *Jewish Marriage and Divorce in Imperial Russia,* 2002

Mark A. Raider and Miriam B. Raider-Roth, editors, *The Plough Woman: Records of the Pioneer Women of Palestine,* 2002

Elizabeth Wyner Mark, editor, *The Covenant of Circumcision: New Perspectives on an Ancient Jewish Rite,* 2003

Kalpana Misra and Melanie S. Rich, editors, *Jewish Feminism in Israel: Some Contemporary Perspectives,* 2003

Farideh Goldin, *Wedding Song: Memoirs of an Iranian Jewish Woman,* 2003

Rochelle L. Millen, *Women, Birth, and Death in Jewish Law and Practice,* 2003

Sylvia Barack Fishman, *Double or Nothing? Jewish Families and Mixed Marriage,* 2004

Iris Parush, *Women's Reading and the Eastern European Jewish Enlightenment*, 2004

Shulamit Reinharz and Mark A. Raider, editors, *American Jewish Women and the Zionist Enterprise*, 2004

Tamar Ross, *Expanding the Palace of Torah: Orthodoxy and Feminism*, 2004

Brandeis Series in American Jewish History, Culture, and Life

Jonathan D. Sarna, Editor

Sylvia Barack Fishman, Associate Editor

Roberta Rosenberg Farber and Chaim I. Waxman, editors, 1999
Jews in America: A Contemporary Reader

Murray Friedman and Albert D. Chernin, editors, 1999
A Second Exodus: The American Movement to Free Soviet Jews

Stephen J. Whitfield, 1999
In Search of American Jewish Culture

Naomi W. Cohen, 1999
Jacob H. Schiff: A Study in American Jewish Leadership

Barbara Kessel, 2000
Suddenly Jewish: Jews Raised as Gentiles

Jonathan N. Barron and Eric Murphy Selinger, editors, 2000
Jewish American Poetry: Poems, Commentary, and Reflections

Steven T. Rosenthal, 2001
Irreconcilable Differences: The Waning of the American Jewish Love Affair wih Israel

Pamela S. Nadell and Jonathan Sarna, editors, 2001
Women and American Judaism: Historical Perspectives

Annelise Orleck, with photographs by Elizabeth Cooke, 2001
The Soviet Jewish Americans

Ilana Abramovitch and Seán Galvin, editors, 2001
Jews of Brooklyn

Ranen Omer-Sherman, 2002
Diaspora and Zionism in American Jewish Literature: Lazarus, Syrkin, Reznikoff, and Roth

Ori Z. Soltes, 2003
Fixing the World: Jewish American Painters in the Twentieth Century

David Zurawik, 2003
The Jews of Prime Time

Ava F. Kahn and Marc Dollinger, editors, 2003
California Jews

Naomi W. Cohen, 2003
The Americanization of Zionism, 1897-1948

Gary P. Zola, editor, 2003
The Dynamics of American Jewish History: Jacob Rader Marcus's Essays on American Jewry

Judah M. Cohen, 2003
Through the Sands of Time: A History of the Jewish Community of St. Thomas, U.S. Virgin Islands

Seth Farber, 2003
   An American Orthodox Dreamer: Rabbi Joseph B. Soloveitchik and Boston's Maimonides School

Amy L. Sales and Leonard Saxe, 2003
   "How Goodly Are Thy Tents": Summer Camps as Jewish Socializing Experiences

Sylvia Barack Fishman, 2004
   Double or Nothing: Jewish Families and Mixed Marriage

George M. Goodwin and Ellen Smith, 2004
   The Jews of Rhode Island

Shulamit Reinharz and Mark A. Raider, editors, 2004
   American Jewish Women and the Zionist Enterprise

Michael E. Staub, editor, 2004
   The Jewish '60s: A Sourcebook

Contents

PART II

PART III

PART IV

Preface

In June 1998 the process of investigating the global interplay between women and Zionism began with a conference at the Hebrew University of Jerusalem that focused on the impact of Jewish women (in general) on the creation of the State of Israel. This conference may have been the first in Israel in which academics were gathered to present research on the history of women in the Yishuv and Israel. A book stemming from that conference was published recently in Hebrew and is currently being translated into English for future publication.* In March 1999 a related conference was held at Brandeis University, focusing on the role of *American* Jewish women vis-à-vis Zionism and the Yishuv. The conferences were cosponsored by the Hadassah-Brandeis Institute and the Jacob and Libby Goodman Institute for the Study of Israel and Zionism, both of which are part of Brandeis University, as well as the Hebrew University of Jerusalem's Lafer Center for Women's Studies. Fifty years after the creation of the State of Israel, the conferences broke new ground and threw considerable light on hitherto neglected facets of Jewish, Zionist, and women's history.

Although *American Jewish Women and the Zionist Enterprise* stems from the Brandeis symposium, it is not an anthology of conference proceedings. Some papers delivered at the conference are not included here, while others were specially solicited for inclusion in this volume.

Since the conference, many individuals, colleagues, and institutions have assisted and supported us in bringing this book project to realization. We thank Phyllis Deutsch, our editor at the University Press of New England, who recognized the significance of *American Jewish Women and the Zionist Enterprise* and offered useful advice from the outset of the project. We owe a debt of gratitude to the many outstanding American, Canadian, European, and Israeli colleagues who participated in the 1998 and 1999 international conferences that spawned this project. We are deeply grateful to Sylvia Barack Fishman, Sylvia Fuks Fried, and Jonathan

---

*Margalit Shilo, Ruth Kark, and Galit Hasan Rokem, eds., *Haivriyot hahadashot: Nashim bayishuv ubazionut berei hamigdar* [The New Jewish Women: Women, the Yishuv and Zionism from the Perspective of Gender] (Jerusalem: Yad Yizhak Ben-Zvi Press, 2001), Hebrew.

D. Sarna for their significant roles in this regard. Thanks are also due to our contributors for their patience and faith in the process that led to the publication of this book. Many other friends and colleagues played critical roles in the volume's production, too. Pamela Nadell and Erica Werfel, a summer intern in the Hadassah-Brandeis Institute, provided valuable assistance with the historical timeline. Mark Schmidt prepared the camera-ready artwork. Sam Bloch of the Herzl Press, David Bodansky, Michael Feldberg of the American Jewish Historical Society, Harriet Korim, and Anita Shapira graciously permitted us to reprint some key items. Kristen Drown, Mary Lou Edmondson, Evyatar Friesel, Miriam Hoffman, Paula Hyman, Stanley Isser, Rafael Medoff, Deborah Dash Moore, Jim Rosenbloom, Shimon Schwartz, Deena Schwimmer, Lyn Slome, Ellen Smith, Judith A. Sokoloff, Jennifer Thomas, Barbara Vinick, and Susan Woodland helped in numerous ways as we readied the manuscript for publication. Last, we are very grateful to Melissa Caro-Ortiz in the Hadassah-Brandeis Institute and Yoel Hirschfeld in the Center for Jewish Studies at the University at Albany, State University of New York, for their cheerful and unflagging technical assistance.

This project also benefited from significant grants and funding provided by the Hadassah-Brandeis Institute, the Jacob and Libby Goodman Institute for the Study of Zionism and Israel, and the Center for Jewish Studies at the University at Albany. Special funding was provided by the Donna Sudarsky Memorial Fund. We are grateful to the aforementioned institutions and agencies, without whose support the project would not have been feasible. Finally, we thank our families for their steadfast interest and encouragement from start to finish.

Waltham, Massachusetts   S.R.
Albany, New York   M.A.R.

Editors' Note

American Jewish Women and the Zionist Enterprise seeks to strike a balance between honoring the integrity of the texts and contributions presented here and the obvious need for an overarching conceptual and structural apparatus that makes the volume useful and accessible for students, scholars, and interested lay readers alike. To this end, we have been careful to use precise terminology throughout the book such as *moshavah, moshav,* and *kibbutz* instead of "colony," "village," or "settlement"—the vague phraseology characteristic of many English-language works on Zionist history and pre-state Israeli society. We also made minor emendations and adjustments to various items in order to unify and enhance the text overall. For example, we modified somewhat the orthography and transliteration of Hebrew and Yiddish, to give English-speaking readers as clear a phonetic equivalent as possible without introducing complex diacritical marks and special linguistic values. Exceptions in this regard are terms and names for which a different usage is highly familiar (e.g., *kibbutz,* Mizrachi Women's Organization of America, Yishuv, etc.). Some common English spellings have been retained for the sake of ease and readibility (e.g., Tiberias, Nablus, Jaffa, etc.). We also included birth and death dates for key figures mentioned in the introductory remarks that frame each section and chapter; however, we did not elect to insert such information into each individual chapter. It is also worth noting that although the glossary of terms attempts to be fairly complete, it does not include phraseology and/or terms that appear infrequently in the book. Rather, to assist the reader, this information has been inserted in the text. Finally, the synonymous place-names *Erez Israel* [Land of Israel], Palestine, Yishuv, and Jewish national home are used interchangeably throughout the book in accordance with the appropriate cultural-political context.

Introduction

Shulamit Reinharz and Mark A. Raider

In 1917, at the height of World War I, the British government issued the Balfour Declaration, effectively recognizing and sanctioning Zionist aspirations for an independent Jewish commonwealth in the postwar Middle East. This shift in British policy marked a dramatic turning point in nearly forty years of Zionist expression and activities in Eastern and Western Europe and, to a lesser extent, in the United States. Thereafter, the Balfour Declaration, which in 1922 was approved by other Allied governments and incorporated into the British Mandate for Palestine, remained hotly contested as Great Britain employed ambiguous strategies to balance competing Zionist aspirations and Arab demands. Tensions continued to rise in the 1930s and 1940s as Britain wavered between appeasing Arab interests, severely curtailing the Zionist enterprise, and exploring possibilities for partioning Palestine. In this period, a small, but increasingly robust Zionist movement developed outside of Palestine in Europe, the United States, and elsewhere. Three decades after the Balfour Declaration, following World War II and the destruction of European Jewry in the Holocaust, Jewish public opinion shifted to an even stronger embrace of Zionism, and an inernational consensus crystallized around the necessity of creating a Jewish state. In 1947, the United Nations voted to partition Palestine and create separate Jewish and Arab states. Following the withdrawal of the British from Palestine and with the support of the United States, the Soviet Union, and other western governments, the Zionist movement immediately established the State of Israel. The Arab bloc rejected the Jewish state, however, and the first in a series of Israel–Arab wars ensued. Thus the State of Israel and the Palestinian Arab nationalist movement arose in the context of a bitter struggle that continues to this day.

Though geographically remote, events in Palestine and the Middle East had a profound impact on diaspora Jewry, including American Jews. American Jews played a significant role in Zionism's development from the 1880s onward and the importance of the American Zionist movement increased swiftly in the years following World War I. Moreover, American Jewish women played roles as important as men did in the pre-state period. In fact, Zionist women's groups in the United States quickly outpaced their

male counterparts and, in many instances, became more significant with respect to grassroots organizing and philanthropy. In 1925, for example,
both the centrist Zionist Organization of America (ZOA) and Hadassah,
the Women's Zionist Organization of America, had countrywide memberships of approximately 27,000. A decade later the ZOA membership had
dropped to less than 17,000 while Hadassah (which declined somewhat
during the Depression) rose to approximately 33,000. Thereafter, Hadassah's membership trajectory stayed well ahead of the ZOA, except for a
brief period on the eve of statehood when the ZOA attained parity with
Hadassah and reached its peak strength of 250,000. A similar pattern is evident with respect to fund-raising and philanthropy, although here the
record is somewhat less clear owing to the fact that Hadassah conducted a
separate fund-raising campaign even as its members participated in the nationwide communal drives of the United Palestine Appeal, which was
headed by the ZOA leadership.[1] As both areas of American Zionist activity
illustrate, American Jewish women played central roles in shaping the
Zionist movement in the United States and determining much of its trajectory. In fact, as the essays in this volume demonstrate, it is virtually impossible to appreciate the scope of pre-state Zionist activity in the United
States—and some key social and political initiatives in Palestine—without
considering the pivotal role played by American Jewish women leaders and
women's groups in advancing and sustaining the Zionist agenda. And yet,
as is true for so many facets of history, the scholarly and popular record is
still remarkably thin in this regard. To rectify this imbalance, our book
seeks to focus attention on American Jewish women and Zionism and, as a
result, to reshape the historical lens through which the pre-state era is generally viewed.

American Jewish Women and the Zionist Enterprise introduces a
range of fresh themes, topics, and approaches to the study of American
Jewish women, Zionism, and the Yishuv (pre-state Israeli society). It also
raises several new and intriguing research questions: What roles did
American Jewish women play as Zionist activists and thinkers? What was
their impact on the creation of the State of Israel? Were they bystanders
or leaders? Did they have a "different voice" from that of American Jewish men who subscribed to Zionism in this period? What were the political, cultural, financial, and social accomplishments of American Jewish
women in the field of Zionism? Though all of these questions cannot be
answered definitively in a single volume, many answers are provided and

---

1. Samuel Halperin, *The Political World of American Zionism* (Silver Spring, Md.: Information Dynamics, 1985), reprint, appendixes IV and V, 325–327.

others are suggested. To this end, the volume is divided into four parts. Part 1 delineates three generational paradigms in the evolution of American Jewish women's understanding of the Zionist idea. Each of the figures singled out here was unique, but not necessarily untypical. In other words, while Emma Lazarus (1849–1887), Henrietta Szold (1860–1945), and Marie Syrkin (1899–1989) were each uniquely talented visionaries, theirs was a Zionism that reflected the myriad concerns, strivings, and dreams of American Jewish women of the times in which they lived, played, and worked.

It is important to note that American Jewish women generally lived under an unusual set of circumstances in the late nineteenth and early twentieth centuries. In stark contrast to their counterparts in much of Europe, Jewish women in the United States enjoyed increasing freedom of individual movement and expression, and some even possessed funds for philanthropic activities. Such liberties and assets were almost totally lacking in eastern Europe, where traditional gender-differentiated Jewish values and systems prevailed and where the possibility for Jewish participation in the host society was marginal. In many situations, Jewish women experienced double oppression—as Jews in an antisemitic milieu and as women in a patriarchal society. The lack of birth control, of opportunities for education, and of a secure income severely restricted the lives of Jewish women in eastern and central Europe. In the United States, these forces were muted.

In fact, in late-nineteenth-century America, Jewish women were able to expand and deepen even their participation in American Jewish religious life. The arrival of 2.5 million East European Jewish immigrants between 1880 and 1924, including many thousands of radicalized young Yiddish-speaking women, helped create the American Jewish labor movement and some of the most important American labor entities including the International Ladies' Garment Workers' Union. Jewish women became involved in the anti-prostitution movement, the Settlement House movement, the suffrage movement, and in the birth-control movement.

The twin themes of female and Jewish liberation also impelled many thousands—and later hundreds of thousands—of American Jewish women to view the new Jewish community in the Land of Israel as a model. This Jewish country could embody, they believed, a reflection of what modern society ought to be: pluralistic, healthy, welcoming, egalitarian, and accessible to all Jews. The fact that very few American Zionist women expected to actually set foot in Palestine did not represent a contradiction for them. It simply meant that their ideology would remain romantic and insulated from the harsh reality of Jewish life in Ottoman and then British Palestine. Zionism for these women became a way of fighting their own assimilationist tendencies, rather than a way of addressing the ideological imperative of emigration.

Although the number of American Zionists who actually immigrated to Palestine was never large, the number of Jewish women who subscribed to the Zionist cause was significant. In fact, as noted previously, women's Zionist organizations in the United States were frequently stronger and more effective than their male counterparts. This was particularly true of the major American Zionist women's groups: Hadassah, the Pioneer Women's Organization, and the Mizrachi Women's Organization.[2] The essays in Part II demonstrate that these and other organizations were diverse in outlook and opened up important new avenues of social, cultural, and political activism for women from all walks of American Jewish life.

A minority of American Jewish women viewed Zionism as a mechanism for self-fulfillment or what came to be known in Zionist parlance as *"hagshamah azmit"* [self-realization]. This idealistic and romantic sensibility of personally participating in the building of a new Jewish society in Palestine resonated with the entire length and breadth of the American Jewish spectrum, and it attracted adherents from all walks of American Jewish life—from secular and religious quarters, from different age groups and social classes, and from a variety of cultural and political orientations. Thus, it is not at all surprising to find (as many of the pieces in Parts II, III, and IV illustrate) a wide array of American Jewish women who found in Zionism an opportunity to revolutionize their own lives and, in the process, participate fully in the construction of a new Jewish social reality—whether as pioneers of Zionist settlement groups like the religious Hashomer Hadati and secular Habonim movements, as political activists who rose through the ranks of American Jewish women's organizations to become political leaders in the Jewish Agency and the Histadrut [General Federation of Jewish Laborers in the Land of Israel], or as devoted social workers, nurses, teachers, and the like who would become influential and innovative figures in a variety of rural and urban settings throughout the Yishuv.

The latter developments stemmed from a groundswell of popular interest in Zionism in the United States, especially among East European Jewish immigrants, which in turn led to the creation of a diverse array of Zionist women's organizations and groups by the 1920s and 1930s.

2. Ibid.

Nonetheless, in this period card-carrying Zionists remained a numerically insignificant minority. The vast majority of American Jews focused on their own swift upward mobility and the promise of prosperity in America, that is, a better life for their children. The challenges and travails of the *other* Promised Land and Palestine's new Jewish society-in-the-making seemed remote and obscure to many, even if it had meaning in a religious or cultural sense. How this relationship was strengthened and evolved among American Jewish women is one of the themes explored in Part II of this volume. By examining many of the key organizational partnerships of American Zionist women in the pre-state period, this book argues that the nexus between American Jewish women, the Zionist enterprise, and the Land of Israel was more broadly and richly developed—and that it began much earlier—than most scholars have previously recognized. As such, this phenomenon must be viewed as a critical component of the American Jewish experience.

Another relationship this volume examines is that between men and women in American Zionism. For example, since its inception in 1897 the Federation of American Zionists (renamed the Zionist Organization of America during World War I) purported to be *the* representative body of the American movement. Though the rank and file consisted of men and women, the organization's leadership was entirely male. Relegated to conventional and secondary roles, female ZOA members performed social functions rather than substantive ones and were shunted to the margins of political activity. In 1912 a few Jewish women had created their own Zionist organization, named Hadassah. As Hadassah grew and flourished, the ZOA leadership demanded that it fold into the male-dominated ZOA. In a remarkable instance of resistance, American Zionist women decided to take matters into their own hands and establish a separate, independent organization rather than allow Hadassah to become the ZOA's female auxiliary. The new American *women's* Zionist organization determined to assume a full range of social, financial, and political roles—challenges that are analyzed by several essays in this volume.

Not only did the ZOA stand to lose a significant portion of its membership and the women's services; it was also threatened with stiff competition. In the event, the ZOA leadership sought to compel Henrietta Szold to merge Hadassah into the organization's ranks. Szold refused. She was interested in mobilizing American Jewish women and foresaw the potential and power of a distinct Zionist women's organization. Indeed, American women's colleges, medical schools, and other institutions had already successfully employed a similar strategy. A crisis ensued, but

Szold held firm. Since that time, Hadassah has grown to become the largest Jewish women's organization in the world. It remains a powerful and, arguably, the most significant Zionist group in the United States. By contrast, the ZOA has enjoyed only sporadic organizational and political success.

With some variation, the scenario described above was repeated in other Zionist quarters. For example, Poalei Zion [Workers of Zion], the American wing of the Russian socialist Zionist party, opposed the establishment of a separate women's organization. Similarly, when Pioneer Women was created in 1925, it too became more successful than its male counterpart. But, as a few essays here demonstrate, Pioneer Women is instructive in an additional way: it highlights the impact of Jewish women *from* Palestine on the mobilization of American Jewish women. In this case, American women's Zionist activity and ideology were not exclusively a product of conditions in America, of Jews generally, or of women. Rather, these spheres were strongly influenced by female emissaries from Palestine, charismatic leaders such as Rahel Yanait Ben-Zvi (1886–1979) and Manya Wilbushewitz Shohat (1880–1961). They, in turn, helped to cultivate "American" leaders like Golda (Meyerson) Meir (1898–1978) and Irma "Rama" Levy Lindheim (1886–1978) who would become significant figures in Zionist and Israeli political circles.

Furthermore, American Zionist women leaders like Henrietta Szold, Golda Meir, Irma Lindheim, and Marie Syrkin traveled back and forth between Palestine and the United States, bringing with them compelling descriptions and instructive reports of life in the Yishuv and forging a bond between the two communities. In general, Hadassah appealed to a new generation of middle-class English-speaking American Jewish women. Pioneer Women attracted working-class first- and second-generation Jewish women from the Yiddish-speaking immigrant milieu. And American Orthodox Jewish women gravitated to the Mizrachi Women's Organization and other Zionist groups within the traditionalist community. In all cases, ranging among the varied classes and religious spheres, American Jewish women understood their Zionist activities in terms of both aiding the Jewish community in Palestine and retaining their own Jewish identity through self-education. In addition, the focus of the women's organizations was on fund-raising and social projects, particularly projects that would aid women and families.

As mentioned above, despite the historical record, the nexus between American Jewish women, Zionism, and Palestine has received only scant scholarly attention. This omission has seriously hampered understanding of Zionist history in general and of women's Zionist activity in particular. Nor has the intersection of American Zionism and American women's history been closely examined. *American Jewish Women and the Zionist Enterprise* begins to fill these gaps.

Thus, the aim of this book is, in part, to prompt scholars to undertake significant new research in a variety of disciplines. It asserts that the relationship between Zionism and American Jewish women was (and remains) multifaceted. Moreover, a variety of methodological and disciplinary approaches are needed such as feminist methods, social history, American women's history, American Jewish history, European Jewish history, Zionist history, and Israel studies. A case in point is the figure of Henrietta Szold, a historical personality whose centrality is evident in many of the essays published here. Szold is an outstanding example of the interplay between the triad of America, Europe, and Palestine in the pre-state era. Her distinct political ideology—reflecting her upbringing as an American Jew of central European ancestry, with several sisters, a rabbi father, and devoted mother—developed long before the success of the American suffrage movement. Clearly influenced by the general ferment among American women who engaged in this significant political project, she was encouraged and influenced by the social activism of Jane Addams (1860–1935) and women in American Progressive circles. Like Addams, Szold was an unmarried and highly educated woman. She forged a meaningful life of her own, developing her own resources to support herself and further the interests of her people. In time, she emerged as a towering leader of American Jewry and the Zionist movement. And yet, notwithstanding the rising profile of Zionist biography as a literary and scholarly genre, there is still no first-rate comprehensive study of the life and times of this remarkable woman.

This lacuna is partly the result of a lack of serious spadework related to women's Zionist history. Cognizant of this vast wilderness, we have assembled here a variety of contributors: men and women, senior scholars and newcomers to the field of Jewish women's studies, and Israelis, Canadians, and Americans. They are historians, sociologists, political scientists, and political activists. Within the context of the volume, they fall into two categories: scholars who provide analytic interpretations *and* individuals who played an actual role in the events under discussion. So, too, the contributions in this book are of two types: scholarly articles *and* eyewitness accounts.

American Jewish Women and the Zionist Enterprise is divided thematically and deals with representative figures, events, and themes of the pre-state era. We hope that this organizing framework makes the subject matter accessible to a broad readership and useful to future researchers. Taken as a whole, the essays in the book have three different foci. Eight pieces are concerned with *significant personalities* (Rose Viteles, Irma Lindheim, Sara Bodek Patliel, Golda Meir, Marie Syrkin, Emma Lazarus, Bessie Gotsfeld, and Henrietta Szold). Several others are concerned with the pivotal role played by American Zionist women's *organizations* (Hadassah-WIZO Canada, American Hadassah, the International Council of Jewish Women, the Pioneer Women's Organization, and the Mizrachi Women's Organization). The remaining essays throw light on *broad themes* and reveal the multidimensionality of the relationship of American Jewish women and Zionism: agricultural and vocational training, religion, ideology, geography, and feminism and femininity.

The inclusion of a variety of personalities and organizations in *American Jewish Women and the Zionist Enterprise* is a distinctive feature of this book. The multiplicity of ideological backgrounds and positions counteracts the parochial and outdated perspective that views the history of American Zionist women through the prism of one organization (i.e., Hadassah). By offering essays on a range of topics, we can better understand the ideological differences among American Zionist women, and we can examine them as thinkers *and* political activists. Women's ideological formulations are no less significant and complex than their actions, and vice versa.

The range of organizations covered in this volume is likewise important. Our contributors deal with socialist, mainstream, and religious branches of Zionism. This spectrum illustrates the fact that some American women's Zionist organizations focused on initiating social and health services while others provided funds to enable women of the Yishuv to create viable political organizations (e.g., nursing stations, women's agricultural training farms, clandestine self-defense groups, etc.).

Furthermore, we contend that a treasure trove of previously neglected and untapped primary materials awaits scholarly investigation. By way of example, we have gathered here several eyewitness documents and personal testimonies, which illustrate the perspectives and voices of American Jewish women who participated in the Zionist enterprise. Together, they represent an aggregate of attitudinal and experiential data requiring careful and systematic scrutiny. No less significant than the corpus of memoirs and literature produced by male Zionist leaders, such data throws light on crucial areas of American Jewish and Zionist history that are virtually uncharted, including the variety of roles played by Zionist women and their self-awareness as participants in one of the most dramatic and consequential episodes in the history of Jewish civilization.

New and innovative analytic tools derived from feminist methods are required in order to plumb the depths of such writings.[3] The fruits of such scrutiny promise to fundamentally reshape our understanding of Zionist history, American Jewish history, and women's history. In the process, we hope that individuals involved in this activity will gather research materials and deposit them in archives for future students of the subject.

This book offers readers various aids to facilitate a fuller understanding of the issues. These include a glossary of terms, a map of the principal locations referred to in the text, illustrations, and a timeline of American Jewish women and Zionism. Each part opens with a prefatory note that places the essays in historical context. Likewise, the chapters themselves are introduced by brief remarks intended to help guide the reader. We also annotated the historical documents that accompany the analytic essays on Emma Lazarus, Henrietta Szold, and Marie Syrkin in Part I as well as the documentary portraits in Part IV. Unlike the contributors' citations, which appear at the end of each chapter, our footnotes appear on the same page as the primary sources in question in order to assist readers unfamiliar with American Jewish and Zionist history. Last, the volume concludes with a bibliographic note that traces the broad outlines of scholarship (in English) on American Jewish women, Zionism, and the Land of Israel in the nineteenth and twentieth centuries. If such tools equip readers to better evaluate the complex and controversial issues at the core of this book *and* prompt students and researchers to mine the hitherto neglected topic of American Jewish women and the Zionist enterprise, our efforts to produce this anthology will have been justified.

3. See, for example, Judith R. Baskin, ed., *Jewish Women in Historical Perspective*, second ed. (Detroit: Wayne State University Press, 1998); Linda K. Kerber and Jane Sherron De Hart, eds., *Women's America: Refocusing the Past*, third ed. (New York and Oxford: Oxford University Press, 1991); Amia Lieblich and Ruthellen Josselson, eds., *Interpreting Experience: The Narrative Study of Lives* (Thousand Oaks and London: Sage Publications, 1995), Ann Oakley, *The Sociology of Housework* (New York: Random House, 1975); Shulamit Reinharz, *Feminist Methods in Social Research* (New York and Oxford: Oxford University Press, 1992).

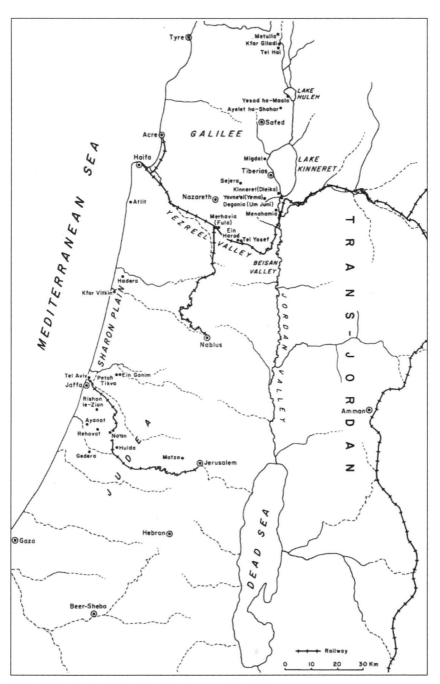

Map of Palestine in the Pre-State Era. Courtesy of Anita Shapira.

Timeline of American Jewish Women and
Zionism in Historical Context, 1848–1948

American Jewish Women and Zionism	American Jewish Affairs	Europe, Palestine, and World Jewish Affairs	General World History
			1848 Central European revolutions Karl Marx and Friedrich Engels publish *Communist Manifesto*
	Mid-19th century Proto-Zionist advocates argue that Jewish settlement in *Erez Israel* is a necessary precondition for the survival and redemption of the Jewish people, marking a radical departure from traditional Jewish attitudes		
	1855 Hebrew Ladies' Benevolent Association founded in San Francisco	**1858** Mortara Affair (Bologna, Italy): After Edgardo Mortara's nurse secretly baptized the six-year-old in her charge, church officials seize the boy, sparks worldwide protests	**1859** Charles Darwin publishes *Origin of the Species*
	1861 Hebrew Free Sewing Society established in Baltimore	**1860** Alliance Israélite Universelle established in France to help Jews worldwide	**1861–1865** American Civil War
	1862 General Ulysses S. Grant issues Order No. 11 expelling Jews from Kentucky, Tennessee, and Mississippi; rescinded by Abraham Lincoln	**1862** First Jewish colonization organization created in Frankfurt am Main, Germany	
	1864 Ladies' Hebrew Widow and Orphan Society established in Denver		

(continued)

American Jewish Women and Zionism	American Jewish Affairs	Europe, Palestine, and World Jewish Affairs	General World History
	1882 First Hovevei Zion [Lovers of Zion] group in U.S.A. founded in New York	**1882** Leon Pinsker publishes *Auto-Emancipation*, lays the groundwork for early Zionist political theory and activity Rise of Bilu socialist Zionist pioneer movement in Russia Hovevei Zion movement (also known as Hibbat Zion) starts in eastern Europe; the first political expression of modern Jewish nationalism; some Hovevei Zion groups establish colonies in Palestine	
	1883 Emma Lazarus's poem "The New Colossus," later inscribed on the Statue of Liberty, welcomes immigrants as "huddled masses yearning to breathe free"	**1882–1903** First Aliyah to Palestine, consisting of traditionalist, lower-middle-class families, results in creation of rural colonies Rishon Lezion, Nes Zionah, Zikhron Yaakov, and Rosh Pinah	
	1884 American branch of Hovevei Zion organized in New York	**1884** Kattowitz Conference results in consolidation of Hibbat Zion movement	

1885
Leaders of Reform Judaism promulgate Pittsburgh Platform, repudiating idea of return of Jews to Land of Israel and Jewish nationalism

1886
Jewish Theological Seminary founded; becomes center of Conservative Judaism

1888
Jewish Publication Society of America established

United Hebrew Trades founded

1889
Reform rabbis organize Central Conference of American Rabbis

1893
Congress of Jewish Women convenes at the World's Columbian Exposition in Chicago; on its last day its members found the National Council of Jewish Women, with Hannah Greenebaum Solomon as head

1896
Rabbi Isaac Elchanan Theological Seminary, later part of Yeshiva

1888
Henrietta Szold joins leadership of Jewish Publication Society of America (JPS); JPS publishes English translations of literature by proto-Zionists and early Zionist figures

1893
Henrietta Szold helps create Baltimore's first Zionist association

1893–1916
Henrietta Szold becomes secretary, actually editor, of Jewish Publication Society's publications committee

1895
Henrietta Szold declares herself a Zionist; one American Jewish newspaper describes it as "a sentiment almost too profound for an American woman"

1895–1899
Rosa Sonneschein, early Zionist advocate, edits *The American Jewess*; she is one of only four Americans to attend First Zionist Congress in 1897

1886
Naftali Herz Imber publishes *Hatikvah* [The Hope], originally titled *Tikvateinu* [Our Hope], in a book of Hebrew poetry

1889
Bnai Moshe group established by the cultural Zionist Ahad Haam in Odessa

1890
Founding of Society for the Support of Jewish Farmers and Artisans in Syria and Palestine (known as the "Odessa Committee")

1891
Jews expelled from Moscow

Jewish Colonization Association created

1896
Theodor Herzl, founder of political Zionism, publishes *Der Judenstaat* [The Jews' State] advocates creation of an autonomous Jewish national home

1894
"Dreyfus Affair": Alfred Dreyfus, French Jewish army captain wrongfully accused of espionage and sentenced to life imprisonment on Devil's Island

(continued)

American Jewish Women and Zionism	American Jewish Affairs	Europe, Palestine, and World Jewish Affairs	General World History
1898 Emma Leon Gottheil attends Second Zionist Congress, later founds first Daughters of Zion study circle in New York	University, begins training Orthodox rabbis National Council of Jewish Women has a national membership of 3370 **1897** Knights of Zion group organized in Chicago, attracts eastern European Jewish intellectuals *Der forverts* [The Forward], leading daily Yiddish newspaper, founded **1898** Union of Orthodox Jewish Congregations established (asserts Zionism can coexist with American patriotism and that Jewish homeland should be used as a refuge) Establishment of the Federation of American Zionists (FAZ), first nationwide American Zionist organization, on July 4	**1897** First Zionist Congress convenes in Basle, Switzerland; World Zionist Organization (WZO) established and Basle Program adopted Bund, Jewish socialist party, founded **1898** Second Zionist Congress **1899** Third Zionist Congress; Jewish Colonial Trust established	**1898** Noted French writer Emile Zola publishes "J'accuse" alleging the French government and military conspired to wrongfully convict Alfred Dreyfus Spanish-American War **1899–1902** Boer War

1900 Sigmund Freud publishes *Interpretation of Dreams*	**1900** Fourth Zionist Congress	**1900** International Ladies' Garment Workers' Union founded; includes sizable number of Jewish immigrants
	First socialist Zionist Poalei Zion [Workers of Zion] groups organized in Russia	
	1901 Fifth Zionist Congress; Jewish National Fund (Keren Kayemet Leyisrael) established	**1901** Joseph Bluestone and Philip Klein withdraw from FAZ and create the United Zionists; Hovevei Zion groups also withdraw
	1902 Mizrahi religious Zionist party founded	**1902** Henrietta Szold studies rabbinics at the Jewish Theological Seminary but will not become a rabbi
	Sejera founded, first experiment in *kibbutz* living	Young Women's Hebrew Association founded in New York City
		In New York City, immigrant Jewish women protest the rising price of kosher meat
	1903 Sixth Zionist Congress	**1903** Establishment of American branch of Poalei Zion [Workers of Zion], offshoot of the Russian Marxist Zionist party
	Disastrous Kishinev pogrom: At least 49 Jews killed and more than 500 injured; worldwide condemnation of the attacks	U.S. government asks the National Council of Jewish Women for

(continued)

American Jewish Women and Zionism	American Jewish Affairs	Europe, Palestine, and World Jewish Affairs	General World History
	assistance in establishing immigrant aid services	**1904** Propelled by the horror of the Kishinev pogrom, Theodor Herzl negotiates with the British to acquire East African territory for Jewish colonization (Uganda Plan); East European Zionists maintain that only Palestine will ensure Jewish survival	
	1904 Conservatives gain control of FAZ		**1904–1905** Russo-Japanese War
		Theodor Herzl dies	
		Manya Wilbushewitz (later Shohat) arrives in Jaffa	
		1904–1918 Second Aliyah (young, single, and primarily male immigrants inspired by socialist Zionism)	
	1905 Zionist societies spring up at Boston University Law School, Tufts, and Harvard	**1905** Seventh Zionist Congress rejects Uganda proposal	**1905** First Russian Revolution
	Eliezer Jaffe founds Hehaluz-Zion Circle, first Zionist pioneering youth movement in the U.S.	Jewish Territorial Organization founded under leadership of Israel Zangwill by Western Jews who withdraw from WZO	Albert Einstein publishes theory of relativity
	Poalei Zion holds first national convention in Philadelphia	Austrian Zionists endorse diaspora nationalism; argue that	Max Weber publishes *The Protestant Ethic and the Spirit of Capitalism*

1906		**1906**
American Jewish Committee founded to defend Jewish civil and religious rights wherever Jews live	Jews should be recognized, culturally and politically as a separate group by diaspora host societies	Dreyfus exonerated
Poalei Zion launches *Der yidisher kemfer* [The Jewish Fighter], weekly Yiddish periodical	Zionist Socialist Workers' Party founded in Russia	
United Zionists merge with FAZ	**1906** Russian Zionists embrace Helsingfors Program to sponsor political and cultural activities for diaspora Jewry; constitutes a major revision of Zionist policy	
Radical anarchist Emma Goldman founds and edits journal *Mother Earth* (until 1918)	Jewish Socialist Workers' Party founded in Russia	
	Poalei Zion Party formally constituted in Russia	
1907	**1907**	
American branches of Mizrachi and Poalei Zion formally declare themselves independent of FAZ; Knights of Zion also declare independent status	Eighth Zionist Congress; declares that groups selling over 3000 shekels (membership dues) worldwide to be recognized as independent	
	World Poalei Zion Party founded at The Hague	

(continued)

American Jewish Women and Zionism	American Jewish Affairs	Europe, Palestine, and World Jewish Affairs	General World History
	1908 FAZ, frustrated with world movement's disregard of American Zionist leadership and positions, nearly votes to sever ties with WZO	1908 Rahel Yanait (later Ben-Zvi) arrives in Palestine	1908 Young Turk Revolution
1909 Henrietta Szold travels to Palestine	1909 New York City Kehillah established	1909 Degania founded, first *kibbutz*	
	Judah L. Magnes founds Achava Club, varied group of Zionist intellectuals committed to diaspora work	Hashomer [The Watchguard] organized	
	20,000 shirtwaist makers, mostly young Jewish girls and women, strike to protest unfair labor practices	Tel Aviv founded	
1910 Henrietta Szold appointed honorary secretary of Federation of American Zionists (FAZ)	1910 Folkshuln [Jewish National Radical Schools] are established by Poalei Zion, emphasize religious and secular subjects and act as Zionist centers	1910 Expulsion of Jews from Kiev	
	In New York, Samson Benderly, head of the first Bureau of Jewish Education, pioneers new methods		

for teaching Hebrew language to American Jewish children

1912
Henrietta Szold founds Daughters of Zion (later renamed Hadassah); Szold serves as Hadassah national president, 1912–1921

Nurses Rose Kaplan and Rachel (Rae D.) Landy are sent by Hadassah to Palestine to offer preventive health care to Jewish settlers (underwritten by Nathan and Lina Straus)

Bertha Landsmen, public health nurse, follows Kaplan and Landy

1913
Jessie Sampter creates Hadassah's education program

1911
Triangle Shirtwaist Factory fire kills 146 women, spurs legal reform of working conditions, and energizes Jewish immigrant women's groups

1913
Knights of Zion reaffiliates with FAZ

Horace M. Kallen founds Perushim [Pharisees], elite Zionist fellowship

Louis D. Brandeis addresses Chelsea Young Men's Hebrew Association, asserts that "multiple loyalties are not objectionable" and Zionism and American patriotism are compatible

Reform Judaism's National Federation of Temple Sisterhoods established, with Carrie Simon as first president

1911
Tenth Zionist Congress approves plan for cooperative Jewish colonies in Palestine

1912
Ada Fishman Maimon arrives in Palestine

1913
Abrogation of U.S.-Russia Treaty due to rift over American Jewish rights

After languishing in a Kiev jail for two years, Menahem Mendel Beilis is acquitted of the charge of ritual murder

(continued)

American Jewish Women and Zionism	American Jewish Affairs	Europe, Palestine, and World Jewish Affairs	General World History
	Atlanta: Leo Frank, a Jewish factory manager from the Northeast, wrongfully accused of murdering thirteen-year-old Mary Phagan; the "Frank Case" buoys southern antisemitism and prompts activism of American Jewish Committee leader Louis Marshall	**1914–1918** World War I forces closure of WZO headquarters and cuts off world movement from Palestine; enormous Jewish suffering as the war engulfs East European Jewry	**1914–1918** World War I, then known as the "Great War"; over 8 million soldiers die; millions of civilian casualties and deaths
1914 Sarah Kussy founds Hadassah branch at Newark, N.J.	**1914** American Jewish Joint Distribution Committee founded to aid Jews caught in the onslaught of World War I		
	American branch of Mizrahi breaks away from FAZ, seeks closer ties to European Mizrahi		
	1914–1918 Provisional Zionist Committee (PZC) created to temporarily assume WZO role; Louis D. Brandeis heads PZC leadership		
	Campaign to elect American Jewish Congress, democratic assembly representing all of American Jewry; Jewish women vote in this election		

1916
Hadassah raises $30,000 for creation of American Zionist Medical Unit in Palestine (AZMU)

1915
David Ben-Gurion expelled from Palestine, comes to U.S. and establishes the Zionist Hehaluz organization

Menorah Journal founded, opens its pages to Jewish intellectuals

Despite inconclusive evidence at trial, Leo Frank sentenced to death; sentence commuted to life imprisonment by Georgia governor; angry mob lynches Frank

East European Jewish immigrant writer Anzia Yezierska publishes *Free Vacation House*

1916
Louis D. Brandeis appointed to U.S. Supreme Court

1917
Elections to American Jewish Congress

Mordecai M. Kaplan advocates political Zionism at convention of Conservative Judaism's United Synagogue of America

1915
Ottoman Turks expel many Zionist pioneers from Palestine who are considered Russian nationals, e.g., David Ben-Gurion, Yizhak Ben-Zvi, and Vladimir (Zeev) Jabotinsky

1916
WZO Actions Committee appeals to American Zionists to send medical personnel and supplies to Palestine

1917
Balfour Declaration: British government supports a national home for the Jewish people in Palestine

1917
U.S. enters war and joins the Allies

Bolshevik Revolution in Russia

(continued)

American Jewish Women and Zionism	American Jewish Affairs	Europe, Palestine, and World Jewish Affairs	General World History
1918 AZMU arrives in Palestine, headed by Alice L. Seligsberg	**1918** American Zionist Conference, Pittsburgh: Louis D. Brandeis reorganizes FAZ into centralized Zionist Organization of America (ZOA), emphasizes economic development of Palestine; Julian W. Mack elected president; Horace M. Kallen drafts the ZOA's "Pittsburgh Program"; ZOA has approximately 150,000 members	**1918** Zionist Commission appointed	**1918** Influenza epidemic begins, kills 20 million worldwide by 1920 Woodrow Wilson supports women's suffrage and calls for new U.S. legislation
1919 Junior Hadassah is formed	American Jewish Congress convenes, is influenced by Zionists to pass resolution calling for a Jewish national home and British mandate in Palestine	**1918–1921** Devastating pogroms against the Jews during the Russian Civil War	**1918–1921** Russian Civil War
Jessie Sampter immigrates to Palestine	Mathilde Roth Schechter founds the National Women's League, Conservative Judaism's sisterhood organization	**1919** Chaim Weizmann, head of the Zionist Commission, and Emir Feisel, son of King Hussein of the Hedjaz, formally agree that Jews and Arabs will cooperate in development of Palestine according to spirit of Balfour Declaration	**1919** Paris Peace Conference;
Mizrachi Women's Auxiliary is founded for Orthodox Zionist women	Mizrachi has 18,000 members	Pogroms in Hungary	Weimar Republic established in Germany
Hadassah establishes School of Nursing in Palestine	Poalei Zion has 7,000 members	**1919–1923** Third Aliyah (young socialist Zionist male and female pioneers organized in collectives)	Treaty of Versailles creates the modern states of Czechoslovakia, Hungary, Rumania, Poland, Lithuania, Latvia, and Estonia
	1919 American Jewish delegation participates in Paris Peace Conference		

(continued)

1920
Henrietta Szold immigrates to Palestine at age 65

1920
Emanuel Gamoran joins staff of the Union of American Hebrew Congregations, promoting Zionism through Reform educational literature

Zeirei Zion Hitahdut [United Youth of Zion] of America established as Hebraist non-Marxist Labor Zionist group

Henry Ford publishes notorious antisemitic canards based on The Protocols of the Elders of Zion

National Council of Jewish Women has a national membership of 28,000

1920
Mandate for Palestine assigned to Great Britain by Supreme Council of peace conference

Histadrut [General Federation of Jewish Workers in the Land of Israel] founded at a countrywide conference of Palestine labor movement

Haganah self-defense organization created

Battle of Tel Hai; Yosef Trumpeldor killed

Women's International Zionist Organization (WIZO) founded in Great Britain

San Remo Conference establishes the framework for the implementation of the British Mandate in Palestine

Arab riots in Jerusalem

Keren Hayesod (Foundation Fund) created by WZO Conference in London

Women vote for the first time in the Yishuv

American Jewish Women and Zionism	American Jewish Affairs	Europe, Palestine, and World Jewish Affairs	General World History
1921 Golda (Meyerson) Meir immigrates to Palestine	**1921** Cleveland Convention highlights Brandeis-Weizmann conflict; "Brandeis group" resigns ZOA leadership and is replaced by Louis Lipsky faction	**1921** Arab riots in Jaffa	**1921** U.S. Congress curtails annual immigration to 3 percent of the number of each foreign national group counted in the 1910 census
Bertha Landsman, Hadassah-sponsored public health nurse, establishes Tipat Halav [Drop of Milk] to provide pasteurized milk to Jewish colonists		Trans-Jordan established	
	ZOA launches new official periodical, *The New Palestine*	Twelfth Zionist Congress	
Manya Shohat, Histadrut representative, creates a Poalei Zion women's committee to raise $10,000 worth of kitchen and laundry equipment for Jewish colonies in Palestine	Brandeis group establishes the Palestine Development Council	Women Worker's Council organized within the Histadrut	
	Histadrut delegation visits U.S., raising money for Jewish colonies in Palestine and making useful political contacts		
Hadassah appeals to Jewish religious school pupils countrywide to "give a penny so a child in Jerusalem can eat"			
Irma Lindheim establishes Intercollegiate Zionist Organization in New York City	**1922** Judith Kaplan, first bat mitzvah in U.S.	**1922** Churchill White Paper	**1922** Fascism emerges as popular political movement in Italy
Alice L. Seligsberg serves as Hadassah president, 1921–1923		U.S. Congress adopts joint resolution endorsing Balfour Declaration, approved by President Warren G. Harding	
		Hapoel Hamizrahi [Religious Worker] party established	

1923 Hadassah creates school lunch program in Palestine Henrietta Szold serves as Hadassah president, 1923–1926	**1923** Geverkshaftn [National Labor Committee for Palestine] campaign is created when Histadrut ends organized labor's opposition to Zionism by allying with United Hebrew Trades Union of Orthodox Jewish Congregations of America establishes a Women's Branch Bnai Brith Hillel Foundation created	**1923** British Mandate confirmed by League of Nations Death of Max Nordau World Congress of Jewish Women convenes in Vienna	
1924 Rahel Yanait (later Ben-Zvi) requests aid from Sophie Udin for women's agricultural training farm in Jerusalem; funds raised by group of seven Poalei Zion female activists (Eva Berg, Leah Brown, Chaya Ehrenreich, Luba Hurwitz, Rachel Siegel, Sophie Udin, Nina Zuckerman)	**1924** Alexander Dushkin, Zeirei Zion activist, appointed head of Chicago's College of Jewish Studies Emanuel Gamoran publishes *Changing Conceptions in Jewish Education*, with curricula on Zionism and Palestine; influences synagogue movements and Jewish schools across the country	**1924** Technikum (later Technion) opens in Haifa First world conference of Hashomer Hazair [Young Guard] movement **1924–1932** Fourth Aliyah (Polish Jewish immigrants, largely urban middle-class families)	**1924** Death of Vladimir Ilyich Lenin Johnson-Reed Act further curtails immigration to the U.S. by reducing it to 2 percent of each foreign nationality represented in the 1890 census
1925 Led by Sophie Udin, female activists secede from Poalei Zion and create new independent women's organization named Pioneer Women; Sarah Feder	**1925** Abraham Cahan, editor of *Der forverts*, visits Palestine and Poland in a trip that prompts him to adopt a pro-Labor Zionist stance	**1925** Hebrew University of Jerusalem is officially opened YIVO Institute for Jewish Research founded in Vilnius	**1925–1927** Adolf Hitler writes and publishes *Mein Kampf* [My Struggle]

(continued)

American Jewish Women and Zionism	American Jewish Affairs	Europe, Palestine, and World Jewish Affairs	General World History
(Keyfitz) serves as national secretary in 1925	United Palestine Appeal (UPA) created to replace Keren Hayesod in American context	Vladimir (Zeev) Jabotinsky founds the World Union of Zionist Revisionists	
Founding of Mizrachi Women's Organization of America, a religious Zionist group	Founding of American Friends of the Hebrew University		
Hannah Hoffman, graduate of Smith College and daughter of a New Jersey Conservative rabbi, travels to Palestine and becomes a pioneer at Tel Yosef	Palestine Economic Corporation established by American Zionist business leaders to encourage investment in the Yishuv; over \$2 million in assets by 1930		
Irma Lindheim visits Palestine for first time	National Council of Jewish Women has a national membership of 52,000		
1926 First national convention of Pioneer Women held in New York City; Leah Biskin serves as national secretary in 1926			
Rose Viteles immigrates to Palestine			
Irma Lindheim serves as Hadassah president, 1926–1928; in 1926 she refuses to cosign a bank loan for United Palestine Appeal, citing ZOA's poor organization and fiscal irresponsibility; Louis			

xlviii

American Jewish Women's History	American Jewish History	Jewish History	World History
Lipsky, ZOA president, rebukes her in the *New Palestine* for abandoning principles of Henrietta Szold; Szold rejects Lipsky's criticism and defends Lindheim			
Bessie Gotsfeld, leader of Mizrachi Women's Organization of America, immigrates to Palestine			
1927 Rahel Yanait (Ben-Zvi) arrives in U.S. as first Moezet Hapoalot emissary to Pioneer Women	**1927** Louis Lipsky asks Brandeis group to return to ZOA and take control of the financial committee	**1927** Death of the influential Zionist thinker Ahad Haam	**1927** Charles Lindbergh makes first solo flight across the Atlantic Ocean
	Al Jolson stars in *The Jazz Singer*, film about acculturation of Jewish immigrant boy, first "talkie"		
1928 Hadassah establishes urban recreation program in Palestine	**1928** Yeshiva University founded	**1928** Jewish settlement of Biro-Bidzhan, in the Soviet Union's far east, begins; planned as a semi-autonomous Jewish region	**1928** Penicillin discovered
Zip Szold serves as Hadassah president, 1928–1930			
Golda Meyerson (Meir) arrives in U.S. as Moezet Hapoalot emissary to Pioneer Women, 1928–1929	**1929** Death of Louis Marshall, president of the American Jewish Committee	**1929** Arab riots throughout Palestine, massacres in Hebron and Safed	**1929** Wall Street stock market crash causes worldwide economic depression
	Palestine Emergency Fund established to aid Jewish community of the Yishuv	Jewish Agency for Palestine expanded to include non-Zionist representation	

(continued)

xlix

American Jewish Women and Zionism	American Jewish Affairs	Europe, Palestine, and World Jewish Affairs	General World History
1930 Rose Jacobs serves as Hadassah president, 1930–1932 Pioneer Women creates division for "single girls" 1930s Hannah Chizhik arrives in U.S. as Moezet Hapoalot emissary to Pioneer Women, 1930–1931 Junior Hadassah reaches countrywide membership of 10,000 and raises $70,000 for Jewish National Fund 1931 Pioneer Women publishes *Vos arbeterns derzeyln* [The Woman Worker Speaks], anthology of writings by Zionist women pioneers in Palestine Hadassah national membership stands at approximately 30,000; approximately $3.5 million raised in previous decade Pioneer Women national membership stands at approximately 3,000	1930 Negotiations with ZOA administrative committee brings Brandeis group back into leadership of American Zionism 1930s During the Great Depression American Jewish membership organizations dwindle in size 1931 Meyer Levin publishes *Yehuda*, first full-length American novel about Zionist pioneers in Palestine Poalei Zion and Zeirei Zion merge to form the United Jewish Socialist labor Party, Poalei Zion–Zeirei Zion (PZ-ZZ) Poalei Zion Yungt and the youth wing of the fraternal order Yidish Nazionaler Arbeter Farband merge to become the Young Poalei Zion Alliance (YPZA)	1930 Shaw and Hope-Simpson reports Passfield White Paper Yevsektsiya, the Jewish section of the Communist Party's Propaganda Department, abolished Mapai (Workers Party of the Land of Israel] founded 1931 Dissent within Haganah causes split and leads to formation of Irgun Zvai Leumi, right-wing Zionist military organization inspired by Zeev Jabotinsky Seventeenth Zionist Congress	1931 Japanese invade Manchuria

1

(continued)

American Jewish Women and Zionism	American Jewish Affairs	Europe, Palestine, and World Jewish Affairs	General World History
1934 Marie Syrkin joins staff of *Jewish Frontier* Rose Jacobs serves as Hadassah president, 1934–1937 Elisheva Kaplan-Eshkol arrives in U.S. as Moezet Hapoalot emissary to Pioneer Women, 1934–1935	**1934** Jewish Labor Committee founded Roosevelt appoints Henry Morgenthau Treasury secretary Poalei Zion-Zeirei Zion launches monthly *Jewish Frontier*, edited by Hayim Greenberg Mordecai Kaplan publishes his magnum opus, *Judaism as a Civilization*, articulating Reconstructionist Judaism **1935** First National Conference for Palestine in Washington, D.C., sponsored by ZOA and several other groups Several hundred Reform and Conservative rabbis issue statement of agreement with policies and practices of Histadrut and Labor Zionism Habonim youth organization founded	**1934** Death of Baron Edmond de Rothschild, patron of Zionist colonies Death of poet Hayim Nahman Bialik Start of Aliyah Bet (illegal Jewish immigration to Palestine) Henrietta Szold becomes director of Youth Aliyah First national conference of Zionist Women's Organization of Argentina, numbering 2000 members **1935** Nineteenth Zionist Congress Revisionist Zionists secede from the WZO and create the New Zionist Organization	**1934** Poland rescinds Minorities Treaties **1935** Italy invades Ethiopia

(continued)

American Jewish Women and Zionism	American Jewish Affairs	Europe, Palestine, and World Jewish Affairs	General World History
1939 Hadassah officially opens its hospital in Jerusalem	**1939** National Conference for Palestine	Austria adopts antisemitic legislation; pogroms in Vienna; deportations begin	**1939** Germany invades Poland; beginning of World War II in Europe
Tamar DeSola Pool serves as Hadassah president, 1939–1943	United Jewish Appeal founded	Orde Wingate organizes Jewish resistance to Arab terrorism	
Young English-speaking women become significant factor in Pioneer Women		Great Britain declares Partition Plan impractical	
The Pioneer Woman becomes a monthly publication		**1939** Nazi "Czech Protectorate" adopts antisemitic legislation	
May Bere (Mereminsky) Merom arrives in U.S. as Moezet Hapoalot emissary to Pioneer Women, 1939–1941		Arab-Jewish Round Table Conference at St. James' Palace in London; final British attempt to reconcile Jews and Arabs	
		MacDonald White Paper restricts both Jewish immigration and land sales to Jews; Zionists deem it a horrifying repudiation of the Balfour Declaration in "the darkest hour of Jewish history"	
		Lohamei Herut Israel (Lehi) founded, clandestine right-wing Zionist military force	

1940 Hadassah joins with the ZOA to form the American Zionist Youth Commission	1940 Sidney Liptzen Foundation established in New York city (first American foundation dedicated to Moezet Hapoalot projects in Palestine)	1940 French Vichy regime promulgates antisemitic legislation	1940 Germany overruns western Europe
Hadassah national membership approximately 73,000		Death of Vladimir (Zeev) Jabotinsky	Winston Churchill becomes prime minister of Great Britain
Pioneer Women national membership approximately 7,000			
Mizrachi Women's Organization national membership approximately 10,000			
1941 Yehudit Simhonit returns to U.S. as Moezet Hapoalot emissary to Pioneer Women, 1941–1943	1941 Death of Louis D. Brandeis	1941 Jewish emigration prohibited by Nazi regime	1941 Germany invades Russia; Japanese attack on Pearl Harbor propels the U.S. into the war
		Slovakia adopts antisemitic legislation	
		Pogroms in Poland, Rumania and Russia	
		Nazi Einstazgruppen begin mass killing of Jews in occupied Russia	
		First Nazi death camps established	
		Palmah organized, clandestine Haganah fighting force	

(continued)

American Jewish Women and Zionism	American Jewish Affairs	Europe, Palestine, and World Jewish Affairs	General World History
1942 Council of Women's Organizations established	**1942** American Jewish Conference endorses the Biltmore Program	**1942** Biltmore Conference, a wartime Zionist gathering held in New York City in lieu of a Zionist Congress, rejects the MacDonald White Paper and advocates creating independent Jewish state in Palestine	**1942** Allied troops deployed to North Africa; battle of El Alamein
Dvorah Rothbard serves as national secretary of Pioneer Women, 1942–1945	Rabbi Stephen S. Wise learns of Nazi plans to exterminate the Jews; after the State Department confirms the report, he announces that 2 million have died, and American Jews hold a Day of Mourning	*Struma* sinks in Black Sea, causing death of 769 Jewish refugees	Wannsee Conference confirms the "Final Solution" for European Jews
Hadassah national membership approximately 86,000		Nazi massacres in occupied Russia continue; Auschwitz, Maidanek, and Treblinka death camps function at full capacity; deportations from ghettos to death camps	
Pioneer Women national membership approximately 10,000	Reform Jewish anti-Zionists organize the American Council for Judaism		
Mizrachi Women's Organization national membership approximately 32,000	Ampal-American Palestine Trading Corporation established; nearly $300,000 in assets	**1942–1944** Mass deportations to Auschwitz from Belgium and Holland	
		1943 Germany declared "*Judenrein*" Mass deportations of Jews from all over Europe to death camps Warsaw ghetto uprising	

1943 Judith Epstein serves as Hadassah president, 1943–1947 Pioneer Women establishes Child Rescue Fund to support Youth Aliyah programs in Moezet Hapoalot schools and farms Hadassah national membership approximately 95,000 Pioneer Women national membership approximately 12,000	**1943** American Jewish Conference established; affirms Zionist goals of Biltmore Conference		**1943** German forces suffer a major defeat at Stalingrad; defeat of German forces in North Africa Surrender of Italy
1944 Mizrachi Women's Organization national membership approximately 35,000 **1944** Hadassah national membership approximately 120,000 Pioneer Women national membership approximately 15,000	**1944** President Roosevelt establishes the War Refugee Board	**1944** Extermination of Hungarian Jewry begins Jewish Brigade organized, sees battle in Italy Irgun and Lehi attack British troops, officers, military installations, and infrastructure in Palestine	**1944** Battle of Normandy; Allies victorious in Eastern and Pacific theaters of war
1945 Pioneer Women led by "presidium of three" (Bert Goldstein, Blanche Mogil, and Dvorah Rothbard)	**1945–1952** Hundreds of thousands of Displaced Persons, who survived World War II, win admission to the U.S.; many are Jews	**1945** Anglo-American Committee of Inquiry created to examine solutions to the question of where to place Jewish refugees	**1945** Surrender of Germany Death of Franklin D. Roosevelt

(continued)

American Jewish Women and Zionism	American Jewish Affairs	Europe, Palestine, and World Jewish Affairs	General World History
Sarah (Kukso) Kafri arrives in U.S. as Moezet Hapoalot emissary to Pioneer Women, 1945–1946		Death of Henrietta Szold	U.S. drops atomic bombs on Hiroshima and Nagasaki; surrender of Japan
Hadassah national membership approximately 143,000		Aliyah Bet and Zionist struggle against British Mandatory intensified	
Pioneer Women national membership approximately 16,000		Haganah and Irgun reach agreement for joint resistance against British Mandatory	
Mizrachi Women's Organization national membership approximately 36,500			
1946 Rivka Yoffe arrives in U.S. as Moezet Hapoalot emissary to Pioneer Women, 1946–1947		1946 Anglo-American Committee of Inquiry recommends new trusteeship of Palestine and rules out statehood for Jews or Arabs	1946 Communists take political control of eastern and central Europe; start of Cold War
Hadassah national membership approximately 177,000		Irgun blows up section of King David Hotel in Jerusalem	Nuremberg Trials begin
		British deport illegal Jewish immigrants to camps in Cyprus	
		Pogroms in Poland	
1947 Hadassah national membership approximately 198,000		1947 Anglo-American Committee of Inquiry declared unsuccessful; Palestine issue submitted to UN	1947 Paris Peace Conference; treaties signed with Italy, Rumania, Hungary, Bulgaria, and Finland

Marie Syrkin publishes *Blessed Is the Match*, first major book in English on wartime Jewish resistance		UN General Assembly creates Special Committee on Palestine (UNSCOP)	
Bert Goldstein elected first "national president" of Pioneer Women		UN General Assembly adopts the UNSCOP's recommendation of partitioning Palestine	
Dvorah Rothbard helps to organize Pioneer Women in Paris, France		Arabs begin attacks on Yishuv	
Yehudit Simhonit returns to U.S. as Moezet Hapoalot emissary to Pioneer Women, 1947–1948			
1948 Shoshana Hareli arrives in U.S. as Moezet Hapoalot emissary to Pioneer Women, 1948–1949	**1948** Founding of Brandeis University	**1948** State of Israel proclaimed May 14, 1948; War of Independence	**1948** Communist coup in Czechoslovakia
Dvorah Rothbard and Sonia Kaminetsky help to create Pioneer Women groups in Argentina, Brazil, Chile, Peru, and Uruguay		U.S. immediately recognizes Israel	
1949 Death of Stephen S. Wise		Moscow "Show Trials"; Jewish life and culture in U.S.S.R. suppressed	**1949** Founding of North Atlantic Treaty Organization (NATO)

Sources: American Jewish Yearbook, vols. 1–50 (1899–1949); *Encyclopaedia Judaica*, vol. 8 (1971), esp. "Chronological Chart of Jewish History"; *Jewish Women in America: An Historical Encyclopedia*, 2 vols. (1997); Marlin Levin and Danielle Lewis, *It Takes a Dream . . . the Story of Hadassah, Timeline of Critical Events: 1840s–Present* (New York: Gefen Books, 1997); Isadore Meyer, *Early History of Zionism in America* (New York: American Jewish Historical Society and Theodor Herzl Foundation, 1958); Mark A. Raider, *The Emergence of American Zionism* (New York and London: New York University Press, 1998); Shulamit Reinharz, *A Contextualized Chronology of Women's Sociological Work* (Waltham, Mass.: Women's Studies Program, Brandeis University, 1993); Shulamit Reinharz, *Timeline of Jewish Women and Women's Issues in Palestine (the Yishuv) and Israel* (draft, July 1998); *The Rise of Israel: A Documentary Record from the Nineteenth Century to 1948*, ed. Howard M. Sachar (New York: Garland Publishing, 1987–1988); Yonatan Shapiro, *Leadership of the American Zionist Organization, 1897–1930* (Chicago: University of Illinois Press, 1971); Melvin I. Urofsky, *American Zionism from Herzl to the Holocaust* (New York: Anchor Press/Doubleday, 1975).

PART I

Three Generations of American Jewish Women and the Zionist Idea

Since the arrival of the Pilgrim settlers and the colonization of New England in the eighteenth century, the notion of rebuilding Zion, although vague, was a persistent theme in American life and letters. The New England settlers considered America itself to be the "New Zion" and the "New Promised Land." Against this backdrop actual projects to create Jewish states or colonies began to appear in the early nineteenth century. For example, in 1825 Mordecai M. Noah (1785–1851), an eccentric diplomat, devised a grandiose scheme to create a Jewish state on an island opposite Buffalo, New York, in the Niagara River. In another peculiar instance, Warder Cresson (1798–1860), a convert to Judaism who briefly served as American consul in Palestine, took the name Michael Boaz Israel and in 1852 established an agricultural colony near Jerusalem.

Not until the fin de siècle, however, did an American woman proclaim the need for a Jewish homeland. We call hers the "voice" of the first generation of American Jewish women Zionists, and it is with her words that we begin this volume. Shocked by the news of murderous pogroms against the Jews of Russia in 1881, and cognizant of the widespread suffering of East European Jewry in this period, Emma Lazarus (1849–1887) advocated the restoration of a Jewish homeland in her lengthy poem, *An Epistle to the Hebrews* (1882–83). Lazarus would become a familiar name in American literary history, and her sonnet "The New Colossus" was to be inscribed at the base of the Statue of Liberty (1903). To this day, it is memorized by schoolchildren across the country. Yet how many recognize that Lazarus was a highly identified and self-aware Jewish woman, and that she herself made an eloquent case for Zionism? As an artist and a public exponent of Jewish nationalism, Lazarus challenged her contemporaries to confront the status of Jews in the modern era. Her explorations of the age-old "Jewish question," in which she publicly probed whether Jews could ever be allowed to live in peace as a minority in any society, helped lay the groundwork for emergent American Zionism. By asking whether the rights and security of Jews could be safeguarded in a time of rising antisemitism, she also posed the question of how to preserve Judaism and Jewish identity in a rapidly changing world. Finally, she contemplated how to meld American patriotism and proto-Zionism, two seemingly irreconcilable values, into a cohesive American Jewish ideology.

Primary among the women who followed in Lazarus's footsteps was Rosa Sonneschein (1847–1932), editor of the *American Jewess,* who attended the First Zionist Congress in Basle, Switzerland, in 1897. Another significant figure was Henrietta Szold (1860–1945), who founded Hadassah in 1912 and directed the Jewish Agency's emergency youth *aliyah* activities during World War II. We have determined to identify Szold as representative of the second generation of American Jewish women Zionists—not only because of her legacy as a Zionist leader but also because of the distinctive American Jewish worldview that impelled her activity in the Zionist enterprise. Just as Lazarus did not live to witness the First Zionist Congress, Szold did not live to witness the birth of the State of Israel, but both women clearly influenced Zionism and the state's creation. Moreover, Szold acknowledged the impact of Lazarus's clarion call on her own ideological development.

Subsequent generations of Zionist women joined the movement inspired by Lazarus and made concrete by Szold. A significant example in this regard is Marie Syrkin (1899–1989), whom we have selected to represent the third generation of American Jewish women in the Zionist enterprise. Syrkin emerged as a Jewish woman activist, Zionist polemicist, and American Jewish public intellectual in the 1930s. As both a thinker and an ideological leader, Syrkin championed American Zionism and the involvement of American Jewish women in the campaign for Jewish statehood. She performed a sizable quotient of Zionist organizational spadework and was close to many of the political leaders who dominated the Histadrut and the Jewish Agency in the decades leading up to the creation of the State of Israel in 1948. In her capacity as an editor of the Labor Zionist journal *Jewish Frontier,* she also played a critical role in politicizing the concerns of American Jews in the pre-state era.

Lazarus, Szold, and Syrkin were visionaries who left a strong public record of their thoughts and achievements. Included in virtually all encyclopedias of American Jewish women, their ideas are necessary reading for understanding the evolution of American Jewish women's Zionist attitudes and behavior. Indeed, as editors we wish to stress women's ideas and intellectual history, in addition to their organizational talent, in the development of the Zionist movement. In sum, these figures demonstrate the centrality of women in the complex relationship of American Jews, the Yishuv, and the Zionist enterprise.

Chapter 1

The celebrated American Jewish poet Emma Lazarus (1849–1897) is best remembered for "The New Colossus," which she composed in 1883:

> Give me your tired, your poor,
> Your huddled masses yearning to breathe free
> The wretched refuse of your teeming shore.
> Send these, the homeless, tempest-tost to me,
> I lift my lamp beside the golden door!

Lazarus's sonnet, originally written to help promote the Bartholdi Pedestal Fund drive in November 1883—a campaign to raise money for the Statue of Liberty's pedestal—is one of the most famous illustrations of American idealism in the fin de siècle. Indeed, for Lazarus the twin conceptions of America as a haven for European immigrants and a beacon for humanity stemmed from her profound belief in the promise of the New World and the prophetic vision of social justice inspired by the Hebrew Bible.

The fourth of seven children born to Esther (Nathan) and Moses Lazarus, a successful German Jewish merchant, Emma was raised in a highly acculturated Jewish household. She grew up in New York and Newport, Rhode Island, and she received a well-rounded modern, private education. Shortly after the private publication of her first book of poetry in 1866, she met Ralph Waldo Emerson (1803–1882), the American writer and philosopher whose poems are regarded as central to the development of modern American thought and literary expression. From this point forward, Lazarus sustained a rich relationship with Emerson, and his influence on her writing was considerable.

Another significant catalyst in Lazarus's development was the outbreak of anti-Jewish violence in Russia and Poland that began in the 1880s. Until this period, Lazarus's writing only infrequently dealt with Jewish themes and issues. Indeed, as a product of the German Jewish elite that prevailed in American Jewish life in the late nineteenth century, Lazarus might have remained detached from the concerns of impoverished East European Jews. But her very position in society provoked in her a sense of noblesse oblige and, after reading Leo Pinsker's proto-Zionist treatise *Auto-emancipation* (1882), she was spurred to activism.[1]

As her numerous essays and poems in this period reveal, the pogroms in eastern Europe not only prompted a radical shift in Lazarus's worldview but channeled her poetic energies. She emerged from relative obscurity to become a highly self-identified and unapologetic American Jewish writer, and she contributed frequently to the well-known periodicals *Lippincotts,* the *Century,* and the *American Hebrew.* In the latter, she published *Songs of a Semite: The Dance to Death and Other Poems* (1882) in serialized form, and she championed "the glorious Maccabean rage" of the Jewish revolt against Antiochus IV (175–164 B.C.E.) in the ancient period, proclaiming, "Let but Ezra rise anew/To Lift the Banner of the Jew!"[2]

It was at this juncture that Lazarus's work attained a distinctive Jewish nationalist tone and even a proto-Zionist scope. Although her prose and poetry tended to be more philosophical than prescriptive, there is little doubt, as Arthur Zeiger asserts here, that she helped to shape the emerging American Jewish public discourse on the issue of the "Jewish question" and the possibility of Jewish national renewal.

Zeiger's essay, written in 1958 and delivered at the first scholarly symposium on the history of American Zionism, is reproduced here in an abridged form because it serves a dual purpose.[3] First, the essay is noteworthy as a pioneering treatment of the history of women in American Zionism. Appearing at a time when American Jewish history was only just beginning to garner recognition as a legitimate scholarly discipline, Zeiger's essay demarcates the interdisciplinarity of American Jewish studies and anticipates many of the themes and methods that would become normative with the growth of Jewish studies and Jewish women's studies in coming decades. In addition to its historiographic value, the substantive value of Zeiger's essay is also noteworthy. Drawing on a variety of original sources, Zeiger, trained as a literary scholar, employs a far-ranging and insightful textual analysis that reveals the complex nature of Lazarus's worldview, particularly her approach to the core problematic of the American Jewish experience: the melding of a new American Jewish identity, which neither privileges nor diminishes the American or Jewish

---

1. We use the phrase "proto-Zionism" to indicate that these ideas predated the emergence of Zionism as a formal political movement but that they anticipated the ideology and structures that crystallized in the Jewish public arena with the appearance of Theodor Herzl a decade later.

2. See the poem at the end of this chapter for the complete text.

3. We have retained the style and language in which it was originally written. The complete essay may be found in Isidore S. Meyer, ed., *Early History of Zionism in America* (New York: American Jewish Historical Society, 1958), 77–108.

inheritance but aspires to a coherent and meaningful synthesis of the two. Finally, the essay demonstrates that Lazarus's vision predated that of Theodor Herzl (1860–1904) and many other European Zionist thinkers, and she helped fertilize the soil of the American Jewish public arena that would later produce such eminent American Zionist leaders as Louis D. Brandeis (1856–1941) and Henrietta Szold (1860–1945).

Emma Lazarus and Pre-Herzlian Zionism

Arthur Zeiger

An Epistle to the Hebrews, comprising fifteen articles written for the *American Hebrew,*[1] is Emma Lazarus' mature confession of faith, the most effective contribution she made to American Jewish thought and policy. Throughout she speaks as a Hebrew to Hebrews: throughout the basic pronoun is "we" rather than (as always before) "they." She writes proudly, with "a vivid sense of the possibilities and responsibilities" of what she considers her "race."[2] At the close of the series, she sums up her purposes:

> My chief aim has been to contribute my mite towards arousing that spirit of Jewish enthusiasm which might manifest itself (1st), in a return to the varied pursuits and broad system of physical and intellectual education adopted by our ancestors; (2nd), in a more fraternal and practical movement towards alleviating the sufferings of oppressed Jews in countries less favored than our own; (3rd), in a closer and wider study of Hebrew literature and history, and finally, in a truer recognition of the large principles of religion, liberty, and law upon which Judaism is founded, and which should draw into harmonious unity Jews of every shade of opinion.[3]

In this paper only five of the epistles (VI, VII, VIII, XII, XIV) are considered: those dedicated to "promoting a more fraternal and practical movement towards alleviating the sufferings of oppressed Jews in countries less favored than our own."[4] The movement has since been named: Zionism. As it had Leo Pinsker (1821–1891) and Theodor Herzl (1860–1904), literary and practical antisemitism led Emma Lazarus to the conviction that the hope of the persecuted Jew lay in regaining nationality—and a place to exercise it. All three had believed in assimilation and progress: these in time's slow course would inevitably bring equality for the Jew. The writings of the Slavophiles and the Odessa pogrom of 1871 disillusioned Pinsker;[5] Eugene Duhring's *The Jew Problem as a Problem of Race, Morals and Culture* and the Dreyfus case "liberated" Herzl;[6] the

Source: Arthur Zeigler, "Emma Lazarus and Pre-Herzlian Zionism," in *Early History of Zionism in America,* ed. Isidore S. Meyer (New York: American Jewish Historical Society, 1958,), 77–108. Reprinted by permission of the American Jewish Historical Society.

Russian persecutions of 1882 and Mme. Ragozin's article in defense of the persecutions[7] were climactic for Emma Lazarus.

Several proto-Zionists had proclaimed, sometimes eloquently, their message—most notably Major Mordecai Manuel Noah (1785–1851), journalist, lawyer, dramatist, United States Consul at Tunis, Grand Sachem of Tammany and Utopian schemer.[8] His famous *Discourse* delivered at the Broadway Tabernacle of New York in 1844,[9] startles through its resemblance to later Zionist writings. Desiring that "by and with the consent of the Christian powers, and with their aid and agency" the land of Israel revert to its "legitimate proprietors," he proposed that the Sultan of Turkey be solicited to grant permission for the Jews to purchase and hold land. He foresaw agriculture and commerce flourishing in the valley of the Jordan after the famous day on which the Sultan issued his *Hatt-i Sherif* [Ottoman reform decree] and did not doubt that the Jews who wanted to reside in the Holy Land and had not the means would be aided by societies constituted for that purpose.[10]

Neither the Major nor any of the minor American proponents of "repatriation" were instrumental in converting Emma Lazarus to the program. It does not appear that any of the Hovevei Zion [Lovers of Zion], the forerunners of Herzlian Zionism, were her ideological ancestors either. Her neglect of them was a function of her ignorance of their achievement. Major Noah, Rabbi Hirsch Kalischer (1795–1874), Rabbi Eliah Guttmacher (1796–1874), Nahman Krochmal (1785–1840), even Moses Hess (1812–1875), were not even names to her. Of the long history of Hibbat Zion [Lovers of Zion Society] she had scarcely a notion.[11]

George Eliot, in Emma Lazarus' account, begot the Zionist idea,[12] an idea now beginning to assume shape and form.[13] She "first spoke practically of re-nationalizing the race." Lazarus' "The Dance to Death" had been "dedicated, in profound veneration and respect, to the memory of George Eliot, the illustrious writer, who did most among the artists of our day towards elevating and ennobling the spirit of Jewish nationality."[14] It was *Daniel Deronda*[15] that stirred Emma Lazarus to the tribute, and the novel continued to be a favorite of hers. Certainly neither the sentimental story of Gwendolyn Harleth's star-crossed love nor the exposition of positivism aroused her enthusiasm. What moved her was the plea for Zionism, for the restoration of the "organic center" to Judaism.

Daniel Deronda exerted an enormous influence on the development of Zionism in the nineteenth century—Perez, Gordon, Smolenskin, Lilienblum, all "made George Eliot's novel their own; translating it into Hebrew, and supplementing it by their own views on the recolonization of Palestine."[16]

It was George Eliot who first spoke the still unspoken word, Lazarus declares, and Laurence Oliphant (1829–1888) who first endeavored to make the word flesh—"who first agitated the question of transporting them [the Jews] to a new political existence from the east of Europe to the west of Asia."[17] He believed that the terrain east of the Jordan, described in *The Land of Gilead*,[18] held the greatest promise to potential colonizers; for not only might its soil be profitably cultivated, but also its surface hid mineral deposits which might be profitably worked. More important than the book, though, were Oliphant's propagandistic articles and letters. Emma Lazarus refers particularly to "The Jew and the Eastern Question" in the *Nineteenth Century* for August, 1882[19]—in essence a pointed abridgment of *The Land of Gilead*—in which he argues for colonization in Syria and Palestine, urging persecution in Russia and *Judenhetze* [Jew hatred] in Germany as the compelling reasons.

Do the Jews themselves want the restoration? The Western or modern Jew does not, Oliphant replies: he spurns an individual Jewish nationality, clings with fervent patriotism to the country which has emancipated him. The orthodox or Oriental Jew, however, does: "subject to contempt, ignominy, injustice, and persecution, culminating in murder and rapine on a terrible scale," he naturally has no such attachments to the country which enslaves him.[20]

Emma Lazarus read Oliphant's whole essay attentively; but one portion she seems to have memorized, so often and so closely does she paraphrase it:

It is an old saying that "every country has the Jews which it deserves." This is true in the sense that the institutions and religion of the country which the Jew may have adopted as his home, no doubt exercise an influence upon his character. Thus, in Russia, where he is surrounded by religious superstition and fanaticism, he is naturally confirmed in the prejudice and bigotry of his own religion. In a country where freedom is unknown he remains relatively ignorant and servile; but he escapes the dangers of indifferentism, and retains a simplicity of character and of faith and a capacity of aspiration which are incompatible with a high state of so-called civilization. Upon purely moral grounds, and putting his material interests aside, I believe he would lose more than he would gain by being suddenly launched upon that chaos of enlightened competition and thought which characterizes the most progressive nation in the world . . . The very exigencies which successful competition involves in America are compatible with the due observance of the requirements of their religion, which render it necessary that the Jews should live in communities.[21]

Quite likely, Oliphant's stress on both the economic and the moral penalties emigration to America would visit on the Jews induced Emma Lazarus to abandon it as one of the three radical "measures . . . for improving the conditions of the East European Jews."[22]

It is doubtful that Laurence Oliphant and Emma Lazarus had met before the *American Hebrew* began serializing *An Epistle to the Hebrews*. In the March issue of the periodical he has a letter dated February 6, 1883, from Haifa (where, commissioned by the Mansion House Fund to supervise Jewish relief work, he had established headquarters), referring to "the gifted lady who has already expressed her sympathy so warmly in favor of the material restoration of Palestine through the agency of her own people," and asking her aid in securing relief for the Rumanian colonists who, laboring under the pressure of the antipathetic Turkish government, inexperience, mismanagement, and very little money, "are in a fair way to starve."[23] But two months later, April 15, 1883, he writes her familiarly, even attempts to enlist her aid in a complex international maneuver: if the American government would represent "through its minister at Petersburg the desirability on political grounds of making a remonstrance with the Porte against the illegal edict it has issued prohibiting Russian Jews from colonizing in Palestine," the Jewish cause would be materially assisted; for Russia entertains power-designs there, and the prejudiced action of the Porte against Russian subjects might be fashioned into a Russian political weapon. That the subjects were the despised Jews, Oliphant appears to have considered immaterial—power politics will seize the pretexts it can. That the weapon American representation might help to fashion would be "one chiefly directed against the political interests of England in the East," Oliphant regards as England's merited chastening—merited because of "its apathy in the Jewish question." And should Russian intervention be attempted and the British government be stirred up as a consequence, "the Jews would be the gainers, it might then become a struggle between the Powers who should protect them most."[24]

Oliphant's scheme sounds like the *Realpolitik* of Graustark; as unreal, surely, is his assumption that she had any way of making "available" his "political idea."[25] The letter he wrote nine days before (Haifa, April 6, 1883) contained a more reasonable message.[26] He warned that the more than three hundred Jewish families stranded at Jerusalem and Jaffa were being provided for by the Christian Missionary Society. "I think," Lazarus quotes him, "that these are people who should rather be looked after by their own co-religionists."[27] She understood the warning, and saw the way of making it available. Her letter to the *American Hebrew* underlines the danger: The fact Mr. Oliphant communicates, she declares,

speaks for itself and seems hardly to require any other comment than the ardent champion of our race so mildly bestows upon it. I cannot resist the hopeful conviction that by merely bringing it to the notice of American Jews through the columns of your paper, it will arouse a deeper sense of the claims that these unfortunate outcasts have upon us, and the extensive necessities of their actual situation. If we have not yet succeeded in proving to Christian missionaries that "converted Jews" are probably not only the most expensive of all marketable commodities but also the most worthless after they are purchased, we might at least raise our own hand to rescue these wretched creatures, who from the pressure of material want, unrelieved by their own kindred, are thus almost inevitably forced into apostasy and moral degradation.[28]

Here and abroad, Oliphant peppered Jewish and other publications, appealing, instructing, denouncing. He was himself denounced plentifully for his colonization plans. *The Jewish Messenger,* which had constituted itself the advance guard of anti-Zionism, was especially vigorous in the attack. In the January 26, 1883 issue the editor ironically admires the strategy—and energy—with which Oliphant or his aides deploy articles on Palestine-settlement:

No sooner had Mr. Oliphant written his views on the topic in *Nineteenth Century,* which of course are industriously copied, when a contribution from him appears in the London *Times,* which likewise makes the rounds of the press. A real book is published, advocating the settlement on a strip of land in Gilead, from the same zealous pen. Suddenly a letter is printed in the *Jewish Chronicle* on the same topic, which is translated in the German and Hebrew papers. And lo, it is Mr. Oliphant-asy again. Then an article with redoubled earnestness. Surely an immense phalanx of writers. But no. It is only Mr. Oliphant-asy once more.[29]

The editorialist finds it necessary (though he somewhat regrets the necessity, because she is "one to whom American Israel is under peculiar obligations") to focus his relentless beam on Emma Lazarus for her indiscretion in "joining Mr. Oliphant-asy's straggling recruits."[30] And again, two issues later, in another lead editorial which the writer, unfailingly witty, heads "Riding an Oliphant," the British journalist and his American recruit are similarly linked. The editorialist, briefly abandoning cleverness for candor, terms "Mr. Oliphant's project of colonizing a strip of land in Gilead a fantasy, and Miss Lazarus' plea for a separate nationality an unwise echo of that fantasy."[31]

Emma Lazarus did not know [Leo] Pinsker's name: his call to action had been anonymously published in Berlin, 1882, under the title, *Auto-Emancipation: Ein Mahnruf an seine Stammesgenossen von einem russichen Juden.*[32] But she knew and admired his pamphlet: "Some practical suggestions towards consolidation are made in a very remarkable pamphlet just printed in Germany, written by a Russian Jew. With his fiery eloquence and his depth and fervor of conviction this anonymous author could scarcely fail to enkindle the imagination of his Jewish readers, even if he stood alone; but re-enforced as he is by so many more influential, if less inspired voices, his appeal for nationality is a pregnant indication of the spirit of the times."[33]

She had heard Zionist views expounded before, by a young Russian immigrant; but it seemed to her then "the audacious vision of an obscure dreamer."[34] Since that time, she confesses,

the incidents of current Jewish history, the swelling voice of Jewish patriotism, the urgent necessity of escape from an untenable position among the nations, have combined to transform me into one of the most devoted adherents to the new dogma. I make this confession the more willingly, because I know it is the history of others as well, or under my own eyes I have seen equally rapid and thorough conversions to the same doctrine: In the minds of mature and thoughtful men, men of prudence and of earnest purpose, little apt to be swayed by the chance enthusiasm of a popular agitation, it has taken profound root, and in some cases overturned the theories and intellectual habits of a lifetime.[45]

The Zionist doctrine of Emma Lazarus may be deduced, with very little remainder, from George Eliot, Laurence Oliphant, and Leo Pinsker. Only one other name is at all significant—Gabriel Charmes, whose *Voyage en Syrie* had recently appeared in the *Revue des deux mondes*,[36] a journal she read devotedly. Charmes traced the evolution of the monotheistic concept in Judaism, its slow growth from a particularist to a universalist religion.[37] Islam and Christianity, he affirms, are the issue of Judaism—being essentially "*grandes heresies juives.*"[38] However, not Charmes' graceful history (based on Renan) but rather his speculations concerning the possibility of a new destiny for the Jews, a resurgence of their moral energy, roused Emma Lazarus. Islam, he wrote, has been engulfed by fatalism, Christianity by otherworldly hopes; but Judaism has always aspired, and aspired now, to a "*felicité générale*" on earth.[39] And modern Jews are attempting to realize an antique dream, to build a community where "progress" and "perfectibility" have actual force. Emma Lazarus echoes Charmes,

The enterprise will succeed if the philosophers do not err who have taught us that violence, crime and injustice are to disappear from this world, to leave room for nothing but virtue and liberty. . .[40]

And she continues, in his vein but not his words,

A race whose spiritual and intellectual influence upon the world has been universally accounted second to none, and whose physical constitution has adapted itself to the vicissitudes of every climate, can be whatever it will.[41]

That Jews are unadaptable to agriculture she regards as an objection no sounder than the one—raised before they gave the world Philo,

Maimonides and Spinoza—that they could be prophets but not philosophers.[42] Another and more serious argument—the Jews themselves do not desire "repatriation"—she is constrained to grant, in part at least. But she continues with the generalization

that even for partial and temporary social reforms it is an almost invariable rule that the class to be benefited have to be instructed before they can understand the nature of the benefit, and generally form in the beginning its most obstinate because most ignorant opponents.[43]

The Russian-Jewish emigrants are men who have sacrificed much for an "Idea, a high spiritual aim." By assuming the mask, converting to Christianity, they could have remained in Russia, life and property secure. Surely these people, at any rate, are "capable of comprehending the principle of consolidation and desiring a restoration"—as, indeed, these already do in great numbers desire it.[44]

What of the Jews in the emancipated countries of Europe, though? Lazarus' reply parallels Pinsker's, except that, like Oliphant and Eliot, she thinks of the restoration as being to Palestine:

There is not the slightest necessity for an American Jew, the free citizen of a republic, to rest his hopes upon the foundation of any other nationality soever, or to decide whether he individually would or would not be in favor of residing in Palestine. All that would be claimed from him would be a patriotic and unselfish interest in the sufferings of his oppressed brethren of less fortunate countries, sufficient to make him promote by every means in his power the establishment of a secure asylum.[45]

Several times during the course of *An Epistle* she iterates her contention: American Jews will retain their American nationality, and practicing binationality is no more practicable than adhering to dual religions.[46] Why, then, does she regard aid to the Russian Jews as a "patriotic" imperative for American Jews? Since nationalism is not the spur—she insists it cannot be—surely "patriotic" is an intrusive and inept term. If American Jews abandoned their East European brethren to their misery while hugging themselves in their prosperity, they might be guilty of inhumanity, "of a narrow selfishness and a short-sighted materialism," as she avers;[47] but, on her premises, they could not be with logic characterized as "unpatriotic."

Comparatively remote "from the scene of agitation, actuated by no base motives of personal gain, free of the "complicated entanglements of European politics," American Jews are enabled to judge "almost with the calmness of postcrity" oppressor and oppressed, as well as to determine coolly the main chances which the international situation affords:

We possess the double cosmopolitanism of the American and the Jew. We see the leashed and greedy hounds of European power straining at their checks, ready to pounce upon the tempting morsel of Egyptian supremacy, or struggling to be freed for the chase and to be "in at the death" of the Ottoman Empire. We have only to watch and wait to put ourselves in readiness for action upon an emergency.[48]

Even if "vigorous, united, and disinterested," such an undertaking might fail. But failure in the attempt would be no disgrace; the disgrace lies in not making the attempt.[49]

It is certainly overstatement to claim that in *An Epistle to the Hebrews* Emma Lazarus "produced a clear-cut and distinctively Zionist program, which along with Pinsker's call, is the second prophetic message addressed to world Jewry."[50] Yet Lazarus' Zionist articles did elicit perturbed responses. Rabbi Abram Samuel Isaacs, editor of the *Jewish Messenger*—which, when it published Lazarus' translation of Nachum's "Spring Songs" four years since, voiced its editor's gratification "that the rich treasures of Hebrew mediaeval poetry have been brought to her attention, and her practiced pen deems them worthy of her skill"[51]—felt aggrieved. He deprecated her advocacy of a separate Jewish nationality. Though complimenting Lazarus on the first half of "The Jewish Problem," which was "a forcible and eloquent glance at some facts in the history of the Jews," he found himself unable to praise the sobriety of her language or the clarity of her reasoning in the second, which was a plea for Zionism.[52] He employs a debater's stratagem, since become very familiar:

It may be new to Miss Lazarus to learn that, strangely enough, the plan she advocates is favored by Stoecker and his followers. At the recent antisemitic congress at Dresden, one of the "planks" in the platform adopted was that the Jews should emigrate from Europe and settle in Palestine. And it is perhaps the mistaken zeal of sincere friends and ardent champions at the eleventh hour, which is intensifying the mischievous and erroneous impression to which the antisemites give every currency, that the Jews are but Semites after all, strangers and aliens in Europe and America, patriots only in Palestine.[53]

It was not new to Emma Lazarus. In Epistle VIII, which had appeared on December 22, 1882, she had remarked on the rare unanimity among Jews and Jew haters. Both believe, she pointed out, in "Re-nationalization, Auto-Emancipation, Repatriation"—the Jews because they wanted to escape the antisemites and the antisemites because they wanted to get rid of the Jews.[54] However, she regarded the curious fact as an argument for her side, whereas the Reverend Isaacs (assuming that what the antisemites wanted, the Jews would do well to disapprove) regarded it on associational grounds as practically Jewish antisemitism.

The opposition of Isaacs, though himself dissident from orthodoxy even in 1883, and later a vigorous exponent of Conservative doctrine, was in general typical of the antagonism toward Zionism exhibited by Orthodox Jews. Jews of the Reform persuasion displayed still less sympathy. Fairly representing their attitude, Rabbi Isaac M. Wise, the principal figure in American Reform, wrote on March 16, 1883:

If Miss Emma Lazarus and others who handle a pen would lay aside their romantic notions of race, nation, Holy Land, Restoration, etc., and assist these practical heads in scratching out of their brains the pervert notions of distinctions between a man and a citizen who believes in Moses and the Prophets, and another who believes in Jesus and his Apostles, they could render good service to their coreligionists and to the cause of humanity, which is disgraced by the blind prejudices of those narrow-minded individuals who see in the Jew a stranger, an indefinable scarecrow of their bewildered imagination . . . We are citizens of the United States, an integral element of this nation, and of no other, with no earthly interests or aspirations different from those who believe in Jesus and his Apostles.[55]

Jews of each sect somehow evaded the limiting logic of their creed, and statements of the pro-Zionist position managed to make their way even into the strongholds of the enemy.[56] To the *Jewish Messenger,* for example, newfangled ideas about the restoration were anathema, but Dr. H. Pereira Mendes, Minister of the Spanish and Portuguese (Sephardic) Congregation, penetrated its columns to support Emma Lazarus in her Zionist campaign:

To Miss Lazarus I pay my tribute of thanks, recognizing how her muse has awakened responsive patriotic vibrations in the Jewish heart. I acknowledge gratefully, very gratefully, that her pen has unveiled the figure of the martyr—nation of the world, properly posed in such a way as accords with truthful history and will command the admiration of ages.[57]

Though he believed, emphatically believed, in a restoration to Palestine, he acknowledged his basis of belief as different from hers. He did not explain the difference; however, one gathers that he perceived a continuum in contemporary plans for the return to Zion and the biblical promise—a perception including, it may be, an element of rationalization, but ideodynamically significant nevertheless, for it furnished the theoretical justification for orthodox acceptance of the modern Zionist idea.[58] The Reverend H. P. Mendes believed, enthusiastically believed (the preacher is manifest in his prose), in the Bible, and "the belief in a restoration rests upon the Bible's assertions, promises, and prophecies." Moreover, he and those sharing his faith, found "the Bible's prophecies echoed by the voice of History, endorsed by the Law of Human Progress, strengthened by the Law of Justice."[59]

Not until the late nineties, after Herzl wrote *The Jewish State,* did Zionism have a considerable impact on the course of American Jewish life. And Herzl, when he wrote, knew nothing of Emma Lazarus, of Leo Pinsker, or of any of the Hovevei Zion, the early proponents of Zionism. Nevertheless, were it not for these, Herzl's call would have been unheard, or heard by few. His message was not inherently more inspiring than Pinsker's, his blueprint for the return no better drawn. Yet the history of Zionism, scarcely distinguishing the dim outline of Pinsker cramped in one of its corridors, focuses on the shining figure of Herzl. The latter succeeded in capturing the effective attention of his people because his way was prepared by the Hovevei Zion. They had formed Hibbat Zion societies everywhere; but, of yet greater importance, they had organized Jewish awareness. And to no "friend of Zion," in fact to no one in nineteenth-century America, belongs so much responsibility—praise or blame—for keeping Zionism alive as to Emma Lazarus. Neither an incisive and original thinker, nor a brilliant and lucid strategist, she was primarily significant as a liaison agent between the first and second generations of political Zionists.

Notes

1. These appeared in the *American Hebrew* from November 3, 1882 to February 23, 1883. For convenience all subsequent notes will be to *An Epistle to the Hebrews,* a reprint from the press of Philip Cowen, Number 6 of the *Publications of the Federation of American Zionists* (New York, 1900). The following table will aid those who wish to locate individual epistles in either the periodical or the reprint (volume, date, and page or pages are listed in that order in the column headed *American Hebrew*):

Epistle	Vol.	*American Hebrew*	*An Epistle to the Hebrews*
I.	XII,	Nov. 3, 1882, 141	7–10
II.	XII,	Nov. 10, 1882, 151	11–15
III.	XIII,	Nov. 17, 1882, 4–5	16–20
IV.	XIII,	Nov. 24, 1882, 16–17	21–26
V.	XIII,	Dec. 1, 1882, 28	27–31
VI.	XIII,	Dec. 8, 1882, 40	32–36
VII.	XIII,	Dec. 15, 1882, 52–53	37–42
VIII.	XIII,	Dec. 22, 1882, 64	42–45
IX.	XIII,	Dec. 29, 1882, 76	46–51
X.	XIII,	Jan. 5, 1883, 88–89	52–57
XI.	XIII,	Jan. 12, 1883, 100–101	58–63
XII.	XIII,	Jan. 26, 1883, 125	64–67
XIII.	XIII,	Feb. 2, 1883, 137	68–72
XIV.	XIII,	Feb. 9, 1883, 149	73–77
XV.	XIV,	Feb. 23, 1883, 17	78–80

Epistles XII, XIII, XIV, and XV are listed as XIII, XIV, XV, and XVI, respectively, in the *American Hebrew,* and an article entitled "The Jewish Problem" which Emma Lazarus wrote for the *Century* (XXV [Feb., 1883], 602–611) is erroneously called "Epistle XII." The article—only portions of which are reprinted in the *American Hebrew* (XIII [Jan. 19, 1883], 119)—not being addressed to "Hebrews" is properly omitted from *An Epistle to the Hebrews.* The *American Hebrew* printed it as an Epistle because Emma Lazarus had had unusual occupations and interruptions "during the week she was to have written the chapter and was unable to meet her deadline" (M. U., *Letters of Emma Lazarus* [New York, 1949], 50; letter dated Jan. 14, 1883). Since the *American Hebrew* had the advance sheets of the "Midwinter Century" containing Lazarus' apposite essay on "The Jewish Problem" in its office, an "Epistle" was born.

2. *Epistle* I, 7.

3. *Epistle* XV, 78.

4. *Epistle* XV, 8.

5. See the "Introduction" by B. Netanyahu to *Road to Freedom: Writings and Addresses of Leo Pinsker* (New York, 1944), 29, 37.

6. See Josef Patai, *Star over Jordan: The Life of Theodor Herzl,* translated by Francis Magyar (New York, 1946), 49, 55–56.

7. "Russian Jews and Gentiles: From a Russian Point of View," *Century,* vol. XXIII (April 1882), 905–920.

8. Lacking detailed evidence in this regard it would appear there is only the military service to justify his title (bestowed at an election for militia officers which he declared was attended only by himself and two others). See Isaac Goldberg, *Major Noah* (Philadelphia, 1944), 73.

9. *Discourse on the Restoration of the Jews* (New York, 1845).

10. Ibid., 35–39.

11. The standard work on the history of Zionism, *Hibbat Zion* by Nahum Sokolow (Jerusalem, 1934), expounds knowledgeably the writings of each of the proto-Zionists mentioned in the text, and dozens of others besides. As a formal organization, it ought to be noted, the Hovevei Zion in America dates from 1882, when Joseph I. Bluestone organized the first group in New York.

12. "Zionism," a term anachronistic in 1882, is nevertheless too convenient to be eschewed.

13. *Epistle* VI, 32.

14. *The Dance to Death: A Historical Tragedy* (New York, 1882), dedication–3; *The Poems of Emma Lazarus* (Cambridge, 1889), 69. The text of the dedication is from the latter volume and differs in small items of punctuation from the former.

15. Published in London, 1876. References here are to the 1888, New York, edition.

16. See Montagu Frank Modder, *The Jew in the Literature of England* (Philadelphia, 1939), 289. (This book is cited, rather than a number of others containing fuller and better analyses, because of its excellent bibliographies.)

17. *Epistle* VI, 32.

18. Full title: *The Land of Gilead: With Excursions in the Lebanon* (New York, 1880).

19. Vol. XII, 242–255.

20. Ibid., 245.

21. Ibid., 246.

22. *Epistle* XIV, 73 ff.

23. Vol. XIV (March 16, 1883), 50–51. The letter is misdated February 6, 1882.

24. Ralph L. Rusk, *Letters to Emma Lazarus* (New York, 1939), 51–52. Rusk says, "Presumably the . . . letter belongs to 1883 or 1884, but I have no conclusive evidence." Schappes (*Letters*, 58 f. n.157), thinks that probably it belongs to 1883. Some of the evidence does point to the earlier years, for the edict of the Porte had recently been issued and Oliphant during the earlier half of 1882 and the latter half of 1883 was much agitated by the prohibition against colonization (see Margaret Oliphant, *Memoir of the Life of Laurence Oliphant and Alice Oliphant, His Wife,* vol. II (New York, 1891), 223 ff.). On the other hand, the tone of the letter might startle an uninitiated correspondent, and there is no evidence of extensive prior exchanges between Oliphant and Emma Lazarus. Moreover, on May 9, 1883, Emma refers to another communication (See footnote 37), dated Haifa, April 6, 1883, she had received from Oliphant—which would mean that Oliphant sent her two letters within nine days, and sent the second before he had received a reply to the first. The date of the letter referred to in the text must therefore remain tentative until other evidence is adduced.

25. Rusk, *Letters to Emma Lazarus,* 52.

26. Schappes, *Letters,* 58, reprinted from the *American Hebrew,* vol. XIV (May 11, 1883), 146. Lazarus addresses the editor of the *American Hebrew,* summarizing in part Oliphant's letter which she has presumably just received. Oliphant's original has not been located.

27. Idem.

28. Idem.

29. "A Problematic Champion," *Jewish Messenger,* vol. LIII (Jan. 26, 1883), 4.

30. Idem.

31. Vol. LII (February 9, 1883), 4.

32. Pinsker, a westernized Russian and an "emancipated" Jew, wrote his pamphlet in German.

33. *Epistle* VI, 34.

34. Idem.

35. *Epistle* VI, 34–35.

36. Max I. Baym, "Emma Lazarus' Approach to Renan and her essay, 'Renan and the Jews,'" *Publications of the American Jewish Historical Society,* vol. XXXVII (1947), 22.

37. "Voyage en Syrie," *Revue des deux mondes,* vol. LVI (June 15, 1882), 888–902.

38. Ibid., 907.

39. Ibid., 911–912.

40. *Epistle* VI, 33. She translates Charmes, *op. cit.,* 912.

41. *Epistle* VI, 35.

42. Idem.

43. *Epistle* VII, 37–38.

44. Ibid., 39.

45. Ibid., 41.

46. Ibid., 42; *Epistle* XII, 66, *Epistle* XIX, 73.

47. *Epistle* XII, 64.

48. Ibid., 67.

49. Ibid., 66.

50. Dora Kobler, *Leo Pinsker and Emma Lazarus* (London, 1943), 8. A thorough investigation of the resemblances between these two writers has long been desired; Miss Kobler's pamphlet, regrettably, leaves the investigation still to be desired.

51. Emma Lazarus, "Spring Songs," *Jewish Messenger,* vol. XLV (Jan. 3, 1879), 1; [s. M. Isaacs] "A Song of Spring," Ibid., vol. XLV (Jan. 10, 1879), 4.

52. "A Problematic Champion," *Jewish Messenger,* vol. LII (Jan. 26, 1883), 4.

53. Idem.

54. *Epistle* VIII, 43.

55. *Sinai to Cincinnati: Lay Views on the Writings of Isaac M. Wise, Founder of Reform Judaism in America,* ed. Dean Wilansky (New York, 1937), 189.

56. The *American Hebrew,* from 1882 on, supported Zionism. Assuredly not Reform and not quite Orthodox, the religious bent of its editorials approximated Conservatism, the movement growing out of the German Historical School. A good statement of the Conservative position is to be found in Robert Gordis's *The Jew Faces a New World* (New York, 1941).

57. "Miss Lazarus and the Restoration of the Jews," *Jewish Messenger,* vol. LIII (Feb. 9, 1883), 5.

58. For an excellent summary of his influence, see David de Sola Pool's biography, "Henry Pereira Mendes," *American Jewish Year Book,* vol. XL (1938), 41 ff.

59. Mendes, *loc. cit.,* 5.

"The Banner of The Jew" (1882)

Emma Lazarus

Wake, Israel, wake! Recall to-day
   The glorious Maccabean rage,
The sire heroic, hoary-gray,
   His five-fold lion-lineage:
The Wise, the Elect, the Help-of-God,
The Burst-of-Spring, the Avenging Rod.*

From Mizpeh's mountain-ridge† they saw
   Jerusalem's empty streets, her shrine
Laid waste where Greeks profaned the Law,
   With idol and with pagan sign.
Mourners in tattered black were there,
With ashes sprinkled on their hair.

Then from the stony peak there rang
   A blast to ope the graves: down poured
The Maccabean clan, who sang
   Their battle-anthem to the Lord.
Five heroes lead, and following, see,
Ten thousand rush to victory!

Oh for Jerusalem's trumpet now,
   To blow a blast of shattering power,
To wake the sleepers high and low,
   And rouse them to the urgent hour!
No hand for vengeance—but to save,
A million naked swords should wave.

*The sons of Mattathias—Yohanan, Simon, Judah, Eleazar, and Jonathan.
† The Mizpeh was a place of solemn assembly for the Jews of Palestine at the time of the Maccabean revolt against Antiochus IV, 175–164 B.C.E.

O deem not dead that martial fire,
   Say not the mystic flame is spent!
With Moses' law and David's lyre,
   Your ancient strength remains unbent.
Let but an Ezra* rise anew.
To lift the *Banner of the Jew!*

A rag, a mock at first—erelong,
When men have bled and women wept,
To guard its precious folds from wrong,
Even they who shrunk, even they who slept,
Shall leap to bless it, and to save.
Strike! for the brave revere the brave!

*See Book of Ezra, Old Testament.

Chapter 2

Among American Jewish women leaders in the pre-state era, none features more prominently in the history of the Zionist enterprise than Henrietta Szold (1860–1945). Born in Baltimore, Maryland, on the eve of the Civil War, Szold died in Jerusalem during the twilight of World War II. In many ways her life mirrored the ascendance and modernization of American Jewry as a whole. A product of the German Jewish milieu that shaped American Jewish life in the nineteenth century, Szold was raised in a liberal but traditional Jewish household. Her parents, Rabbi Benjamin and Sophie (Schaar) Szold, saw to it that she received a proper American education through high school as well as private instruction in German, Hebrew, and traditional Judaism. Although she aspired to be a teacher—and even established a night school for East European Jewish immigrants—her many talents quickly impelled her to enter a variety of Jewish intellectual, cultural, and political spheres. A brief overview of her trajectory reveals a woman passionately committed to the ideal of Jewish social activism and the values of American Progressivism.

In 1888 Szold joined the publications committee of the newly established Jewish Publication Society of America, where she served as the only woman of the nine-member group and played an instrumental role in the issuance of a number of seminal English-language publications on Jewish history, religion, and philosophy as well as the classic JPS Hebrew Bible project and the *American Jewish Year Book*. Next she enrolled in the Jewish Theological Seminary in New York City, where she was required to affirm in writing that she had no intention of training for a rabbinic career. (The American rabbinate would remain a male preserve well into the twentieth century.) In 1897 she became active in the Federation of American Zionists, the first countrywide centrist Zionist group in the United States, later renamed the Zionist Organization of America (ZOA). After traveling to Palestine in 1909 at the invitation of her friend and colleague Rabbi Judah L. Magnes (1877–1948), she founded the Daughters of Zion-Hadassah Chapter of the ZOA. What was at first regarded by the organization's male leadership as a ladies' auxiliary swiftly emerged as an independent women's Zionist organization that blossomed into the largest and most successful of all American Zionist groups. Among Hadassah's primary objectives was the establishment in Palestine of the Hadassah Medical Unit, a precursor of the Yishuv's emerging medical care infrastructure and the Hadassah Hospital on Mount Scopus in Jerusalem.

From the 1920s until her death, Szold lived in Palestine and served in a variety of Zionist leadership positions including the three-member Palestine executive of the World Zionist Congress, where she was responsible for the movement's education and health portfolios. In the 1930s she held the social welfare portfolio of the Vaad Leumi, the Yishuv's semi-autonomous legislative body. In these capacities, Szold collaborated with the Yishuv's prevailing Labor-led political coalition and spearheaded a wide range of social, educational, and health initiatives that led to significant reform of the country's educational system, the introduction of social-work activities, and the establishment of modern health care facilities.

Szold was also among the first Zionist leaders to comprehend the magnitude of the Nazi threat to European Jewish life. Her work as head of the Zionist movement's Youth Aliyah department resulted in the immigration to Palestine of thousands of refugee children and, as a consequence, hers became a household name in every town, village, and colony of the Yishuv. She also became an advocate of Arab-Jewish reconciliation, even at the risk of strenuous opposition to such progressive policies among many of her followers in Hadassah.

In the chapter that follows, Allon Gal, a leading student of American Zionism, investigates Szold's worldview and illustrates her centrality as an independent Zionist leader and thinker in the first half of the twentieth century. Drawing on a wealth of primary materials and some recent scholarship concerning Szold and Hadassah, Gal examines the Americanized quality and context of Szold's Zionist perspective and illustrates her steadfast commitment to social justice in the new Jewish society-in-the-making in Palestine. We have also included a revealing glimpse of correspondence between Szold and a young admirer. The exchange highlights Szold's exceedingly modest demeanor and underscores an aspect of female Zionist leadership that stood in stark contrast to male Zionist leaders of the pre-state period: a readiness to sublimate one's personal ego and legacy for the sake of the greater good. This was certainly one of Szold's most enduring qualities. It may also help to explain, at least in part, why she and other women have yet to command the scholarly attention of other major Zionist figures, each of whom has been the subject of first-rate full-length biographies.

The Zionist Vision of Henrietta Szold

Allon Gal

Henrietta Szold's Zionist views were basically a product of the democratic qualities of American culture. Antisemitism played almost no part in shaping her Zionist outlook. On the contrary, she believed that American society was genuinely democratic and amenable to reform. If its Jewish citizens had problems, there were pragmatic remedies. In addition, she deeply loved her native state of Maryland; and she never disparaged the American Jewish diaspora. Rather, she believed America complemented Jewish life.[1]

At the same time, Szold was aware of the danger of assimilation and did not regard America as the ideal place for Judaism to revive and flourish. Rather, Judaism could best develop in a fully integrated Jewish setting—the Jewish homeland. For these reasons, her communal Jewish activity and her Zionist work in America developed simultaneously. This ideological course was rather characteristic of mainstream American Zionism.[2]

Organizationally, too, Szold was anchored in the mainstream of American Zionism. She was the admired founding-mother of Hadassah, the largest continuous Zionist movement in America. She served as its president for a decade and a half during its formative years (1912–1921, 1923–1926) and as its honorary president for the rest of her life. During her *Erez Israel* period (in intervals between 1920 and 1945), she maintained ties with American Zionists, particularly Hadassah members. While abroad, she kept in touch with such Zionist leaders as Harry Friedenwald, Israel Friedlaender, Judah L. Magnes, Stephen S. Wise, Mordecai M. Kaplan, Louis D. Brandeis, and Julian W. Mack. Throughout most of her life, a wide audience of American Zionists received her warmly.[3] At the same time—as this article will elucidate—Henrietta Szold did have her own path, her genuine Zionist philosophy and personal dream.

Zionism as Judaism

Her commitment to Judaism was at the very core of her Zionist vision, therefore Szold's style of Zionism should be emphatically distinguished from European Zionism, which promulgated a revolt against traditional

Judaism and Jewish values that had evolved in the centuries-long *galut* [exile]. Szold's Zionist course strove to preserve core traditions and the spirit of historic Judaism.[4] In 1896, at the centennial memorial of the death of Moses Mendelssohn, the philosopher of the German Enlightenment and spiritual leader of German Jewry, Henrietta Szold delivered an intriguing lecture, "A Century of Jewish Thought," that placed her as a link between Mendelssohn's legacy and modern Zionist ideology.

According to Mendelssohn, Szold suggested, the secret strength of Jewish national survival derived from three sources: the laws of Torah, the heritage of the prophets, and the Bible's continuous vitality. Similarly, the Hebrew language was not abandoned in 2,500 years. Modern Jewish nationalism consecrates the secular but could not be entirely secular. Having set down these premises, she depicted Mendelssohn as the pioneer of Jewish national renaissance.[5]

Szold felt the greatness of Mendelssohn's group lay in their reviving the Hebrew language and culture, while avoiding the "trap of national conceit and Chauvinism." Leopold Zunz, one of the commanding figures of Jewish scholarship in the nineteenth century, also followed the path of eschewing assimilation and Jewish chauvinism. The Zionist movement enthusiastically adopted this delicate line. Szold saw in Zionism a love for the Jewish cultural inheritance, an essentially humanistic and universalistic national endowment. This heritage stemmed from the ethical message embedded in "Hebrew ideals that are amiable, noble, and peace-oriented."[6]

Szold developed this fundamental theme methodically in a 1901 article in the *Maccabaean,* the periodical of the Federation of American Zionists. Here she claimed that the Jewish people was facing an internal danger of national dissolution that could be countered by the revitalization and modernization of "the Talmudic system." To achieve revitalization, the movement should emphasize two factors: the revival of Jewish ideals and the advancement of the creative role of the Jewish community in *Erez Israel.* According to Szold, uniting the Jewish people with Judaism should be Zionism's historic mission.[7]

Szold's conception of Zionism was profoundly spiritual rather than solely political or practical. In "The New Year of Trees," an article written on the festival of *Tu Bishvat* [Fifteenth of *Shvat*] in 1903, she peculiarly justified the holiday—the redemption of the land for the Zionists in Palestine—as follows:

. . . Trees are a symbol, as a sign for the whole of God's nature. The Jewish religion wants us to have our eyes wide open for all things in the world of man, the past and the present, the Jewish world and the non-Jewish world, but no less it wants us to give heed to what passes in the world of nature. . . . Life is made up not only by the objects seen . . . the most powerful forces are those that work unseen, with patience, with perseverance, and in silence. . . . Let [us] apply [our] mind and study how the sap rises, brings life to the driest stick, clothing it with verdure and color, and [we] will at the same time learn that beside the life of material things . . . there is a hidden life, which we call the life spiritual, the Godly life, full of the beauty of holiness, a life of love, of charity, of hope, of faith in God, of noble self-sacrifice.[8]

Shortly after a failed love affair with the world-renowned Talmud scholar Professor Louis Ginzberg, Szold traveled to Palestine with her mother in 1909. As is well known, the visit was instrumental in leading to the creation of Hadassah, the Zionist women's organization dedicated to practical work in *Erez Israel*. However, the tenor of Szold's spiritual Zionism did not change. She would often recall that during her historic visit, she decided to remain a Zionist because she discovered in Palestine not just the challenge of relieving misery and disease but also the opportunity to achieve an "intellectual life, coupled with idealism, enthusiasm, and hope. Only Zionist activism carried out on the soil of *Erez Israel* could realize the dream of Judaism's future and salvation."[9]

In a letter to Mrs. Julius Rosenwald, years after the establishment of Hadassah, Szold identified "the cause of Palestine" with "the cause of the Jew and, most important of all, of Judaism." She went on to define the Zionist enterprise in Palestine as "the need of a center from which Jewish culture and inspiration will flow." This center will not only

bring immediate blessing to those now in distress and in terror of life, and [it will be] a blessing for all future times redounding to the benefit not only of those who will make use of their sanctuary rights in Palestine [but] also those who like ourselves, [remain] in a happy, prosperous country, [who] will be free to draw spiritual nourishment from a center dominated wholly by Jewish traditions and the Jewish ideals of universal peace and universal brotherhood.[10]

Her universalistic interpretation of Judaism notwithstanding, Szold tended to shun such American Progressive Zionists as Brandeis, for whom traditional Judaism was of minor importance. Nevertheless, Szold's efforts in Palestine received Brandeis's all-out blessing, as well as the backing of the Brandeis-Mack group. In the conflict between the American Zionists and the European-based Lipsky-Weizmann group, she chose to "throw in [her] lot with the Mack-Brandeis party." Still, she could not bring herself to fully identify with their attenuated links to Judaism and what she termed their "half-hearted" approach to cultural-educational Zionist work in the diaspora.[11]

A More Beautiful Torah

Szold fervently believed that Zionism was the only way to safeguard an ethically meaningful Jewish religious life. She revealed these sentiments in an expressive address to the Zionist Organization of America's (ZOA) Administrative Committee in 1936, elaborating on the roots of her affiliation with Zionism. She explained how she had declared herself a Zionist as early as 1891, "five years before Herzl." Her commitment stemmed from the atmosphere in which she was raised with its emphasis on the living, modern, ethical *halakhah* that could evolve only within an independent Jewish framework. "I had been prepared for it [to be drawn into Zionism] by my conception of Jewish development . . . a conception that I got from my father's interpretation."

My father was in the habit of interpreting the daily events of life Jewishly to his children—by the *halakhah*—that such and such is the Jewish point of view. I remember for instance that we had a murder trial in Baltimore, and my father took that trial and demonstrated to us point by point how differently that would have been handled by Jewish law. That is what impressed me tremendously—the abnormality of the Jewish people and the need to restore the Jewish people to normality. But for me normality was in those days, the development of the Jewish laws under the circumstance of modern life. That was my entrance to Zionism. [12]

Szold bemoaned the shameful backwardness of Jewish law regarding women's rights and expressed hope that Zionism would institute changes: "Take the question of the *agunah* [a woman] who is neither wife nor widow. There are thousands of *agunot,* particularly after the World War, and our rabbis and great *gaonim* [sages] have not even touched that phase, despite the fact that we have the possibility for a normal development. That is the way I came to Zionism."[13]

Szold had joined the Zionist movement only after being convinced that it could overcome a tendency toward zealotry and mass chauvinism. Szold believed Palestine held the highest potential for Judaic development and protection of the Jewish people from moral failing. "For saving the spiritual, intellectual things . . . there is nothing but Zionism. . . ."[14]

Szold's vision of Zionism was faithful to its ethical-Judaic origins. For example, she concluded her famous 1906 article, "How the Torah Grows," with the hope that the Torah would

help Jews . . . to lead clean, wise, and useful lives. . . . And if God in His good time will lead the Jews back to our land we shall carry thither with us what we took thence—a Torah, but a greater and a more beautiful Torah than it was two thousand years ago. Even there, in our comfortable home, our first and chief duty, the purpose for which we live, the thing that will continue to be our wisdom and our understanding in the sight of the nations, will be to take care of our inheritance from the days of Moses, to add to it, to enrich it, and to pass it on to posterity, to an endless chain of "sons of the Law," the great Congregation of Jacob.[15]

Szold supported the Zionist Pittsburgh program of 1918 that perceived Jewish Palestine as a largely cooperative endeavor and persistently advocated its incorporation into the text of the British Mandate for Palestine.[16]

Szold's understanding of Prophetic Judaism was human-centered and linked to a free society. She sided with the secular camp in the Yishuv's blistering religious struggles, such as observance of the Sabbath, in order to bolster the democratic foundations of society and to consign religion to a purely voluntary and ethical sphere.[17]

Szold rejected displays of nationalism and messianism in Zionism, and loathed the appearance of these elements in the religious teachings of Abraham Isaac Kook, the Ashkenazi chief rabbi of Palestine from 1921 to 1935. In one of her letters she went so far as to portray the chief rabbi as a man "who has not an iota of grace or even humanness."[18]

Mutual suspicion characterized her relationship with the Mizrahi, the Yishuv's mainstream, religious Zionist movement at the time. Szold was painfully disappointed by the state of religious affairs in Palestine. Addressing the special meeting of the ZOA Administrative Committee in 1936, Szold expressed her frustration that religion in Palestine had not been developing in a more creative, modern, and socially responsive way.[19] Nevertheless, she subtly avoided confrontation with the religious establishment in Palestine by loyally attending a modern, socially active synagogue in Jerusalem with a similarly minded circle of friends.[20]

The Stubborn Crusade

For Szold, *aliyah* was not a radical phase in Zionism; rather, Jewish immigration and settlement in *Erez Israel* was a process in which old and new elements intermingled. Fascinated with the Jewish presence in *Erez Israel* before Zionists came to settle the land, she published an article on this subject in 1915 demonstrating that *Erez Israel* had been developing along Jewish lines throughout the nineteenth century. In her words, "The Old Settlement looks upon itself as the religious 'representative' of the secular Jewish world outside. The New Settlement strives to build up a self-sufficient Palestinian Jewish community. In evaluating the New Palestine, all the elements composing the two Settlements are equally important."[21]

On one hand, she argued, Palestine should be settled in an innovative way; on the other hand, she insisted, it should be "hallowed by the past." According to this synthesis "more values and more positive values [would] be created": "A compact Jewish community, composed of members happy through untrammeled Jewish self-expression, must reconstitute a Palestine spiritually worthy of the unique place it has occupied in the history of human thought. *Ex Oriente lux* must again be a true saying, that the sacrifices in Palestine and outside of the land may have been worthwhile."[22]

Nevertheless, she did not conceive of Palestine as the crucible for the shaping of "a new Jewish personality," as most European pioneers did. On the contrary, she viewed the diaspora Jew and Jewish history of the Middle Ages in a positive light; the Jew of the *galut,* according to Szold, had been resourceful, dynamic, assertive, and at the same time a meaningful participant in the surrounding world. She specifically included the ghetto Jew in this category.

The Jew will return [to *Erez Israel*] bringing with him experiences gathered in the countries in which he dwelt, and finding in his native environment the spirit according to which his experiences will be molded anew. . . . Jewish vitality—the vital abilities of the Jew and the vital force of Judaism—will be poured like a stream into the sciences, the industries, the arts, the literature, the political activity, the daily human walks of the Jew. His going up and his going down in the land will be Jewish. If Zionism is, indeed, a spiritual force, then it has the power to make its adherents not only shout until they are red in the face, but also live out Jewish ideals in religion, in philosophy, in government, in business, in every work of hand and brain.[23]

Erez Israel, then, was for Szold not just a territory to be settled by enthusiastic inhabitants; rather, it was the ideal setting for the reestablishment of a human-being-centered and God-loving Jewish civilization. But Judaism is far more. It is a system of living, an all-embracing theory, a varied, multifarious civilization, providing for every human emergency, equal to every human need, with room for every human endeavor—and holding out every divine hope.[24]

It comes as no surprise that Szold combined her "practical work" in Palestine with the moral improvement of Jewish life and values there. Her medical project became merged in her eyes with her care for general education. In a letter summing up her first year in the new country in 1921, she wrote, "I still find the moral atmosphere here stifling, whether among the orthodox or in the new Yishub [*sic*]. The education of the children is false. We are raising an arrogant, self-sufficient generation." And she went on to elaborate on the ways to bring up "to heights, the two systems, the medical and the educational, [that] have the same requirements to ensure their perfection."[25]

Szold maintained this Zionist vision while, for example, discussing Hadassah's work in Palestine in 1928:

... The Zionist ideal is larger even than Palestine itself. The upbuilding of Palestine is a symbol, the concrete expression of your Zionist conviction that Judaism must be changed back from a creed to a way of life. Even a successful economic upbuilding of Palestine will remain an empty shell unless you and the whole of Jewry fill the work for Palestine with Jewish content—with high ethical aspirations, with just thinking and just action, with adherence to the behest of an exalted conception of life, which defines idealism as unswerving honesty and truth. . . . you must participate in the shaping of an honest, noble Zionist policy.[26]

In the same vein she wrote in 1932:

More and more it becomes clear to me that only insofar as the bearers of Zionism are penetrated through and through with the spirit of Judaism can there be value to the movement. That is the reason I put Judaism in juxtaposition to Zionism. I had always looked forward to the realization of Zionism as the opportunity for translating Judaism into terms of practice.[27]

While she strove for humanistic and attainable goals in the Yishuv, Szold persisted in her crusade for a social-work system. This stood in stark comparison to the dogmatic anti-*galut* ideology of Labor Zionism, which proclaimed that after the new society in Palestine was nurtured on labor unionism and socialism, all social ills would automatically be solved. Opposed to this, Szold pointed out the need for social responsibility in *Erez Israel* similar to the role of U.S. Jewish welfare organizations and American Jewish contributions to social welfare at large.

When in 1930 the Vaad Leumi came into existence there was no social service. The Zionists dogmatically opposed it. They said we do not want to do what we did in the *galut*, base life on charity. We want justice and social righteousness and that is not charity and therefore they invited the JOINT to do this nasty piece of work, admitting that it had to be done and not realizing that nothing was more unjust and unsocial than to deny [it] to those who needed advice and relief. Therefore I was put in this position of having to start a piece of work. I started in institutional work. . . .[28]

She then went on to describe how she had labored without a budget and how "Mr. Ben-Zvi, sat the head of the table [*sic*], a big broad man, and shrugged his shoulders and he said out of the hollow which he created with his shoulders, 'We are going to offer them [the socially deprived] work and *nigmar*—finished—let them take it or leave it.'" Szold returned to the need for social services, dealing with health care and broken families. But only in 1935, at the Nineteenth Zionist Congress, was a commission for social programs set up. No money was allocated for the budget, however, and Szold, in a two-year protest, refused to attend the weekly meetings of the Zionist Executive.[29]

Getting the Zionist movement to agree to implement social services in the Yishuv was a great victory for Szold. The stubborn crusade she waged derived from her social experience in the United States and the influence of American Progressivism. And significantly, in contrast to Ben-Zvi's rigid socialist Zionism, Szold respected the compassionate characteristics she found in Jewish history.[30]

Ironically, Szold's actual identification with *Erez Israel* did not go very deep. Precisely because her *aliyah* was grounded in a goal "larger than Palestine," her presence there seemed elusive and flighty. At moments of disappointment and personal crisis that occurred all too frequently, she longed to return "home" to America.[31] Sadly the spiritual side of the Promised Land never lived up to her expectations.

No matter how earnestly she tried to attach herself to the landscape of her adopted country, she never stopped yearning for the natural beauty of Maryland and the warmth and familiar smells of her parents' home. "In the dry season, one thinks of Elijah and Job and Amos. Now in the spring-like winter [the letter was written in December], it is Ruth as Botticelli might have painted her, and the Psalmist in his non-militant mood, and a little bit of Jeremiah at his tenderest."[32]

In an odd way Judaism served as an intermediary between herself and her natural surroundings. It tied her to the scenery insofar as she imagined it as biblical countryside. The actual physical geography of Palestine was subordinate to Judaism. She revered the personalities of Ruth, the author of Psalms, and of Jeremiah, urging the inhabitants to live up to these ideals. Szold endorsed the Torah's exhortation that *Erez Israel* be given to the Jewish People on condition that they remain God-loving and moral. Of all the prophets, Szold was attracted especially to Jeremiah, the thundering moralist. On arriving in the Holy Land, she admitted to her close friend Alice L. Seligsberg that "we are studying Jeremiah"; and by this she meant they were pursuing Jeremiah's spiritual path. Later she penned, "The Jews, whom Jeremiah and myself criticize unmercifully, are a wonderful people. . . ." Hadassah's motto, chosen by Szold with Israel Friedlaender's help, was taken directly from Jeremiah's chastising lament: "Behold the voice of the cry of my people from a land that is very far off . . . Is there no balm in Gilead? Is there no physician there? Why then is not the healing of the daughter of my people accomplished?"[33]

A reader of Szold's voluminous correspondence from Palestine may search in vain to find allusion to concrete descriptions of the country and its battlefield past. Instead, Szold was chiefly interested in the beauty facet of the country's landscape, especially the flowers "over here," in relation to those in her beloved Maryland. Many of Szold's letters intertwine motifs of Maryland wildflowers and images of the pristine scenery of ancient Palestine. In a letter to her sister in 1936 she wrote: "Over the fence of the little fruit garden of my Youth Aliyah office a honeysuckle vine drapes itself. I have been bringing bunches of the blooms home with me and making myself homesick as I draw in the fragrance that fills my room."[34]

In 1940, utterly homesick, she wrote to her family about her garden's desperate struggle for survival:

I had a gardener, Perles, the grandson of our father's best friend! re-pot my window plants. Most of them are now arranged on the table of my porch. The fuchsias bloomed, but wanly. There is too much sun, too little moisture for them; they are now standing under the table for protection. Mr. Perles insists upon keeping the begonias and the amaryllis indoors. Do you remember the begonia that bloomed so incessantly? It is still blooming. The other one, from Ayanot, is gorgeous as to leaf and bloom. . . . The most luxuriant pot next to the Ayanot begonia is the one planted with a little slip by Adele from the Ehrlich garden. Your enumeration of the spring blossoms in Eva Leah's woods made me homesick beyond words. But it was right for me to stay here![35]

An intriguing reference to Maryland vegetation and the divine promise of Palestine is reflected in a 1941 letter from Jerusalem to her sister: "To think of Golden Bantam corn and fish with flavor, and a walk through ferny woods! It is like hearing about the glories of the ancient Temple service and not having the privilege of witnessing them."[36] The highest goal, reserved for the Holy Temple, always remained intangible.[37]

Education and History

Szold envisioned the day when a highly educated society would develop in *Erez Israel*.[38] To advance her ideas, she labored vigorously for an educational system that would advance democracy and individual responsibility in the public sphere. Her model was Jewish education of the Second Temple Period characterized by small classes and direct, value-oriented teacher-pupil relationships. Her plan was to synthesize the ancient Jewish heritage with the modern American ideal of a pluralistic-democratic society as described in the works of educator John Dewey and social philosopher Horace Kallen. Alexander Dushkin, a distinguished Jewish educator associated with Szold in the New York Kehillah [community] experiment (1908–1922), understood her attempt to reform educational programs in the Yishuv. In the 1920s Dushkin and Szold succeeded in bringing to Palestine Dr. Isaac Berkson, an outstanding scholar and proponent of cultural pluralism.[39]

Whereas the Palestinian pioneers focused on ancient epochs of national sovereignty, especially the First Temple Period, Szold preferred to seek expressions of the national ethos in Jewish history of the Middle Ages. She persistently claimed that medieval Jewish history, tortured as it was, had bequeathed a legacy of social compassion and sensitivity to the vulnerability of the weak.[40] As national president of Hadassah in 1925, she was asked to speak at the inauguration of the Hebrew University on Mount Scopus. On this historic occasion she delivered an eloquent speech embellished with historical-ethical references summarizing her aspiration for a merger between spiritual Zionism and humanistic education.

Not dry-as-dust learning do we ask for. We long for life. We long to know how to live life in the diaspora as it will and must be lived by the Jew in the homeland—wisely, justly, truly, beautifully, and nobly. Let our sons and daughters enter your research laboratories to learn under your guidance how to extract the Jewish spirit from the varied heritage of all the Jewish ages. Chaldea, Egypt, Babylonia, Assyria, Persia, Greece, Rome, Spain, Russia, all the remotest recesses of our abiding-places, make them yield up what is life-giving. Sublimate the experiences of a hundred generations of faith, thought, law, literature, action, and suffering—yes, suffering, too, since of poignant suffering there was so much, and its purging fires may not be extinguished in our memory, lest we forget and wax proud. Transmute into terms of modern Jewish living all that has happened to us in the lands of our sojourn, all the ideas, which the centuries of events have engendered in us. Thus shall our sons and daughters become a blessing to us and to those who consort with us. They will be fathers and mothers of virile generations who will live consciously as the heritors of an eternal way of life. They will be teachers who know how to pierce to the minds and hearts of little children and implant the spirit you have bestowed upon them. Teach them harmonious living—how to transform theory into practice, thought into act, aspiration into progressive fulfillment, love into life.[41]

In her lofty view of the Jewish people, the vast sweep of its history was to be mobilized toward the ideal of a harmonious Jewish society.

In similar fashion, Szold endorsed a liberal attitude toward revival of the Hebrew language. As a Zionist, she was committed to the modernization and development of Hebrew and used it in daily discourse. At the same time, she was fascinated by the multilingual panorama of the Yishuv and considered it an invaluable Jewish asset. She abhorred the nationalistic slogan *rak ivrit!* [Only Hebrew!] rampant in the Yishuv. This aggressive cultural obligation had become especially demanding under the fiery leadership of Menahem Ussishkin.

Szold was not alone in rejecting this passionate cry. Most of the tiny community of Americans in Palestine disparagingly labeled Ussishkin "Menahem Pasha" or "Tsar Menahem," even though the majority of the Yishuv, particularly those of East European origins, viewed him admiringly as "the man of iron." Szold, in her gentle way, yearned for a living Hebrew that would flourish amiably side by side with other languages, rather than excluding them. She shed tears of remorse when Eliezer Ben-Yehudah, the pioneering linguist in restoring Hebrew as a modern language, demanded that public life in the Yishuv be purified of traces of English.[42]

Hebrew was not Szold's first language. She had to labor to deliver a formal address. Nevertheless, her "compromising" attitude to the revival of Hebrew stemmed from her *Weltanschauung,* not personal linguistic difficulties. She viewed the ancient tongue as she viewed the entire Zionist enterprise in Palestine. Both were refined improvements of aging traditions rather than revolutionary ideologies separating from the *galutic* past.[43]

Cultural Osmosis

Szold's vision of Judaic revival through Zionism had points in common with Ahad Haam's, without being identical. Her American Jewish background made the difference. The classic, European, cultural Zionist constantly warned against "assimilation through imitation,"[44] whereas Szold, ardent, Hebraic-Judaic revivalist as she was, sought an intensive exchange between Jewish national culture and the civilized world. "Osmosis" became a dominant motif in Szold's dialogue with Zionism.

In a significant 1916 speech, Szold expanded on this theme of Jewish cosmopolitanism: "the inner history of the Jews shows . . . a constant process of osmosis, a transfusion of elements from the outside. . . . Once it had assimilated, it gave forth new stimuli, that is the true cosmopolitanism of the Jew. Such cosmopolitanism cannot be destroyed by nationalism. On the contrary, nationalism, the recognition of one's own nature and need, fosters it.[45]

For Szold, as well as for many American Jews, the concept of Zionism (particularly in pre-Holocaust times) included a commitment to general (i.e., not only Jewish) social improvement. She constantly pursued a meaningful Jewish-Zionist contribution to world civilization. As she stated in 1914,

It is because he [today's Zionist] . . . declines to win favor for his people by virtue only of past service, past nobility, and past martyrdom; because he is convinced that it [contemporary Zionism] is capable of present service and present nobility, as it has shown itself capable of present martyrdom, that he seeks, in these modern days to be more than merely a martyr. He asks a fair chance qua Jew to be once more a contributing factor to civilization.[46]

In Szold's Zionist outlook, Jewish contribution to modern world civilization was a major goal. She often elaborated on the Jewish potential for bringing various nations together in a constructive way.

By virtue of his/her historical diffusion among the nations and unique communal experience, the modern Jew, she believed, had a special role to play in the rapprochement of East and West. She referred to this task as the noblest of missions for Jewish nationalism. She astutely pointed out that assimilatory pressures in Western, democratic, capitalist societies could, paradoxically, lead to the revival of Jewish communal ideas. This would occur because "the right to live in a community must be recognized as inherent in the idea of liberty."[47]

Szold concluded her 1916 programmatic lecture by announcing that the Jewish, "Oriental" contribution to society must be based on communality and justice:

These are the visions that have not departed from the hearts of the Zionist Jews. Almost his first achievement for the land of the fathers was the establishment of the National Fund, based on the law of social righteousness characteristic of Jewish law. . . . With his peculiar nationality guarded and permitted to develop, he will not lose in cosmopolitanism but only gain in force—more than ever become the intermediary between the Orient and the Occident. Osmosis will not cease. It will again, be reinforced by modern opportunities, which annihilate time and space, become a reciprocal process. And the creative play of a group in the East will stimulate the creative play of group in the West.[48]

Jewish nationalism, then, with its "osmotic" or absorptive nature, would forever create a diversified culture in *Erez Israel*. Conscious of the two millennia the Jews dwelt among the nations and absorbed their positive influences, Szold felt that Jewish life in *Erez Israel* had to be heterogeneous and pluralistic. It comes as no surprise that diversity for Szold was "a sign of health and modernity."[49]

Internationalist Zionism

Szold's Zionist mission in *Erez Israel* never lapsed into narrow nationalism. Under her leadership, the Hadassah organization's services were offered, on principle, to all the inhabitants of Palestine, Jewish and non-Jewish. This stood in contrast to the restrictive policy of the leading Labor Zionist health program Kupat Holim [Workers Fund] toward the Arab population.[50]

Since arriving as a new immigrant in 1920, Szold gradually became convinced that Arab nationalism contained just aspirations. She repeatedly recommended a policy of Jewish-Arab reconciliation. But despite her somewhat maudlin inclinations she never became a blind advocate of Arab nationalism. Rather, she sharply criticized the desultory pace of progress in Arab society toward civil and individual rights.[51]

Szold's social criticism, however, did not interfere with her empathy for Arab nationalist aspirations or their efforts to modernize their society. The lofty tone of her internationalist convictions is evident in her speech at the groundbreaking ceremony of the Hebrew University in 1925:

And with them [the Jewish students] the sons and daughters of our Arab kinsmen will go up, to dwell in the halls of science, of the sciences which together with us, in a day gone by, they expounded to a Europe that was arid, parched, and thirsty. They will drink deep of the waters of their philosophy, of the wine of their poetry of love and adventure, of the rich, strong sap of their idiom. . . . For our Hebrew University shall be builded as a house of learning for all the peoples of the earth. Like Abraham's tent, it shall be open on every side. A hospitable welcome shall greet all that is genuine in study, all who crave knowledge in truth and sincerity. Over its portals the words will gleam: "Ho, every one that thirsteth, come ye for water."[52]

Szold's interest in internationalism was not confined to Zionist ideology. She was a serious student of the subject and even became a disciple of Hans Kohn, the scholar of nationalism, who made his home in Jerusalem during the second half of the 1920s. Kohn raised some basic objections with the Zionist leadership on the Arab question. Szold came to the conclusion that since Arab nationalism was historically legitimate, then it would be both wise and moral for the Zionist movement to look it squarely in the face.[53]

In the wake of the 1921 Arab riots, Szold warned that the absence of constructive relations between the two peoples would bring about a genuine Zionist tragedy. By this she meant not only the heavy political price that such neglect would exact but also the irreparable social and moral injury to the very nature of Zionism in *Erez Israel*. Years later, in the background of escalating Arab violence, the assassination of the moderate Labor Zionist statesman Hayim Arlosoroff, and the subsequent trial of three fanatical Zionists (who were eventually released for lack of evidence), she returned to her theme. Sensing the approach of internal catastrophe, deeply anguished by the havoc in the Yishuv resulting from the Arlosor-off trial, she felt that Jewish civil society had grown dangerously lawless. In a long letter to her sisters in 1934 she laments the turn of events:

I am heart-broken because the Jews don't seem to realize that the Arab question and the way they are going to solve it are the supreme test—I hate the nagging way the Jews here adapted towards the English Government, whether the question be the big one of restriction of immigration or petty daily inadequacies—I am unhappy because we Jews here have no feeling for order, system, self-discipline, character-building in our educational work, indulge in unending partisan bickering, while arrogantly believing ourselves superior to all others with whom we come in contact. . . . [54]

The situation appeared volatile because of the fierce nationalist conflict: "Arab nationalism [is] embittering the nationalism of [our] Jewish teachers," that is, Jewish society increasingly gives vent to violent responses. "You should listen to the 'political' quarrels of the children in the kindergartens . . . and you will understand my depression," she wrote grimly to her sisters.[55]

Indeed, what disturbed Szold most in Zionist relations with the Arab world was what she considered the insular, overly nationalistic pattern the Yishuv had imposed upon itself. Following the Arab riots of 1936 and the closing of the Port of Jaffa to Jews, the authorities had an alternative Jewish port constructed in Tel Aviv, but Szold resented this independent project, despite its enthusiastic celebration in the Yishuv.

Matters are not going to be mended if the alienation between us and the Arab population is emphasized. Now a stock company for marine business in Tel Aviv has been formed and in four years 70,000 UK pounds worth of stock has been sold. It is not the way—this way of creating race-compartments—of healing the breach, of destroying the seeds of race-hatred.[56]

In 1937 the British Peel Commission proposed partitioning Palestine into a Jewish state, an Arab state, and a British zone. While mainstream Zionists grudgingly accepted the offer, Henrietta Szold rejected the proposal outright because of the social-ethical dangers she believed were inherent in a two-state solution. She saw partition as a victory for Jewish particularism while "they [the Zionist leaders] consider that the first step has been taken towards the genuine 'redemption' of the Jewish people." She lamented that "Jews did not stand the acid test of finding the way to the solutions of a racial [Arab] problem," and called on her brethren "to come to their senses" and face this historic challenge, "which could have justified the nationalism of Zionism."[57]

Politically, Szold sympathized with Brit Shalom [Covenant of Peace], the "peace movement" of the 1920s and 1930s that supported Arab-Jewish rapprochement and binationalism. In the early 1940s, after the demise of Brit Shalom, she joined the five-person presidential board of its successor, Ihud [Unity], of which Judah L. Magnes was president and Martin Buber a member. Szold did not budge from her position despite intensive pressure from American and Palestinian Zionists, including sections of Hadassah.[58]

Throughout her life Henrietta Szold remained faithful to the vision of Arab-Jewish cooperation. Until her death in early 1945, she actively planned Hadassah's health and welfare clinics for Jews and Arabs.[59]

The Ladder in the Garden

This article has documented that some of the basic features of Henrietta Szold's vision were characteristic of genuine American Zionism. She understood Zionism as a slowly evolving movement rooted in Judaism, committed to the revival of the historic Jewish homeland. American Zionists generally believed that a multitude of values associated with American civilization were integral elements of Jewish national existence. A similar view was held regarding their concept of Zionism's universal mission.[60]

Still, Szold's Zionism was especially refined, very highly conscientious, often even agonized. Several months after she immigrated, she wrote to her close friend Alice Seligsberg about her vision of Jacob's ladder as a symbol of Zionism. A Jeremiah-like prophet was needed, she lamented, "one who can scourge and console, refine and stimulate. . . . We are still on the lowest rung of the ladder—[though] we had thought ourselves near the top!"[61] Henrietta Szold persistently climbed the ladder while she dealt morally with the challenges of the time and place; she consistently envisioned a free, ethical, peace-oriented, flourishing Jewish society—perhaps a subconscious allusion to her Maryland flower garden. She was always painfully aware of the next rung on Jacob's ladder.

Notes

Abbreviations used in notes:

AJH   *American Jewish History*
CZA   Central Zionist Archives, Jerusalem

HA   Hadassah Archives, New York City
HN   *Hadassah Newsletter*
NLJ   National Library, Givat Ram, Jerusalem
NP   *The New Palestine*

1. Joan Dash, *Summoned to Jerusalem: The Life of Henrietta Szold* (New York, 1979), 5–44 and passim; Michael Brown, *The Israeli-American Connection: Its Roots in the Yishuv, 1914-1945* (Detroit, 1996), 133–160; Eric L. Goldstein, "The Practical as Spiritual: Henrietta Szold's American Zionist Ideology, 1878–1920," in *Daughter of Zion: Henrietta Szold and American Jewish Womanhood,* ed. Barry Kessler (Baltimore, 1995), 17–33; Baila R. Shargel, *Lost Love: The Untold Story of Henrietta Szold* (Philadelphia, 1997), 3–29, 315–335, passim.

2. For Szold see esp. Brown, *The Israeli-American Connection,* 133–137, 147–150; for American Zionism, Allon Gal, "Aspects of the Zionist Movement's Role in the Communal Life of American Jewry, 1898–1948," AJH, LXXV, no. 2 (Dec. 1985), 149–164, and idem, "American Zionism between the World Wars—Ideological Characteristics," *Contemporary Jewry* [Hebrew], V (1989), 79–90.

3. See note 1, supra, and Baila R. Shargel, *Practical Dreamer: Israel Friedlaender and the Shaping of American Judaism* (New York, 1985), 91–92 and passim. See also Melvin I. Urofsky, *American Zionism from Herzl to the Holocaust* (Garden City, N.Y., 1975), 107–144 ff., and idem, *We Are One! American Jewry and Israel* (Garden City, N.Y., 1978), 198, 267.

4. For the European scene, see Nathan Rotenstreich, *Modern Jewish Thought* [Hebrew] (Tel Aviv, 1987), vol. 1, 159–215; Jacob Katz, *Jewish Nationalism: Essays and Studies* [Hebrew] (Jerusalem, 1979), 72–106; Arnold M. Eisen, *Galut: Modern Jewish Reflection on Homelessness and Homecoming* (Bloomington, Ind., 1986), 148–180. For the American background, see Allon Gal, "The Motif of Historical Continuity in American Zionist Ideology, 1900–1950," *Studies in Zionism,* XIII, no. 1 (Spring 1992), 1–20; Arthur A. Goren, "Spiritual Zionists and Jewish Sovereignty," in *The Americanization of the Jews,* ed. Robert M. Seltzer and Norman J. Rose (New York, 1995), 165–192.

5. Henrietta Szold, "A Century of Jewish Thought," read before the Baltimore section of the National Council of Jewish Women, January 26, 1896 (Baltimore, 1896), 4–6. The Zion Association of Baltimore published the paper that was read before the non-Zionist NCJW.

6. Ibid, 10–16.

7. "The Internal Jewish Question: National Dissolution or Continued Existence," *Maccabaean,* I, no. 2 (Nov. 1901), 57–61.

8. H. Szold, "The New Year of Trees," [1903], CZA, A125/268.

9. H. Szold ltr. to Alice L. Seligsberg, Milan, Dec. 12, 1909, CZA, A375/291; and see Goldstein, "The Practical as Spiritual," 17–33.

10. H. Szold ltr. to Mrs. Julius Rosenwald, Jan. 17, 1915, in Marvin Lowenthal, ed., *Henrietta Szold: Life and Letters* (New York, 1942), 84–88, quot. p. 86.

11. H. Szold ltrs. to family, June 22, Aug. 18, 1921, CZA A125/257; Harry Barnard, *The Forging of an American Jew: The Life and Times of Judge Julian W. Mack* (New York, 1974), 103 and passim.

12. Address at Special Meeting of ZOA Administrative Committee, Jan. 9, 1936, CZA A125/315, 1–2.

13. Ibid., 2–3.

14. Ibid., 1, 3.

15. *Maccabaean,* X, no. 4 (Apr. 1906), 155.

16. H. Szold ltr. to Thomas Seltzer, Jan. 25, 1922, CZA, A125/258; quot., Lowenthal, *Henrietta Szold,* 108.

17. H. Szold ltr. to family, June 12, 1931, CZA, A125/263.

18. H . Szold ltr. to family, Jan. 26, 1922, CZA, A125/258.

19. Jan. 9, 1936, Hotel Astor, CZA, A125/315; and see comments in Dash, *Summoned to Jerusalem,* 195–220, passim.

20. See Alexander M. Dushkin's sympathetic biography, *Living Bridges: Memoirs of an Educator* (Jerusalem, 1975), 284 ff.; and see Israel Goldstein, *My World as a Jew: The Memoirs of . . .* (New York, 1984), vol. 1, 79–80; see also Shargel, *Lost Love,* 331–332.

21. *American Jewish Year Book* 5676 (Philadelphia, 1915), 28–158, quot. p. 31.

22. Ibid., 156.

23. H. Szold, "The Internal Jewish Question," 60–61.

24. Ibid, 60.

25. H. Szold ltr. to family, Sept. 14, 1920, CZA, A125/256; and ltr. to H. Friedenwald, Mar. 16, 1921, in Lowenthal, ed., *Henrietta Szold,* 168–170.

26. *A Message from Henrietta Szold to the Women of Hadassah, Addressed to the 14th Annual Convention, Pittsburgh, June 27–29, 1928,* a brochure at the NLJ, quot. p. 3.

27. H. Szold ltr. to Junior Hadassah, Sept. 20, 1932, HA, 7/1, Box 18, Folder 196.

28. H. Szold, Talk at Hadassah Natl. Bd. Meeting, Jan. 2, 1936, CZA, A125/315, 5; for background see esp. Robert Morris and Michael Freund, eds., *Trends and Issues in Jewish Social Welfare in the United States, 1899–1952* (Philadelphia, 1966), 3–230.

29. H. Szold, Talk at Hadassah Ntl. Bd. Meeting, 1936, 7, 8, 16.

30. Cf. Brown, *The Israeli-American Connection,* 150–155. For a sympathetic treatment of Szold's contribution to social work in the Yishuv, see Katharine F. Lenroot (chief of the Children's Bureau, U.S. Dept. of Labor) in the 1945 "Henrietta Szold Issue" of HN. Accordingly, the methods of social organization that Szold brought to the Yishuv were conspicuously American, but their roots were Jewish. Lenroot concludes her essay with Szold's view of the progress to be made with "peoples of all races in the homeland of the Jews," which was based on Isaiah 58; see "Henrietta Szold—Social Pioneer," HN (Dec. 1945), 20, 22; and see also Dash, *Summoned to Jerusalem,* 227–229.

31. "Perhaps I shall survive this terrible war and join you in America," she wrote to her sister Bertha as late as Sept. 17, 1941, CZA, A125/268.

32. H. Szold ltrs. to family and T. Seltzer, Mar. 23, 1920, and Jan. 25, 1922, CZA, A125/257, A125/258, resp.

33. See note 35, supra; H. Szold ltrs. to Alice Seligsberg and Benjamin and Sarah Levin, Jan. 3, 1921, Oct. 1, 1935; Lowenthal, ed., *Henrietta Szold,* 160, 283, resp.; cf. Dash, *Summoned to Jerusalem,* 107.

34. H. Szold ltr. to sisters, May 1, 1936, CZA, A125/265.

35. H. Szold ltr. to Bertha Szold, June 14–17, 1940, CZA, A125/267.

36. H. Szold ltr. to Bertha Szold, Oct. 3, 1941, CZA, A125/268.

37. A great number of Szold's letters contain floral descriptions that attest to

the motif of the questionable attainability of the Holy Land. See ltrs. to family, Aug. 21, 1936, Oct. 17, 1941, CZA, A125/265, A125/268, resp. Her identification with the land never revealed a possessive or fanatic inclination. Marvin Lowenthal has noted that in her letters Szold avoided the Hebrew term *kibush* [conquering, overcoming], which was widely applied by the pioneers to denote countless facets of Zionist settlement; see his *Henrietta Szold*, 145.

38. Dushkin, *Living Bridges,* passim; idem, "'and Thou Shalt Teach Them Diligently': Impressions of Henrietta Szold as a Jewish Educator," HN (Dec. 1945), 17–19.

39. Dushkin, *Living Bridges,* 8, 24–25, 61–62 and passim; idem, "Szold as a Jewish Educator," 17–19. From his early activism in New York in 1918 until his death in Jerusalem in 1976, Dushkin held a foremost position in promoting Zionist education and pedagogical scholarship in both countries. For the American dimension, see Brown, *The Israeli-American Connection,* 147–150.

40. Gal, "The Motif of Historical Continuity in American Zionist Ideology," 1–20; idem, "The Historical Continuity Motif in Conservative Judaism's Concept of Israel," *Journal of Jewish Thought and Philosophy,* II (1993), 157–183; for Hadassah and Szold see idem, "The Motif of Historical Continuity in Zionist Ideology," 6–9 and note 44, infra.

41. H. Szold, "Our Own Alma Mater," NP, VIII, no. 13 (Mar. 27, 1925), 334.

42. H. Szold ltr. to Harriet Levin Terrell, July 2, 1922, CZA, A 125/9; Dash, *Summoned to Jerusalem,* 148–154, 174–177.

43. H. Szold ltr. to Bertha Szold, Oct. 17, 1941, CZA, A125/268. A Letter to the Editor of the *Nation,* August 13, 1914 [3 pp.], in HA.

44. Jacques Kornberg, ed., *At the Crossroads: Essays on Ahad Haam* (Albany, 1983), xv–xxvii, 3–45, and passim; cf. Evyatar Friesel, "Ahad Haamism in American Zionist Thought," loc. cit., 133–141, and Gal, "Aspects of the Zionist Movement," 150 ff.

45. H. Szold, "Zionism: A Progressive and Democratic Movement," an address at the People's Institute, Cooper Union, HA, Szold Collec., Box 31, Folder 358, 6; cf. Irving Fineman, *Woman of Valor: The Life of Henrietta Szold, 1860–1945* (New York, 1961), 278–284.

46. Allon Gal, "The Mission Motif in American Zionism (1898–1948)," AJH, LXXV, no. 4 (June 1986), 363–385; H. Szold, "The Promised Land," *Nation,* Aug. 13, 1914 [3 pp.], in Szold Collec., HA.

47. H. Szold, "Zionism: A Progressive and Democratic Movement," 11.

48. Ibid.

49. H. Szold, "The Promised Land," 2.

50. Dash, *Summoned to Jerusalem,* 225–226.

51. Arthur A. Goren, ed., *Dissenter in Zion: From the Writings of Judah L. Magnes* (Cambridge, Mass., 1982), 47, 73, 81 and passim; Joan Dash, "Doing Good in Palestine: Magnes and Henrietta Szold," in *Like All the Nations? The Life and Legacy of Judah L. Magnes,* ed. William M. Brinner and Moses Rischin (New York, 1987), 99–111; H. Szold ltrs. to family, Apr. 27, Dec. 3, 1921, CZA, A125/257.

52. H. Szold, "Our Own Alma Mater," 334.

53. H. Szold ltrs. to Rose A. Herzog, Oct. 2, 1931, and Anna Kaplan, June 7, 1932, quoted in Lowenthal, *Henrietta Szold,* 235, 236, resp. (Kohn was born in

Prague in 1891, emigrated to the U.S.A in 1931, and died there in 1971); cf. Brown, *The Israeli-American Connection,* 138–140.

54. H. Szold ltrs. to family, Dec. 3, 1921, CZA A125/257, and June 22, 1934, CZA, A125/264.

55. Ibid.

56. H. Szold ltr. to sisters, June 5, 1936, CZA, A125/265.

57. H. Szold ltr. to sisters, July 9, 1937, CZA, A125/266.

58. Dash, *Summoned to Jerusalem,* 208, 297–299; for Szold's polemic with Tamar de Sola Pool, president of Hadassah (1939–1943), see her letters to de Sola Pool, Sept. 7, 1942, Nov. 8, 1942, Jan. 1, 1943, CZA, A125/151–152.

59. See I. F. Stone, "For Jews and Arabs Alike," HN (Dec. 1945), 32–33.

60. See notes 1–4, supra, and note 65, infra. It would be instructive to undertake a comparative study of Szold and other Hadassah activists who immigrated to Palestine such as Jessie Sampter and Irma Lindheim; see Bertha Badt-Strauss, *White Fire: The Life and Works of Jessie Sampter* (New York, 1956), and Irma L. Lindeim, *Parallel Quest: A Search of a Person and a People* (New York, 1962). See also Brown, *The Israeli-American Connection,* 134–137; Allon Gal, "Hadassah and the American Jewish Political Tradition," in *An Inventory of Promises: Essays on American Jewish History in Honor of Moses Rischin,* ed. Jeffrey S. Gurock and Marc L. Raphael (Brooklyn, N.Y., 1995), 89–114.

61. H. Szold ltrs. to Alice Seligsberg, Jan. 3, 1921, and to Bertha Szold, Sept. 20, 1941, in Lowenthal, ed., *Henrietta Szold,* 160–161, and CZA A125/268, resp.

"Keeping the Torch Burning" (1936)

An Exchange of Correspondence between Beatrice Barron and Henrietta Szold

52 Lee Street
Cambridge, Massachusetts
August 24, 1936

My Dear Miss Szold,

I am the leader of a girls' Young Judaean club which has been named in your honor. The club is now going on its fourth year of existence, and I feel it is my duty as the leader of these girls to tell you what we have been doing in the past four years especially as you have been the inspiration for the existence of this club.

The ages of these girls are from twelve to fourteen years. When a girl enters the club, a Candle Light Ceremony is conducted. This ceremony is very beautiful and impressive. The girls assemble in a large circle; white is worn as a symbol of purity, and blue and white banners are worn across their breasts bearing your name. Each girl holds a candle which is lit with the exception of the person who is to become a member of the club. The president then lights the candles saying these words, "As I light this candle I hope that you may keep the spirit of Judaism burning forever and that someday you too may do as much for your people as Henrietta Szold has." We try to hold such a ceremony on your birthday.

Recently, a study of Palestine was made which included the study of important Palestinian cities, their industries, and the important people now living in Palestine. A survey of the Palestine Scout movement was made as all the girls are scouts including myself. A reenactment was made of the Palestine and American scout movement as a means of raising money for Keren Hanoar [Youth Fund].

Dramatics, debating, and the learning of current Hebrew favorite songs take up a great part of the Saturday evening meetings. Your life accomplishments were reenacted recently to show what great things you have done.

I recently asked them what they have gained since they have joined

Reprinted by permission of Hadassah, The Women's Zionist Organization of America.

with or in the Young Judaean ranks. The answers were much the same being that they feel more at home with their own kind of people, they've learned things about the Jewish people that they would not have learned otherwise, and that they want to carry on the work that you have started.

I hope that I may hear from you soon so that I may convey to the girls the courage that you have of keeping the torch burning so that we also, no matter what hardships we have to confront with, will keep your kind words of advice and encouragement in our minds.

    With Young Judaea greetings, I am,
    Beatrice Barron

The Jewish Agency for Palestine
Central Bureau for the Settlement of German Jews
Jerusalem, P.O.B. 92
September 14, 1936

Dear Beatrice Barron,

I thank you for your letter of August 24, 1936 in which you give me a description of your Young Judaea Club and its doings. Naturally, I am touched by your kind thoughts of me, and your associating my name with your group. I confess if you had asked my permission to use my name, I might have told you that I am not greatly in favor of honoring living persons in so distinguished a way. Even now I would warn you not to fall into the hero-worshipping habit. We are all mortal together, all of us apt to commit errors. It is better to keep one's mind directed to great, moving ideas than to attach our thoughts to persons. If persons realize ideas, their actions should doubtless be recognized as valuable, and their due need of praise should not be withheld, but our chief occupation, I think, should be to understand and value and illustrate great ideas.

I was encouraged to write in this strain by the last sentence in your letter, in which you invite words of advice from me.

Give my cordial regards and good wishes to all the members of your club. I hope it will continue to prosper and help its members to prepare themselves for a life of usefulness and idealistic striving.

    With wishes for a happy New Year,
    Yours sincerely,
    Henrietta Szold

Chapter 3

The twentieth century witnessed the catastrophic losses of World Wars I and II as well as the dramatic rise of the State of Israel. By midcentury, the widespread anti-Jewish violence of Europe and the magnetic effects of America's bounty had caused nearly 2.5 million European Jews to immigrate to the New World. The momentous and dramatic changes of this era reshaped American Jewish life in significant and unprecedented ways. In recent decades, the story of East European Jewish migration has been told by feminist scholars who emphasize "the complex role for women in the adaptation of immigrant Jews to American conditions."[1] Among the political strategies available to Jewish women in the New World, Zionism proved to be an especially fruitful avenue for empowerment and claiming positions of public leadership and responsibility.

While figures such as Emma Lazarus (1849–1887) and Henrietta Szold (1860–1945) are rightly considered pioneers of American Zionism, others such as Marie Syrkin (1899–1989) were among the movement's chief pathfinders—women who helped define the contours of the emerging American Zionist sensibility in the twentieth century. To a considerable degree, as this chapter demonstrates, Marie Syrkin's life illustrates the experience of the third generation of American women Zionists.

Born in Switzerland, she was the only child of the well-known East European socialist Zionist theoretician Nahman Syrkin (1868–1924), whose voluntaristic and utopian brand of Jewish nationalism deeply influenced East European Zionist groups in Europe, America, and Palestine. Raised in the ferment of the dynamic East European Jewish intellectual milieu of the fin de siècle, young Marie was fluent in five languages by the age of ten—Yiddish, Russian, German, French, and English. The American public education system also had a profound impact on her upbringing, and her facility with language ultimately led to a college career in literature. At the same time, she became active in American Zionist affairs and emerged as a significant voice in Labor Zionist circles. She joined the staff of *Jewish*

---

1. Paula E. Hyman, "Eastern European Immigration," in *Jewish Women in America: An Historical Encyclopedia*, ed. Paula E. Hyman and Deborah Dash Moore, vol. 2 (New York: Routledge, 1997), 351.

Frontier in 1934, where she worked closely with the Labor Zionist thinker Hayim Greenberg (1889–1953) and other significant Jewish public intellectuals, and she very quickly earned a reputation as a keen Zionist polemicist. During this period, she also ghostwrote speeches for such major Zionist figures as Chaim Weizmann (1874–1952) and Golda Meir (1898–1978). In later decades, she would become known for her pioneering studies of the American public education system, Jewish resistance during the Holocaust, and the fate of Jewish Displaced Persons after the war. Nor did she shy away from public controversy, as exhibited in her spirited assessments of Palestinian Arab nationalism in the 1970s, the antisemitism of British historian Arnold Toynbee (1889–1975), and the alleged Jewish self-hatred of the German refugee scholar Hannah Arendt (1906–1975).

In this chapter, Carole S. Kessner, a scholar of American Jewish literature and biographer of Marie Syrkin, provides a detailed analysis of Syrkin's trajectory and her complex legacy as a Zionist thinker and a combative Jewish public intellectual. We have also included an essay written by Syrkin herself in 1946 on the eve of the partition of British Mandatory Palestine into separate Jewish and Arab states. The piece not only highlights her sharp analytic skill and erudition but also reflects the considerable degree to which her vantage point—as a woman, an American, and a Labor Zionist—dovetailed with the ascendant pragmatic Zionist strategy of the Jewish Agency's political leadership. In the essay, Syrkin makes the case for acceptance of the partition scheme and brings into sharp relief the competing agendas of different American Zionist factions at one of Zionism's most fateful junctures.

Marie Syrkin: An Exemplary Life

Carole S. Kessner

At the end of her life, Marie Syrkin said, "Today I can write with as much passion about old age as I once could about love."[1] The following verse, from a poem entitled "Of Age," written when she was nearly eighty, is, however, about both love and age:

> Women live longer than men;
> The few that I loved are dead.
> Had I the power to summon,
> Whom would I bring to my bed?[2]

Her question goes unanswered, although there were indeed a few good candidates for the position. But more to the point is the fact that since Marie Syrkin *did* live longer than most of her male colleagues, it left her, in the last decade of her life, having to justify her past as an idealistic polemicist for the Labor Zionist movement, as an apologist for the words and actions of her friend Golda Meir, as an antagonist of the New Left, as a bewildered but vocal adversary of the ascension of Likud, as an unshaken believer in her own interpretation of history in the face of the new revisionist historiographers, and as an idiosyncratic feminist. Doubtless, in her long life of one month short of ninety years—she died on February 1, 1989—she made mistakes; but the significance of her life perhaps lies less in her polemical stances, and, in the assessment of Irving Howe, "more in the kind of life she led, a life committed to values beyond the self."[3]

Marie Syrkin led a life that reads like a gripping novel, full of romance, history, poetry, and action, all quickened by intellect, conviction, and, most of all, wit—both ironic and self-deprecatory. Born in Switzerland in 1899, two years after the First Zionist Congress and six years before the 1905 Russian Revolution, she was the only child of Nahman and Bassya Osnos Syrkin. Nahman Syrkin met his wife Bassya Osnos at the Second Zionist Congress in Basle in 1898, where both were studying medicine. This, their daughter has pointed out, "gives some idea of how far my

Source: Carole S. Kessner, "Marie Syrkin: An Exemplary Life," in *The "Other" New York Jewish Intellectuals,* ed. Carole S. Kessner (New York and London: New York University Press, 1994), 51–70. Reprinted by permission of New York University Press.

mother was emancipated."[4] Moreover, in 1898 Syrkin had written his seminal work, *The Jewish Socialist State* (one year after Herzl's *The Jewish State*), in which he expounded his vision of the synthesis of socialism and Zionism; this ultimately would become the program of the founders of the State of Israel. Bassya Syrkin, though a tubercular who would die in America at the age of thirty-six when her daughter was only sixteen, was herself a headstrong revolutionary activist.

To be born the only daughter of two such professional idealists could not be without consequences, both positive and negative. Psychobiography has to take into account the daughter's love-hatred for her father who was an erudite moralist, yet who was possessed of a blazing temperament that vented itself publicly in scathing argument and privately in what his daughter has described as a zealous "dedicated hardship."[5] It would also have to take into account the model of feminist activism and egalitarianism provided by her mother, for Bassya Syrkin held the conviction that women should have independent careers and that they should not be "shackled by men and society and should be free."[6]

One might go so far as to claim that Marie Syrkin's attraction to Golda Meir was influenced by the model of Bassya Syrkin. In the introduction to Marie Syrkin's biography of Goldie Myerson (Golda Meir), published in 1955, the author describes her friend as "the rare type that one might simply describe as the effective idealist. . . . Among the remarkable personalities who created the State of Israel, I met a number of such men and women—individuals who responded to a world in chaos neither passively as 'alienated' intellectuals, nor as energetic cynics. For me, this translation of belief into life became one of the few sources of moral affirmation in our time."[7]

Notwithstanding Bassya Syrkin's conviction that women should have independent careers, she soon discovered that the birth of her child one year after marriage, the demands of her husband's political life which necessitated frequent moves from one country to another, and concerns for her poor health resulted in the abandonment of her medical studies. But it did not stop her from continuing activities in behalf of socialist Zionism; during the first few years of her marriage, at the time of the 1905 Revolution, Bassya Syrkin twice returned to Russia carrying revolutionary pamphlets in the false bottom of her trunk.

These were years, moreover, when the Syrkins' peripatetic life meant that by the time Marie was ten, she had lived in five countries—Switzerland, Germany, France, Russia, and the United States. The family finally moved to America in 1908 because, as Marie Syrkin herself quipped, "Papa was always getting exiled—so we traveled a lot."[8] By this time she was fluent in five languages—Russian, French, German, Yiddish, and English—which she quickly picked up in school. One might note here that Hebrew was *not* among the languages she learned, despite the fact that when she was a child her father would make sporadic attempts to instruct her in Spinoza in Latin, Marx in German, and the Bible in Hebrew. She later lamented the fact that Hebrew was never to become one of her languages. In her eighties, in a response to a remark by Trude Weiss-Rosmarin that Marie was fortunate to be, after all, the daughter of Nahman Syrkin, she snapped back, "yes, but one thing he failed to provide me. He did not teach me Hebrew at an age when one could have learned it. It's maddening. . . . That he didn't teach me Hebrew was a serious loss."[9] This lack, she later claimed, was a major reason for her own failure to make *aliyah*. The more compelling reason, however, was her refusal to give up joint custody of her child.

Not only was Marie Syrkin an unusually beautiful child, as she was a beautiful mature woman and handsome into old age, but she was exceptionally intelligent and treated as a prodigy by her parents. Yet in these early years, if she admired her parents' dedicated poverty, she did not seem the slightest bit interested in the politics that inspired their chosen financial condition. She was fast developing a passion for romantic poetry equal to her parents' passion for radical politics. Nor did she show any signs that she was to develop a writing style that more often than not would be characterized as acerbic. Her diary for the year 1915, when she was barely sixteen, reveals the usual adolescent propensity for romantic sentimentality, though it also demonstrates an unusually lush and rich vocabulary. The following is an example from the diary.

All day that sad line from Keats' immortal poem has been ringing in my brain. "Where but to think is verily a vale of tears." This world is verily a vale of tears, tears which can never be dried. I find myself continually thinking of W. . . . The remembrance of my dream kiss still burns my lips; I feel sullied, outraged, my whole soul is seared, and yes, I would willingly dream it again and again. The dominant note in my entire being has become the primitive call from man to woman, the first hushed whispering of love.[10]

There is nothing at this stage to suggest that Marie Syrkin would become the "doyenne of Labor Zionism." If anything, her diary suggests that she might become a woman of *belles lettres;* this is no doubt what would have happened, had she not made a conscious career choice to use her literary gifts in the service of Zionism and the Jewish people. She liked to tell a story about the time, a few years after the death of her mother, when Nahman Syrkin, who disapproved of her literary bent, blazed out at her because he thought she was frittering away her abilities. When she was about nineteen, she happened to be quietly reading a novel by H. G. Wells. The newspapers at that time were full of the exploits of a young woman criminal who had been dubbed "the bobbed-haired bandit." When this female outlaw was not busy committing crimes, she was reputed to have spent her time reading novels. Syrkin, upon seeing his daughter leisurely reading her novel, exploded, "What difference is there between you and the bobbed-haired bandit? She has short hair and you have short hair; she reads novels and you read novels!" It was just at this time, moreover, that Nahman Syrkin remarked somewhat sardonically, "There is a woman in our movement who is a remarkable speaker. I thought you'd be like her." The unnamed woman was, not surprisingly, Golda Meir.[11]

Marie Syrkin's passion for poetry was to inspire her first serious romance, but also it caused a confrontation with her father, for which she would never quite forgive him. The summer after Bassya Syrkin died of chronic tuberculosis, Nahman moved himself and his sixteen-year-old daughter into a couple of rooms in the apartment of some impoverished ladies. He would spend most of the day at the 42nd Street Library, before he went to his meetings at night. Anxious to spare his daughter the loneliness and the unpleasantness of the hot New York summer, Nahman Syrkin sent his daughter off for the season to the Atlantic Hotel in Belmar, New Jersey. It happened to be owned by Syrkin's friend, and it was frequented by the Jewish intelligentsia, so Syrkin felt safe. Although there was a distinct difference between Syrkin's theoretical views in favor of the freedom of women and his overbearing, overprotective, Victorian attempt to control his daughter's life, he nonetheless sent her away for the summer of her sixteenth year.

But the mere delight of a summer vacation away from the hot city was not the real reason for Marie Syrkin's nostalgia for "that fabulous summer."[12] This, it appears, was the precise moment when Nahman Syrkin's daughter was to act on the mixed message that her father had communicated: on the one hand was his general message of independence and equality for the sexes; on the other, was his personal effort to maintain strict control over Marie's activities. She was to decide in favor of asserting her own independence—whatever the consequences; and this would be a lifelong characteristic.

It was during this summer that she met a young man of twenty named Maurice Samuel. He had come to the Atlantic Hotel to visit a friend. Not only was he handsome, and by the sixteen-year-old's standards, an older man, but every poem Marie loved, Samuel knew by heart. He introduced her to the poetry of Francis Thompson (which was to become the subject of her master's thesis at Cornell many years later). The two fell headlong in love, and the intensity of their romance culminated in their elopement in 1917 when Marie was barely eighteen. Maurice was twenty-two; he had enlisted in the army and was about to leave for France. Nahman Syrkin, however, instantly had the marriage annulled, claiming that his daughter was underage. This time he successfully exercised his will, but it resulted in a resentment that his daughter never conquered. In fact, Marie Syrkin and Maurice Samuel's common interest in Zionism and their activities in its behalf led to a brief resumption of their relationship in later years.

Nahman Syrkin's admonitions notwithstanding, Marie went off to pursue her literary studies at Cornell in 1918 as her father went off to Versailles to represent the socialist Zionists at the Peace conference. He wrote to her constantly from Paris, sending her money, warning her about further *"affaires de coeur,"* fussing over her health, and moralizing. On June 12, 1919, after she had written to him that she had just married a young instructor of biochemistry named Aaron Bodansky, Nahman wrote back, "I'm so proud of the nobel [sic] desires which are filling your exceptional soul. Maryetchka, if nobody believes in you, I believe in your talents and your future. Some deep feeling, an intuition, prophesies me that you will develop a nobel [sic] and sublime attitude of life. . . . Read only good inspiring books, every book in its original text, read and reread every book and try to conceive not only what the great writer had outspoken, but what he had concealed. . . ." A paragraph later he writes, "Darling, I understand much your excitement about the change of your name. Of course, I would like very much that you should wear the name Bodansky-Syrkin and write under that name."

Gradually, at Cornell, Marie Syrkin's public commitment to Jewish life and to Zionism began to emerge. While at the university, she had been a member, though not an active one, of the pan-collegiate International Zionist Association (IZA). Her merely tangential association with the IZA is explained in an article she published in the *New Palestine* in 1925, in which she praises the new student movement Avukah [The Torch]. In a prose style foreshadowing the sharp ironic wit alongside the roseate idealism that would later characterize her writing, she describes the IZA as

a kind of painless dentistry which temporarily filled spiritual cavities of a special nature. . . . A Jewish student of a certain type went to the IZA meeting to sing the *Hatikvah* [The Hope] when he remembered Zion. To remember Zion in a vague ineffable way, was the chief function of the Zionist student groups. . . . A too platonic love for Zion, rather than a sense of living alliance with a concrete Palestine was the unsubstantial basis on which the IZA failed to flourish.[13]

In praise of the new Jewish student movement, Syrkin pointed out that the prewar student movement was animated by the desire for conformity and full Americanization; but the new movement arose out of post-mandate conditions and was quickened by the "beat of the *haluzim* pick-axes in Palestine." Avukah arose when "Zion emerged from the hazy distance of a Utopia to the disconcerting clarity of a reality. To declare oneself a Zionist meant more than merely to sing the *Hatikvah* or bethink oneself of Israel. It was the definite statement of national allegiance. It was also the affirmation of national individuality."[14]

This appears to be the earliest example of Marie Syrkin's Zionist writing. Stylistically it is embryonic Syrkin. In connection with the prose of John Milton, one critic has identified such a style as the rhetoric of zeal;[15] that is, it is a mode that see-saws between extravagant idealism and rapier thrust. Of late, Syrkin has been criticized for having spoken in the language of naive and sentimental early Zionism, but this overlooks the point that such a double-sided rhetorical style is characteristic of the zealous writer from the prophets through John Milton and polemicists of the sixties. Only the idealist with a sense of high moral purpose can turn the carpet over to expose a rough underside of moral indignation. The cynic has only one texture.

During the early 1920s, Marie Syrkin continued to write her own verse and to translate Yiddish poetry into English. She was, in fact, among the very first to do so. Of course, this was one way of reconciling her love of poetry and her emerging sense of Jewish purpose. By the time she was twenty-four, she had already published translations of the poetry of Yehoash in *Menorah Journal*. These were praised by Yehoash himself. It was with regard to these translations, moreover, that the editor of *Menorah Journal,* Henry Hurwitz, sent her a note asking for biographical data. Syrkin wrote back with the following revealing self-description: "As to myself, I am the daughter of Dr. Syrkin and the wife of A. Bodansky who teaches here. I have my B.A. and M.A. from Cornell and, God willing, I may some day get a Ph.D."[16] She never did; but by the time she was twenty-eight, she had such a long list of publications that she was asked to become associate editor of the short-lived publication *Reflex*, edited by S. M. Melamed.[17]

Throughout the 1920s, Marie Syrkin's professional activities were restricted primarily to poetry, journalism, and teaching. Her personal situation—the tragic death of her first son, the birth a few months later of her second son, the death of her father, her separation and subsequent divorce from Bodansky, and her return to New York with her surviving child—necessitated self-support, which she accomplished by teaching English at

Textile High School in Manhattan. This was a job that she utterly detested, but which she kept out of economic necessity until 1948. These circumstances, including her marriage in 1930 to the poet Charles Reznikoff, with whom she lived, on and off, until his death in 1976, made anything more than writing a virtual impossibility.

By the early thirties, however, the more urgent the world situation became, the more Marie Syrkin became intent upon doing on-the-spot reporting. In 1933, when she was granted a sabbatical from Textile High School, Syrkin took herself off for the first of her innumerable trips to Palestine. On this voyage, the romance of the *haluziut* seemed more powerful than the news that she heard over the ship's radio about Hitler's edicts. "The Nazi menace," she later reported, "in its initial phase seemed somehow unreal. It was too preposterous; it would blow over."[18] But the great experiment in socialist Zionism sent her into rhapsodic wonderment at the smallest achievement in the *kibuzim* of the Jordan and Galilee: "The rapture of a young woman who ran up to me with the first radish grown in her settlement, the *hora* danced on the Sabbath on the streets of still uncrowded Tel Aviv along whose shores camels slowly made their way,"[19] she waxed eloquent. Today, some may be a bit embarrassed by such "purple prose," but Marie Syrkin was responding ingenuously.

Most Jewish intellectuals (and non-intellectuals) of this period in America and Europe were not especially attracted to the spartan life in Palestine, nor to the Zionist cause itself. They kept their emotional distance. Syrkin, however, returned from her summer visit inspired and eager to work. It was at this time, moreover, that she met Golda (Myerson) Meir, who had come to America both to seek medical care for her daughter and to be a *shlihah* to Pioneer Women. The friendship of the two women was natural and complementary, for as much as Syrkin admired Golda Meir for her rare effective combination of activism and idealism, Meir certainly admired Marie Syrkin for her combination of intellect and idealism. They were, furthermore, both unself-conscious feminists of the same stripe.

After she returned from her 1933 sojourn among the pioneers, Syrkin's career took the signal turn that would propel her into an activist role as commentator, speechmaker, speechwriter for others, witness to great events, and firsthand reporter from the zone of conflict. While maintaining her job at Textile High School, she assumed a position on the editorial board of the newly established journal of the Labor Zionists, the *Jewish Frontier*. The intensity of her commitment to the purpose of this publication is evinced by the fact that for her thirty-five years of editorial service she received no pay. In her capacity as an editor of *Jewish Frontier* she worked closely with the editor, Hayim Greenberg, with whom she had a deep personal relationship.

Among Marie Syrkin's articles in this critical decade were firsthand reports from Palestine on the Arab disturbances, attacks on Jabotinsky and the Revisionists, on the pro-Nazi Mufti, a long stream of articles in praise of the *haluzim* and Youth Aliyah. Among her most prized achievements was her exposé of the Moscow show trials. At the suggestion of Hayim Greenberg, Syrkin read through the six hundred pages of the Russian stenographic typescript of the trials; this resulted in a remarkable full analysis which appeared in the *Jewish Frontier* in January 1937. "By now," she wrote, "everyone is familiar with the set-up":

The chief figures of the Bolshevik Revolution admit to a collection of crimes among which murder is the most attractive. This wholesale confession is indulged in by all of Lenin's closest associates and collaborators with two exceptions—Stalin and Trotsky. Stalin is in the Kremlin and Trotsky in Mexico, the rest are in their graves or about to repose in them. Just how complete the liquidation of the Old Bolsheviks has been, may be judged from glancing at the membership of the Central Committee of the Communist Party during the crucial years of 1917 to 1920. With the exception of a few who retired from political life, all the surviving members have been shot as counterrevolutionaries—again barring Trotsky and Stalin.[20]

Thus, Syrkin concludes, the defendants' confessions were false and the trials were Stalin's method of liquidating dissent. Today that conclusion does not seem so remarkable, but the writer's insistence that "no service is done to socialism or to Soviet Russia by refusing to face what one conceives to be the truth"[21] was not so easily faced by the Left. And when some believers in the Revolution finally did, it required a complete repudiation not only of Stalinism but of socialism, and then of liberalism as well.

During the war years Syrkin wrote a stream of essays, and poetry too, pressing for the opening of the gates of Palestine, demanding liberalization of immigration quotas; she wrote a speech for Chaim Weizmann to deliver at a Madison Square Garden rally, and articles and speeches for Golda Meir, all the while holding down her teaching job. As detestable as that job may have been, it gave her the raw material for her widely acclaimed book, *Your School, Your Children* (1944),[22] which was a vanguard analysis of the American public school system. In fact she wrote a number of essays on democracy and the schools in *Common Ground,* the official organ of the Common Council for American Unity. It was, moreover, this early interest in the American education system that later led her to speak out against the "politically correct" position in the 1970s on the issue of the black civil rights movement, affirmative action, and their effects on the university. In 1970, at a conference held at the home of the president of Israel on the subject of "Jews Confronting Antisemitism in the United States," and again in an article in the *New York Times* magazine, and once more in 1979 in the *New Republic,* Syrkin took the unpopular view among liberals that ethnic proportional representation, which really is a racial quota, destroys the merit system and thereby undermines the democratic belief that protection of the individual holds the best promise for meeting the needs of all minorities within a democracy. "The abrogation of individual rights," she asserted, "would mean curtailment of free entrance into the professions and sciences in accordance with ability and intellectual zeal." The implication for Jews, who constitute only 3 percent of the population, she claimed, is that they would be the chief losers.[23]

Perhaps the most celebrated episode in Marie Syrkin's entire journalistic career, and the one she was most proud of, occurred in 1942 when the State Department received a cable from the Geneva representative of the World Jewish Congress to be forwarded to Rabbi Stephen Wise, president of the American Jewish Congress. The message contained the truth about Hitler's plan to annihilate European Jewry. As editors of the *Jewish Frontier,* Marie Syrkin and Hayim Greenberg were invited in August of 1942 to attend a small private meeting of Jewish journalists, where they learned of the perplexing report from Geneva that the mass extermination was already under way. Despite all that they had been aware of for the last nine years, and despite the *Frontier's* continual reportage of conditions in Germany and Europe, the entire group was unable to assimilate this new information. Their immediate response was shock and skepticism. This—in face of the fact that only a week earlier the *Frontier* itself had received a document from the Jewish Socialist Bund which was an account of mass gassings at Chelmno. Later, Marie Syrkin openly admitted that she and Greenberg were unable to assimilate either account, and she confessed that "we hit on what in retrospect appears a disgraceful compromise: we buried the fearful report in the back page of the September issue in small type, thus indicating that we could not vouch for its accuracy. But by the next issue the small staff of the magazine had uncovered enough material so that the truth had to be acknowledged."[24] The October issue was omitted and the November issue appeared with black borders. Syrkin wrote the following editorial remarks:

In the occupied countries of Europe, a policy is now being put into effect whose avowed object is the extermination of a whole people. It is a policy of systematic murder of innocent civilians which in its ferocity, its dimensions and its organization is unique in the history of mankind. . . . [25]

This editorial was the first American report of the systematic annihilation that Syrkin claimed was already in force. It is also a succinct formulation and anticipation of later arguments for the uniqueness of the Holocaust, such as that of the historian Lucy Dawidowicz.[26]

In 1945, when the war was over, Marie Syrkin took the first available ship to the Middle East for another of what she claimed were her "firsts." This time she went to gather material for her book on Jewish resistance, *Blessed Is the Match*.[27] This was, in fact, the first of the eyewitness accounts of partisans, ghetto fighters, and Jewish Palestinian parachutists. In this volume of personal interviews, the mother of Hannah Senesh describes her daughter's last days in the Hungarian prison. Marie Syrkin's account of the heroism of the young Hannah Senesh, already a legend in Palestine, brought this story to the American public for the first time, and Syrkin's translation of Senesh's poem "Blessed Is the Match" became the authoritative one:

> Blessed is the match that is consumed in
>   kindling flame.
> Blessed is the flame that burns
>   in the secret fastness of the heart.
> Blessed is the heart with strength to stop
>   its beating for honor's sake.
> Blessed is the match that is consumed
>   in kindling flame.

The volume also contained an interview with Joel Brand who told of his negotiations with Adolf Eichmann for the ransom of European Jewry in the famous "goods for blood" episode.

During the 1945–46 sojourn in Palestine, Syrkin had her own personal adventure with underground activity when she was recruited to give the first English-language broadcast over the secret radio of Kol Yisrael [the Voice of Israel]. She always insisted that, unlike Golda Meir, she herself was not a true activist, that she merely did what she had to do; that is, she put her gift for writing in the service of her moral and political convictions. Perhaps this is why she took particular delight in dramatically recounting her adventure with "undercover" activism. Proudly she would display two books given to her in 1946 by "comrades of the Haganah." The dedication reads: "Receive the blessings of the sons of the homeland for your voice that added color to the announcement of the redemption. When the day comes when the wall of evil crumbles in the storm, your reward will be the opening of the gates."

In November of 1946, in anticipation of the Twenty-Second Zionist Congress which was to be held the following month in Basle, Syrkin published an urgent plea for partition which she knew would be among the acute issues on the agenda. Zionist leaders were busy aligning themselves pro and con prior to the Congress, and Syrkin felt compelled to make the case for partition in advance. In words that carry some resonance today, she summed up her argument with a clever twist of a well-known biblical story: "In 1937 partition was called a Solomon's judgment. Today we must perhaps consider that the child is a Siamese twin whose life can only be saved by drastic operation."[28]

The 1946 Zionist Congress was a profoundly emotional experience. Urged by Ben-Gurion and Golda Meir, who insisted that so important was Marie Syrkin's participation in this Congress that they would cover her expenses, she attended the meeting as a delegate of the American Labor Zionist Party. This Congress, the first since 1939, was marked by the twin traumas of loss and reunion. The participants mourned the many delegates of the 1939 Congress who had not survived, and they took bittersweet pleasure in reunion with those who had remained alive. They also met a group of delegates who arrived from the DP camps.

The 1946 Congress was Marie Syrkin's first encounter with Displaced Persons. Her next experience came in 1947 when Abram L. Sachar, then the director of Hillel, asked her to take an assignment to help screen suitable candidates from among the young survivors in the DP camps for admission to American universities. They would be permitted, under these circumstances, to enter the United States beyond the restrictions of the prevailing immigration quotas.

The assignment was challenging in the extreme, for the job of making "selections" had connotations from the immediate past. Syrkin was warned not to allow herself to be too emotional, but the grim tales she heard from the scores of hopeful applicants from whom she could choose only fifty, from the physically stunted and psychologically scarred young people who looked at her with pleading eyes, tore at her heart.

For a woman who claimed to be without great physical stamina and less than adventuresome, Marie Syrkin's actual activities in these years belied her protestations. After her strenuous stint in the DP camps, she went back to Palestine in the wake of the siege of Jerusalem. Her fears for the life of the nation had been expressed in the poem entitled "David," written at the time of the Arab attack:

> Suppose, this time, Goliath should not fall;
> Suppose, this time, the sling should not avail
> On the Judean plain where once for all

Mankind the pebble struck; suppose the tale
Should have a different end: the shepherd yield,
The triumph pass to iron arm and thigh,
The wonder vanish from the blooming field,
The mailed hulk stand, and the sweet singer lie.

Suppose, but then what grace will go unsung.
What temple wall unbuilt, what gardens bare;
What plowshare broken and what harp unstrung!
Defeat will compass every heart aware
How black the ramparts of a world wherein
The psalm is stilled, and David does not win.[29]

Once back in Palestine immediately after the siege, Syrkin was assigned
the task of compiling data for the official report to the United Nations on
the flight of the Arabs from Israel and responding to accusations that the
Israelis had desecrated the Christian and Moslem Holy Places. She
traveled throughout the territory and finally drew the conclusion, derived
from personal interviews with clergy and community leaders whom she
named, that for the most part the Arabs had responded to the direction of
their own leaders, that they were being used by the Arab states as pawns,
that the flight was simultaneously a deliberate part of Arab military strategy, and also an uncontrollable stampede which Arab leadership strove
unsuccessfully to check when they realized the level it had reached. There
had been no Jewish master plan to expel them, and there had been no
Jewish plan to desecrate the Holy Places. Moreover, Syrkin argued that
"for the Arab, Palestine is a geographic fact, not an historic concept—and
a very recent geographic fact, at that,"[30] Further, she held that the nomenclature "Palestinian" for the Arab group is artificial and she questioned the existence of Palestinian nationalism as distinguished from an
attachment to the hometown. "Village patriotism," she argued, "was
made into a national cause."[31] This, she was to argue later in defense of
her friend, was the meaning of Golda Meir's oft-quoted remark that
"there are no Palestinians."

Syrkin believed in what she regarded as the absolute justice of Israel's
case: that Israel did not appear as a conquering invader and that at the
start it believed it could live in peace with the Arabs; that the truncated
State of Israel represents a necessary but not entirely just second partition
of the original area designated by the Balfour Declaration; and that the
state represents the culmination of decades of peaceful settlement sanc-
tioned by international agreements.[32] For these convictions, Marie Syrkin
later found herself attacked by the political left and accused of being an
apologist for Golda Meir, who held the same opinions.

Yet despite these firmly held beliefs, like her father before her, Marie Syrkin was not doctrinaire. She was quite aware that there was a distinction to be made between the justice of Israel's case and the practical need to work out a solution. She could have enough empathy for those who were suffering to say, "certainly it is true that the Palestinian Arabs left homes and villages dear to them, and no supporter of Jewish nationalism like myself has the right to minimize the intensity or equivalent dignity of Arab nationalism."[33] As recently as April 1988, less than a year before she died, Syrkin said in print that

Since 1967 the Labor Party and its adherents have argued that no matter how compelling the legal claim to the West Bank as part of the original territory designated for a Jewish homeland may be, and no matter how deep the religious attachments to the biblical patrimony of Judea and Samaria, these considerations had to give way before the danger to the Jewish or democratic character of the Jewish State that would be posed by the incorporation of over a million hostile Arabs. . . . To save the Jewish State from the progressive corrosion of being an occupying power and from engaging the talent and energy of its people in the unhappy task of maintaining formidable military power able to repeat the miracle of victory against monstrous odds, rational avenues towards a truce, if not full peace, should be explored.[34]

At the age of fifty-one, Marie Syrkin began a new career; or, one might say, she was granted the career she had long ago dreamed of. Again at the invitation of Abram L. Sachar, who was now president of the newly established Brandeis University, Syrkin became the first female professor of an academic subject on the faculty of Brandeis. She was appointed a professor of English literature.

It was here, moreover, that the New York Jewish intellectuals and the "other" New York Jewish intellectuals came face to face; Marie Syrkin, Ludwig Lewisohn, and Ben Halpern became the colleagues of Irving Howe and Philip Rahv. Though Howe, as Syrkin believed, initially opposed her tenure on the grounds that she was a journalist and not a scholar, and although Rahv complained that she was not an intellectual, remarking sarcastically that she thought *The Great Gatsby* was a book about bootleggers, Howe eventually grew to admire and honor her. He wrote in the special issue of *Jewish Frontier* (January/February 1983) in tribute to Marie Syrkin, "I value [Syrkin's] good humor, I value her self-irony, but most of all, I think of a remark someone once made about Thomas Hardy—that the world's slow stain had not rubbed off on him. There can be no greater praise, and I think it is true for Marie."

While at Brandeis, Marie Syrkin instituted one of the first courses in Holocaust literature and in American Jewish fiction to be taught in the universities. As early as 1966, in an essay in *Midstream,* she argued a point that later would become a commonplace of the genre: "The literature of the Holocaust . . . eludes the usual classification because of the very nature of its theme. The accepted literary categories—novels, plays, verse, essays—are unsatisfactory because they assume a measure of formal achievement to warrant consideration. . . ."[35] In *The American Jew: A Reappraisal,* edited by Oscar Janowsky, she wrote a pioneering essay on American Jewish fiction, and a re-evaluation of Henry Roth's *Call It Sleep* when that work was republished in 1964. She wrote in praise of Nellie Sachs and in sharp criticism of Philip Roth's *Portnoy's Complaint,* an attack Roth himself peevishly referred to in his later novel *Professor of Desire.* All the while she continued to write her own verse—two poems were to be anthologized in the *New York Times Book of Verse,* edited by Thomas Lask, an anthology of the best poetry to have appeared in the *Times* between 1920 and 1970.

In 1955 Syrkin published a biography of her dear friend Golda Meir, a memoir of her father, and edited an anthology of the writing of Hayim Greenberg. She continued her polemical arguments in the pages of many journals, taking on such formidable adversaries as Arnold Toynbee, I. F. Stone, and Hannah Arendt; she also debated the latter in a public forum.

When Marie Syrkin retired from Brandeis in 1966 as professor emerita, she returned to New York to resume her life with Charles Reznikoff. In this penultimate phase of her life, she assumed a desk at the Jewish Agency, became the editor of Herzl Press, and was elected a member of the World Zionist Organization. Now sixty-seven years old, she continued to lecture around the country and in Israel, to serve on the editorial boards of *Midstream* and the *Jewish Frontier,* to write for such diverse publications as *Commentary, Dissent,* the *Nation, Saturday Review,* the *New York Times* magazine, and the *New Republic.* She kept up her periodic trips to Israel and in 1973 went there to write a major piece for Golda Meir who was now prime minister, and for whom Syrkin had become a speechwriter. The article "Israel in Search of Peace" appeared in *Foreign Affairs* in April 1973. She also edited an anthology of Meir's speeches; and after she flew to Israel on the presidential airplane as an official delegate of the United States at the funeral of her friend Golda Meir, she expressed her grief in the following poem, "For Golda":

> Because you became a great woman
> With strong feature
> Big nose
> and heavy legs,
> None will believe how beautiful you were,

> Grey-eyed and slim-ankled.
> The men who loved you are dead.
> So I speak for the record.
> Indeed you were lovely among maidens
> Once
> In Milwaukee and Merhaviyah,
> And sometimes in Jerusalem.[36]

These busy, productive, and personally satisfying post-academic years, however, were to last only ten years. With no warning, on January 12, 1976, after Marie Syrkin and Charles Reznikoff had enjoyed a pleasant dinner together, he complained of indigestion. A doctor was called in and diagnosed a massive coronary. Reznikoff was rushed to the hospital where he died within hours. In her touchingly spare poem, "Finality," Syrkin describes his death and her loss:

> Death, the great kidnapper,
> Snatched you suddenly
> Asking no ransom.
> We were at dinner chatting,
> He broke in with two gentle, black attendants
> and a noisy ambulance.
>
> When I came back before dawn,
> The cups were still on the table
> And I was alone.

It is interesting to compare this poem with one that Syrkin had written over half a century earlier, after the death of her first-born son. Although, of course, the emotional content is different in kind as well as degree, the curious fact is that some fifty years later, death is once again experienced as a kidnapper.

> They should not have done what they did:
> The two men with gloves
> And faces I cannot remember
> Who came to carry you off
> Before my eyes.
> Silently they seized you,
> Kidnappers,
> (A hospital dreads the dead.)
> They should not have done what they did.[37]

In her last years, Marie Syrkin lived in Santa Monica—a move she had earlier planned to make with Charles Reznikoff. Here she would escape the rigors of New York City living and be close to her half-sister, her son, her grandchildren, and great-grandchildren. From here she continued to write on political issues, to keep up with current ideas and events, to publish a collection of her essays, *The State of the Jews,* and to publish a volume of her own poems, *Gleanings: A Diary in Verse.* In her final years, she would continue to confound her critics on the left and right, first by signing the first *Peace Now* statement, and then, by resigning after its first issue, from the board of *Tikkun.*

To the very end Marie Syrkin remained the consummate pragmatic idealist. Aware of current trends in historiography, she asserted, two weeks before her death on February 1, 1989, that those who now proclaim that the "myth" of Israel is dead are mistaken. Israel, she maintained, is an exemplar of what can be done. "Even if it lasts only forty, fifty, years, what that State achieved can never be erased because it shows the potential of idealism. . . . The adaptation of the dream to realities is merely the price of survival."[38]

Notes

1. Marie Syrkin to Carole Kessner, January 1989, unpublished interview.

2. Marie Syrkin, *Gleanings: A Diary in Verse* (Santa Barbara: Rhythms Press, 1979). 13. Hereafter called *Gleanings.*

3. Irving Howe, "For Marie," *Jewish Frontier* (January/February 1983): 8.

4. Marie Syrkin, personal interview.

5. Marie Syrkin, *Nachman Syrkin: Socialist Zionist* (New York: Herzl Press, 1961), 153.

6. Ibid., 60.

7. Marie Syrkin, *Way of Valor: A Biography of Goldie Meyerson* (New York: Sharon Books, 1955), 7. Syrkin's attitude toward the stance of the New York Intellectuals is reflected in her reference to "alienated" intellectuals.

8. Marie Syrkin, personal interview.

9. "Marie Syrkin and Trude Weiss-Rosmarin: A *Moment* Interview," *Moment* 8, no. 8 (September 1983): 40.

10. Marie Syrkin, *Diary,* March 28, 1915–June 4, 1915. This quotation is from the entry on March 29, 1915. On April 10, she identifies "W" as Weinstein.

11. Marie Syrkin, personal interview.

12. Syrkin's characterization of that summer was made when she was eighty-eight.

13. Marie Syrkin, "The New Youth Movement," *The New Palestine* (August 14, 1925): 140.

14. Ibid.

15. Thomas Kranidas, in his essay "Milton and the Rhetoric of Zeal," *TSLL* 6 (1965): 423–32.

16. Unpublished letter, dated May 23, 1923, from the Marie Syrkin–Henry Hurwitz Correspondence, American Jewish Archives, Cincinnati, Ohio.

17. According to Charles Madison in *Jewish Publishing in America: The Impact of Jewish Writing on American Culture* (New York: Sanhedrin Press, 1976), 226, *Reflex* was started in 1927. "In the early issues the articles were of current

interest and written by journalists and scholars who were in the limelight or who later attained prominence. Among them were Alexander Goldenweiser, Moses Gaster, Marie Syrkin, S. A. Dubnow, Isaac Goldberg, Franz Oppenheimer, Maximilian Harden, and Maurice Samuel."

18. Marie Syrkin, *The State of the Jews* (Washington, D.C.: New Republic Books, 1980), 2.

19. Ibid.

20. Reprinted in *Jewish Frontier* (January/February 1983): 23–27.

21. Ibid.

22. Marie Syrkin, *Your School, Your Children* (New York: L. B. Fischer, 1944).

23. Syrkin, *State of the Jews*.

24. Marie Syrkin, "What American Jews Did During the Holocaust," *Midstream* 84, no. 8 (October 1982): 6.

25. Ibid.

26. Lucy Dawidowicz, "The Holocaust Was Unique in Intent, Scope, and Effect," *Center Magazine* (July/August 1981).

27. Marie Syrkin, *Blessed Is the Match* (Philadelphia: Jewish Publication Society, 1947).

28. Marie Syrkin, "Why Partition?" *Jewish Frontier* (November 1946), reprinted in *State of the Jews,* 80.

29. Syrkin, *Gleanings,* 70.

30. Marie Syrkin, "The Arab Refugees," *State of the Jews,* 128.

31. Marie Syrkin personal interview.

32. Ibid.

33. Ibid.

34. Marie Syrkin, "Doublespeak about Israel," *Congress Monthly* 55, no. 3 (March/April 1988): 11.

35. Syrkin, *State of the Jews,* 297.

36. Marie Syrkin, "For Golda," *Jewish Frontier* (November/December 1984): 13.

37. Syrkin, *Gleanings,* 92–93.

38. Marie Syrkin, personal interview.

"Why Partition?" (November 1946)

Marie Syrkin

There is a strong likelihood that the coming Zionist Congress[1] will be another "Partition Congress."[2] That is to say, the question of a Jewish state in a part of Palestine will probably be among the acute issues before the delegates. This possibility is already an alignment of forces: parties are going on record in their official platforms as to whether they oppose or accept partition; Zionist leaders are committing themselves pro and con. . . .

. . . In the present deadlock, the Jewish Agency[3] has openly advanced the compromise formula of a "viable Jewish state in an adequate portion

Source: Marie Syrkin, "Why Partition?" in *Jewish Frontier*, 13:11 (November 1946), 4–6. Reprinted by permission of David Bodansky.

1. The reference is to the Twenty-second Zionist Congress, which met the following month in Basle, Switzerland. The congress would prove to be the scene of an open and bitter political conflict between two competing Zionist factions. The "moderates," led by Chaim Weizmann (1874–1952), the architect of the Balfour Declaration of 1917 and later the first president of Israel, favored a gradualist approach to state building within the constraints of the British Mandate. The "militants," led by David Ben-Gurion (1886–1973), who later served as Israel's first prime minister, with brief interruptions, from 1948 to 1963, and the American Jewish leader Rabbi Abba Hillel Silver (1893–1963), championed a combative approach. In the event, a majority of congress delegates rebuffed Weizmann's moderate policy, sided with Ben-Gurion and Silver, and affirmed a new postwar Zionist political strategy of working for a viable Jewish state in Palestine. The congress also rejected Britain's call for a Jewish-Arab conference in London—fearing that such a gathering would undermine support for Zionist aspirations in Palestine—and the Morrison-Grady Plan, which proposed the cantonization of Palestine. Consequently, Weizmann resigned the presidency of the World Zionist Organization, and Ben-Gurion and Silver assumed power as chairmen, respectively, of the Zionist Executive and the newly created American Section of the Jewish Agency.

2. The reference is to the Twentieth Zionist Congress, held in Zurich in August 1937, which debated the British Royal Peel Commission's original proposal to partition Palestine into separate Arab and Jewish states. The Arabs of Palestine unequivocally rejected the proposal. Meanwhile, it caused deep division among the Zionists, who split over the issues of sovereignty and maximalism. The continuation of Arab violence, which lasted from 1936 to 1939, eventually prompted the British government to abandon the plan.

3. The Jewish Agency was legally recognized by the League of Nations in the Mandate for Palestine as "a public body for the purpose of advising and cooperating with the Administration of Palestine in such economic, social and other matters as may affect the establishment of the Jewish national home and the interests of the Jewish population in Palestine, and subject always to the control of the Administration, to assist and take part in the development of the country" (British Mandate for Palestine, Article 4); for the complete text, see Paul Mendes-Flohr and Jehuda Reinharz, eds., *The Jew in the Modern World: A Documentary History,* 2nd ed. (New York and Oxford: Oxford University Press, 1995), 593–594. In its first decade, Chaim Weizmann headed the Jewish Agency. Starting in the mid-1930s,

of Palestine" as a basis for discussion.[4] It is this formula which has precipitated the familiar charges of "treason" and "timidity," raised both by the ideological opponents of partition and the political adversaries of the Jewish Agency. . . .[5]

It should be superfluous to state that every member of the Agency Executive in Paris[6] who voted for the partition formula did so with a full sense of the immense and bitter sacrifice of Jewish rights implicit in this proposal. . . . None know this as well as the political representatives entrusted with the burden of defending Jewish interests before the [British] Mandatory Power.[7] The only relevant question is whether better terms than partition can be secured in the present crisis. The situation of both the Yishuv and of the Jews of Europe is too grave to admit of a rhetorical maximalism which has no prospect of realization within the predictable future.

. . . Of course, partition must have more to recommend it than a hypothetical acceptability to the British. It has to offer Zionism definite immediate advantages for the losses we incur. Perhaps such advantages become clearer if we venture to look back upon the past decade. Let us suppose that partition had been accepted in 1937 and a Jewish state had been es-

---

however, the Jewish Agency was dominated by a Labor-led coalition under David Ben-Gurion. With the establishment of the State of Israel in 1948, the Jewish Agency was reorganized as a nongovernmental organization responsible for many of Israel's overseas activities including education, fund-raising, and *aliyah*.

4. In the course of its deliberations, the Twenty-second Zionist Congress softened the language of the resolution to appease those factions, notably centrist American groups like Hadassah and the ZOA, which balked at the term "Jewish state" and preferred the locution "a Jewish commonwealth integrated into the world democratic structure."

5. The reference is to the Revisionists who rejected partition and insisted on "a Jewish state within the historic boundaries of Palestine, based on a Jewish majority"; quoted in *American Jewish Year Book*, vol. 49 (1947), 254. The Revisionist Zionist party (also known as the Union of Zionist Revisionists) was founded in 1925 by Vladimir (Zeev) Jabotinsky (1880–1940). It originally advocated a revision of the Zionist Executive's conciliatory policy toward the British Mandatory and stepping up the pace of the Jewish settlement in Palestine. Jabotinsky, a brilliant writer, orator, and polemicist, considered himself the true heir to Herzl's legacy of classical Zionism. He was a staunch opponent of Labor Zionism and placed a premium on the notions of territorial maximalism, military strength, armed resistance against the British, and retaliation by Jews in Palestine against Arab attackers.

6. The Jewish Agency Executive met in Paris in August 1946 owing to the fact that some of its members, including David Ben-Gurion, would have otherwise been arrested by the British in Palestine or in Great Britain as part of the Mandatory's policy of crushing anti-British activity in the Yishuv. Indeed, several Zionist leaders, including Moshe Shertok (1894–1965), were detained by the British in a jail in Latrun. The Paris meeting focused on the issue of partitioning Palestine but also deliberated on the Morrison-Grady Plan (see note 1 above), prevailing British restrictions on Jewish immigration to Palestine, and the release of Jewish prisoners in Latrun.

7. Following World War I, the Supreme Council of the Paris Peace Conference assigned the Mandate for Palestine to Great Britain. The British assumed legal control of Palestine in 1920, and the country remained in British hands until 1948.

tablished in a part of Palestine. It is not easy to be wise even after the event, because we have no post facto knowledge of what other concomitant developments might have taken place had such a state been established. But it seems reasonable to assume that even a small Jewish state in part of Palestine would have meant the salvation of hundreds of thousands of Jews destined to perish in the crematoriums and gas chambers. A Jewish state would have had the right to determine the rate of immigration into its boundaries. And we may also assume that even a small Jewish state would have been represented at the San Francisco Conference, and would have enjoyed membership in the United Nations, just as Lebanon does.[8] For reasons which appeared valid to us then, our decision on partition was deferred. No one could foresee the catastrophe that would engulf the Jewish people. . . .

We cannot blame ourselves for having not been seers. But if we may be forgiven for lacking foresight, we cannot afford to neglect the indications provided by hindsight. That too is a form of vision. We now know that a status in Palestine which will create possibilities for immediate immigration and which will offer Jewish independence is the primary need of the Jewish people.[9] It might be sensible to seek to delay a final political solution if there were any likelihood that an interim period would provide for

8. The Conference of International Organizations, which met in San Francisco from April 25 to June 26, 1945, laid the groundwork for the United Nations. At Chaim Weizmann's request, Nahum Goldmann (1894–1982), who was then living in the United States, and his assistant Eliahu Elat (1903–1990), an expert on Arab affairs, represented the Jewish Agency at the conference.

9. Syrkin is referring to the desperate plight of Jewish refugees, known as Displaced Persons. "Displaced Persons" (also "DPs") was the euphemism used to describe the millions of European refugees, including many thousands of Jewish survivors, who suddenly came under the jurisdiction of the victorious Allied occupation forces with the conclusion of World War II. The magnitude of the refugee crisis prompted the Allies to establish scores of DP camps, including several camps designated for Jewish DPs in the American and British military zones in Italy, Germany, and Austria. Although many Hungarian and Czech Jewish DPs opted to be repatriated, approximately 65,000 other Jewish DPs were unable to do so owing to the intensity of antisemitism in their former communities. Indeed, the number of Jewish DPs rose steadily as many thousands of Jews who did attempt to return to their pre-war homes were forced to seek refuge in the wake of continued regional anti-Jewish violence, especially in Poland, where a series of pogroms occurred in the summer of 1946. By 1947 there were over 200,000 Jewish DPs in the Allied camps. Still, severe British restrictions on Jewish immigration to Palestine precluded the possibility of Jewish resettlement in Palestine. The alarming situation attracted widespread international attention, and President Harry S. Truman placed increased pressure on the British to allow for Jewish immigration to Palestine. Meanwhile, however, the Haganah smuggled many DPs into Palestine as part of Aliyah Bet. The British intercepted many Haganah vessels, and the captured passengers were held in detention camps in Cyprus. An especially noteworthy episode in this period was that of the *Exodus*, a ship whose passengers included a sizable number of DPs. Intercepted by the British while trying to reach Palestine, the *Exodus* was forced to return to

such immigration and would improve Zionist prospects for better ultimate aims. But all evidence points to the contrary. . . .

The objection has been raised by some American Zionists that it was bad tactics for the Jewish Agency to make its partition offer. Shrewd bargainers hold out for the maximum and then they scale down their terms, if they have to. Those who advance this curious argument seem willfully to forget that the Zionist movement has been engaged in endless heart-rending negotiations with the British. . . . It is ludicrous to pretend that the Jewish Agency pulled a compromise out of a blue, unclouded sky. The discussion [with the British] had been proceeding rapidly to a disastrous conclusion when the Executive made its supreme effort to stay the collapse.

Those who are already seeking to hamstring the deliberations of the forthcoming Congress by binding their members to a priori positions belong to various camps. They are the political doctrinaires who hold to the purity of their faith with theological fervor. The undiscouraged proponents of a binational state, who still expect to dwell in connubial affection with the Arabs despite the negative response their suit receives, oppose partition.[10] On the other hand, the "maximalists" of long standing, who will surrender no jot of their claim to a Jewish state on both sides of the Jordan [River], are equally adamant.[11] Religious Zionists, who feel that they cannot barter with the Lord's promise, are split on the issue of

---

Europe, where its weary and half-starved passengers were beaten off the ship with clubs by British forces, all in the glare of the world media. The tragic episode signaled a major public relations defeat for the British and a turning point in support for the Zionist enterprise.

10. Following World War I, several prominent Zionist figures and left-wing Zionist groups began espousing a binational solution to the land question in Palestine. The proponents of binationalism envisioned a state framework in which Jews and Arabs would enjoy political parity while maintaining their communal autonomy. Three key groups advocated binationalism: Brit Shalom [Covenant of Peace], founded in 1926 by Arthur Ruppin (1876–1943) and other intellectuals; the Ihud [Union], established in 1942 by the philosopher Martin Buber (1878–1965), the Hebrew writer Moshe Smilansky (1874–1953), and Youth Aliyah director Henrietta Szold (1860–1945); and Hashomer Hazair [The Young Guard], a Marxist Zionist pioneer movement.

11. The reference here is to the political tension between the leaders of the Jewish Agency and the right-wing Revisionist Zionist party, which dated back to the late 1920s (see note 5 above) when Vladimir (Zeev) Jabotinsky became the main voice of opposition to Chaim Weizmann's leadership as well as the policies of the World Zionist Organization and the Vaad Leumi in Palestine. In this period, the Revisionists' growing strength in Poland and elsewhere, combined with mounting tension between the right-wing Zionist groups, on the one hand, and Weizmann and the emergent Labor-led majority in Palestine, on the other, prompted Jabotinsky and his followers to secede from the World Zionist Organization. In 1935 the Revisionist movement founded the New Zionist Organization (NZO)—an alternative framework to the WZO. The NZO combated the proposed partition of Palestine in 1937 and proffered its own policies for rescuing Jews from Nazi-occupied Europe and opposing the British Mandatory regime in Palestine. The NZO disbanded after the war, and in 1946 the Revisionists rejoined the WZO.

partition.[12] These factions are theoretically committed to the particular solutions they have been advocating since their inception. They are intellectually and spiritually obstinate—the modern Zealots.

However, the real danger that the Congress may be stratified into anti- and pro-partition blocs which will paralyze its functioning stems from another source. It is not the ideological doctrinaires who represent the real threat. One may as well say it plainly. There are sectors of the Zionist movement, particularly the American Zionist movement, who are not averse to making political capital for their own partisan ends out of the present crisis.[13] Partition is popular with no one. To seek to transfer the indignation engendered by such a necessity for considering such a sacrifice to those who labored under the bitter obligation of making such a proposal is a discreditable maneuver.

Partition must not become a stick with which to attack the Zionist Executive or the Jewish Agency. Personal antagonisms and party rivalries can no more be avoided in the Zionist movement than in other movements. But there are moments in history which impose their responsibilities and restraints. This is one of them. Every Zionist aware of the desperate plight of the Jews of Europe and of Palestine must bear in mind that partition may represent the only immediate, realistic means of preventing the British from carrying out their unconcealed effort to liquidate Zionism. In 1937 partition was a Solomon's judgment. Today we must perhaps consider that the child is a Siamese twin whose life can only be saved by a drastic operation. At any rate, let American Zionists approach so fateful an issue, free from petty and essentially irrelevant considerations.

12. The twenty-seventh annual convention of American Mizrachi [sic] met in early November 1946 and rejected the notion of partitioning Palestine. Instead, Mizrachi pledged to work for the "historical claim of an independent Jewish state with its historic boundaries as ordained by the Torah"; quoted in *American Jewish Year Book*, vol. 49 (1947), 250. At the same time, however—especially after the Twenty-second Zionist Congress—several factions in the world Mizrahi movement, including elements from the party's American wing, gradually yielded to the Jewish Agency Executive's formula of establishing a "viable state" in Palestine according to modern political boundaries.

13. The reference here is to the so-called Bergson group, led by Hillel Kook (1915–2000), a right-wing militant Zionist activist who adopted the pseudonym Peter Bergson. From 1940 to 1945, Bergson spearheaded the Revisionist Zionist movement's opposition to the Zionist leadership in the United States. Known for provocative public statements and gestures, the Bergson group attracted a talented and distinguished circle of adherents including former U.S. Senator Guy M. Gillette (1879–1973), the publicist and screenwriter Ben Hecht (1893–1964), and U.S. Congressman Will Rogers, Jr. (1911–1993). The Bergson group created several American front-organizations, notably the Committee for a Jewish Army of Stateless and Palestinian Jews (1941), the Emergency Committee to Save the Jewish People of Europe (1942), the American League for a Free Palestine (1943), and the Hebrew Committee of National Liberation (1944). The groups raised funds, staged public rallies, organized protest marches, published ads in major American newspapers, and generally lobbied throughout the United States to promote the rescue of European Jewry.

PART II

American Jewish Women's Organizations and the Zionist Enterprise

Jewish women in the Progressive Era (circa 1890–1920) behaved very similarly to their Christian neighbors by creating reform organizations for personal uplift and the assistance of others. The vast numbers of illiterate, unskilled, and poor immigrants who left the Old World for the New, starting in the 1880s, reached the fifteen million mark before the U.S. Congress abruptly closed the "golden door" in 1924. As the social and ethnic makeup of American society changed, ugly interethnic, social, and political conflict ensued. At the same time, America was shifting rapidly from an agrarian to an industrial society. Advances in transportation and communications swelled the American economy, and allowed newcomers to participate, integrate, and even acculturate. The immigration influx produced two loosely defined types of American Jews—old-timers (largely of German ancestry) who were relatively well-off, spoke English well, and knew how to be American; and newcomers (largely of Russian and Polish ancestry) who were poor, spoke Yiddish, and were uncertain of how to meld their American and Jewish identities. Against this backdrop, many American Jewish women of the former category organized into an effective movement that fought for civic and legal equality, including the right to vote, while the newcomers gravitated to working-class concerns and fought for the rights of labor. Both sought in various ways to reform America.

World War I brought many of the strivings and activities associated with these arenas to an almost complete standstill. With respect to Zionist objectives, however, the wartime crisis proved to be uniquely propitious. Even as the United States was plunged into the chaos of European maelstrom, the Balfour Declaration of 1917 made it clear that the British government recognized the aspirations of the Zionist movement to create an autonomous Jewish national home in Palestine. For the first time, an international superpower publicly declaimed the possibility that Jewish statehood might be attained in the near future. After the war, Great Britain supplanted the Ottoman Empire and was granted the Mandate for Palestine by the League of Nations. This new political configuration seemingly placed Zionist aims within reach, a turn of events that prompted vehement Arab protests and widespread hostility. In this context, American Zionism, formerly an idea with adherents in only a tiny fraction of the population, achieved a new degree of recognition, legitimacy, and urgency.

As the chapters in this section demonstrate, American Zionist organizations were relatively small in this period. Most significant, however, is the fact that American Jewish women who had begun to work for Zionist ideas understood that they could be most effective in organizations of their own, rather than as members of male-dominated Zionist groups or as members of the women's auxiliaries of such groups. The realization of the need for separate sex-based Zionist organizations is one of the most important features of American Zionist history; however, it was not an easily won achievement. A general pattern emerged of vociferous male-led opposition to Zionist women's organizations; similar phenomena influenced the development of Hadassah, the Mizrachi Women's Organization, Pioneer Women, and the Women's International Zionist Organization (WIZO). Ironically, these organizations became not only strong—in large measure because they were separate—but also more robust and durable than Zionist organizations created by American Jewish men.

American Jewish women's Zionist organizations were further differentiated by the social, religious, and political leanings of American Jewish women in the pre-state period. Perhaps because of the limited opportunities for regular paid employment at the time, a large array of talented women activists—spanning the broad and multifaceted spectrum of American Jewish life—became forceful political and economic leaders for these organizations. Leah Brown (1890–1970), Bessie Gotsfeld (1888–1962), Lotta Levensohn (1882–1972), Irma Levy Lindheim (1886–1978), Golda (Meyerson) Meir (1898–1978), Jessie Sampter (1883–1938), Alice L. Seligsberg (1873–1940), Henrietta Szold (1860–1945), Sophie Udin (1896–1960), Nina Zuckerman (1889–1984), and many others built, sustained, and steered their respective Zionist women's organizations, both in the United States and in Palestine. Drawing on the Jewish traditions of communal voluntarism and the pursuit of social justice, American Zionist women leaders exploited specific social, religious, and political factors to make their organizations large, well run, and financially successful. They understood and exploited the urban concentration of America's Jews, the tax laws that encouraged philanthropy, the predisposition of American ethnic groups to think and act as organized blocs, and the desire of Jews to socialize with one another, build up the ranks of voluntarism, and see their philanthropic dollars spent wisely. In time, American Zionist women's organizations also established partnerships with Jewish women overseas and put their skills to work building many of the central institutions of the Yishuv.

The articles in this section analyze organized American Jewish women's Zionist practical activity in the pre-state era and the early years of statehood. Baila Round Shargel examines the rise of the Mizrachi Women's Organization, an independent women's religious Zionist group that served as a counterbalance to the male-dominated American Mizrachi party. Mary McCune examines the techniques and tactics Hadassah employed to build an effective organization in American society, specifically by counteracting the anti-Zionism of other Jewish women's organizations and recruiting like-minded members into its own ranks. Mark A. Raider's study of the Pioneer Women's Organization, the American Labor Zionist women's framework, adds a discussion of social class and collectivist ideology to this discourse of organizational analysis. He focuses on the ties between working-class Jewish immigrant women in the United States and the female members of the nascent Palestine labor movement. Esther Carmel-Hakim explains the powerful influence of Canadian Jewish women on Zionist projects for women in Palestine. Nelly Las demonstrates through an examination of the International Council of Jewish Women that, aside from recruiting women from non-Zionist organizations into Zionist ones, the non-Zionist organizations themselves were deeply influenced by Zionism's rise. Finally, Mira Katzburg-Yungman shows how Hadassah created and solidified the health care system of Palestine's Jewish society-in-the-making and discusses the instrumental role played by American Jewish women in this countrywide endeavor. In sum, the chapters in this section demonstrate that American Jewish women's Zionism was not a monolithic movement. Rather, like American Zionism as a whole, the Zionist efforts of American Jewish women included distinctive political, cultural, and religious groupings. Moreover, the key tensions for American Zionist women were larger than simply those between male and female Zionist groups. Tensions and rivalry existed among secular, traditional, and socialist Zionist women's groups, within various Zionist camps, and among American Jewish women less concerned with Zionism than they were with North America.

Chapter 4

In 1901 the Fifth Zionist Congress met in Basle, Switzerland, and resolved to embark upon a new approach to Jewish cultural and educational affairs. The decision to deviate from exclusively political work was in large part the product of intensive lobbying by the Democratic Faction of the World Zionist Organization (WZO), a group of young men who asserted that Zionism was a Jewish renaissance movement. In response, many East European traditionalists who objected to the WZO's prevailing secular orientation resolved to create a separate religious Zionist faction of the WZO. Led by Rabbi Isaac Jacob Reines (1839–1915), the traditionalist wing of the Zionist movement gathered in Vilnius in 1902 and established the Mizrahi religious Zionist party, the first recognized independent political federation within the WZO.

Since its inception, the slogan of the Mizrahi party has been "The Land of Israel for the people of Israel according to the Torah of Israel." The name Mizrahi is an acronym for the Hebrew phrase *merkaz ruhani,* meaning "spiritual center"; it is also the Hebrew term for "eastward."

In 1914 Rabbi Meir (Berlin) Bar-Ilan (1880–1949) founded the American branch of the Mizrahi party. Bar-Ilan, the party's guiding spirit, hailed from Volozhin, Russia. Unlike many of his Zionist contemporaries, he maintained a positive attitude toward the American Jewish diaspora and lived in the United States from 1913 until his own immigration to Palestine in 1926. Notwithstanding the political infighting that characterized this early period in American Zionism's development, Bar-Ilan oversaw the growth of the Mizrachi Organization of America to roughly twenty thousand members countrywide by the mid-1920s.

Much of American Mizrachi's success from this point forward, as Baila Round Shargel argues in the chapter that follows, was due to the vigorous and strategic activity of the party's female members. Shargel singles out Bessie (Goldstein) Gotsfeld (1888–1962) as a particularly influential Mizrachi women's leader. A native of Przemysl, Poland, Gotsfeld was the eldest daughter of an enlightened Talmudic scholar, and she received "a religious education at home and a secular education in a Catholic school."[1]

---

1. Ava F. Kahn, "Bessie Goldstein Gotsfeld," in *Jewish Women in America: An Historical Encyclopedia*, ed. Paula E. Hyman and Deborah Dash Moore, vol. 1 (New York: Routledge, 1997), 545.

She immigrated to the United States as a young woman and soon gravitated to the Mizrachi party, where she emerged as a leading advocate for the establishment of a separate religious Zionist women's organization. The new group, named the Mizrachi Women's Organization, boldly asserted its independence in philanthropic and political affairs, a highly radical departure from the normative pattern of traditional East European Jewish life—a phenomenon, however, not dissimilar from the trajectory of other American Zionist women's groups. Shargel examines the extent to which the Mizrachi experience meshed with Zionism's American pattern. She also throws considerable light on how and why Gotsfeld came to be known as "the Henrietta Szold of Mizrachi Women."

"Never a Rubber Stamp": Bessie Gotsfeld, Founder of Mizrachi Women of America

Baila Round Shargel

Bessie Goldstein Gotsfeld never considered herself a feminist or a revolutionary. Indeed, all her endeavors were intended to advance the causes of Orthodox Judaism, first in America, then in the Holy Land. At the same time her life's work stretched the borders of the Orthodox power structure to incorporate women into one important domain. Under her leadership, passive acceptors of a patriarchal religious structure became active decisors in the area of education and culture.

Born in 1888, Bessie Goldstein was the firstborn child of a Galician rabbi who educated his sons and daughters in religious and secular subjects. While still in Poland, Bessie completed a secondary course of instruction in an advanced Polish-Catholic "gymnasium."

In 1905 the Goldstein family migrated to New York, where a cultured Orthodox young man instructed the children in the English language and literature. Mendel Gotsfeld, the Australian-born tutor, fell in love with Bessie, who was as clever as she was attractive. They married in 1909 and moved to Seattle, where Mendel's clothing store brought prosperity to the young couple, happily married but sadly childless. In 1919, after Bessie suffered the first of many episodes of diabetic shock, they returned to New York. Mendel established himself in the jewelry business while Bessie found solace in the company of her large and warm extended family.[1]

Despite persistent illness, Bessie worked strenuously for a cause that she had already espoused: religious Zionism. The Gotsfelds had met Rabbi Meyer Berlin when he undertook a nationwide tour on behalf of the newly established Mizrachi Organization of American. The rabbi's later reflections describe Seattle as a city with "men and *women*" (my emphasis) of great Zionist potential, some favorably inclined toward Mizrachi.[2] Since his memoirs seldom mentioned women, one can reasonably assume that this was a reference to Bessie Gotsfeld, around whose family table he met potential members.[3] The encounter must have taken place between 1915 and 1918.[4] At that time, the charismatic young rabbi was in the process of convincing American Orthodox Zionists to withdraw from the Federation of American Zionists (FAZ), the umbrella American Zionist organization, and affiliate with the world Orthodox Zionist body.[5] By the same token he persuaded the impressionable young Bessie to abandon Hadassah, the women's General Zionist organization, and devote her efforts exclusively to Mizrachi.

Resettled on Manhattan's Lower East Side, Gotsfeld honed her skills as a fund-raiser for Mizrachi-run institutions in Palestine, primarily synagogues and *yeshivot*. Despite their lack of formal education and immigrant status, women supporters of Mizrachi were cognizant of injustice and chafed at the fund-raising system. They were acculturated enough to grumble over taxation without representation. It was not right, they murmured, for outsiders, even respected rabbis, to dictate the beneficiaries of their money collections. With encouragement of Rabbi Berlin, who remained close to the Gotsfeld-Goldstein clan, they formed a local group called Ahios Mizrahi [Sisters of Mizrachi] in 1924.[6] Adela Goldstein, Bessie's stepmother, took the helm.

Ahios Mizrahi in New York was created with autonomy as an objective. But to the rabbis and other male money collectors, the new organization was simply a more effective fund-raising engine. At a meeting attended by 130 women, Rabbi Yehudah Leib Fishman (later Maimon), the Palestinian representative of Mizrahi, addressed the women. He thanked them for their success, then held out his hand for the money. Bessie Gotsfeld, better educated and more articulate than most members, and resolutely tactful, broke the embarrassed silence that followed. Masking her anger with a controlled smile, she rose, thanked him for his very *interesting* speech, then told him that the ladies would consider what she called his "request" and inform him of their decision at some other time.[7]

Of course Rabbi Maimon never saw the money. Instead Gotsfeld volunteered to go to Palestine and survey local conditions. The object was to ascertain a suitable project for the Mizrachi Women's Organization of America, the autonomous national organization of Orthodox Zionist women, newly formed with the blessings of Rabbi Berlin.[8] Travel to Palestine in 1926 was not a simple affair, especially for an ailing, diabetic women. But once Bessie decided to do something, nothing would stand in her way. Her first visit, personally financed, lasted for six months.

Mizrahi had been founded in Europe under the leadership of Rabbi Isaac Jacob Reines, an educational innovator within the Lithuanian *yeshivah* world. Reines was prominent among the minority of European rabbis who responded to Herzl's call for an end to Jewish homelessness and landlessness. But he soon parted ways with General Zionism. What precipitated the split was a resolution passed at the Fifth Zionist Congress (1901) advancing educational goals that were strictly national and secular. At that juncture Reines's followers held a breakaway conference and formed a new party within Zionism. They called it Mizrahi, meaning "east" and implying the Land of Israel, but also an abbreviation of *merkaz ruhani:* spiritual center. This new branch of Zionism would continue to participate in the movement's physical and material ventures: rebuilding the land, establishing new communities, and advancing the cause of statehood. Already pledged to revive Hebrew as the common language of everyday speech and literature, the Mizrahi party would also bolster that endeavor.

The rabbis, however, rebelled against what they considered the extreme secularism of most Zionists. Demanding that Zion be rebuilt in "the spirit of Torah," they chose the motto *"Erez yisrael leam yisrael, al pi torat yisrael"* [The Land of Israel for the people Israel according to the Torah of Israel]. Since they were unable to dominate the Zionist establishment, they settled for control of the education system and cultural agenda of the religious minority in the Yishuv.[9] By 1921 a Mizrahi network of schools was in place. (With the exception of a few years when Labor Zionism, representing the anti-religious, agricultural ideal, managed a third education system, two Zionist school systems have historically functioned in Palestine/Israel, one secular, the other religious.)

Before the break with the FAZ,[10] American Mizrahi groups, acting in concert, had promoted Jewish education "for boys and girls" in every American city with a sizable Jewish population.[11] By contrast, the European rabbis who emigrated to Palestine did not trouble themselves with female education. For Americanized Bessie Gotsfeld, herself progressively educated in Poland and America, this was deplorable neglect. But where in the Yishuv was the model for education along Orthodox lines for young women? To be sure, the new secondary schools were modern and coeducational. But Bessie knew that these schools were too freewheeling for Orthodox Zionists. She observed that the religious Zionist establishment had responded to Zionist secular education by creating a modern Orthodox secondary school. The Tahkemoni school in Jaffa offered both general and Judaic subjects, with Hebrew as the language of instruction.[12] Other schools along that line would soon follow. And, of course, *yeshivot* of every stripe and on all levels were in place.

Orthodox schools, however, educated only boys. Orthodox girls had scant opportunity to gain knowledge or skills that would equip them to function in the new Jewish society in Palestine. With only grade school training, energetic female adolescents from religious families had the choice of languishing at home helping their mothers with housework and child care while waiting for a proper *hoson* [bridegroom] or working at low-level jobs as maids or laborers in the few textile mills of the country.

In light of this predicament, Bessie suggested that the Mizrachi Women's Organization of America (MWA) sponsor a technical school for Orthodox girls in Jerusalem. The project both mimicked the parent body and challenged it. I say "mimicked" because it recapitulated the motive behind Mizrachi's separation from General Zionism: the demand for religious control of education and culture, at least for Orthodox Jews.

The choice of female education presented a distinct challenge. Orthodox men and women had always supported institutions that sustained the elite Talmudic culture. By contrast, the proposed secondary school for young women conveyed a double message. The first message was gender solidarity: women helping girls. The second message was a practical female sensibility, need-driven rather than ideology-directed. Instruction in Mizrachi Women's institutions would satisfy the requirements of multiple groups: of young women who otherwise would have remained ignorant and unemployable; of the Yishuv, which required skilled workers in the city and on the farm; and finally, of religious Zionists at a time of secular triumph. Graduates, competent in several fields, would put a new face on Orthodoxy and help ensure continuity into the next generation.

To forestall possible objections, the curriculum was couched in conventional terms. It exploited the fact that the so-called technical courses were extensions of work performed by homebound women. New occupational courses could thus be seen as conservative, training women in traditionally feminine pursuits.

"Domestic Science" was the name of the first curriculum in cooking, baking, housework, laundry, and sewing. Young women who opted for the agricultural curriculum received additional instruction in raising poultry, vegetables, and flowers,[13] In years to come additional courses were offered in crafts and secretarial skills. All were needed in the workplace. But to satisfy traditionalists uneasy over women functioning in the public sphere, publicity wisely proclaimed a secondary objective: instructing future housewives to function efficiently in kitchen, laundry, and garden.[14]

Bessie Gotsfeld easily convinced the MWA to support the vocational school. The national body then authorized her to return to Palestine as its official representative, purchase a suitable building in Jerusalem, obtain permits for construction, hire a director and staff to run the school, and recruit suitable teachers and students.

In 1933 the first Beit Zeirot Mizrahi [House of Young Women of Mizrahi] opened its Jerusalem doors. It provided a two-year course, and by

December 1935 Gotsfeld could happily report: "So far every girl that left our school got employment and is pretty well paid."[15] By that time she had decided to settle permanently in Tel Aviv with her husband. She would remain there until her death in 1962. Life in Palestine would, however, often be interrupted by trips abroad. Recurrent illness forced Bessie to consult European medical specialists and find respite in European spas. An additional obligation was attendance at Mizrachi Women's American conventions. Especially in the lean Depression era, only Bessie's charisma could loosen the purse strings of women struggling to keep their own families afloat. Events in Europe presented new challenges. Beit Zeirot Mizrahi was already educating German girls escaping Nazi humiliation and deprivation. To meet their needs and those of resident Orthodox girls, a second school was required, this time in Tel Aviv. Gotsfeld repeated the strenuous efforts to establish the facility and put it on its feet.

In the 1930s and 1940s, times of unprecedented catastrophe for the Jewish people, the demand for educational institutions to instruct and also house young women grew apace. Without hesitation, Gotsfeld rose to the challenge. She persuaded American backers to underwrite new institutions and wheedled local British and Jewish officialdom into endorsing them. The American Mizrachi Women's Organization also took upon itself the housing and education of child refugees from European Orthodox families who gained admission to the country with Youth Aliyah numbers. Among them were several children's villages for German refugee children, then the famous Children of Teheran,[16] then orphaned Holocaust survivors. The most ambitious undertaking, founded in 1947, assumed Gotsfeld's name: the Bessie Gotsfeld Children's Village and Farm School—in Hebrew, Kfar Batya. (Batya was Bessie's Hebrew name.) Eventually, the MWA would become the official sponsor of religious technical education in Israel.

Institutions under MWA sponsorship provided cultural enrichment as well as vocational training. For Beit Zeirot Mizrahi–Jerusalem, Gotsfeld recruited the very talented Torah teacher Nehama Leibowitz as classroom teacher and supervisor of the Judaic studies curriculum. All the schools added instruction in English, physical training, and intramural clubs. Beit Zeirot Mizrahi–Tel Aviv became a community center for cultured Orthodox Europeans. Both resident and commuting students were encouraged to attend the evening lectures and concerts.

These activities place Bessie Gotsfeld firmly in the camp of what sociologist Samuel Heilman calls modern Orthodox syncretism. While those whom he terms "Orthodox rejectionists" are suspicious of contemporary secular culture and prefer to isolate themselves from it or at least consign it to an inferior position, Orthodox syncretists value modernity on its own terms. They enjoy the benefits of modernity and make every effort to reconcile traditional behaviors and ideologies with contemporary consciousness and conditions.[17]

Gotsfeld represented Orthodox syncretism on four levels: modernist/ scientific, aesthetic, personal, and political. To begin with the modernist/ scientific: The curriculum for the Batei Zeirot announced the intent "to bring . . . to the task in the home a scientific approach."[18] Every skill, no matter how humble, made use of the latest and best technology. The stoves in the student kitchen, imports from America, were state-of-the-art; kitchen classes were not lessons in how to follow recipes but instruction in the chemical properties of various foods. Graduates of the program in "domestic science" found jobs as food purchasers for large institutions, dieticians, and nutritionists. Finding scientific staff for a Zionist and Orthodox technical school was not easy. A letter to Bessie's sister-in-law and confidante Belle Goldstein complained:

We still did not succeed getting the right spiritual directress. There is always something lacking. If she has the proper training she is not religious. If she is religious, she knows no Hebrew. If she knows Hebrew, she has not the training.[19]

Gotsfeld remained committed to female education, but when the need arose, she included boys. Kfar Batya's coeducational system was progressive. Its overall director was Hayim Zvi Enokh, an innovative educator who modeled the school after the Pestalozzi School near Zurich, Switzerland. The system promoted "natural learning" and "personal independence." The school at Kfar Batya became a model for progressive education in Israel.[20]

On the aesthetic level, Kfar Batya was a showplace; buildings and grounds attracted visitors from Israel and abroad. For Bessie Gotsfeld, aesthetics were not a frill but an integral element in education. When planning a youth village, children's home, or synagogue for an institution, she consulted top European-trained architects. School directors, counselors, and supervisors were expected to maintain the buildings and gardens. Several of these individuals had reputations as martinets for cleanliness and orderliness. Former students recall the school principal at Kfar Batya, a real "*yekke,*" who enforced tidiness with a slight twist of an errant student's ear.[21]

Beit Zeirot Mizrahi–Tel Aviv, a graceful L-shaped building two (later three) stories high, was equally attractive. An expert gardener, professionally trained in Germany, tended a neat plot. The entrance of polished stone gleamed like marble. Counselors at resident facilities followed instructions to discard chipped plates. Sabbath tables were adorned with flowers. Inside the classroom and out, students at all Mizrahi women institutions assimilated Bessie's good taste.[22]

On the next level, the political, Bessie labored incessantly to maintain the independence and strength of her organization. Her first difficult task was to wrangle funds from the women she represented. That she sometimes resorted to psychological blackmail is indicated in the following excerpt. After acquiring a prime property for Beit Zeirot Mizrahi–Tel Aviv, she badgered the New York office with the following:

> I must stress again that we would have never gotten the lot if we did not say that we are prepared to build (immediately).

She sweetened the demand for more funds with a tribute:

> At this time of unemployment, it was a great inducement to be able to give employment to people.[23]

Out of deeply felt necessity Gotsfeld developed expertise in manipulation. Encountering officials within the Yishuv—British or Jewish, religious or secular, municipal or national—her manner was always pleasant and conciliatory. The velvet words, however, could not conceal her steely resolution. David Ben-Gurion, recovering from an exhaustive and exhausting conversation with Gotsfeld, was rumored to have wished she were in *his* camp.[24]

Within the Palestinian Orthodox network, Gotsfeld allied herself with the modernists. Rabbi Yehudah Leib Maimon, director of the Department of Religious Affairs, remained indifferent to female education. His insensitivity, in fact, had triggered the very creation of the MWA.[25] Sidestepping Maimon, Bessie Gotsfeld enlisted the aid of Meir Berlin (later Bar-Ilan), the cultured European rabbi who had introduced Bessie to Mizrahi. Serendipitously, at the time that Kfar Batya was planned, he administered the Jewish National Fund.[26] In that capacity he secured the beautiful Raananah site for the Children's Village and Farm School.[27]

Gotsfeld's toughness surfaced in her dealings with another Orthodox group, women supporters of Hapoel Hamizrahi. On the surface the two organizations cherished common values: Zionism, religious traditionalism, and Hebrew labor. Indeed, in *Erez Israel* the two groups cosponsored a few settlements. Gotsfeld's quarrel concerned the American, not the Palestinian, scene. Letters to her sister-in-law indicate displeasure at the efforts of Hapoel Hamizrahi to create a national women's organization in the United States. A 1931 letter urged:

Should they still come to our women for money they should not hand it to them and against this we must make the most strenuous propaganda.[28]

Five years later, when the two organizations were planning a joint effort in Palestine, she exclaimed:

If they think that I am just going to accept whatever program they make without meeting with my understanding about it, they will be greatly disappointed. I never in my life was a rubber stamp and don't expect to be.[29]

The political became the personal:

I hope you see their point very clear. The object is to have your representative in Palestine out of the picture.[30]

That, of course, never happened. Furthermore, though the Boston society of Hapoel Hamizrahi and similar groups in other American cities continued to function, they did not federate into a national organization until 1948.

The most prominent competitor for the hearts and hands of Orthodox women Zionists was not the weak and localized Hapoel Hamizrahi but rather Hadassah, American Jewry's largest, strongest, and most admired organization. At the urging of founder Henrietta Szold and national president Rose Jacobs, Hadassah became the fund-raising agency for Youth Aliyah. The MWA was one of the four agencies to secure Youth Aliyah children, yet this fact was not well known.[31] In the course of receiving and settling German children, Gotsfeld frequently contacted Szold, who directed Youth Aliyah in Palestine. Bessie respected the older woman but at the same time resented the organization with which her name remained associated.[32] Hadassah's policy, she confided to her sister-in-law, was "to swallow every other group."[33] She particularly objected to the participation of American Orthodox women in Hadassah.[34]

In the case of Bessie Gotsfeld and the MWA, it is impossible to disentangle the political from the personal. Prompting the inception of the organization was a craving for group autonomy that flowed from individual women's quests for personal freedom and self-fulfillment. Bessie became a role model; when Mizrachi women read portions of the Gotsfeld-Goldstein correspondence published in the MWA's *News Bulletin,* they considered her advance toward organizational and personal independence and achievement as their own. This, in turn, allowed each member to fulfill an original objective: "the desire of self-expression and self-assertion in her work for Palestine."[35] Clearly, the Zionist ideal of *hagshamah azmit* [personal realization] was as decisive for Orthodox women who supported the Yishuv as it was for secular Zionists.

Because of Orthodoxy's patriarchal culture, Mizrachi women faced more vigorous opposition than their more acculturated Zionist sisters. But there were compensations. Programs under their sponsorship satisfied an inchoate yearning for enfranchisement within Orthodoxy. Education had always been the exclusive preserve of Orthodox men. Institutions sustained by the MWA signified that education, albeit of a different type, could also be of, by, and for Orthodox women.

In contemporary Orthodox Zionist circles, Bessie Gotsfeld is often designated "The Henrietta Szold of Mizrachi Women."[36] I think the comparison diminishes the founder of the organization, today called Amit Women. Bessie Gotsfeld was as charismatic a personality and as influential in Orthodox circles as Szold was in General Zionism. As I continue to research Gotsfeld's life, moreover, I uncover new correlations between the lives and work of these two pioneering American Zionist women. But that is another paper. I close here with a statement by Zalman Abramov, a historian of religion-state tensions in modern Israel: "Jewish self-government (in the Yishuv) scored its greatest successes in the field of education and health services."[37] If we accept this generalization, then this pair of American Jewish women, who devoted their lives to the education and physical well-being of Jews in the Yishuv and early state, are even more pivotal than heretofore considered.

Notes

1. Much of the data about Bessie Gotsfeld's personal and organizational life is culled from *Bessie,* a pamphlet written by Leona M. Goldfeld and distributed by Amit Women. Mrs. Goldfeld is Bessie Gotsfeld's great-niece.

2. See Meir Bar-Ilan's memoir, *From Volozhin to Jerusalem* (Ramat Gan: Bar Ilan University, 1971), 465. To Berlin, Seattle was "an island" in a sea of western un-Jewishness.

3. Goldfeld, *Bessie,* 8.

4. Ibid. Actually the man who took credit for introducing Mizrachi to the West Coast was Rabbi Wolf (Zeev) Gold. See his "The First Days," in *Mizrachi Jubilee Publication of the Mizrachi Organization of America, 1911-1936,* Pinchas Churgin and Leon Gellman, ed. (New York: Posy-Shouslon Press, 1936), Hebrew section, 42. Berlin's travels to "the Far West"—he mentioned Seattle, Denver, and San Francisco—must have taken place during his second sojourn in America, 1915-1918, not the first, 1913-1914, when he visited the East and Midwest. See *From Volozhin to Jerusalem,* 469. In Berlin's published letters the most westerly point represented was Minneapolis. See Nathaniel Katzberg, ed., *Rabbi Meir Bar-Ilan, Letters* [Hebrew] (Ramat Gan: Bar-Ilan University, 1976), Vol. I., Letter #18, 69.

5. For information on the beginnings of the Mizrachi Organization in America see Zeev Gold, "First Days," 40–44, and Zechariah M. Kerstein, "The Beginning

of Mizrachi in America," Yiddish section, 233–242, both in *Mizrachi Jubilee Publication.* Whether Berlin (later Bar-Ilan) organized a national movement or merely regularized an existing one is in dispute. Evyatar Friesel found no lasting Mizrachi presence in America until Rabbi Meyer Berlin's arrival in November 1913; *The Zionist Movement in the United States, 1897–1914* [Hebrew] (Tel Aviv: Hakibbutz Hameuhad, 1970), 135–137. Shoshana Dolgin-Beer disagrees. She cites evidence of a solid Mizrahi organization in the immigrant neighborhoods of New York, Pittsburgh, and St. Louis between 1909 and 1912, with some contact between the European rabbis who headed them. See "The Formative Years of the Mizrahi Movement in America, 1884–1918" (M.A. thesis, Touro College, 1997), chs. I and II. Her point-of-view coincides with that of Nathaniel Katzberg, who credited Berlin with separating American Mizrachi from the FAZ. See his Introduction to *Rabbi Meir Bar-Ilan, Letters,* Vol. I, 20. Melvin I. Urofsky, the premier contemporary historian of American Zionism, does not enter the fray. Indeed, he devotes little space to the founding of Mizrachi or its early activities. See his *American Zionism from Herzl to the Holocaust* (Lincoln: University of Nebraska Press, 1995), 102.

   6. By this time a number of Mizrachi auxiliary societies flourished in various cities. Kerstein ("The Beginning," 235) mentions "Ahios Zion," a Pittsburgh group.

   7. Goldfeld, *Bessie,* 11. On Fishman's contributions to the men's organization, see Gold, "First Days," 43.

   8. The Mizrachi Women's Organization of America was founded at the Eleventh Convention of the Mizrachi Organization of America, Cleveland, 1925. See the subsection of Kerstein's "The Beginning" entitled "The Mizrachi Woman's Organization," Yiddish section, 244–245; Mrs. Abraham Shapiro, "The Mizrachi Women in America," in *Mizrachi Jubilee Publication,* English Section, 45–6; and Dolgin-Beer "Formative Years, " 62.

   9. See Jessie Sampter, *Guide to Zionism* (New York: ZOA., 1920), 103–105; Ehud Luz, *Parallels Meet: Religion and Nationalism in the Early Zionist Movement, 1882–1904,* Philadelphia: Jewish Publication Society, 1988, 237–246; and Geula Bat-Dror, "The Question of Culture in Sefer Shragai," chapter in *Research on Religious Zionism and Aliyah to Erez Israel* [Hebrew] (Jerusalem: Mosad Harav Kook, 1981) 66–81.

   10. Leftist Zionist groups also broke with the weak FAZ, for example Poalei Zion. I thank Mark A. Raider for this datum.

   11. See Marnin Feinstein, *American Zionism, 1884–1904* (New York: Shulsinger Brothers, 1965), 268.

   12. See S. Zalmon Abramov, *Perpetual Dilemma: Jewish Religion in the Jewish State* (Cranberry, N.J.: Associated University Press, 1976), 73. Dolgin-Beer (*Formative Years,* 25) notes that as early as 1910 American supporters of Mizrahi discussed "matters relating to Tahkemoni." Several of Rabbi Meir Berlin's letters from America requested funding for the Jaffa school (*Letters* 27, 28, and 30). Furthermore, Rabbi Fishman devoted a considerable portion of his time in America to raising funds for the school.

   13. Pioneer Women, the female organ of the Poalei Zion Party was also founded in 1925. It sponsored a network of training farms and agricultural schools. See Mark A. Raider, *The Emergence of American Zionism* (New York: New York University Press, 1998), 54–57.

14. See Shapiro, "The Mizrachi Women in America," 45–46 and Mrs. Bessie Gotsfeld, "The Mizrachi Vocational Institute" 77–82, both in *Mizrachi Jubilee Publication,* English Section.

15. Bessie Gotsfeld to Belle Goldstein, 1 December 1935, Bessie Gotsfeld Papers, Amit Women Archives, New York City.

16. About a thousand East European children, mostly orphans who had fled from Poland, traveled on foot through Russia, reached Iran, traversed the Red Sea to Egypt. They finally reached Haifa, to the acclaim of every Jew in Palestine.

17. Samuel Heilman, "The Many Faces of Orthodoxy," *Modern Judaism* 2:2 (May 1982): 172–198.

18. Gotsfeld, "Mizrachi Vocational Institute," 77.

19. Gotsfeld to Goldstein, 2 August 1936, Gotsfeld Papers.

20. David Eliach, head teacher of Judaic subjects at Meshek Yeladim Moza and Kfar Batya (both under MWA sponsorship), and Yaffa Sorenson Eliach, his erstwhile student. Interviews by author, New York City, 1 October 1998.

21. Ibid; Judith Alter Coleman and Mira Bramson, interviews by author, New Rochelle, N.Y., 2 February 1999. These women were refugee students at Beit Zeirot Mizrahi and other institutions supported by MWA.

22. To the point of secretly ridiculing the extravagant hats worn by visiting American Mizrachi women. Ibid; Yaffa Eliach made the same point.

23. Gotsfeld to Goldstein, 2 August 1936, Gotsfeld Papers. Portions of letters such as this one were intended for publication in the organization's *News Bulletin.*

24. Eliach interview.

25. I am speculating here, but his views on modernist women could be attributed to anger at his sister's defection from Orthodoxy; Ada Maimon was a prominent leader of the secular Jewish women's labor movement in *Erez Israel.*

26. See Yael Ilan, ed., *The World Zionist Organization: The National Institutions, Structure and Functions* (Jerusalem, World Zionist Organization, 1997), 6.

27. Israel Friedman, address at "Mrs. Bessie Gotsfeld Memorial Meeting," New York City, 23 July 1974; interview by author, New York City, 24 February 1999.

28. Gotsfeld to Goldstein, 6 November 1931, Gotsfeld Papers.

29. Idem., 2 August 1936.

30. Ibid.

31. The four constituent agencies of Youth Aliyah were Hadassah, Mizrachi Women's Organization, Pioneer Women, and the United Palestine Appeal. See Archives of Youth Aliyah, RG1/B2 (1945), Hadassah Archives, New York.

32. By the 1930s Szold had long since left Hadassah leadership to concentrate on administrative duties for the Yishuv. On Hadassah's role in Youth Aliyah, see Marlin Levin, *Balm in Gilead: The Story of Hadassah* (New York: Schocken Books, 1973), 112–135. That the Mizrahi leadership was at first lukewarm about Youth Aliyah is indicated by Rabbi Yehuda Leib Fishman-Maimon's siding with the Zionist leaders who voted against Hadassah's "Special Campaign" for the project (see 126). Mizrahi officials were convinced that Hadassah deliberately placed Orthodox children in non-Orthodox settings. See Minutes of a Hadassah Board Meeting on the subject, 11 March 1936, Archives of Youth Aliyah RG1/B13/F66; and Szold to Hadassah president Judith Epstein, reporting a meeting with an angry Rabbi Meir Berlin, 3 July 1936, RG1/B1/F1. A current advocate of this thesis is Sandra Berliant Kadosh. She maintains that for Szold and others in

Youth Aliyah leadership, *kibbutz* life was the desideratum, facilitating absorption of young immigrants and crucial for the upbuilding of the Yishuv. Because this concept overrode all other considerations, she argues, Szold made no effort to help youngsters from Orthodox homes resume religious practice upon resettlement. "Ideal vs. Reality; Youth Aliyah and the Rescue of Jewish Children during the Holocaust Era," Ph.D. diss., Columbia University, 1995. Kadosh's thesis merits further investigation.

33. Gotsfeld to Goldstein, 17 November 1936, Gotsfeld Papers.

34. Idem, 2 July 1936.

35. Statement of the founding objectives of the MWA (1928) in the Amit Women Archives.

36. Israel Friedman address, op. cit.; Leona Goldfeld, Address at Amit Women, New York Office, 9 December 1997.

37. Abramov, *Perpetual Dilemma*, 113.

Chapter 5

It is commonplace to observe that Hadassah, the centrist American Zionist women's organization established in 1925, is today the largest and most successful of all American Jewish organizations. What began as a loosely connected array of women's study groups on the eastern seaboard in the early twentieth century emerged by the eve of Jewish statehood in 1948 as the single most powerful Jewish philanthropic and membership organization in the United States. What accounts for the magnetism of Hadassah in the pre-state era? How did the organization mobilize its resources and why did Hadassah's public relations strategy prove so spectacularly effective? Finally, what does Hadassah's evolution reveal about the relationship between American Jewish women and the Zionist enterprise? These are some of the core issues explored by Mary McCune in the chapter that follows.

McCune asserts that Hadassah's recruitment strategy between World Wars I and II reflected a new "gendered Zionism," a distinctive approach that placed a premium on women's "perceived talents and interests" and appealed to women "in seemingly nonpolitical ways"—a combination that dovetailed with the ascendant middle-class interests and sensibility of most American Jews. Her study focuses on Hadassah's recruitment efforts vis-à-vis the National Council for Jewish Women (NCJW), a non-Zionist American Jewish women's organization founded in 1893 by Reform Jews generally uninterested in Jewish nationalist programs and ideas. Deploying a historical lens, McCune uses the relationship between the two groups as a test case, tracing some of the ways Hadassah promoted Henrietta Szold's (1860–1945) vision of the "women's interpretation of Zionism" and steadily made inroads into NCJW circles at the local and national levels.

That Hadassah's philanthropic, social, and political program generally resonated with a broad cross section of American Jewish women is evident from McCune's analysis. Indeed, the organization's surge from roughly 27,500 members in the mid-1920s to 250,000 members in 1948 amplifies her assessment. But McCune also emphasizes the distinctive quality and effectiveness of Hadassah's ideological worldview in combination with the group's dynamic organizational strategy. Such a synthesis, she demonstrates, was not only attuned to the rhythms of American Jewish life but also prefigured Zionism's shift from the margins to the very center of the American Jewish experience.

Formulating the "Women's Interpretation of Zionism": Hadassah Recruitment of Non-Zionist American Women, 1914–1930

Mary McCune

Introduction

Responding to criticism that Hadassah should limit its work to Zionists, Henrietta Szold wrote to a colleague in March 1925 that "if we did not penetrate into non-Zionist circles, it would be impossible to raise the huge sums we do raise." She further suggested that some people in Palestine might actually benefit from coming to the United States to "take a hand in the 'black work' of collecting funds."[1] While Hadassah leaders like Szold recognized the importance of raising money, not all Zionists of the period concurred. Some male leaders, though envious of Hadassah's ability to raise such large sums of money, publicly discounted the group's success, considering its work mere charity and nearly devoid of serious Zionist content. But Hadassah leaders felt that their medical work, and the fund-raising that supported it, amounted to the feminine element in Zionism, crucial both for Palestine and for building the movement at home in the United States. This gendered perspective on Zionism, one that emphasized the complementary ways men and women contributed to the movement, stressed women's practical nature, their concern for what Hadassah leaders called "the facts of life, birth and bread and shelter and disease." Fund-raising for their projects, they believed, contributed to the Zionist mission in Palestine and could also be utilized effectively to spread the Zionist message back home.[2]

By the mid-1920s, reaching out to new constituents had become a central priority for the women's organization. Membership in the Zionist Organization of America (ZOA) fell throughout the decade from a wartime high of nearly 200,000 to a mere 13,500 by 1931. Szold and the rest of Hadassah's leadership appreciated the necessity of gaining new recruits both to augment their own organizational coffers but also to aid in bolstering the American Zionist movement in general. The women's methods resulted in extraordinary success. In this period of ZOA decline, Hadassah saw its own membership skyrocket from 2,710 in 1917 to 44,000 by 1931.[3] This achievement had significant results not only for their own organization; it also played a central role in sustaining, and building, the American Zionist movement during a period when the male-led movement seemed unable to win new recruits.

Hadassah's methods of attracting new members have much to tell us about the ways that middle-class American Jews became Zionists and the messages they found appealing. A crucial element of Hadassah's appeal lay in its ability to construct an image of itself that fit neatly alongside that of other women's organizations of the period, both Jewish and non-Jewish. Rather than underscoring what distinguished their group from others, Hadassah women approached non-Zionist American Jews with projects familiar to all American women involved in club work and reform initiatives. Stressing what united women enabled Hadassah to attract non-Zionist allies to support its own programs. After drawing them into cooperative endeavors, Hadassah women then strove to convince these non-Zionists of the fundamental importance of the larger political and ideological mission. The group's methods resulted in tremendous growth for this wing of the American Zionist movement.

Hadassah's recruitment strategy centered on clearly articulating its gendered Zionism, a form of Zionism that valorized women's perceived talents and interests. Rather than discuss Zionist ideology or the political ramifications of establishing a Jewish homeland in Palestine, Hadassah attracted non-Zionists by engaging their interests as women. Hadassah publications stressed its services to women and children, its devotion to medical work, and its ability to heal the breach between Arabs and Jews. These projects, though clearly aimed at promoting Jewish Palestine, resembled work pursued by a wide variety of contemporary women's organizations. In the postwar era when many women's groups, both Jewish and non-Jewish, turned their attention overseas by joining such organizations as the Women's International League for Peace and Freedom, or Carrie Chapman Catt's National Committee on the Cause and Cure of War, Hadassah promoted its own involvement in international and peace issues. Like many other women's groups, Hadassah presented itself as involved in a politics that differed substantially in focus and method from that of men. By appealing to women in seemingly nonpolitical ways, highlighting those topics and undertakings common to so many middle-class women, Hadassah was able to attract a large number of new recruits to the Zionist movement during the interwar period.[4]

Hadassah leaders particularly recruited members of the National Council of Jewish Women (NCJW), an organization resolutely non-Zionist until after World War II. These groups participated in similar work and used analogous rhetoric and imagery to describe their projects. Their reliance on maternalist themes and visions of gender difference linked both groups to non-Jewish women's voluntary efforts of the period.[5] These commonalities worked to Hadassah's benefit. Just as the NCJW had long before established close ties to the National and International Councils of Women, so too in the 1920s many of its members volunteered to assist Hadassah without feeling any particular conflict of interest. By moving Hadassah into the mainstream of female organization activity, its leaders ultimately succeeded in making Zionism an ideology acceptable to middle-class American Jews. Hadassah's work, although often perceived as being apolitical, philanthropic, and feminine, in the end played a significant role in helping Zionism begin its move from the fringes to the center of American Jewish life.

Concern for Jewish "Girls" and Mothers

The National Council of Jewish Women, founded in 1893, sought to promote knowledge of Judaism and Jewish culture, to fight religious and other persecutions, and to involve women in social reform.[6] The majority of its leadership, if not its early membership, was composed of Reform Jews who were disinclined to support Zionism. Despite the leadership's coolness to Zionist ideals, the organization avoided taking any firm position on this issue, a policy applied to all controversial topics that might cause division among members. Throughout the 1920s, the NCJW retained a membership of several thousand women, making it one of the largest Jewish women's organizations in the United States. Although the NCJW initially considered itself a religious organization, the group soon became involved with communal charity work, particularly among those segments of the population overlooked by existing organizations. Services for women and children, especially single immigrant women, seemed to be the area of most glaring inadequacy in the leadership's opinion. An 1897 publication announced that "women's work ought first to turn toward the condition of women and children, the two most helpless classes." The Department of Immigrant Aid, founded in the NCJW's first year, worked with immigrants at the ports and in their transition to a new life in the United States.[7] The NCJW soon broadened its services to the immigrant community by initiating health care programs, providing information and

legal advice on the citizenship process, advocating secular education including sex education in the public schools, supporting private religious
training for girls, and starting programs for the often forgotten rural Jews.
Leaders felt it was their duty to help the immigrants maintain a strong religious identity while facilitating their transformation into patriotic U.S.
citizens. This led to the sponsorship of an Americanization program,
which grew once the NCJW shouldered responsibility for assisting immigrant women to become properly educated American voters.[8]

During World War I, the NCJW was quite active in raising relief funds
for Jewish war victims, and this interest in international affairs did not flag
with the signing of the Versailles Treaty. The NCJW grew ever more involved in international affairs in the interwar period, setting up a Reconstruction Unit to aid Jewish refugees in various port cities throughout Europe and spearheading the World Congress of Jewish Women in 1923.[9]

Hadassah, founded shortly before World War I, remained a small organization with only several thousand members until after the war. In its
first years of existence, the group quickly distinguished itself in the field
of medical care by raising significant sums of money and sending a Medical Unit to Palestine. In November 1918, Hadassah opened a school for
nurses at the same time that its Medical Unit moved into the Rothschild
Hospital in Jerusalem.[10] The extent of disease and malnutrition in Palestine after the war compelled the women to broaden the range of
Hadassah's medical services, especially to children. During the 1920s,
Hadassah entered into antiepidemic work, such as the antimalarial program funded by Louis D. Brandeis. As part of this effort, the women's organization assisted with land reclamation and reforestation projects
aimed at lowering the recurrences of malaria that were ravaging the
population. By the time the British mandatory government stepped in to
take over the routine extermination of mosquitoes in 1931, it relied solely
on Hadassah-trained professionals to assist with the task.[11]

During the interwar period the organization opened additional hospitals in Safed, Jaffa, and Haifa and expanded its medical services for children, including several infant welfare clinics established in the Old City of
Jerusalem and eventually in fifteen other areas by 1926. Under the leadership of public health nurse Bertha Landsman, Hadassah also engaged in
a milk distribution program called Tipat Halav [Drop of Milk] which
produced and distributed the first pasteurized milk in Palestine. When too
few mothers came to the distribution stations, Landsman devised a
means by which to bring the milk to them personally: the Donkey Milk
Express. Parents who could afford the milk were assessed a fee in order to
cover the costs of free distribution to the poor. One young woman whose

husband balked at paying this assessment managed to convince him to change his mind by abstaining from the *mikveh* [ritual bath]. "I absolutely *refused* to go until he gave me the money for milk. He won't refuse again," she confidently told the nurses.[12]

Both Hadassah and the NCJW involved themselves in work commonly associated with women, such as nursing, which targeted women and children as clients. The organizations sought to improve the health and living conditions of immigrant populations and endeavored to make these people's transition to their new lives a process with as few obstacles as possible. Priding themselves on their practical and effective projects, both groups argued that fund-raising was a crucial component of their larger mission, one that enabled the very survival of valuable programs. In the years following World War I, Hadassah and the NCJW expanded their organizations' agendas, the NCJW by turning its attention overseas and Hadassah by significantly broadening its Palestine program. This growth in work required an increase in dues-paying members. Each organization sought to augment its membership, and hold on to its old members, by stressing how its programs had made a unique contribution to Jewish life. Ultimately, women in both organizations found that their perspectives on women's work, although aimed at achieving politically divergent ends, contained notable similarities.

In 1918 Hadassah submerged itself within the ranks of the ZOA, relinquishing a great deal of its autonomy. In explaining the new structure to members, Henrietta Szold took the opportunity to underscore Hadassah's importance, stressing the group's singular and gendered mission. She declared that although a totally separate Zionist women's organization had ceased to exist in the United States, Hadassah's methods would continue to produce significant results. Reiterating the common Hadassah theme that women were more practical than men, Szold maintained that propaganda among women would always require special means that highlighted "concrete purposes." Women and men could be in a single organization, yet Szold felt they would work toward the same goal by using distinct means. She argued that Hadassah had "introduced the sex line into Zionism when it had never existed there before. . . . We only gathered ourselves together because it seemed that the men who had been existing for sixteen years had not been able to get the women in."[13] This gendered outlook, a commitment to Zionism that appealed directly to women, had proved successful in drawing women to the movement in the past. In the future, Hadassah leaders believed, recruiting women would still require these "special means" even if Hadassah was a part of the ZOA.

Hadassah did not long remain submerged in the ZOA. In 1921, and later in 1928, leaders battled to regain some measure of autonomy. At the same time they began a zealous campaign to reach out to other women's groups involved in work similar to their own but which were officially non-Zionist in character. This interest in building its membership base became ever more critical as Hadassah began to bear greater financial responsibility for its own projects. By the time that the American Jewish Joint Distribution Committee (JDC), the Keren Hayesod [Palestine Foundation Fund], and ZOA withdrew support from the Hadassah Medical Organizations in 1927, thereby making the unit Hadassah's obligation alone, the women's organization had positioned itself as central to the maintenance of health care throughout Palestine. Reflecting on the change in the unit's status and in Hadassah's general program, Henrietta Szold commented in 1929 that "the Hadassah Medical Organization came into the country as a war relief organization and remained in the land as a peace organization."[14] No longer providing temporary crisis relief, by 1930 Hadassah's programs were indispensable to the provision of medical services in Palestine. Such an expansion in the group's program could not have been undertaken had the organization not successfully recruited new members and new funding sources back home.

The NCJW was a perfect group on which to focus Hadassah's efforts. Despite their official differences on the matter of Zionism, much united the women in the two groups. The leaders came from similar social backgrounds, and before the war the organizations had engaged in comparable social welfare, educational, and health programs. The refugee crisis of World War I led many NCJW members to begin to think about Jews concretely as a people, rather than as simply members of a common religious faith. During the war, NCJW members, who had long concerned themselves with the plight of immigrant girls, expanded their purview to include overseas work as well. Their involvement in European affairs led to a greater awareness of antisemitism and influenced them to reconceptualize their understanding of Jewish identity. Reflecting on such changes, prominent NCJW leader Rebekah Kohut commented that "whether we will or no, the consciousness of our Jewishness is forced upon us. We may glory in it, we may try to evade it, but it is inescapable. We are forced to consider ourselves as one tribe." No matter how far some Jews strayed from Judaism, they nevertheless remained "members of the family."[15] Taken together, the NCJW members' experiences during the war, their growing awareness of antisemitism, and their greater knowledge of European Jewish life allowed many of them to become more responsive to the Zionist message in the postwar period.

Common Themes, Common Needs

The two groups envisioned their work in similar fashion, relying heavily on language filled with common themes and imagery. Like other middle-class American women's reform groups, maternalism and assertions of women's natural practicality imbue both NCJW and Hadassah publications of the period even in the case of women who, like Henrietta Szold, were never mothers themselves. For instance, in 1921 Szold urged Hadassah women to devote themselves to "motherhood work." She suggested that if the first aim of the group was the development of Palestine, "let our second aim be to make our land 'A Joyful Mother of Children.'"[16] Similar phrases were common in Hadassah and NCJW publications before and after the war. Echoing Hadassah's interest in practical and maternalistic work, a representative to NCJW's 1929 Texas State Conference claimed that "the average woman is not content with work accomplished by her money—she must see the 'work of her hands.' It is the woman's nature to 'mother' something, whether it be a child or a cause, and the cause that is closest to her heart, is the cause that she can see accomplished."[17] Like Hadassah, NCJW also articulated a vision of complementary gender relations. Men and women performed distinct tasks, but each remained vital to the overall success of their joint project—the general advancement of Jews in the United States. As early as 1913, Sadie American outlined this concept of gender cooperation and interrelatedness:

We women have time in the daytime to come together, and the men have time in the evening to come together, and the time will come when we will fully realize that each needs the other, for advice, for their different points of view, male and female, the men contributing that which is virile, if you please, but the womanly influence equally valuable, equally necessary; . . . we women not looked upon as simply doing women's work, but [both men and women] cooperating for progress.[18]

Both the NCJW and Hadassah stressed women's inherent maternal concern for children, their sympathetic responses to other women, and all women's natural propensity for practical endeavors. Both organizations considered fund-raising for their projects to be vital work, not frivolous, as well as a concrete expression of women's concern for others. Finally, both organizations championed women's voluntary endeavors and supported an equality with men that allowed for gender difference. This common viewpoint, this shared perspective on gender roles and the importance of women's contributions to public life, enabled rank-and-file Hadassah and NCJW women to breach the political divide that formally separated their organizations.

As the NCJW and Hadassah bolstered their programs, each realized how essential it was to maintain a large membership in order to keep its revenue stream constant. A healthy, growing membership would also enhance the power of each group in American Jewish organizational life. The campaign drives pursued by Hadassah and the NCJW in the 1920s ultimately caused tensions between the leadership of the groups as each sought to promote its vision of American women's role in aiding Jews worldwide. As both organizations scrambled to retain members and garner new ones after the war, each repeatedly asserted its intention to enroll every American Jewish woman in its own group. In 1921, for instance, the NCJW proudly announced in the inaugural edition of its journal, the *Jewish Woman,* that it would "endeavor to induce every Jewish woman in our communities to affiliate with us."[19] The following spring, the NCJW declared that it wanted to attract over 50,000 women to the organization, thereby raising its total membership to 100,000.[20] The group fell short of achieving these lofty goals; in 1923 the extension committee stated that although 600,000 Jewish women lived in the United States, only 48,000 were NCJW members. The committee proposed encouraging higher levels of recruiting by presenting a special pen to those members who brought in more than twenty-five newcomers.[21] Such premiums seem not have done the trick, as later the extension committee linked the very survival of the NCJW's work to its members' capacity to recruit others. An advertisement in 1924 warned members: "The Need of the National is Urgent! Can your Section afford to jeopardize our broad program by failing to meet your quota?" These campaigns continued throughout the decade as the NCJW sought to maintain its preeminence among American Jewish women.[22]

In similar fashion, Hadassah's recruitment campaigns attempted to strengthen the organization's power and ability to pursue its overseas program. But, unlike the NCJW, Hadassah saw its post-1921 membership drives as aimed at a larger goal; the leaders regarded inducting new members into their organization as a critical component of strengthening the American Zionist movement. NCJW leaders certainly had their own conception of American Jewish identity, which they encouraged through their organization and its work, but they did not see themselves as an intrinsic part of a larger political movement like Zionism. Hadassah women, on the other hand, committed themselves to Zionist ideals and believed that their work served a higher purpose than simply providing useful services to needy populations. Hadassah then challenged the NCJW not only by seeking to lure away its members but also by attempting to change their minds about the noncommital, non-Zionist stance of the NCJW's national leadership.

Recruiting Non-Zionist NCJW Women

Announcing a drive to raise membership late in 1926, Hadassah's *Newsletter* reported that there were thousands of women in America who "must be changed from passive, if amiable, spectators into collaborators in the upbuilding of Palestine."[23] This desire to build its membership was inextricably linked to Hadassah's commitment to promote Zionism. Just as fund-raising laid the foundation for life in Palestine, so did new membership augment the strength of Zionism in the United States. Henrietta Szold believed that fundraising helped the Zionist mission because "where money goes[,] the heart follows."[24] Women might start out apolitical, uncommitted to Zionism per se, but through their interest in helping Jews overseas, Hadassah leaders believed, they could be brought around to supporting Zionism. Cooperation would encourage the transition to full-fledged commitment.

Hadassah leaders focused recruitment efforts on ventures that united women in both groups, such as immigrant aid, health care, and social work. Despite the organization's adherence to Zionism, Hadassah campaigns most frequently presented the group's work in nonpolitical tones and linked it explicitly to work pursued by other relief organizations. A 1923 Hadassah chapter's plan to solicit donations from a variety of sources, even non-Jews, illuminates the organization's attempt to place its work within the broader context of international relief. A Chicago delegate reported to the national convention that her local group had grown weary of ceaseless fund-raising drives and the expense they entailed. Looking at the methods of nonsectarian relief organizations, these women had concluded that "if people all over the world, and so many Jewish people, contribute to the Red Cross for health work, we have a perfect right to appeal to Jews to contribute to health work in Palestine." Women had set out across the city asking numerous individuals and organizations for donations, presenting Hadassah's Palestine work in this nonsectarian manner. By the end of the first drive they had raised $6,500 with an expense of only $200. In 1923 the campaign raised $12,000 with an outlay of only $300. The Chicago success led the national convention to approve a motion urging Hadassah's board to "aid the chapters in securing annual contributors to Hadassah, Zionist or non-Zionist, Jewish and non-Jewish, as the case may be. . . ."[25] The promotion of Hadassah's work as nonpartisan at heart, embracing health and welfare initiatives but not political ideology, proved an expeditious means to raise money.

Even before this national commitment to raising funds among non-Zionists and non-Jews, the leaders had realized the utility of stressing common cause with other middle-class Jewish women's organizations. Informal meetings, they averred, were among the best means by which to bring non-Zionist women slowly into the movement. Criticizing the large-scale efforts of the male-led Zionist movement, Hadassah leaders argued that most people did not join Zionism because of "much-lauded mass meetings" but rather through routine participation in small groups. Particularly during the war years, Hadassah leaders urged members to reach out to others through a shared interest in relief activities. A wide array of women, they argued, might be persuaded to assist Hadassah with relief work despite their reluctance to embrace Zionism forthrightly. With time, leaders believed, such sympathetic women would "perceive [that] there is a greater task before them than that of providing raiment for the children of Palestine—that of providing a home for the Children of Israel."[26] By talking to women one-on-one and asking them to participate in relief work for Jews in Europe and Palestine, Zionist women could change the minds of newcomers.

The most effective means of promoting non-Zionist active involvement in Hadassah's work was through the sewing circles, groups that provided clothing for those in Palestine. Pittsburgh and Chicago claimed the two largest and most organized of these circles, and both included NCJW members. Hadassah leaders quickly realized the utility of these circles for recruitment and urged all chapters throughout the nation to start their own circles in order to further spread Hadassah's message among non-Zionists. In 1926 Ruth Cohen, reporting on the success of the sewing circles, asserted that these small groups had proved indispensable in attracting women to the movement. "In many Jewish women's organizations not under the auspices of Hadassah," she noted, "the sewing circle is the only link with Palestine. It is often the e[n]tering wedge for Hadassah in a city and the kernel about which the whole chapter is built."[27] Cohen bluntly admitted that the sewing circles served a larger purpose than mere relief provision; these circles allowed Zionist women a forum to talk to others about the movement and its mission in Palestine. Hadassah leaders recognized the importance of the small group, of bringing women together in pursuit of feminine, charitable activities. By attracting women with such seeming apolitical and nonideological work as preparing infants' clothes to send overseas, Hadassah activists could introduce non-Zionist Jewish women to their ideals in a relaxed and nonthreatening atmosphere.

The group realized great success with such efforts. In 1924 Hadassah reported 547 sewing circles acting in cooperation with the Palestine Supplies

Department. Among these circles numbered 25 sections of the NCJW, even though the national leadership still refused to take an official position on Zionism.[28] By 1927 Hadassah claimed that more than 700 sewing circles existed throughout the United States and that over the course of ten years the circles had contributed $500,000 in goods and donations to Palestine.[29] The sewing circles proved invaluable in terms of monetary and material sustenance but also, and more important, by introducing potential members to Hadassah's work. Commenting on the success of the sewing circle as a recruitment tool, the Hadassah leaders proudly proclaimed in January 1927 that "there is a 'Hadassah-spirit,' a spirit of harmony and unification which has attracted women from all ranks, even anti-Zionist women, and has made of them first, Hadassahites, and then convinced Zionists, to whom nothing Jewish in Palestine or outside of Palestine is strange."[30] The path to Zionism for many women, according to these leaders, could begin with traditional women's volunteer work pursued under the auspices of Hadassah. While this work seemed on the surface to be nonpolitical, the clear intent was to succeed in winning new recruits to the Zionist cause through the most effective means possible, even if such methods struck some Zionists as overly philanthropic and insufficiently serious.

Along with recruiting through fund-raising campaigns and the sewing circles, Hadassah pursued more frequent, and formal, interaction with other national Jewish women's organizations in the attempt to facilitate the growth of its own membership. Drawing on the success of the sewing circle model, in 1923 Hadassah formed a committee charged with devising a plan to encourage collaboration on Palestine projects between Hadassah and the other national Jewish women's organizations.[31] A similar resolution passed the following year directed each chapter to "form a committee to enlist the interest and cooperation of other organized groups of Jewish women in their respective communities." The movement to recruit new Zionists one by one was to proceed simultaneously on both local and national levels.[32] These resolutions also reflect Hadassah's growing interests in American Jewish organizational life, especially the world of women's associations. By further systematizing the process they had developed among the sewing circles, Hadassah leaders hoped to bring more women into the Zionist movement while increasing the prominence of their own organization among the other national Jewish women's groups.

One particularly useful arena for such interaction was the Conference Committee of National Jewish Women's Organizations, a group formed at the biennial convention of the National Federation of Temple Sisterhoods

(NFTS) in January 1925. This group grew out of the NFTS Committee on Friendly Relations and involved all the major Jewish women's groups including the NCJW, Hadassah, the Women's Branch of the Union of Orthodox Jewish Congregations, and the Women's League of the United Synagogue of America. By August Hadassah's involvement in the group had already proved fruitful. A notice in the *Newsletter* reported that discussion of Palestine appeared prominently on Conference Committee agendas at the local level. Hadassah's leaders exhorted members to continue with such promising work, reminding them that bringing the Zionist message to non-Zionist women was "fully one-half of our task."[33]

A year earlier, Henrietta Szold attended a conference of Jewish women's organizations held in Pittsburgh. After returning from this speaking engagement, she asked the 1924 Hadassah convention delegates, "how can we interpenetrate the other Jewish women's organizations?" Aware that sections of the NCJW and other groups had been cooperating with Hadassah on the local level for years, she proposed that the national office keep a table listing the major Jewish women's organizations and noting the extent of collaboration taking place between Hadassah and local sections. Armed with incontrovertible evidence of rank-and-file support for Zionist projects, Hadassah's national leadership could then approach the leaders of these groups to request that they take an official position on Zionism. The national leadership would have to recognize the Zionist character of many of their own constituents or be forced to act in opposition to trends occurring on the grassroots level. Stressing the common theme inherent in all Hadassah's recruitment campaigns, Szold asserted that "we must work from below upwards." Singling out the NCJW in describing her proposal, Szold argued that if 90 of the 120 NCJW sections could be shown to support Zionism, then the organization's national leadership would be hard-pressed to continue its reticence on the subject. Other Hadassah members agreed that a visible representation of NCJW support for Zionism at the grassroots level could be extremely useful in pushing the leadership to alter its resolutely non-Zionist stance.[34]

Szold and others at the 1924 Hadassah convention realized that they had a difficult task before them if they wished to influence the NCJW's official position on Zionism. A Boston delegate, Mrs. Lurie, alerted members to the fact that the NCJW had recently passed a resolution to limit the sums it dispensed to outside groups. This delegate stated that she had approached the NCJW requesting a donation in light of the fact that Hadassah was a relief organization just like the Red Cross. Using methods that had proved quite fruitful in Chicago, this delegate tried to present Hadassah's work as nonpolitical and nonsectarian relief similar to the

NCJW's own program. Her efforts, however, did not result in success.[35] This tale touched off a round of grumbling in which some delegates referred to NCJW women as having "stone hearts." A Mrs. Cheiffetz felt compelled to respond to such charges. Explaining that such opinions had forced her, an NCJW member for twenty-four years, to "analyze my heart," she concluded that "it was beating and I was certain it wasn't stone." She further asserted that some 95 percent of the delegates to this very Hadassah convention held membership in the NCJW. Although the NCJW as an organization refused to endorse Zionism, Cheiffetz reminded the convention that its members supported Palestine by joining in Zionist projects one by one.[36] Hadassah leaders urged the membership to take Cheiffetz's message to heart. They reminded members that significant cooperation occurred on the local and state levels between the two organizations regardless of the NCJW national office's coolness.[37] Evidence suggests that one by one NCJW women did make notable contributions to Hadassah's work. The "Chapter Notes" section of Hadassah's *Newsletter* reveals an observable growth in local chapters reporting cooperation with the NCJW sections, testifying to the success of Hadassah's effort to "interpenetrate" other Jewish women's groups, especially the "stone-hearted" NCJW.

One city where cooperation between the groups proceeded apace was Pittsburgh. At a luncheon sponsored by the Pittsburgh chapter at Hadassah's 1924 convention, Szold reiterated a long-standing theme that women's contribution to Zionism involved more than fund-raising and philanthropy. Szold asserted that Hadassah's work had important objectives both for Zionism and for American Jewry. She stated that "Hadassah has begun to heal the spiritual breach among our people, our women, our Jewish women here [in the United States]." Urging the members to forge ever stronger bonds with their sisters in the NCJW, Szold told them that the Pittsburgh head of the NCJW had conveyed to her how common it was for the two groups to assist one another. Szold took this as evidence that NCJW members gave "intellectual allegiance to the Zionist ideal, [and] it remains true that if you offer them the opportunity of working for our Jewish Homeland, they will welcome it wherever they see it, and join hands in order that that home may become a reality."[38] Pittsburgh NCJW members, like so many others, came to Hadassah through an interest in women and children and over time grew more amenable to the larger goals of Zionism.

Throughout western Pennsylvania, NCJW sections supported Hadassah's work and came together to push the leadership of the two groups into closer relations. The Pennsylvania statewide NCJW conference, held in Lancaster in October 1924, passed a resolution stating that whereas Palestine is assuming importance in the solution of the world problems of the Jewish people, particularly in relation to the tasks which the National Council of Jewish Women has adopted as its province, viz.: immigration, women on farms, and the welfare of unprotected girls, therefore, Be it resolved that the Pennsylvania State Conference recommends that the Board of the NCJW invite to its meeting an accredited representative of Hadassah, the Women's Zionist Organization of America.[39]

Although the Hadassah board reported to its convention that this resolution had led to an "amicable" meeting with NCJW president Rose Brenner and Hadassah's executive secretary Estelle Sternberger in Brooklyn on January 14, 1925, it concluded that "no hope of immediate participation in Palestine work was held out."[40] Yet the official spin on the event, later presented in the *Newsletter,* assured readers that "such occurrences herald a time when it will be recognized that Palestine, the center of Jewish life, is the concern of all Jews."[41]

NCJW president Rose Brenner presented a much cooler version of the meeting to her own board in November 1925. Indeed, the text of her presentation made it quite clear that she felt the entire meeting should never have taken place. In the text of her prepared speech, Brenner noted that this meeting had occurred only because the Pennsylvania sections "most unwisely" passed a resolution requesting it. "A long and amicable conversation was held," she stated, "and clearly demonstrated that Hadassah's work has no place in the program of the National Council." She further concluded that these organizations could maintain friendly relations only when each confined itself to its own sphere of activity.[42] Surely aiming to remind its upstart sections of the NCJW's purview, Brenner asked the board to endorse a policy reiterating the group's dedication to "the Jewish woman, in America, AND ON HER WAY TO AMERICA; . . ." [emphasis in the original].[43] Brenner urged her board to underscore that the NCJW was an organization concerned with American Jewish women and immigrants. While the war had heightened the group's interest in international affairs, the official program was to remain limited to those projects connected to the United States, not Palestine.

Certainly, Brenner's actions displayed her desire to maintain control over the vision and agenda of her organization. Yet while she abjured NCJW participation in Zionist work, at least on an official basis, she did not entirely move her organization away from action on other international and political issues. In the same speech advocating that the NCJW confine itself to work with American Jewish women, Brenner asserted that the most important interorganizational alliance the NCJW had made in the previous year was with the Conference on the Causes and

Cure of War. Brenner proudly noted that the NCJW had been one of nine national women's organizations to sign the call for the conference, and she counseled her own board to make peace a priority.[44] This is but one example of the NCJW's move into the political arena in the postwar world. The organization also joined the Women's Joint Congressional Committee and took official positions on a wide range of issues such as the Cable Act, the Sheppart-Towner Act, and more. Nevertheless, Brenner could not ignore the Pennsylvania sections, which in 1925 claimed the largest number of sections per state in the nation. By 1925 she and the rest of the NCJW leadership could not exclude all relations with Hadassah or Zionism.[45]

Throughout the 1920s, Hadassah continued recruiting locally, bringing NCJW women into cooperative projects and thereby encouraging them to join the organization directly. To reduce conflict with the NCJW, Hadassah leaders employed language, patterned after Rose Brenner's, that advanced the notion of a noncompetitive partnership between the two groups. In 1926 Hadassah president Irma Lindheim sent greetings to the NCJW's Triennial. In her message Lindheim claimed that the NCJW and Hadassah pursued similar work but in distinct arenas: where the NCJW helped immigrants on their way to the United States, Hadassah brought aid to immigrants settling in Palestine. "May a strong bond unite these two great sister organizations," she proclaimed. "In the purposes which they share in common let them cooperate, in the purposes which are specifically their own, let them complement each other."[46] Borrowing Brenner's message to undercut her ultimate intent, Lindheim argued that the NCJW and Hadassah did not have to compete. Together they could aid Jewish women around the globe.

In a symposium titled "Cooperation among National Women's Organizations" published in the *Jewish Woman* in 1928, Hadassah board member Rachel Natelson presented the "Point of View of Hadassah." Following Lindheim's model, Natelson argued that a variety of organizations sought to meet the diverse needs of the Jewish people around the world. In Palestine ideological differences further escalated the potential for duplication of services. She believed that American Jewish women grew confused when they received numerous appeals from a variety of groups proposing to aid development in Palestine. Natelson urged NCJW members to consider Hadassah the safest "medium, if not the object, of material interest in Palestine" and assured them that Hadassah was taking steps to coordinate women's groups in that land. Her objective was surely, at least in part, to establish Hadassah's primacy among American Jewish women interested in Zionism.[47]

Alluding to tensions between Hadassah and the Women's International Zionist Organization (WIZO), Natelson informed NCJW readers that these two Zionist groups had agreed not to propagandize in each other's "territory." Yet she declined to comment on the relations between Hadassah and the NCJW, because she felt such a topic "deserves a chapter in itself." She concluded that the future demanded that all Jewish women's organizations "as time goes on, work in ever closer harmony," even holding up the General Federation of Women's Clubs as a model for them to follow.[48] In her view, women should seek to streamline the provision of services. But while Hadassah and WIZO might fight turf battles, she assured NCJW members that they need not fear the encroachment of Hadassah on their own work.

The NCJW's submission to the symposium propounded a similar ideal of mutual, if more aloof, cooperation. President Ida W. Friend also focused her attention on the speedy and efficient dispensation of aid. She argued that Jewish women's organizations needed to develop mechanisms to avoid duplication and to cooperate in fulfilling their general goals. Yet the example she set forth in support of her ideas betrayed not a little disdain for life in Palestine. Presenting a tale of one woman to illustrate how Jewish organizations could work together, she described how a girl in Palestine had received Hadassah's assistance but wanted to go to the United States to find her fiancé. The NCJW provided the young woman with advice on immigration, helped her to locate her fiancé, and eventually settled the two in the United States. After introducing the young woman to the local section of the National Federation of Temple Sisterhoods, Friend stated that "we thus have the completed circle of cooperation in which each organization within its sphere has contributed to the happiness of a deserving sister who without such aid might still be languishing in a distant village of Palestine."[49] While the overall goal was to reduce overlap, it seems that another implicit aspiration was to help young girls leave Palestine, not emigrate there.

Friend's example along with Brenner's earlier coolness to Hadassah in general reflect a distrust of Hadassah and its work that was characteristic of a core of the NCJW leadership. While many of their rank and file were moving closer to Hadassah's ideals, most of the leadership maintained a chilly distance, fearing not only the loss of their ability to set the organization's agenda with regard to political issues but also losing members to the Zionist group. Distrust arose particularly among those NCJW leaders who did not believe Hadassah's commitment to mutual cooperation was sincere, fearing that Hadassah wanted to augment its own membership rolls above all else. At a 1927 board meeting, Florine Lasker stated that "we may just as well be perfectly candid about the fact that Hadassah wants a good deal more than just moral support." Another member concurred. Lillian Burkhart Goldsmith told the NCJW board that for three years the South California NCJW members had tried to involve Hadassah members in their work, but during that time only one Hadassah woman had offered her help. Most Hadassah members, Goldsmith maintained, refused to assist the NCJW in any meaningful way.[50] Hadassah seems to have been more successful in attracting volunteers for its projects than the NCJW was in garnering Hadassah's assistance for its domestic endeavors. Hadassah's recruitment tactics called for cooperation, but a cooperation with a definite end in mind: bringing more women to the Zionist movement. While they might have paid lip service to aiding the domestic projects of the NCJW, Hadassah women focused their considerable energies on building Palestine and bolstering the American Zionist movement.

Despite the NCJW leaders' suspicion regarding Hadassah's ultimate motive, by 1929 the Zionist women's group had achieved major success in bringing new members into the movement. By 1931 Hadassah rivaled the NCJW in size, claiming forty-four thousand members, an increase of forty-two thousand that had occurred in only fourteen years. Hadassah proudly discussed instances of heightened cooperation between the two groups in its "Chapter Notes" column. The comparable column in the NCJW's publication, the *Jewish Woman,* maintained a stony silence about Zionist activism in its local sections. By the late 1920s, however, the NCJW could no longer ignore Zionism as an issue of importance to American Jewish women. Even if it avoided advertising for Hadassah in its own pages, the NCJW publication did begin to present stories on Zionist topics. The World Congress of Jewish Women, spearheaded by NCJW leader Rebekah Kohut, also witnessed a dramatic growth in the Zionist presence between its 1923 and 1929 Congresses. Finally, late in 1929, several NCJW leaders themselves attended Hadassah's convention, including NCJW president Ida W. Friend and Rebekah Kohut. And in 1930, for the first time, a Hadassah representative was invited to attend the NCJW's Triennial.[51]

Conclusion

Hadassah's promotion of a gendered Zionism, of what Szold called the "women's interpretation of Zionism," appealed to large numbers of American women. By concentrating on what many Americans considered to be women's natural aptitude for social welfare work, particularly among women and children, Hadassah was able to frame its devotion to Zionism within a structure and rhetoric familiar to other middle-class women. Hadassah leaders highlighted projects that resembled the work being pursued by the most prominent women's organizations of the period. Moreover, Hadassah's recruitment efforts focused on women individually, allowing them forums whereby they might assist Zionist work before deciding whether or not to join the movement directly. These methods were especially effective with NCJW members, who by the mid-1920s had immersed themselves in international affairs and concerned themselves with the needs of Jews worldwide. By 1929, although Hadassah leaders had not succeeded in altering the NCJW's official position on Zionism, they and their energetic local membership had done a great deal to draw the NCJW rank and file into their work and all too often, especially in the view of NCJW leaders, into official membership in Hadassah itself.

Hadassah's effective recruitment tactics played a significant, if until recently overlooked, role in sustaining the American Zionist movement through a period of membership decline and heightened disinterest among many middle-class American Jews. While the ZOA lost official members during the 1920s, Hadassah proceeded with a vigorous and successful campaign to enroll ever growing numbers of new recruits while at the same time continuing such voluntary activities as the sewing circles. Recognizing from their organization's inception that traditional strategies to draw in new members did not work nearly as well with women as they did with men, Hadassah leaders devised alternative means by which to bring women into the Zionist fold. They downplayed the more overtly political aspects of their program, those that middle-class women would tend to find the most controversial, in favor of nonthreatening cooperation in projects women of the era believed were their special, feminine province.

Employing these tactics, however, did not mean that Hadassah itself was anti-ideological or disengaged from politics; rather, the organizational leaders perceptively used their knowledge of women in order to attract them and slowly draw them into the ideology of the movement. The leaders' major goals were never merely to sew clothes for destitute children or raise money for medicinal supplies, but to promote Jewish settlement in Palestine and to build the Zionist movement at home. Yet they understood that more American women would rally to the cause of children than would embrace outright the more provocative elements of the Zionist plan. Leaders correctly surmised that over time these volunteers could be counted on to adopt Zionist views and officially join the movement. Membership growth in the 1920s reveals that, through the utilization of seemingly nonpolitical means, Hadassah leaders succeeded in achieving their political ends.

Notes

1. Henrietta Szold to Nellie Straus Mochenson, 23 March 1925, Record Group 2, Box 62, Folder 1, Hadassah Archives (hereafter HA).

2. "The Woman in Zionism," *Maccabaean* 30 (February 1917): 148, located in Record Group 4, Box 2, Folder 20, HA. Joyce Antler employs the term "gender-based Zionism" in her recent work on Hadassah. See Joyce Antler, *The Journey Home: How Jewish Women Shaped Modern America* (New York: Schocken Books, 1997). For other works examining the importance of gender in Zionism, see Michael Berkowitz, "Transcending 'Tzimmes and Sweetness': Recovering the History of Zionist Women in Central and Western Europe, 1897–1933," in *Active Voices: Women in Jewish Culture*, ed. Maurie Sacks (Urbana: University of Illinois Press, 1995), 41–62; and *Western Jewry and the Zionist Project, 1914–1933* (Cambridge: Cambridge University Press, 1997), 175–93; David Biale, "Zionism as an Erotic Revolution," in *People of the Body: Jews and Judaism from an Embodied Perspective*, ed. Howard Eilberg-Schwartz (Albany: State University of New York Press, 1992), 283–307; Paula E. Hyman, *Gender and Assimilation in Modern Jewish History: The Roles and Representations of Women* (Seattle: University of Washington Press, 1995), 144–149; Mary McCune, "Social Workers in the *Muskeljudentum*: 'Hadassah Ladies,' 'Manly Men' and the Significance of Gender in the American Zionist Movement, 1912–1928," *American Jewish History* 86 (June 1998): 135–65; Claudia Prestel, "Zionist Rhetoric and Women's Equality (1897–1933): Myth and Reality," *San Jose Studies* 20 (Fall 1994): 4–28; and Margalit Shilo, "The Double or Multiple Image of the New Hebrew Woman," *Nashim: A Journal of Jewish Women's Studies and Gender Issues* 1 (Winter 1998): 73–94.

3. Melvin I. Urofsky, *American Zionism from Herzl to the Holocaust* (New York: Doubleday, 1975), 305, 345. Numbers for Hadassah's 1917 membership are from the "Report of the Proceedings of the Fourth Convention," 2, Record Group 3, Box 1, Folder 4, HA. The religious Zionist group Mizrachi also grew during this period, though not as dramatically as Hadassah. In 1925 Bessie Gotsfeld helped establish the Mizrachi Women's Organization of America, which split formally from Mizrachi in 1934. Now known as AMIT, the group is the largest religious Zionist organization in the United States. See Ruth Raisner, "AMIT," in vol. 1 of *Jewish Women in America: An Historical Encyclopedia*, ed. Paula E. Hyman and Deborah Dash Moore (New York: Routledge, 1997), 48–49.

4. Like other women's leaders, those who headed Hadassah were consummate politicians even as they disavowed male political culture. While they may have focused on different issues than their male counterparts, they proved themselves able to act similarly when necessity demanded. On the redefinition of what constituted "political" activism in the years following the passage of the Nineteenth Amendment, see Kristi Anderson, *After Suffrage: Women in Partisan and Electoral Politics before the New Deal* (Chicago: University of Chicago Press,

1996). On women's clubs and organizations of the period, see Karen J. Blair, *The Clubwoman as Feminist: True Womanhood Redefined, 1868-1914* (New York: Holmes & Meier Publishers, 1980); and Anne Firor Scott, *Natural Allies: Women's Associations in American History* (Urbana: University of Illinois Press, 1991). For examples outside the United States see Leila J. Rupp, *Worlds of Women: The Making of an International Women's Movement* (Princeton, N.J.: Princeton University Press 1997); and Nancy R. Reagin, *A German Women's Movement: Class and Gender in Hanover, 1880-1933* (Chapel Hill: University of North Carolina Press, 1995). For a discussion of the NCJW in relation to other women's clubs of the era see Anne Rugles Gere, *Intimate Practices: Literacy and Cultural Work in U.S. Women's Clubs, 1880-1920* (Urbana: University of Illinois Press, 1997).

5. On maternalistic rhetoric and female reform see Seth Koven and Sonya Michel, eds. *Mothers of a New World: Maternalist Politics and the Origins of Welfare States* (New York: Routledge, 1992); Molly Ladd-Taylor, *Mother-Work: Women, Child Welfare, and the State, 1890-1930* (Urbana: University of Illinois Press, 1994); Robyn Muncy, *Creating a Female Dominion in American Reform, 1890-1935* (New York: Oxford University Press, 1991); and Lynn Y. Weiner, et al., "Maternalism as a Paradigm," *Journal of Women's History* 5 (Fall 1993): 95-131.

6. Faith Rogow, *Gone to Another Meeting: The National Council of Jewish Women, 1893-1993* (Tuscaloosa: University of Alabama Press, 1993), 23-24; Seth Korelitz, "'A Magnificent Piece of Work': The Americanization Work of the National Council of Jewish Women," *American Jewish History* 83 (June 1995): 178.

7. *1897 Program of Council of Jewish Women*, convention publication, 25, Box 4, Folder 1, Hannah G. Solomon Collection, Library of Congress (hereafter LC). Ellen Sue Levi Elwell, "The Founding and Early Programs of the National Council of Jewish Women: Study and Practice as Jewish Women's Religious Expression" (PhD. diss., Indiana University, 1982), 97-125; Korelitz, 179-81; and Rogow, 138-52.

8. Korelitz, 188-95; Rogow, 133-54.

9. *Council Pioneer: A History of Council in the Vanguard of Social Advance* (n.p.: National Council of Jewish Women, 1955), 2-3, 13; Rebekah Kohut, *My Portion* (New York: Albert & Charles Boni, 1927), 267-69.

10. Marlin Levin, *Balm in Gilead: The Story of Hadassah* (New York: Schocken Books, 1973), 69-72.

11. Levin, 73-80. On Brandeis's antimalarial efforts see Philippa Strum, *Louis D. Brandeis: Justice for the People* (Cambridge, Mass.: Harvard University Press, 1984), 279.

12. Levin, 84.

13. "Report of the Proceedings at the Fifth Convention," June 1918, 7, 10-11, Record Group 3, Box 1, Folder 5, HA

14. Quoted in Levin, 64.

15. Rebekah Kohut, *As I Know Them: Some Jews and a Few Gentiles* (Garden City, N.Y.: Doubleday, Doran & Company, 1929), 40.

16. "Letter from Henrietta Szold," 1921 Convention Proceedings, 5, Record Group 3, Box 2, Folder 4, HA.

17. Mrs. Joseph Utay, "Texas State Conference," *Jewish Woman* 9 (July-September 1929): 43.

18. Sadie American, "Report of Executive Secretary," *Official Report of the Council of Jewish Women Seventh Triennial,* December 1914, 25, Box 4, Folder 5, Solomon Collection, LC.

19. Mrs. William Loeb, Chair of the Extension Committee, *Jewish Woman* 1 (October 1921): 11.

20. Mrs. William Loeb, Chair of the Extension Committee, "Vigorous Extension Campaign," *Jewish Woman* 2. (April 1922): 2, The NCJW goal was to reach 300 sections and 100,000 members in 1923. In the same issue Rose Brenner stated that the organization currently had 45,000 members. Rose Brenner, "The Great Interpreter," *Jewish Woman* 2 (April 1922): 4.

21. Mrs. Clarence E. Mack, "A Challenge to Our Women," *Jewish Woman* 3 (February 1923): 18–19.

22. *Jewish Woman* 4 (April 1924): 21. See also *Jewish Woman* 4 (April 1924): 36; *Jewish Woman* 5 (March 1925): 28–29, and *Jewish Woman* 9 (January–March 1929): 33–34.

23. "Hadassah Sabbath," *Newsletter* 7 no. 2 (November 1926): 2.

24. "Report of Proceedings of the Fifth Convention," June 1918, 10–11, Record Group 3, Box 1, Folder 5, HA.

25. "Proceedings and Resolutions of the Ninth Convention," 1923, 9–23, Record Group 3, Box 3, Folder 2, HA.

26. *Hadassah Bulletin,* no. 26 (November 1916): 2–3.

27. Ruth Cohen, "Report of Miss Ruth Cohen, Executive Secretary of Hadassah," 1926 Convention, 2, Record Group 3, Box 5, Folder 2, HA.

28. Ruth Cohen's 1926 report notes that "naturally the Council has not yet taken action regarding Palestinian work." See her report to the 1926 convention, 17, Record group 3, Box 5, Folder 2, HA. For sewing circle figures see "Palestine Supplies Bureau Report," 1924 Convention Proceedings, 1, Record Group 3, Box 3, Folder 4, HA.

29. Ruth B. Fromenson, "A Decade of Sewing," *Hadassah Newsletter* 7, no. 6 (March 1927): 9.

30. *Hadassah Newsletter* 7 no. 4 (January 1927): 3.

31. "Proceedings and Resolutions of the Ninth Convention," 1923, 8, Record Group 3, Box 3, Folder 2, HA.

32. "Proceedings of the Tenth Convention," 1924, 189, Record Group 3, Box 3, Folder 3, HA.

33. *Hadassah Newsletter* 5, no. 9 (August 1925): 1. On formation of the Conference Committee see notice in *Jewish Woman* 5 (March 1925): 56; and *Hadassah Newsletter* 5, no. 5. (March 1925): 7.

34. "Proceedings of the Tenth Convention," 1924, 232–37, Record Group 3, Box 3, Folder 3, HA.

35. Ibid., 241–43.

36. Ibid.

37. Ibid., 245–46.

38. "Address delivered by Miss Henrietta Szold," 2 July 1924, 5–6, Record Group 3, Box 3, Folder 4, HA.

39. "Report of the National Board of Hadassah, the Women's Zionist Organization of America," 1924–1925, 8, Record Group 3, Box 4, Folder 2, HA.

40. Ibid.

41. *Hadassah Newsletter* 5 no. 9 (August 1925): 3.

42. Typescript report to Board of Managers by Rose Brenner, November 1925, 2–3, Box 100, Klau Library, Hebrew Union College. The handwritten words "most unwisely" were added to the typed speech but were also crossed out.

43. Ibid., 9.

44. Ibid., 3–4.

45. *Jewish Woman* 5 (March 1925): 28–29. Membership campaign information reports that the organization included 229 sections, 43 of which were in Pennsylvania. The next in line were New York with 22 and New Jersey with 21. On NCJW's postwar political work, see Rogow, 167–75.

46. *Official Report of the Eleventh Triennial,* November 1926 (New York: National Council of Jewish Women, 1927), 9–10.

47. Rachel Natelson, "Point of View of Hadassah," *Jewish Woman* 8 (April–June 1928): 6–7.

48. Ibid., 7.

49. Ida W. Friend, "Point of View of the National Council of Jewish Women," *Jewish Woman* 8 (April–June 1928): 4–6.

50. "Proceedings of the Meeting of the Board of Managers of the National Council of Jewish Women," January 1927, A29–30, Box 3, Folder 2, NCJW collection, LC.

51. *Hadassah Newsletter* 10, no. 2 (December 1929): 5, located in Record Group 3, Box 6, Folder 3, HA; Rose Jacobs handwritten notes, Record Group 7, Reel 4, HA. See also *World Congress of Jewish Women, Vienna, May 6–11, 1923* (Wien: A. G. Steinmann, 1923); *Protokoll der Gründungsversammlung des 'Weltbundes jüdischer Frauen' vom 4.-6. Juni 1929* (Record of the Founding Meeting of the "World Congress of Jewish Women" from 4–6 June 1929) (Berlin: B. Levy, 1929); and Nelly Las, *Jewish Women in a Changing World: A History of the International Council of Jewish Women* (ICJW), 1899–1995 (Jerusalem: A. Harman Institute of Contemporary Jewry, 1996). Note especially the dramatic increase in Zionist topics discussed at the later meeting as compared with the 1923 Congress.

Chapter 6

Zionism was forged on the anvil of East European Jewish life in the fin de siècle. In this period, there evolved in imperial Russia and Poland a branch of the Zionist movement that emphasized Marxist and utopian socialist notions of building the Jewish national home. In Palestine, where by the early twentieth century Zionist plantation farmers of the First Aliyah (1881–1903) had obtained a colonial foothold, there quickly developed a unique Hebrew workers' culture as a result of a wave of Jewish immigration known as the Second Aliyah (1904–1914). The youthful Second Aliyah pioneers—known in Hebrew as *haluzim*—possessed an exceptional esprit de corps and championed collectivist values, including the significance of nonexploitative Jewish labor and the transformation of the economic and occupational makeup of contemporary Jewish life. For the *haluzim,* such a transformation portended a complete personal revolution and was intended to form the basis of the new Jewish society-in-the-making in the Land of Israel.

American soil also proved to be fertile ground for many East European Jewish immigrants who sustained, in part or whole, aspects of the socialist Zionist agenda. Concurrent with the rise of the countrywide Palestine labor movement, there emerged in the United States a small but vigorous Labor Zionist movement that viewed itself as an extension of the pioneering Zionist ethos. Like its sister movements in eastern Europe and Palestine, American Labor Zionism coalesced around distinctive ideological camps such as the youth groups Gordonia, named for the Labor Zionist philosopher A. D. Gordon (1856–1922), and Hehaluz [The Pioneer]; the political parties Poalei Zion [Workers of Zion] and Zeirei Zion Hitahdut [United Youth of Zion], which represented, respectively, Marxist Zionist and non-Marxist socialist Zionist perspectives; and the fraternal order known as the Jewish National Workers' Alliance-Farband. As the colorful names reveal, American Labor Zionism was really a loose coalition of subgroups, each of which maintained differing attitudes toward the key Jewish social, cultural, and political issues of the day, including the debates over Marxism and voluntaristic socialism, Yiddishism and Hebrew, and territorialism and Zionism.

Drawing on their prior experience in eastern Europe, Yiddish-speaking immigrant women in the United States continued to play a significant role in the fledgling Labor Zionist movement. But like women active in other American Zionist circles, such as the religious Mizrachi and centrist Hadassah organizations, as well as their female socialist contemporaries in Palestine, American Labor Zionist women soon discovered that only an autonomous women's entity would provide them with the organizational and political leverage they desired. In this chapter, Mark A. Raider examines the pre-state history of the Pioneer Women's Organization (since renamed Naamat USA). He also traces the complex relationship between Labor Zionist women in the United States and the Yishuv, and demonstrates the extent to which the former were influenced by the proactive efforts of *shlihot* [emissaries] sent by the women's division of the Histadrut [General Federation of Jewish Workers in the Land of Israel], known as Moezet Hapoalot [Working Women's Council]. Such emissaries included Manya Shohat (1880–1961), Rahel Kaznelson-Shazar (1888–1975), and Golda Meir (1898–1978), women who emerged as central figures in Palestine's (and later Israel's) political landscape. Their ability to rally broad American Jewish support for the Yishuv and the Palestine labor movement was initially and, according to Raider, in large measure dependent on the efforts and achievements of the Pioneer Women's Organization. In the decades prior to statehood, such a foothold in American Jewish life proved to be an important factor in the success of the Zionist campaign.

The Romance and *Realpolitik* of Zionist Pioneering: The Case of the Pioneer Women's Organization

Mark A. Raider

3rd woman: Well, Goldie Meyerson knew that we are five million Jews in America and when things began to boil in Palestine, she was told by our *shlihim* [emissaries] who came here that the [United Jewish Appeal] had scheduled a campaign to raise $250 million dollars for the Yishuv and European needs.

2nd woman: Was she pleased that we had pledged to raise so much money?

3rd woman: She hit the ceiling, because the *shilihim* came back to Palestine without the money right there and then.

2nd woman: For goodness sakes, what did she expect? The appeal wasn't officially opened and people, I am sure, are still paying off last year's pledges.

3rd woman: Well, from what I heard, Goldie knew that the Yishuv couldn't wait until America began raising money. Jewish lives were at stake, the Arabs weren't going to wait until whenever to start murdering Jews. Money for arms and all forms of Haganah work was needed immediately.

2nd woman: Yes, now I can imagine how she felt. Phooey on the men. When it comes to doing the actual work, leave it to the women, so Goldie Meyerson came to get the money herself.

3rd woman: You are so right. Goldie Meyerson is an aggressive, impatient woman. Our *haverim* [comrades] are sincere and have done much for the Jewish state, but Goldie is an exceptional woman.[1]

—"Information, Please" (c. 1944)

The playlet "Information, Please" was one of dozens of homespun hands-on educational materials developed by the Pioneer Women's Organization in the 1940s. What is striking about the skit, intended for performance at club meetings, is the extent to which it reflects a highly Americanized sensibility, namely, the crisp American locutions, the plainspoken emphasis on finances and fund-raising, the sidelong glances at self-important male Zionist groups, the mythologization of Golda Meir. Such romanticism, combined with a sizable quotient of political savvy, is also reflected in the observations made a decade earlier by Rebekah Kohut, a leader of the National Council of Jewish Women:

Immediately upon [Pioneer Women's] inception, information was disseminated among the Jewish working women here, telling them of the life and needs of the Jewish working women in Palestine, the important part she plays in the moral and economic growth of the country, the heroism she has shown in overcoming the difficulties under which she has had to rear her family while doing her work, etc., etc. As a result, the Pioneer Women's Organization . . . has become the buttress of spirit and substance of the working woman in Palestine, so that the latter uses her new freedom to the best advantage in doing her share, if not more than an equal share with the man, in improving the living conditions of the worker. Those who have visited Palestine in the past few years speak with the utmost admiration of the *haluzah* [female Zionist pioneer], who with face uplifted toward the Eastern sun, her shoulders straightened by the new freedom, with her hands eagerly mothers the neglected soil which she loves so dearly. And the lot of this *haluzah* has been greatly improved thanks to the efforts of the Pioneer Women's Organization.[2]

Kohut's remarks throw light on both the Americanization and the residual national consciousness of Yiddish-speaking Jewish immigrant women in the first half of the twentieth century. Indeed, an examination of Pioneer Women illustrates the shift in American Jewish priorities vis-à-vis Palestine's Jewish society-in-the-making and the increasing importance of ties between American Jews, the Yishuv, and the Zionist enterprise. These phenomena, as this study argues, were interrelated and became central to American Jewish life much earlier than is generally recognized by historians of American Jewry and Zionism. Never a mass movement nor a major channel for fund-raising in behalf of the Yishuv, Pioneer Women was most effective as a direct conduit to the Jewish community in Palestine for American Jews. The organization also provided an early and secure foothold for many important female Zionist leaders from Palestine with whom American Jews had otherwise strikingly little contact. Manya Shohat, Goldie Meyerson (later Golda Meir), Rahel Kaznelson-Shazar, and Elisheva Kaplan Eshkol, to name just a few, were among the dozen or so prominent Histadrut [General Federation of Jewish Workers in the Land of Israel] and Moezet Hapoalot [Women Workers' Council] leaders who spent extended time in the United States and would emerge, in time, as key political figures in pre-state Israeli society and later the State of Israel.

The Pioneer Women's Organization of America—renamed "Pioneer Women" in 1947, today called "Naamat USA"—was officially founded in 1925. (Naamat is a Hebrew acronym for "Working and Volunteer Women.") The new group sought to elevate the public profile of the *haluzot* [female Zionist pioneers] in the Yishuv [pre-state Israeli society] and "to help pioneer women's cooperatives in Palestine" through American-based philanthropic efforts.[3] Pioneer Women considered itself the sister movement of Moezet Hapoalot, the Palestine women workers' movement. It embraced the latter's vision of "expand[ing] the boundaries of the Jewish woman's role" in the Yishuv and "secur[ing] her full and equal participation in the process of Jewish national reconstruction."[4]

Pioneer Women also emphasized the importance of women in the American Zionist enterprise and provided a forum for working-class Jewish immigrant women who sympathized with the aims and ideals of socialist Zionism and the fledgling Yishuv. In time, the organization opened up new channels of communication between the Palestine labor movement and the Jewish community in America. It became a significant force in American Jewish life and played a central role in American Zionism in the decades preceding the establishment of the State of Israel in 1948.

The Spadework of Manya Shohat

"The entire movement here is worthless!" lamented the Zionist leader Manya Shohat in 1921. Thus Shohat, a member of the first Histadrut delegation to the United States, described the American branch of Poalei Zion [Workers of Zion], an offshoot of the Russian socialist Zionist party. Shohat decried the inactivity of the local party and informed her Palestine comrades that the American movement was but a "tempest in a teacup." "They are fed up with the way they have worked thus far," she explained,

and [the party newspaper] *Die zeit* [The Times] . . . is folding . . . And all this is not because . . . there is no place for a newspaper such as this, on the contrary it is needed and very important. It is because the administration of the newspaper is totally ineffective.[5]

The eventual closure of *Die zeit* proved to be a source of profound demoralization for the American movement.[6] Under the present circumstances, Shohat asserted, the American party could hardly be depended upon to promote investment in Palestine. Additionally, as she quickly discovered, any fund-raising conducted by Histadrut delegates inadvertently competed with the American movement's existing drive to send tools and farm machinery to the Palestinian *kvuzot* [workers' colonies] as well as the comparatively well-organized Keren Hayesod [Palestine Foundation] campaign.[7]

In order to avoid overtaxing the movement's scarce internal resources, Shohat created an ad hoc committee of female movement members that proposed to raise $10,000 worth of kitchen and laundry equipment for the struggling *kvuzot* from the community at large. The women's committee elicited the interest of a cadre of female Poalei Zion members who worked hard to achieve their goal. But neither the campaign nor the women's committee was a top priority for Shohat. In fact, she devoted most of her energy to a clandestine campaign to procure weapons for the Jewish self-defense organization in Palestine known as Hashomer [the Watchguard]. Nevertheless, Shohat's efforts laid the groundwork for the creation of an activist Labor Zionist women's organization in the United States.

From Tree Nurseries to Labor Zionist Women's Organization

In 1924, when the Zionist pioneer leader Rahel Yanait (later Yanait Ben-Zvi) sought American Jewish financial support for an agricultural school and tree nursery near the Ratisbonne monastery in Jerusalem, she naturally turned to the women who had participated in Manya Shohat's committee two years earlier. The nursery was one of several such projects organized by the Palestine labor movement. Yanait requested assistance for the construction of a well. In this way, she hoped to become independent of the British Mandatory, which controlled Palestine's limited water supply and allocated an insufficient amount of water to the nursery.

With the assistance of the Jewish National Fund, the Zionist agency responsible for land acquisition and development in the Yishuv, Yanait drew up plans for digging a well. Next, she enlisted the support of Sophie Udin and six other Poalei Zion activists: Eva Berg, Leah Brown, Haya Ehrenreich, Luba Hurwitz, Rahel Segal, and Nina Zuckerman. The group, which coalesced around the urgent needs of Yanait's nursery, recognized the potent political value of such an undertaking for the Palestine labor movement. They also sought to exploit Yanait's call for financial assistance in order to assert their own agenda within the male-dominated Poalei Zion Party. Like many of their contemporaries who experienced the swift social, economic, and political transformation of American women in the 1920s, the cohort grouped around Udin reasoned that their objectives would best be advanced through an autonomous Labor Zionist women's organization. To this end, they published a carefully crafted letter written by Yanait in *Der tog* [The Day] on March 8, 1924. In the letter, Yanait opined that "our tree nursery cannot exist without a well."

The little trees need water. The municipal water supply is insufficient . . . The *kvu-zah* [worker's commune] must have a well to collect the rain water and to hold it for the rainless dry season. In the last two years more than 130,000 saplings from our *kvuzah* have been planted in 17 points in Galilee and Judaea. . . . It costs about 150 [British] pounds to build [a well], and we want to obtain a loan from America. With utmost responsibility, we take it upon ourselves to repay this sum in six or seven years.[8]

The letter, in its endearing simplicity, proved highly effective. The image of female Zionist pioneers tending "saplings" and reclaiming the wilderness of the Yishuv struck a responsive chord among working-class Jewish immigrant women in America. Udin and her followers suc-ceeded—not only in raising the sum requested by Yanait, but also in using the enthusiastic response of Jewish immigrant women to buttress their campaign within the party for the creation of a separate Labor Zionist women's organization.

Poalei Zion's male leadership was generally opposed to the creation of a separate women's organization. The party leaders feared that such a structure would undermine Poalei Zion's credibility in the eyes of the im-migrant community. Having long since "emancipated" the female mem-bers and endowed them with equal rights and obligations, the party leaders argued, there was no need to sponsor a new socialist Zionist women's organization.[9] Such specious reasoning, however, did not deter Udin, Berg, Brown, Ehrenreich, Hurwitz, Segal, and Zuckerman. They asserted that only in an autonomous organization would women be able to fully realize their potential and assume greater responsibility for the movement as a whole. Other factors also influenced the decision to establish Pioneer Women. The Poalei Zion Party ranks were small, elitist, and largely dominated by men. Consequently, many female party leaders felt a strong need to expand their own constituency. They argued that the minuscule number of women in Poalei Zion actually in-hibited new women from joining the party. With the support of Manya Shohat, Rahel Yanait, Goldie Meyerson, and others, the women mem-bers of Poalei Zion fought to create a totally new and independent vehi-cle for outreach.

In 1925 Sophie Udin appealed to the fifteenth annual Poalei Zion con-vention to approve the formation of a separate women's organization. "I explained, in the name of a small group of members," Udin later recalled, "our desire to be a part of the party, an organic part, but independent."[10]

The first national Pioneer Women convention was held in New York City in 1926. Leah Biskin was elected the new organization's "national secretary," an office akin to that of secretary-general of a European-style socialist party. The convention, in defiance of a sizable segment of the Poalei Zion Party, declared Pioneer Women to be completely autonomous in its organizational and educational work. At the same time, it adopted much of the traditional socialist Zionist program and affiliated with the World Union of Poalei Zion, the Socialist International, and the World Zionist Organization. Pioneer Women's founders also stressed the ideological and political tasks of the organization over its philanthropic activities. The 1926 convention articulated the following goals:

1. To help create a homeland in Palestine based on cooperation and social justice;

2. To give moral and material support to the Moezet Hapoalot;

3. To strive through systematic cultural and propaganda work to educate the American Jewish woman to a more conscious role as co-worker in the establishment of a better and more just society in America and throughout the world.[11]

At the outset, Pioneer Women mobilized twenty clubs with approximately three thousand members.[12] The organization's ranks were initially comprised of Yiddish-speaking women who possessed an exceptional esprit de corps. These idealistic, committed, and liberal young working women made time for organizational activities as well as fund-raising for women's agricultural training schools in Petah Tikvah, Nahlat Yehuda, and Hederah, places most of them never expected to actually see. Golda Meir, who was sent by the Moezet Hapoalot as an emissary to Pioneer Women in 1928, later recalled: "Suspicious of frivolity, it was a long time before the earnest women tolerated purely social gatherings where the ladies might play bridge instead of listening to a lecture on A. D. Gordon, Borochov or other socialist Zionist theoreticians."[13]

Pioneer Women and the American Jewish Landscape

During the interwar years, American Jews began to view the Zionist enterprise with great interest and enthusiasm.[14] In fact, between the end of World War I and the establishment of the State of Israel in 1948, the number of women enrolled in the American Zionist movement grew tenfold, from approximately thirty thousand to over three hundred thousand. The meteoric rise of Hadassah, originally an offshoot of the Zionist Organization of America, was nothing short of remarkable, and it swiftly became the largest Zionist group in the United States.[15] Notwithstanding its seemingly nonpartisan General Zionist orientation, Hadassah, like many American Jewish groups, was profoundly influenced by the Zionist pioneering enterprise in Palestine. The largely native-born constituency of Hadassah saw in the pioneers an extension of their own American idealism. This perspective is revealed, among other places, in the popular Zionist literature of the period. In 1925, for example, Sarah Kussy, a junior Hadassah member and founder of the organization's first branch in Newark, New Jersey, posed the following rhetorical question: "Do our Jewish pioneers work as did the Pilgrim Fathers in Massachusetts in 1620?"[16]

Do they, too, cut down trees, build log cabins, make paths through thick forests and hunt game? Well, they work at least as hard as did the early settlers of America, though not exactly in the same way. Our pioneers, too (*haluzim* they are called) must build their own homes, but, they do that not by felling trees, for the forests of Palestine were cut down long ago and never replaced. Their task is much harder. They build of stone instead of wood, of stone that is firmly imbedded in the soil from which it can be removed only with the greatest difficulty. These stones must be cut and shaped for building, which takes much longer than sawing logs. Nor can the settlers live by hunting, since game does not abound in Palestine. They must wrest food from the earth by the sweat of their brows, by ploughing the fields, and planting and reaping the harvest.[17]

Kussy depicted the *haluzim* not only as role models but as the very embodiment of American Jewish values and ideals. She merged hard work, thrift, self-sacrifice, and industriousness—all equally suggestive of the *haluz* and the American icon Horatio Alger—into one integrated American Zionist sensibility. To this must be added Kussy's depiction of gender relations in Palestine, which reflects her own bias as well as the place of women in emergent Zionist culture. At one o'clock in the afternoon, she noted, the *haluzim* she had visited would break for lunch.

The men stopped their labor and with tools over their shoulders came along making their way to the common dining room of the settlement. Did they have to cook their own meals? No, that task was spared them, for *haluzot* [female pioneers], young women workers and settlers, were there to do that for them. These girls cook, wash house, mend for the men and help them in other ways as well. . . . "Do you find your work hard?" I asked a girl. "Not very," she answered, then shrugging her shoulders added with a smile, "We are doing it for ourselves, for the Jewish people, not for strangers."[18]

FIGURE 1. Masthead from *Di pionern froy* (December 1928). Courtesy of Naamat USA.

The foregoing description provides a glimpse of the way American Jews perceived the Zionist enterprise in Palestine during the interwar years. In other words, although the Zionist pioneers were generally considered dynamic and revolutionary, Zionist women pioneers were most often thought of in a quasi-traditional context. In this way, the complex reality of the Palestinian setting was transvalued to reinforce social patterns and norms acceptable in the American context.[19]

In sharp contrast to the outlook described above, which typified that of Hadassah and the Zionist mainstream in America, Pioneer Women promoted a radical image of independent, sexually liberated *haluzot*. For example, the masthead of the organization's journal *Die pionern froy* [The Pioneer Woman] conveys an unapologetic and forthright egalitarian message (fig. 1). A *haluzah* [female pioneer] carrying a basket and rake sets out to toil in the fields. The image is framed by date palms while in the background the sun rises over the tents of a pioneer settlement. (The union bug beneath the illustration is also revealing!) The masthead articulates a simple and direct theme, namely, that working-class, Yiddish-speaking women were playing an important and central role in building the Yishuv. Finally, the unpretentious quality of the illustration resonated with the values of hard work, physical toil, and sisterhood so central to the self-perception of Jewish immigrant women and their Americanized

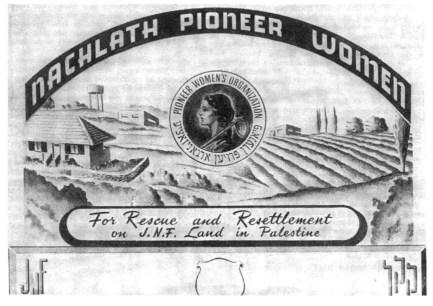

FIGURE 2. Cover illustration from *The Pioneer Woman* (January 1945). Courtesy of Naamat USA.

daughters.[20] Such images of female Zionist pioneers retained their currency well into the pre-state period (figs. 2 and 3) and were given form in everyday life by the train of Moezet Hapoalot emissaries, most of whom displayed a conspicuous lack of concern for American middle-class fashions and sensibilities.

Pioneer Women sought to consolidate its ranks by tapping the vast reservoir of potential American Jewish female support for Labor Zionism. In many respects, the groundwork had already been laid by the International Ladies' Garment Workers' Union (ILGWU) and certain highly placed Hadassah members who publicly endorsed the Histadrut and the workers' settlements in Palestine. In 1930 Pioneer Women issued the following statement in English:

> The modern woman is taking her place in the front ranks of social life. Woman is playing a considerable role in the development of modern industry and production and strives side by side with man for the betterment of living and working conditions of toiling humanity and for a better social order.
>
> The Jewess, no less than the Jew, is now active in the various phases of our life, and the Jewish girl and mother aids powerfully in the upbuilding of Palestine in her own peculiar way—constructive, educational and stimulating way. . . . The *haluzah* is right in the thick of the work of the rising Jewish commonwealth in Palestine. . . .

The Pioneer Women's Organization is not just one more organization of women, doing what others do. . . . It is an organization of women with a distinct task of furthering the economic emancipation and the national rehabilitation of the Jewish masses on the foundations of free labor and social justice. . . .

Through our affiliation with the labor wing of Zionism we back the interests of the Palestine workers. . . . Our own independent sphere of activity. . . . is raising funds for the women pioneers in Palestine. . . .

The progressive Jewish woman, the worker or the helpmate of the worker, has found for herself in our organization an opening for her energy and spiritual craving that nothing else could satisfy in equal measure. We have learned to think and act independently. Our sense of responsibility of Socialism, the cause of the Jewish Homeland, has been heightened. The great liberating ideal and its modern and creative womanhood added to our self-esteem and enhanced the value of our contribution to humanity. Through association with so many comrades in our organization we have grown in moral and mental stature and found a source of joy nothing else could give.

Deep enjoyment, unexcelled spiritual gain and opportunity to learn—that is the triple benefit the Pioneer Women's Organization gives to its members. Join our ranks! Share our ideal and our joy! Be a Pioneer![21]

FIGURE 3. Logo from *The Pioneer Woman* (October 1950). Courtesy of Naamat USA.

Despite the fact that the "Aims and Objectives of the Pioneer Women's Organization" was published in English, its awkward syntax and inelegant grammar betrays Pioneer Women's inescapable immigrant character. The text is also replete with references to self-improvement and education, and reveals the group's latent Americanizing aspirations. Although Pioneer Women did not want to be "just one more organization of women," its members did increasingly imitate the social and philanthropic behavior of mainstream American Jewish women's groups like Hadassah and the National Council of Jewish Women. To be sure, the latter were not especially receptive to immigrant women, nor were they particularly concerned with the range of social and economic issues working-class women faced in their everyday lives. By contrast, it is noteworthy that while the pages of the *Pioneer Woman* reveal with increasing frequency instances of "donor parties," "parlor meetings," and "sewing and knitting classes," such concerns are totally overshadowed by articles and features with titles like "Women in Overalls," "Equal Pay for Equal Work," and "Here's to Women Workers!" That Jewish women's educational and economic advancement remained a paramount issue for the organization is evident in the front-page article of the December 1931 issue of the *Pioneer Woman*. "The problem of the women employed in our industries," explained Fannia M. Cohn of the ILGWU, [is] "one of the most perplexing problems before us, [and] must be met squarely and with open-mindedness."

By dodging it, we will never solve it. It is too complicated for an easy-going answer. The first step, and most necessary one, in solving a complicated problem is to admit that it exists . . . Through workers' education, if purposely directed, more and more women will become aware of the importance of their position in our industrial society. . . .

Those of them who suffer not so much from lack of ability as from lack of confidence in their ability, may through such information come to appreciate the important place they occupy in our economic structure. Because they may learn of the millions of women workers who fill our factories, mills and offices, and upon whose labor and management industries producing hundreds of millions of dollars worth of goods depend they may come to know the important role that women play in our retail distributive activities—that American department stores, for example, famous the world over for size and management, are made possible by the labor not only of diligent saleswomen behind the counter, but also of competent, far-seeing women administrators; that offices in which the exchange transactions which form so integral a part of our present economic system are mainly in hands of women who each year assume more important functions. Such a picture of women, working and contributing so vastly to our economic life, will help develop in working women a consciousness of their own importance.[22]

The seamless melding of Pioneer Women's agenda with that of the ILGWU illustrates the resonance in both arenas of the themes of class consciousness, feminism, labor solidarity, and egalitarianism—core values of the working-class Jewish immigrant community. In short, for many female immigrants joining Pioneer Women was tantamount to being not only a *haluzah* but an American in the fullest sense.

The Broadening of Pioneer Women's Activism

In the 1920s and 1930s Pioneer Women was bolstered by a talented host of *shlihot* [emissaries] sent by Moezet Hapoalot. Manya Shohat and Rahel Yanait Ben-Zvi, who spent extended time in the United States during and following World War I, were succeeded by Golda Meir (1928–1929), Hana Chizhik (1930–1931), Rahel Kaznelson-Rubashov (later Shazar) (1932–1933), Elisheva Kaplan Eshkol (1934–1935), Hasia Kuperminz Drori (1937–1938), Yehudit Simhonit (1938–1939, 1941–1943, 1947–1948), May Bere Mereminsky (Merom) (1939–1941), Sara Kafri (Kukso) (1945–1946), Rivka Yoffe (1946–1947), and Shoshana Hareli (1948–1949). Together with these Palestinian spokeswomen, Pioneer Women's American leadership—notably national secretaries Sophie Udin (1924–1925), Sara Feder (Keyfitz) (first half of 1925, 1936–1938, 1951–1955), Feigel Benson (second half of 1925), Leah Biskin (1926–1931), Nina Zuckerman (1931–1932), Golda Meir (1932–1934), Dvorah Rothbard (1938–1945), Blanche Fine Mogil (1945–1947), and Bert Goldstein (1945–1951)—embarked on a concerted and persistent recruitment campaign aimed at both Yiddish- and English-speaking Jewish women in the United States and Canada.

In 1931, for example, the organization published *Vos arbeterns derzeyln* [The Woman Worker Speaks], an anthology of personal reminiscences by *haluzot* [pioneers] about their experiences in Palestine. The volume was (and remains) a veritable treasure trove of information about the nexus between women and Zionism.[23] An extraordinary and compelling amalgam of memoirs, prose, reflections, diary entries, testimonials, and letters, it is, at once, uplifting and tragic, dramatic and seemingly banal, public and private. It vividly depicts and records the reality, experiences, and perspectives of a cohort of East European Jewish women who matured in the turbulent decades spanning the nineteenth and twentieth centuries, and whose lives were forged in the crucible of pogroms, revolution, and state building. The book includes essays about the early years in several *kvuzot* [communes]; life in Palestine during World War I;

impressions of the philosopher A. D. Gordon, the poet Rahel Blaustein, and other notable figures of the Second and Third *Aliyot;* Jewish family life in agricultural colonies; and several hitherto unpublished photographs of *haluzim* and Jewish colonies. The volume was well received, and in 1932 Pioneer Women published an English translation titled *The Plough Woman.* The latter opened a window on Jewish life in Palestine to a largely uninformed English-reading audience.

Appearing at the height of the Depression, a period that coincided with the Yishuv's rapid growth and economic expansion, *The Plough Woman* presented a poignant alternative to the misery and hardship of American society and the Jewish working class in the United States. It purported to point the way to individual fulfillment and collective national redemption, and it was tailored to appeal to an East European Jewish immigrant community increasingly sympathetic to the aims and ideals of Labor Palestine. It gave concrete expression to the concerns of a wide array of Jewish women confronted by the universal challenges of modernity—in the American, Jewish, immigrant, and Zionist settings.

The Plough Woman may be profitably compared with the contemporaneous writings of other East European Jewish women. In another context, it has been demonstrated that the Polish Yiddish weeklies *Froyen-shtim* [Women's Voice] and *Di froy* [The Woman] "featured primarily female authors and proclaimed the importance of what we may call self-emancipation." *Di froy,* in particular, sustained a "specific Jewish orientation [that] was Zionist as well as feminist, [as] indicated by its . . . focus on pioneering in Palestine and the building of a new life based on Jewish national culture."[24] Similarly, the Yiddish poet and Zionist activist Aliza Greenblatt, who lived in the United States, constructed her autobiography *Baym fentster fun a lebn* [At the Window of a Life] in order to position herself "at the center" of the Jewish public arena, underscoring the value of authorship as "a key component" of the social hierarchy. Her autobiography, in other words, was intended to be "both personal memoir and collective history."[25] Like *Froyen-shtim, Di froy,* and *Baym fentster fun a lebn, The Plough Woman* illustrates not a new female identity per se but rather "the confused outline of merging worlds—a new sense . . . of the bounds of geographic, social, and psychological representations."[26] The text invites us to explore the changing self-perceptions of Zionist women and reimagine the world in terms of the protean social and political possibilities they imagined in their everyday lives.

The Plough Woman, with its veneration of the Zionist women pioneers, was something of a cross between an account of everyday life and a sacred text. True believers revered these women as exemplars of the new irreligious Jewish religion (the text is replete with expressions of their holiness and saintly behavior); Rahel Kaznelson-Shazar, Manya Shohat, and others were its high priests; and "departed" comrades—many of whom had died tragically as a result of illness, suicide, or skirmishes with Palestinian Arabs—such as Sarah Lishansky, Pessie Abramson, and Rahel Blaustein—were anointed as its martyrs.[27] Maurice Samuel accentuated the valorization of the Zionist women pioneers in his English translation.

Like the plethora of Zionist propaganda and iconography that steadily penetrated the Jewish public arena in this period, *The Plough Woman* was calculated to evoke sympathy and identification with the Zionist pioneers and the Yishuv.[28] However, although the Zionist pioneer was a unique Labor Zionist creation, the image of the pioneer was far from monolithic. It was adapted and used to exploit a range of complex attitudes to modern Jewish life, including broad themes that resonated with the experiences of Jewish immigrant women in the United States. Such images gave concrete expression to the mythology of Zionist women—on the one hand, brawny, weather-beaten, rugged pioneers living off the land; on the other, maternal, nurturing, feminine caretakers whose domestic roles were transvalued to suit the needs of the new Jewish society-in-the-making. This dualism helped to elevate the notion of *haluziut* [pioneering] to the position of a hallowed Zionist and Jewish feminist ideal.

In time, however, as Pioneer Women's membership became increasingly Americanized, the organization gradually became less doctrinaire and shifted to an English-speaking orientation. As the organization grew, so did the proceeds of its fund-raising campaign on behalf of the Moezet Hapoalot. In its first decade, Pioneer Women transmitted over $383,000 to Histadrut-related projects in Palestine. By 1939 it had 170 chapters in seventy cities and approximately 7,000 members. Of the 170 clubs, 85 were categorized as "Yiddish-speaking" and contained 4,500 members.[29] It also sustained a monthly publication, the *Pioneer Woman* (which was sprinkled with modern Hebrew terms like *haluz, kibbutz, aliyah, kibush haavodah* [conquest of labor], *hakhsharah* [agricultural and vocational training], and *haluziut*), and initiated several Hebrew-speaking clubs. In 1941 Pioneer Women maintained 250 clubs with a total membership of 10,000.[30] In addition to its traditional Zionist orientation and support for the Palestine labor movement, the organization now concentrated on bringing in new members from all walks of Jewish life. The younger acculturated members, wrote Rose Kaufman (later national president, from 1965 to 1969) in 1942, "like teas, attractive settings, flowers on the table, luncheons in a hotel—why not?"[31] In a similar vein, new ventures like the nationwide Tozeret Haarez Consumers' League—intended to support the Yishuv's commercial industries—gradually replaced the strident political campaigns of previous decades.

It was evident by the end of World War II that the increasing number of English-speaking clubs had emerged as the main points of entry for new and younger members between the ages of thirty and thirty-five. This included a preponderant number of recruits from outside the movement's "traditional" ranks, women who were never previously affiliated with a Zionist or labor organization. For example, a typical published report of the national executive noted that in January 1945 "*Haverah* Sara Feder, co-chairman [*sic*] of the National Organization Committee, visited Tulsa, Milwaukee, Chicago, St. Louis and Kansas City in the past few months in connection with the membership drive." In Chicago alone, Feder (later a national president) "addressed nine English-speaking clubs." By contrast, in Kansas City "she had meetings with both Yiddish-speaking clubs" and "helped strengthen Club 3 of English-speaking younger women."[32]

But Pioneer Women did not abandon its record of social activism. During World War II, it mobilized a countrywide network of volunteers who participated in civil defense efforts, Red Cross activities, war bond sales, blood drives, salvage work, and victory gardens. Such activities demonstrated Pioneer Women's commitment to American Jewry's wartime efforts and enhanced the organization's national visibility. The wartime campaign, explained the June 1944 issue of the *Pioneer Woman,* also benefited the organization. "It added zest to the *Erez Israel* program; it introduced non-Jewish [read: non-Yiddish] speakers; it helped attract women who were under the impression we were interested in only the *Erez Israel* program."[33]

In this period, when news of the destruction of European Jewry became well known, the organization also created emergency fund-raising initiatives such as the Child Rescue Fund of 1943 and the Building Fund of 1944, both of which were targeted at the needs of European Jewish refugee children in the Yishuv. After the war, the campaign was widened to include orphans and children born in "DP" (Displaced Persons) camps. At this juncture, Pioneer Women also drove forward the process of putting several specific projects in Palestine on solid footing. Thus, it increasingly focused its energies on establishing and maintaining social service facilities in urban and rural locations throughout the country that directly benefited women and children, including new training farms, children's homes, vocational schools, and immigrant absorption centers.[34]

Pioneer Women after World War II

Following World War II, Pioneer Women expanded its range of national and overseas activities. Indeed, the North American organization played an active role in establishing new branches of Pioneer Women in Argentina, Brazil, Chile, Uruguay, and Peru. (It had established a group in Mexico City as early as 1936.)

With the establishment of the State of Israel in 1948, Pioneer Women also broadened the scope of its American activity. It embraced a cultural educational agenda that revealed growing concern about Jewish continuity in the New World. It moderated much of its original socialist and feminist ideology as well as its philosophical and political orientation. "We have *haluzic* [pioneering] [*sic*] work to do right here," opined Bert Goldstein in the October 1951 issue of the *Pioneer Woman*. "We must bring to American Jewish women that *ruah hanefesh*, that spiritual warmth which . . . makes the essential difference between the Zionists in Israel and the Zionists here in America. To attain that quality we cannot be merely fund-raisers."[35] In this way, the organization reflected the changing character and concerns of a sizable segment of American Jewish women while continuing its work with labor and progressive groups on behalf of liberal domestic causes (e.g., the fight against McCarthyism, the championing of civil rights, the battle to increase state and federal funding for public housing, etc.).

In the post-state era, Pioneer Women proved to be an important partner for the Labor Zionist movement in Israel as well as a key player in American Zionism. The organization continued to work very closely with Moezet Hapoalot and the Jewish Agency for Israel. It promoted American Jewish tourism to the new state, conducted numerous independent and collaborative fund-raising campaigns, spearheaded efforts on behalf of vocational and educational centers for Jewish and Arab women and girls, helped create a vast network of day-care centers for Israeli working families, actively participated in Zionist political affairs, and served as a conduit to American Jewish society for Israel's rising women's movement. On the American front, too, Pioneer Women assumed responsibility for a multiplicity of Labor Zionist causes that encompassed the movement's on-going educational, cultural, and political concerns in the United States.

In recent decades, Pioneer Women (reestablished as Naamat USA in 1981, the name of its sister organization in Israel) has experienced a gradual decline in membership. From a peak of approximately fifty thousand members in the 1970s, the organization has been reduced by nearly half, or roughly to the size of Pioneer Women in 1948. This trend is due, in part, to the fact that many of Naamat USA's functions and goals—like those of the Zionist Organization of America, Hadassah, Mizrachi, and other American Zionist groups—have been steadily adopted by mainstream American Jewish groups and institutions.

To sum up, before the establishment of the State of Israel, Pioneer Women anticipated the shift in American Jewish priorities vis-à-vis the Jewish national home and the increasing importance of Labor Zionism and its significant impact on world Jewish affairs. It was distinguished in the American context by the fact that it alone served as a channel for Jewish immigrant women who sympathized with the aims and ideals of the labor movement in Palestine as well as progressive causes in the United States. It also provided an important American foothold for many Zionist leaders in the decades before the cause of the State of Israel became an integral component of the American Jewish consensus. In more recent years, however, as Naamat USA and other Zionist groups have struggled to maintain their place in the evolving American Jewish landscape, the organization has gradually shed much of its distinctive character. Nonetheless, it remains the voice of Labor Zionist women on American soil and an outpost of a progressive and egalitarian Zionist vision of diaspora Jewry.

Notes

1. From a typescript of a skit titled "Information, Please" (c. 1944), 2. Naamat USA Archives.

2. Rebekah Kohut, "Jewish Women's Organization in the United States," *American Jewish Year Book,* vol. 33 (1932), 188.

3. *American Jewish Year Book,* vol. 29 (1927), 184.

4. Dafna N. Izraeli, "The Women Workers' Movement: First Wave Feminism in Pre-State Israel," in *Pioneers and Homemakers: Jewish Women in Pre-State Israel,* ed. Deborah Bernstein (Albany: State University of New York Press, 1992), 183.

5. Letter from Manya Shohat to Rahel Yanait, September 21, 1921, in Rachel Yanait Ben-Zvi, ed., *Before Golda: Manya Shohat,* trans. Sandra Shurin (New York: Biblio Press, 1989), 174.

6. Marie Syrkin, *Nahman Syrkin: Socialist Zionist; A Biographical Memoir and Selected Essays* (New York: Herzl Press and Sharon Books, 1961), 207–208.

7. Leib Spizman, ed., *Geshikte fun der zionistisher arebeter bavegung in zfon amerike*, vol. 2 (New York: Farlag Yidisher Kemfer, 1955); Anita Shapira, *Berl: The Biography of a Socialist Zionist* (Cambridge: Cambridge University Press, 1984), 120–121.

8. Translated from *Der tog*, March 8, 1924.

9. A similar situation obtained in Palestine, where Histadrut leaders vigorously opposed the creation of Moezet Hapoalot. See Izraeli, "The Women Workers' Movement," 198–199.

10. Quoted in Thea Keren, *Sophie Udin: Portrait of a Pioneer* (Rehovot: Published by the author, 1984), 37.

11. Cited in *Pionern froyn konstitushn suvenir-bukh*, 1930. Naamat USA Archives.

12. *American Jewish Year Book*, vol. 29 (1927), 184.

13. Golda Meir, *My Life* (New York: Dell Publishing Company, 1975), 125; Meron Medzini, *Hayehudiyah hageah: Golda Meir rehazon yisrael, biografiyah politit* (Jerusalem: Edanim, 1990), 76.

14. See Mark A. Raider, *The Emergence of American Zionism* (New York and London: New York University Press), ch. 3.

15. Samuel Halperin, *The Political World of American Zionism*, reprint (Silver Spring, Md.: Information Dynamics, 1985), 327.

16. Sarah Kussy, "The Conquest of the Soil: A Visit to a Pioneers' Settlement in Palestine," *Young Judean* (February 1925): 10. I-61, Jewish Student Organizations, American Jewish Historical Society.

17. Ibid.

18. Ibid.

19. See Matthew Frye Jacobson, *Special Sorrows: The Diasporic Imagination of Irish, Polish and Jewish Immigrants in the United States* (Cambridge, Mass. and London: Harvard University Press, 1995), 105.

20. See Susan Glenn, *Daughters of the Shtetl: Jewish Immigrant Women in America's Garment Industry, 1880–1920* (Ithaca, N.Y.: Cornell University Press, 1990); Sydney Stahl Weinberg, *World of Our Mothers: The Lives of Jewish Immigrant Women* (New York: Schocken Books, 1988), esp. ch. 10.

21. See "Aims and Objectives of the Pioneer Women's Organization," *Pionern froyn konstitushn suvenir-bukh*, 1930. Naamat USA Archives.

22. Fannia M. Cohn, "Woman's Eternal Struggle," *Pioneer Woman*, no. 24 (December 1931): 1–2.

23. See *The Plough Woman: Records of the Pioneer Women of Palestine; A Critical Edition*, ed. Mark A. Raider and Miriam B. Raider-Roth (Hanover, N.H., and London: University Press of New England, 2002).

24. Paula Hyman, "East European Jewish Women in an Age of Transition, 1880–1930" in Judith R. Baskin, ed., *Jewish Women in Historical Perspective*, 2nd ed. (Detroit: Wayne State University Press, 1998), 280–281.

25. Susanne A. Shavelson, "Anxieties of Authorship in the Autobiographies of Mary Antin and Aliza Greenblatt," *Prooftexts* 18 (1998): 162, 184.

26. Germaine Brée, "Autogynography," in *Studies in Autobiography*, ed. James Olney (New York and Oxford: Oxford University Press, 1988), 177.

27. See Anita Shapira, "The Religious Motifs of the Labor Movement," in *Zionism and Religion*, ed. Shmuel Almog, Jehuda Reinharz, and Anita Shapira (Hanover, N.H., and London: University Press of New England, 1998), 251–272.

28. See Raider, *The Emergence of American Zionism*, ch. 3.

29. *American Jewish Year Book*, vol. 41 (1939), 499.

30. *American Jewish Year Book*, vol. 43 (1941), 585.

31. Quoted in Judith A. Sokoloff, "Naamat USA through the Decades," *Naamat Woman* 10 (September–October 1995): 21.

32. "In the National Executive," *Pioneer Woman*, no. 103 (January 1945): 11.

33. Quoted in Sokoloff, "Naamat USA through the Decades," 22.

34. "Buildings Erected in Israel, 1945–1949," *Pioneer Woman*, no. 145 (June 1949): 12, 24.

35. Quoted in Sokoloff, "Naamat USA through the Decades," 26.

Chapter 7

The history of Canadian Jewry differs in significant and distinctive ways from that of American Jewry. Until 1850, Canadian Jewry was centered on the small Jewish community of Montreal and numbered not more than 250 souls. However, as was the case with the United States, the outbreak of pogroms in tsarist Russia in 1881–1882 and the ensuing waves of mass East European Jewish migration to North America marked a turning point in the size and composition of the Canadian Jewish community. Thereafter, several thousand East European Jewish immigrants settled in the provinces of Quebec and Ontario. By the time of the Canadian census of 1891, the Jewish population had risen to nearly 6,500 total, including the beginnings of Jewish settlement in the provinces of Manitoba, British Columbia, Alberta, and New Brunswick. In the ensuing decades, Canadian Jewry's natural population growth was substantially augmented by a net increase in East European Jewish immigration. By the decade of the 1920s, the period examined in the following essay by Esther Carmel-Hakim, the Jewish community had grown more than twentyfold to over 125,000 nationally.

Several efforts were made at the turn of the nineteenth and twentieth centuries to establish a Canadian branch of the Zionist movement. However, the real impetus for the development of the Zionist Organization of Canada (ZOC) came in the wake of the influx of sizable numbers of East European Jewish immigrants to the cities of Montreal, Toronto, and Winnipeg, where a broad spectrum of Yiddish-speaking social, cultural, and political organizations took root and flourished. The Zionist scene developed rapidly and reflected all of the major parties and organizations active in the World Zionist Organization and the Yishuv. The small size of Canadian Zionism seems to have fostered intramovement cooperation. In contrast to American Zionism, particularly during the years following World War I when the political clash between Louis D. Brandeis (1856–1941) and Chaim Weizmann (1874–1952) divided and subsequently ruptured the American movement, Canadian Zionism as a whole was notable for its relative lack of internecine conflict and strife. Indeed, a significant achievement of the Canadian Zionist movement was the 1927 purchase of a 30,000-*dunam* tract of land in the Hefer Valley, a valley that stretches between Hederah and present-day Netanyah on the coastal plain. The ZOC transferred ownership of the land to the Jewish National Fund, which in 1929 purchased contiguous tracts of land in the region and initiated a new plan for Jewish colonization of the valley.

Less well known are several key philanthropic and land acquisition initiatives orchestrated by Canadian Zionism's vigorous constituent groups that prefigured the Hefer Valley project. For example, at the urging of Hannah Meisel (later Meisel-Shohat) (1890–1972), an early leader of the women's Zionist pioneer movement in Palestine, Canada's Hadassah and Women's International Zionist Organization (WIZO) groups embarked on a joint fund-raising project in 1921 to help establish a women's agricultural training farm in Nahalal, one of the first in the Yishuv. In the following chapter, Esther Carmel-Hakim asserts that this collaborative effort stemmed from the understanding by Hadassah and WIZO that "women can depend only on the support of other women to carry out projects designed to improve women's conditions and status." To this end, they set aside their organizational differences for the greater good and created a model of collaboration emulated by the broader Canadian Zionist movement.

Hadassah-WIZO Canada and the Development of Agricultural Training for Women in Pre-State Israel

Esther Carmel-Hakim

The contributions of Hadassah and the Women's International Zionist Organization (WIZO) to the medical care and education of the Jewish population in Palestine are well acknowledged. Less is known, however, about the unique contribution made by Hadassah Canada to the establishment of agricultural training schools for women in Palestine, and especially Hadassah Canada's help in the creation and maintenance of the first agricultural school for women, founded in Nahalal in 1923 by Hanna Meisel.

This essay examines the background and the beginning of Hadassah-WIZO Canada's contribution to setting up the school.

Most women's middle-class organizations at the beginning of the century were involved with traditionally philanthropic activities and charity concerning women's and children's welfare such as health care, clothing, and food supplies. In Canada under the leadership of Lillian Freiman, Hadassah took an unusual and new direction: it financed and supported agricultural training of women in Palestine. The goal of such training was to educate pioneer women and enable them to take an active part in the Zionist enterprise and rural settlement. This course of action by Hadassah Canada was not only an innovation but also a deviation from the common philanthropic and charitable activities of other women's organizations at the time.

Three features differentiated Canadian Jewry from American Jewry in this period.

1. Canadian Jewry felt more threatened. Antisemitism was virulent in Quebec and elsewhere in Canada.[1]

2. The vast majority of Canadian Jewish communities were centered in three big cities, Montreal, Toronto, and Winnipeg.[2]

3. Most of the congregations in Canada were observantly Orthodox in religious practice.

Zionism in Canada from the 1890s did not have to compete, as it did in both Britain and the United States, with previously established organizations. The Zionist movement in Canada thrived since there were not competing nationalisms and no opposing Reform ideology.[3]

Two main Zionist women's organizations existed in the early years of the century: Hadassah[4] and WIZO.[5] The first Canadian Hadassah chapter was formed in March 1917 in Toronto during a visit from Henrietta Szold, the president of American Hadassah. The movement grew quickly in all parts of Canada, not least because Hadassah was an expression of the earliest impulse among Canadian Jewish women for independence from what they perceived as a male-led establishment. Canadian women wanted to choose their own priorities. In January 1919, the sixteenth convention of the Canadian Zionist Organization was held in Toronto.[6] Here Archie Freiman was elected National President of the Zionist Organization. At the same time his wife, Lillian Freiman[7] was appointed to head the newly created Helping Hand Fund to assist homeless and destitute Jews living in Palestine. Lillian Freiman played a prominent role in a wide range of charitable and philanthropic activities of both a Jewish and nonsectarian nature. In 1934[8] she received the prestigious Order of the British Empire in recognition of her important volunteer work. She was the first Canadian Jew to be honored in this way. However her Zionist work was closest to her heart, and she was astonishingly successful in fund-raising for the "Helping Hand Fund Campaign." Freiman firmly believed that, instead of charity, productivity should be fostered, and she consequently suggested sending sewing machines and material instead of clothing to the Yishuv. As she put it, "We must concentrate on the work of rehabilitation and reconstruction."[9] While traveling through Canada for the Helping Hand Fund Campaign, Freiman urged women to organize into chapters whose aim would be help in the rebuilding of Palestine. These chapters became the Canadian Hadassah Organization.

During this period, the Women's International Zionist Organization was established in England. The initiators of WIZO were the wives of the Zionist leaders in Great Britain. The Balfour Declaration of 1917, the British conquest of Palestine at the end of World War I, and the increasing importance of the Zionist Organization's headquarters in London contributed to the awakening of Zionist women's activities in England. In 1919, after returning from a visit to Palestine, Rebecca Sieff, Vera Weizmann, Edith Eder, and several colleagues associated with the Women's Federation of Great Britain decided to establish an International Federation for Zionist Women.[10]

These events coincided with the Third Aliyah, which brought a new wave of immigration to Palestine. Among the immigrants were women who hoped to participate in the building of a new Jewish society. Generally speaking, there were three main approaches to the issue of women's participation in the Zionist movement in Palestine.

   1. One approach was that women should fulfill their traditional role of maintaining the household support-system: cooking, laundry, childcare and health care.

   2. At the other extreme was the belief that there should be no difference between men's and women's activities: women are as strong as men both physically and mentally and should take part in all necessary work.

   3. The third way, represented by Hannah Meisel,[11] saw women's main area of activity as the household but also believed that they must contribute to the Zionist agricultural revolution by developing those agricultural branches which women traditionally had engaged in.

Meisel's idea was that by learning how to manage vegetable plots and dairies and raise poultry, women could perform productive, profitable labor in the new settlements of the pre-state period.[12] Moreover, those agricultural branches generally were not well developed in the Jewish settlements. Meisel rejected the idea, so widespread at the time, that because women lacked the physical strength to work in the fields with the men, they should remain in the kitchen, laundry, and nursery.

Only two years after her arrival in Palestine, Meisel put her vision to work in a new institution: a training farm for women, founded in 1911 in Kinneret. There, Jewish women from Europe who had no experience in physical labor could acquire agricultural training.[13] Meisel raised the necessary funds for the farm from a Jewish women's organization in Germany. The farm was closed in 1917 with the onset of World War I. Meisel met the founders of WIZO in London in 1919, where she influenced the direction of the new Jewish women's organization and became a member of its Executive.[14] The seeds for the establishment of the agricultural school for women in Nahalal were planted then.

In February 1921, the first convention of Hadassah Canada took place, and a letter from Hannah Meisel was read by the Zionist leader Dr. Shmarya Levin.[15] In the letter, Meisel challenged the new organization to take under its patronage the establishment of an agricultural school for women. In her words: "The Jewish village could never be built without the active participation of the woman and this participation could not be prosperous without previous preparation. . . . The first work of Zionist women should therefore be the immediate establishment of a central agricultural school for women in this country, of which, in the course of time, branches could be extended all over the country."[16]

The first national convention accepted the challenge set by Meisel and adopted the following resolution: "That Canadian Hadassah be directly associated with one specific undertaking in Palestine and that this be to establish a school for Household Science, as outlined in Meisel's letter."[17] Within half a year $88,000, a considerable sum for the period, was collected to help establish the school. The funds were regarded as sufficient to build an agricultural school for sixty students, including the buildings, the farm, and inventory. However, because no land was set aside for the school the money was in fact used by Keren Hayesod for other purposes![18]

On the first visit of Chaim and Vera Weizmann to North America in 1921, Vera met Lillian Freiman, who had become the dominion president of Hadassah, and persuaded Hadassah Canada to become part of the new WIZO organization that had been established nine months earlier in London.[19]

At the Twelfth Zionist Congress in Carlsbad, which now included a combined WIZO-Hadassah Canada delegation, a budget of 20,000 Egyptian pounds[20] was approved for the establishment of the agricultural training school for women. This was one of the first times money was specifically designated for women workers in Palestine. The WIZO-Hadassah Canada delegates played an important role in this decision.

The sum of 20,000 Egyptian pounds (EP) appears in the budget for the World Zionist Organization's Agriculture and Settlement Department in 1921–22.[21] Although the importance of such a school was clearly acknowledged, once again no land was allocated, and the money that had been set aside to establish the school was diverted to other projects. Finally, at the end of 1922, 500 *dunams* of land were given for the school to be built near Nahalal,[22] but this time there was no budget. Out of the original sum of 20,000 EP allocated by the Zionist Congress in Carlsbad, only 400 EP were ultimately given to Meisel.[23]

With these funds Meisel began her preparations. The first women workers arrived in Nahalal in March 1923 and lived in tents. They then moved into structures that had been built for the poultry. The first two cows were sent to the school by the Dutch WIZO,[24] and practical work began. Conditions improved only at the end of 1923, after the second WIZO convention, when WIZO decided to pay a monthly stipend of 100 EP to the school.[25]

However, arguments between WIZO and the Zionist Executive over the ownership and supervision of the school soon broke out. The Zionist Executive was unwilling to recognize WIZO's ownership and supervision of the school in Nahalal.[26] The Executive insisted on being reimbursed for the initial investment. The cornerstone of the first school building was laid in January 1924 because of the financial support of Hadassah Canada. The official opening of the school took place in April 1926.[27] The school was very modern and a source of pride for the whole Yishuv.

Another milestone in the development of the school and Yishuv was Lillian and Archie Freiman's first visit to Palestine in 1927.[28] Impressed by the school and its achievements, Lillian Freiman convinced Hadassah Canada to undertake full financial responsibility for what she called the First Agricultural College for Women in Palestine. At the fifth Hadassah conference held in Winnipeg in July 1927 it did just that, including paying back former investors. At this point, ownership of the school was officially transferred to Hadassah Canada, and it became the organization's main project in Palestine. In appreciation of the Freimans' assistance to the Yishuv, two settlements in Israel bear their names: Havazelet Hasharon, named for Lillian, and Bitan Aharon, for Archie.[29]

In an era that placed a premium on rural colonization, the agricultural training of Jewish women was a foremost Zionist concern and was achieved with the support of Hadassah Canada. The school at Nahalal, a center of agricultural training for women in the twenties, prepared its graduates to settle in all types of rural settlements as well as to become agricultural instructors. By giving women a chance to learn and develop agricultural skills, the school also encouraged independence and enabled its graduates to take the first step toward equality. And indeed, many of the founders of the women workers' movement in Palestine were graduates of such agricultural training initiatives, including Ada Fishman, Yael Gordon, Hannah Chizhik, and Sara Malkin, to name a few.[30]

In sum, over time Hadassah Canada changed its direction from philanthropy and charity to production and development. While other middle-class women's organizations supported health care projects, Hadassah Canada established an agricultural school. Although both the Zionist Congress (in 1921) and the World Zionist Organization's Agriculture and Settlement Department recognized the importance of agricultural training for women, they were satisfied with merely declarative support. Twice the money allocated for the establishment of the school was diverted by the Zionist authorities for other projects. Only the support of women's organizations in the diaspora made agricultural training for women possible at both the farm in Kinneret and the school in Nahalal. Without such crucial support, no agricultural training for women would have been possible in this period. That support came from dedicated groups of women, often consisting of the wives of Zionist leaders, who established separate women's organizations and decided their own priorities for helping Jewish women in Palestine.

The lesson of Nahalal might be that women can depend only on the support of other women to carry out projects designed to improve women's conditions and status. Agricultural training for women in pre-state Israel could not have taken place without the moral and financial support of the women's organizations of the diaspora.

As Lillian Freiman herself put it: "Ladies first, in ordinary parlance, has become merely a form of courtesy, a sort of graceful tribute from the gentlemen to the feminine frailty of women. But these two innocent-looking words take on an entirely different meaning when spoken in certain Zionist circles. They stand for something definite. They are a tribute not to feminine frailty but to feminine ingenuity."[31]

Notes

This article was written for the Hadassah-Brandeis Institute in 1999. I would like to express my thanks to my advisers Prof. Yaacov Goldstein and R. Margalit Shilo, as well as to Dr. Deborah Bernstein, for their advice and input. I would like to thank Nancy Rosenfeld and Nancy Peled for their assistance with the English version of this article.

1. Antisemitism grew after 1933. G. Tulchinsky, *Taking Root: The Origins of the Canadian Jewish Community* (Toronto: Lester Publishing, 1992), xix.

2. Tulchinsky, *Taking Root*, xix–xxi.

3. Under the leadership of Clarence de Sola, a member of the Spanish Portuguese "aristocracy" of Montreal Jews who headed the Canadian Zionist Federation from 1898 to 1919, the movement grew. From a population of 16,000 in 1901 Canada's Jewish population reached 75,000 in 1913. The Canadian Zionist Federation became a kind of national Jewish congress because of its countrywide support. Zionism thus went deeper into the Canadian Jewish context than into the American one, because of the conjuncture of separate and distinctive cultural, demographic, and political factors, and because of the unique constitutional and racial structure of Canada. Canadian Jews, in reaction to French Canadian antisemitism and nationalism, may even have absorbed some nationalistic influences from the French Canadians in Montreal. Tulchinsky, *Taking Root*, xxiv–xxv.

4. Hadassah was founded in the United States by Henrietta Szold in 1912. Fay Grove-Pollak, *The Saga of a Movement, WIZO, 1920–1970* (Tel Aviv: WIZO, 1970), 115.

5. Women's International Zionist Organization, founded in London in 1920. The first women's organization that was involved in actual work for the benefit of women in Palestine was the Women's League for Cultural Work in Palestine, founded in 1907 by the wives of the Zionist leaders of Germany.

6. *Canadian Jewish Chronicle*, 6:31 (December 12, 1919), 1; Bernard Figler, *Lillian and Archie Freiman Biographies* (Montreal, 1961), 34.

7. Lillian Freiman was born in 1885 in Mattawa, Ontario. She was only seventeen when she attended her first Canadian Zionist convention in Montreal in 1903. This was the third Canadian Zionist Convention, and she was the delegate of the Ottawa Daughters of Zion Group. She never missed, a convention after this one. Lillian Freiman was experienced in fund-raising, since she was involved in fund-raising and work for the Red Cross and other organizations during World War I. Figler, *Lillian and Archie Freiman Biographies,* 2–24, 33.

8. *Ottawa Evening Citizen,* January 2, 1934, 4. Figler, *Lillian and Archie Freiman Biographies,* 18–19.

9. Figler, *Lillian and Archie Freiman Biographies,* 9. There is still room to investigate whether or not Lillian Freiman herself is the origin of Hadassah's acceptance of agricultural training for women as the focus of its activity in Palestine.

10. CZA Z4/2073. A letter from December 30, 1919, from the temporary committee of the Federation of Women Zionists in Britain to other women's organizations. They announce their intention to establish a Zionist Women Organization. In the fall of 1919 Rebecca Sieff, Vera Weizmann, and Edith Eder visited Palestine for a month, and a letter from Rebecca Sieff to the federation gives an idea of the direction the new organization will take. *First Annual Report of the Federation of Women Zionists of the United Kingdom,* June 1920, London, 2. CZA Z4 1927.

11. Meisel, who was born in Russia and received agricultural training in Switzerland and France, was the initiator of agricultural training for women in Palestine since she came in 1909. Rina Farber, *The Echo of the Lake of Galilee Came this Far* [Hebrew] (Tel Aviv, 1980), 3–45.

12. Hannah Meisel Shohat, "The Rural Education of Young Women," *At This Time* 3 [Hebrew], 1916.

13. Margalit Shilo, "The Women's Farm at Kinneret, 1911–1917: A Solution to the Problem of the Working Woman in the Second Aliyah," in *Pioneers and Homemakers: Jewish Women in Pre-state Israel,* ed. Deborah S. Bernstein (Albany: State University Press of New York, 1922), 19–44.

14. CZA WIZO History File. A letter from Meisel to Froinlich dated November 14, 1971, mentions the meeting of Meisel and the leaders of WIZO.

15. Figler, *Lillian and Archie Freiman Biographies,* 77–78.

16. CZA S15 20/100, June 1920, translation of the original letter that was written in Hebrew.

17. Figler, *Lillian and Archie Freiman Biographies,* 8.

18. Farber, *The Echo of the Lake of Galilee Came this Far,* 9–60.

19. WIZO was founded in July 1920 by Vera Weizmann, Rebecca Sieff, Edith Eder, and Romana Goodman after the first three came back from a visit to Palestine in November 1919. Israel Sieff, *Memoirs* (London, 1970), 22–23.

20. The currency used in Palestine.

21. CZA L3 658. The budget for the year 1921, a sum of 20,000 EP, appears for the agricultural school for girls.

22. CZA S15/21111, a letter dated October 27, 1922, from Moshav Nahalal agreeing to give the land for the school.

23. Nahalal School archive, a letter from the Zionist Executive dated January 1, 1923, giving Meisel the first 200 EP for the school.

24. Chaya Brasz, Irgun Olei Holland, Jerusalem, 1993. 10.

25. See CZA Z4. A letter from the secretary of WIZO dated February 8, 1924, declaring WIZO responsibility for the school.

26. See CZA Z4, letter from the Zionist Executive to WIZO from February 27, 1924.

27. Chaim Weizmann, Lady Samuel (who congratulated in Hebrew), and representatives from the Histadrut and all the other workers' parties were there.

28. Figler, *Lillian and Archie Freiman Biographies,* 5–10; *Canadian Jewish Chronicle,* 25:3 (1927), 9.

29. *Emek Hefer* [Hebrew], ed. Yizhak Ben-Zvi (1970), 42, 244.

30. Ada Fishman, *The Women's Workers Movement* [Hebrew] (Tel Aviv, 1929), 8–32.

31. Figler, *Lillian and Archie Freiman Biographies,* 22–23.

Chapter 8

The International Council of Jewish Women (ICJW) was created in 1899 following the widespread success of the National Council of Jewish Women (NCJW) in the United States, a countrywide organization founded by Hannah Greenebaum Solomon (1858–1942) to unite American Jewish women and promote religious, educational, and philanthropic endeavors. The NCJW was established in 1893 at the conclusion of a four-day Jewish Women's Congress that took place as part of the World Parliament of Religions at the World's Columbian Exposition in Chicago.

Like the NCJW, the ICJW served as a vehicle for the social and political expression of Jewish women in Canada, Europe, Latin America, Australia and New Zealand, and Africa. In most respects, the ICJW followed in the footsteps of the NCJW, its well-organized and affluent sister organization. Before World War I, both groups maintained neutral positions vis-à-vis the issues of Zionism and Jewish colonization in Palestine. However, neither group ever went so far as to articulate an anti-Zionist stance similar to that of many male-dominated Jewish groups and societies in the West, nor did they discourage contact between Jewish and Zionist organizations in the philanthropic arena, even in relationship to the fledgling Yishuv.

The Balfour Declaration of 1917 as well as the tremendous Jewish suffering in the eastern war zone, including antisemitic violence that continued unabated in the postwar years, prompted the NCJW and ICJW to view Palestine as a practical option for alleviating the plight of East European Jewry. This attitudinal shift, Nelly Las asserts in the following chapter, occurred during the interwar period and paved the way for the two organizations' increasingly pro-Zionist activities and policies. In part, this gradual transformation reflected the broader context of the day, namely, growing worldwide Jewish popular support for the Yishuv and the Zionist enterprise. But it was also the result of deliberate efforts and political assessments made by the NCJW and ICJW organizational leadership. For example, NCJW leader Rebekah Bettleheim Kohut (1864–1951) proved to be a formidable influence on the group's conversion to Zionist sympathies.

The process described above reached its zenith in the late 1920s, when the NCJW and ICJW championed the so-called expansion of the Jewish Agency to include active non-Zionist representation and participation. Indeed, this episode marked a crucial turning point in relations between the World Zionist Organization (WZO) and virtually all major non-Zionist Jewish leaders and groups in the West. WZO president Chaim Weizmann (1874–1952), together with Louis Marshall (1856–1929) and Felix Warburg (1871–1937), the preeminent American non-Zionist leaders and philanthropists in the United States, spearheaded this venture. It was not only unprecedented but essentially committed all the major Jewish organizations of the West to building the Jewish national home. The idea of an expanded Jewish Agency found considerable support, as Las points out, among the NCJW and ICJW leaders and their respective constituencies. Strictly speaking, throughout the pre-state era both the NCJW and ICJW remained neutral on matters of official Zionist policy making. Nevertheless, they engaged fully in the mounting Jewish public campaign to promote the Yishuv and assist in its stabilization and development. By the eve of World War II, the NCJW and ICJW were deeply involved in several social service and charitable projects in Palestine. Following the war's end, news of the Holocaust and the European Jewish refugee crisis hastened the adoption of nominally Zionist orientations and programs by both organizations. That they did so without in any way diminishing their diaspora commitments is testimony to the organizational elasticity, ingenuity, and stewardship of the NCJW and ICJW.

The Impact of Zionism on the International Council of Jewish Women, 1914–1957

Nelly Las

The study of the Zionist contribution of the International Council of Jewish Women can appear paradoxical when we consider that this organization never defined itself in terms of Zionism, despite all the events of this century, and despite its bond with Israel.

Since Theodor Herzl's publication of *The Jewish State*,[1] Jewish attitudes to Zionism have been complex. Jewish women, who began to develop independent public activity at the turn of the century, were not exempt from debating the issues raised by Zionism. At the time, some Jewish women tried to extend their social and humanitarian services to Jewish communities abroad and to create an international organization. After successive attempts and a long break during World War II, a structured institution with well-defined principles and aims was finally established in 1949.[2] Today, the International Council of Jewish Women is an umbrella organization for forty-seven affiliates representing approximately two million members throughout the world.[3] It defines itself as working "for the benefit of all humanity, with the emphasis on Jews, women and the State of Israel."[4]

This essay deals essentially with the period before the establishment of the State of Israel and during the first decade of its existence. It should be noted that before the idea of a Jewish state was widely accepted, all official support by Jewish organizations was considered a positive "contribution" to the Zionist cause.

Zionism was in fact not of focal importance to the basic ideology of the International Council of Jewish Women when it was established. However, in any study of organized Jewish solidarity, since the First Zionist Congress, it is impossible to ignore the Zionist aspects, whether positive or negative.[5] As the Zionist movement and the Zionist enterprise expanded and developed, most of the important Jewish organizations were forced to express their views on Zionism. Some supported Zionism wholeheartedly, several were prepared to support Jewish settlement in *Erez Israel* without political Zionism, and others were fiercely opposed to it.

This essay focuses on attitudes and disputes regarding Zionism within a non-Zionist organization[6] that moved, over the time, from ambivalence to strong support to the Zionist enterprise. This study combines two important issues in contemporary Jewish history: the participation of women in Jewish communities through their organizations, and the attitudes of diaspora Jews to Zionism from a women's perspective.

Jewish Women's Organizations: A New Model of Jewish Sisterhood

While some research has been carried out in recent years on the relationship between Jewish organizations and Zionism, research into women's organizations is still in its early stages. A basic question that often arises regarding research into women's organizations is its relevance to larger questions. Studies of organizations run the risk of getting bogged down by descriptions of the bureaucracy inherent in the routine life of an organization. However, this kind of research can also yield insights, as the history of a Jewish women's organization reflects general trends in Jewish society. These insights reveal the status of Jewish women in the community as well as processes at work in the Jewish world at large. In addition, they are the best yardstick of Jewish women's involvement in the community and in society. In contrast to biographies, which emphasize the achievements of unique women, research into women's organizations provides information about ordinary Jewish women—not only women who are considered feminists and revolutionaries, but homemakers like our mothers and grandmothers, those women who do not necessarily leave traces in history. At the end of the nineteenth century, Jewish women organized themselves for the first time on a national scale. The pioneer organization was the National Council of Jewish Women in America (NCJW), which was followed by many others around the world. Some of them defined themselves as "Zionist," like Hadassah and the Women's International Zionist Organization (WIZO), with the primary purpose of assisting the Zionist enterprise. Others concentrated on providing humanitarian and philanthropic assistance at the local level but nevertheless expressed various opinions regarding Zionism.

Since the beginning of the twentieth century, some of these local Jewish women's organizations tried to establish activities on an international level, following the initiative of the American National Council of Jewish Women. They modeled themselves after the International Council of Women, which was established in America in 1888.[7] Whenever the International Council of Women held a meeting, it invited the leaders of the Jewish women's organizations. These conventions gave Jewish women an opportunity to meet, to strengthen their bonds, discuss problems common to Jews in various countries, study organization methods, and try to devise solutions to local and global concerns.

After the meeting of the International Council of Women held in London in 1899, Hanna G. Solomon, president of the National Council of Jewish Women in America, encouraged the creation of the Union of Jewish Women of England. At the next meeting in Berlin in 1904, she helped to create the German Jewish women's organization, the Jüdischer Frauenbund.

That same year, in an address to Temple Israel in Saint Louis, Hannah G. Solomon expressed the importance of an international bond among Jewish women: "And so we need internationalism for Jewish women, that shall bring them together to utilize their strength in perpetuating the great moral truths we hold for the world. . . ."[8]

In May 1914, at a conference of the International Council of Women held in Rome, the leaders of the three Jewish women's organizations, from America, Britain, and Germany, decided to establish a worldwide organization of Jewish women. A brief notice to this effect appeared in the *American Jewish Year Book* of the same year, announcing the establishment of an International Society of Jewish Women.[9]

A great deal of courage and daring was needed to establish an international women's organization at this time. For one thing, travel from one distant country to another was not as developed and as safe as it is today. Furthermore, the magnitude of the task was overwhelming. Many Jews the world over, in dire straits caused by poverty, persecution, and pogroms, sought refuge in friendlier countries. Among the waves of Jewish immigrants, women were the most vulnerable, especially single women: young girls traveling alone, abandoned wives *(agunot)*, and destitute women. By this time, Jewish women's organizations were providing extensive social services and humanitarian assistance in their own countries: helping immigrants, the sick, and the elderly. Under the auspices of an international organization, these humanitarian services could be elevated to a new level: they were now available to tens of thousands of Jews in distress throughout the world, in particular eastern European Jews who needed help desperately.

During those years, in addition to humanitarian services and philanthropy, a new way to help Jews was suggested by the Zionist movement: instead of finding refuge in a foreign country, to build a homeland in *Erez Israel*.

Jewish Women's Organizations and Zionism: Ambiguous Attitudes

What was the position of the new international organization of Jewish women on Zionism? Although it had no official position on Zionism, its leading members had strong opinions on the subject.

When the ICJW was created in 1914, Zionism was still a theoretical concept, a kind of utopia. Herzl's dream of statehood lost impetus after his death in 1904. A small minority of Jews supported the Zionist movement, but many opposed it.

For example, we know that Bertha Papenheim, who headed the Jewish women's movement in Germany for almost twenty years, the Jüdischer Frauenbund, was fiercely opposed to Zionism. As a German patriot, she was convinced that she already had a homeland. She claimed that Zionism led to the breaking up of families, had no respect for Jewish tradition, and in addition was not sufficiently concerned by the problems of women.[10] However, within her organization, which numbered thirty-five thousand in 1914, the question of Palestine was often debated.[11] Regardless of the president's opinion, support of Palestine was added to the organization's platform after World War I.[12] The Zionist question was also discussed within the leadership of the American National Council of Jewish Women, especially after the establishment of the competing organization of Zionist women, Hadassah. Although the official position of the National Council was neutral, various opinions can be found among the members. Many of them, essentially Reform women, were opposed to Zionism in accordance with the trends of the American Reform movement.[13] Others, like Rebekah Kohut who was "converted" to Zionism by Herzl (whom she met on one of her visits to Austria), had a positive attitude.[14]

Those who held strong Zionist views shifted their affiliation to Hadassah when it was founded.[15] It is important to note, though, that the Council's founders were on excellent terms with the founder of Hadassah, Henrietta Szold, who was universally admired. Long before her Zionist conversion, Szold delivered a speech at the first Congress of American Jewish women in 1893, at which the National Council of Jewish Women was founded. Years later, she delivered her very first Zionist speech to the Baltimore group of the Council, and after she founded Hadassah, she often invited NCJW leaders to visit Palestine.[16]

The 1923–1929 Congresses of Jewish Women: Forging an International Bond in a Time of Violence

At first, the international organization of Jewish women established in 1914 remained theoretical. The opportunity to become truly an international Jewish sisterhood would occur in 1920, when the American NCJW sent delegates to Europe to study the problems of European Jewry in the aftermath of World War I and to explore ways of assisting those in distress. This Reconstruction committee was headed by Rebekah Kohut, a founder of the NCJW.[17]

The year 1920 was far different from 1914, the year the ICJW was formally established. Europe lay shattered and bleeding in the wake of a harsh, cruel war. However, Jews had also experienced some positive changes during this period: Jewish settlement in *Erez Israel* had been expanded, and the Balfour Declaration of 1917 had legitimized Zionism, which until then had been considered by many to be merely a theoretical concept.

The misery and suffering of the Jews of eastern Europe stood out in sharp relief against the background of these political gains. The situation of the Jews was desperate. Thousands had been massacred in the Ukraine, thousands more were hunted and persecuted in Poland, and masses of refugees were wandering from town to town throughout Europe. In the large cities of Germany, Austria, Belgium, Holland, they crowded into hostels run by Jewish communities, which were unable to cope with such vast numbers.

In 1920 and 1921 the American NCJW sent two teams of professional social workers to Europe who tried to help the many orphans and to guide candidates seeking to emigrate. They organized English classes to facilitate the integration of the future immigrants into the United States. Rebekah Kohut initiated the establishment of Jewish women's organizations in Riga, Rotterdam, The Hague, Amsterdam, and Antwerp, in order to guarantee emigration services in all the ports.[18]

Another task was to organize a World Congress of Jewish Women to renew ties with European Jewish women, which had been suspended during the war. This was to be the forum for deliberations on the urgent problems facing postwar European Jewry. The congress was scheduled to be held in May 1923 in Vienna, where the city's notorious antisemitic shock troops had gone about pasting virulent anti-Jewish posters on the walls.[19]

The history of the International Council of Jewish Women between the two world wars can be summarized by two impressive conferences of Jewish women held in Vienna in 1923 and in Hamburg in 1929. These meetings were initiated and financed largely by the NCJW of America, which sent large delegations. The president of these World Congresses of Jewish Women was Rebekah Kohut.

The first Congress of Jewish Women convened in Vienna in May 1923 in an impressive setting and with massive press coverage, in the presence of the Austrian president, the mayor of Vienna, the chief of police, and many Viennese literary figures and politicians. Delegates from Jewish women's organizations from over twenty countries were present, as well as leaders of the local Jewish community.

The five main topics discussed over six days were the duties of the Jewish woman within the community, the problem of refugees and orphans, the situation of homeless girls, aid for emigration, and support of Palestine.[20]

The frightening sights witnessed by some congress attendees brought the hardships and suffering of thousands of Jewish refugees and orphans into sharp relief. Pogroms and persecution had rendered many of them homeless. At one point during the congress, when the representatives from eastern Europe reported on the terrible plight of Jews in Russia and the Ukraine, emotions were so intense that proceedings were halted for a few minutes.

Among the suggestions for relieving Jewish sufferings, Zionism was accepted as a practical option, although political action was still rejected. Relocation to Palestine was a humanitarian solution and a way of providing sanctuary for the refugees.

During the congress, the women raised various suggestions concerning Palestine. The representative from Holland directed attention to the need to take part in the work of reconstructing Palestine, which she designated as the duty of the whole of the Jewish people. Ms. Margulies from Berlin submitted a resolution, which was accepted, in favor of aiding the *halu-zim*.[21] Among the final resolutions adopted by the congress, the Palestine proposal was adopted unanimously with great acclamation:

By the Balfour Declaration and its acceptance in international law, by the Treaty of San Remo and the acceptance of the Palestine Mandate by Great Britain, Palestine has become the homeland of the Jews. It appears, therefore, to be the duty of all Jews to cooperate in the social-economic reconstruction of Palestine and to assist in the settlement of Jews in that country. By declaring themselves prepared to take part in this work, the Congress of Jewish Women emphasizes that it does not bind itself thereby in any way to any political program.[22]

The resolutions made at the congress attest to the unanimous support expressed by the women's organizations for settlement in *Erez Israel*. Jewish hardship and distress, on the one hand, and the Balfour Declaration and settlement expansion on the other, legitimized and justified the Zionist enterprise, as a humanitarian solution.

Despite their admiration for the political achievements of the Yishuv, however, the leaders of Jewish women's organizations found it difficult to support Zionism in practice. They went with the flow, never being daring or original in their attitude to Zionism. In practice, they were identical to other non-Zionist organizations. This ambivalence and confusion is evident in Hannah G. Solomon's autobiography *Fabric of My Life (1946)* where she describes her visit to *Erez Israel*:

. . . and, at last, Jerusalem! Zionist and non-Zionist unite in deepest tribute to the magnificent achievement in Palestine. . . . Miss Szold introduced us to the wonders wrought in Palestine, and perhaps our most poignant memory of our World Tour was the revelation of the "Promised Land," present and future. Of course, we were prepared for great accomplishment, and found it, but there were unimaginable surprises, everywhere: Pagliacci, sung in Hebrew; a Jewish Woman's Club, advocating "equal rights for women"; . . . Since my visit, I believe in a Zionist state less than ever, but I do hope all the persecuted may find sanctuary there, under adequate protection. And I admit that what the Zionists already have done is the greatest adventure of the century. To take a country, a wasteland, and make it bloom again in the hope of its becoming a resting place for hunted people, with the ideal of Jewish education and culture, to spread this ideal throughout the world, is an unmatched goal in human history! Most of us are satisfied to let destiny guide, believing God holds the reins. Now, we know we must act, as well as pray.[23]

The second World Congress of Jewish Women was convened in 1929 in Hamburg, Germany. As in 1923, the event was a show of Jewish women's solidarity on an international scale. This congress was attended by two hundred representatives, including a large delegation of very dynamic and energetic German women. Delegates from fourteen countries came together to discuss subjects of common interest and to form a world organization of Jewish women, as agreed upon in the previous congress.

Congress participants were welcomed warmly by the mayor of Hamburg and by the local Jewish community. The various sessions dealt with general concerns of Jewish communities and with problems faced by Jewish women in particular: Jewish education, the struggle against antisemitism, and the tragedy of abandoned wives (*agunot*).[24]

This time, the question of Palestine was more accentuated than in the previous conference. The burning issue of the year was the cooperation of Zionists and non-Zionists within the framework of the Jewish Agency for Palestine, which would constitute a bridge between philanthropy and political Zionism.

At the start of the congress, a telegram was read from Louis Marshall, president of the American Jewish Committee. He expressed "the hope that Jewish women would decide to take part in the work of the Jewish Agency." Anita Mueller-Cohen, a leading Viennese philanthropist, spoke about the work accomplished by Jewish women in Palestine and said it was the duty of women of all countries to help develop Palestine. Irma Lindheim, the president of Hadassah, who was present at the congress, urged the congress to participate in the efforts carried out by the Jewish Agency. Rebekah Kohut also declared herself in favor of the Jewish Agency, "because Felix Warburg and Louis Marshall were members." A heated debate followed. Finally, the most important resolution taken at the congress was "to cooperate in the work of building Palestine."[25]

These two international Jewish women's congresses attracted a great deal of publicity but were not immediately followed by action. These inspiring meetings enabled Jewish women to meet and exchange views. The delegates had the opportunity of expressing themselves on important issues and participating in determining the destiny of the Jewish people. They were recognized by Jewish communal leaders and by the most prestigious Jewish institutions. However, this success was not converted into practice, and the activities of Jewish women's organizations were not renewed until after World War II. Clearly, international action was extremely problematic given the conflict and crisis in Europe. After the rise of Nazism, most European women's organizations were inoperative, especially the organization of German women. The others lacked means and support. Organizations that were able to pursue their activity did so independently. The American National Council of Jewish Women participated in social action and rescue work. On the question of Palestine, it vacillated between neutrality and formal support. For example, at the American Jewish Conference of 1943, the NCJW took a neutral position. However, some months later, it published a declaration strongly condemning the White Paper of 1939 and reaffirming its support of the upbuilding of Palestine in the spirit of the Balfour Declaration.[26]

The Reconstitution of the ICJW (June 1949): From Discontinuous Congresses to a Unified Organization

Immediately after World War II, the American National Council of Jewish Women decided to revive its overseas program and to take part in the rescue actions of the Joint Distribution Committee.[27] At the NCJW convention held in Dallas in 1946, Mildred G. Welt, the president of the NCJW at the time, proposed that the international Jewish women's organization which was never formally structured and which had been effectively dead for nearly twenty years, be reestablished. Her proposal was unanimously accepted.[28]

The first problem facing this initiative was to revive the organization after so much time. Who could even remember its brief existence? Twenty years had elapsed, years of extermination, of clandestine activity and massive displacements of Jewish populations. Some of the European activists had disappeared; others had resigned from public life. Some, however, remained convinced of the necessity of reestablishing the international Jewish women's organization in accordance with the principles that had guided its creation at the beginning of the century.

The International Council's last president, Rebekah Kohut, was still alive. For the sake of continuity, she was asked to head the organization, even if only in name. Although she was too old and not in good health, she agreed to accept the position.

The International Council's Reconstitution Committee set to work immediately. It began by sending letters in the name of the president of the American NCJW to Jewish women's organizations that had been in contact with the NCJW in previous years. Letters sent to France, England, Mexico, Switzerland, Belgium, Australia, South Africa, and Brazil made the following appeal:

We in the United States believe that there is a great need for the opportunity of meeting with the Jewish women of the world whose interest, work and problems undoubtedly are similar to ours. We realize how much we can gain from each other. . . . [29]

Enthusiastic replies were received from organizations such as those in Australia, England, South Africa and Switzerland:

The responses indicated that the women outside the United States are eager—are hungry for any assistance, stimulation, inspiration we could give them through meeting together. The promptness with which the replies came in and the contents of their letters showed that the Jewish women all over the world look to us for any ray of hope we can offer them . . . [30]

After two years of preparation, the international meeting was held in Paris from May 29 to June 1, 1949, at the Council Home, a home for single women that the American NCJW had founded as part of its overseas program.

Officially represented Jewish women's organizations included the National Council of Jewish Women of America, the National Council of Jewish Women of Canada, the Union of Jewish Women of South Africa, the Union of Jewish Women of Australia, the Union of Jewish Women and the League of Jewish Women of England, and the Union of Jewish Women of Switzerland.

These organizations formed the nucleus of the new international council. The other delegates were from Holland, Greece, North Africa, and Italy. Israel was represented by the Israeli ambassador's wife, who was invited at the last minute.[31] The participants did not reach any major decisions, but the meeting helped to give the ICJW some of its basic structures and to define its principles, most of which are relevant to this day.

The ICJW was defined as a federation of national women's organizations, independent of each other and apolitical in nature. Its objects were essentially "to promote friendly relations and understanding among Jewish women of all countries; to further the best and highest interests of humanity; to uphold and strengthen the bonds between Jewish communities throughout the world; to support the principles of the United Nations Bill of Human Rights; and to improve the status of women."[32]

The vague and general character of these initial aims can be explained by the need to include many organizations with a wide range of opinions in order to bring the organization into being. There is barely any reference to Judaism, and no reference at all to the recently created State of Israel. Among the basic principles of the ICJW, the concern with projecting an image of objectivity and of distance from Zionism was maintained, as was the concern with being a humanitarian organization.

Strengthening Ties with Israel

Theoretical principles do not always stand firm in the face of reality. The situation of European Jews after the *Shoah,* and the difficulties confronting the newly born State of Israel, helped to shape the agenda of the Jewish organizations of the diaspora, especially with regard to Israel.

The newly created State of Israel intrigued and excited the members of ICJW. Most of its affiliated organizations had begun developing various aid programs for Israel, each according to its character. Major funds were devoted to the Hebrew University of Jerusalem, a symbol of Jewish culture and education. Even non-Zionist women envisioned the State of Israel as a source of Jewish culture rather than a political center.

After the 1954 convention of the ICJW, the "Council of Women's Organizations in Israel" joined the ICJW. This opportunity to develop a relationship with Israeli women was warmly welcomed by diaspora Jewish women.[33]

Still, it took until 1957 for the ICJW to pass a resolution supporting Israel, which was done at its convention in Jerusalem. The resolution stressed that "ICJW urges its affiliate organizations to give their support to the continuing social, economic and cultural upbuilding of Israel."[34]

This declaration of support for Israel was not a clear profession of Zionist faith. The ICJW continued to set itself apart from Zionist organizations, although its activists maintained excellent ties with their Zionist colleagues. Aid to Israel was not yet a central concern, but one of many. With time, a formal beginning paved the way to personal friendship between the women of Israel and the diaspora, which eventually led to greater involvement and finally to an unconditional support of Israel by the ICJW itself.

Conclusion

The period I have focused on could be called the "prehistory" of the ICJW as we know it today. Although this activity did not leave many traces in the history books, the first stages of Jewish women's public action on a worldwide scale are historically significant. The drama of the ICJW during this period stems from the huge and seemingly impossible tasks it aspired to, on one hand, and the tumultuous events that were to stand in its way on the other.

The ICJW was ambivalent toward Zionism. Nonetheless, like many other groups at the time, it contributed to Zionism by supporting Jewish settlement as a haven for Jews in distress, rather than as a focus of political action.

General enthusiasm for Zionism was apparent at the 1923 and 1929 congresses. Though delegates were sent by many different countries representing organizations with different points of view, resolutions were almost unanimously in favor of assisting the settlement enterprise. The women were united in a feeling of common purpose: to help Jews in need. They differed regarding the way to achieve this goal or the terms to be used. This philanthropic approach, which only partially supported Zionism, was widespread among Jews at the time.

The Zionist leadership, then confronted with a large opposition within Jewish communities, welcomed any expression of support with delight. Supportive declarations, in a public forum with press coverage, could have great impact. In addition to their political value, they could benefit fund-raising for Palestine, which was of critical importance.

For a historian observing a community in transition, efforts to sustain the status quo can be as significant as change. The International Council of Jewish Women was reestablished in 1949. Although the momentous events of the Holocaust and the establishment of the State of Israel had occurred in the interim, the views of the ICJW did not undergo a drastic change.

More than formerly, the ICJW defined itself as a universal, nonsectarian organization, without giving priority to Jewish causes or to the newly established State of Israel. This position was not a result of indifference to historical events, but quite the opposite. In a period that followed atrocious events, many Jews experienced a lack of self-confidence and feelings of anxiety. Diaspora Jews did not know what the consequences of the establishment of a Jewish state would be for them. ICJW leaders felt they had to stress their "universality" in order to avoid accusations of dual loyalty and sectarianism. In a climate of great change and anxiety, it was also important to maintain a consensus and an atmosphere of pluralism within the reborn organization.

Still, these views were not only the product of rational thought but were also deeply ingrained in the ideology of the organization. Since its conception at the beginning of the century, this ideology was based on the Jewish sense of morality, and a firm belief in the particular moral and educational mission of women, "for the higher good of humanity."

Over the next few years, this universalism was to give way to involvement in particularly Jewish missions and with the State of Israel. It would appear that it is difficult for Jews to maintain objectivity and universality when faced with the distress of their people. This "slippage" is in fact a process of discovering one's Jewish identity. "Jewish revival" or "self-discovery of one's Jewish identity" has periodically occurred in times of crisis: after the Dreyfus case, after the Kishinev pogroms (1903–1905), after the Ukrainian pogroms (1918–1921), after the Arab riots of 1929, after the *Shoah,* and after the successive wars in Israel since the establishment of the state. The ICJW was not immune to this historical process, and it too has become successively more "Jewish" and "Zionist."

In fact, as has been shown, the Yishuv and subsequently the State of Israel became early focal points of identification for women active in Jewish organizations, although their terminology (i.e., "Zionist," "non-Zionist," or "philanthropist") did not always reflect this identification.

The ICJW's ambivalence toward Zionism was resolved over time by several factors that combine Jewish solidarity with historical events. The achievements of the State of Israel, on the one hand, proved its capacity to save Jews in danger, while at the same time a new kind of animosity in the name of "anti-Zionism" appeared. Meanwhile, the close ties the ICJW leaders developed with their colleagues in Israel gave diaspora women a better understanding of the needs and the existential dilemmas of the Israeli citizens.

Today, in the United Nations where they are represented, WIZO, ICJW, and other Jewish organizations are virtually indistinguishable in their attitude toward Israel. Paradoxically, what began as an apparent preconception that equated "Jewish" with "Zionism" has become a historical truth. However, this particularism does not mean sectarianism. When the situation of Israel improves, the International Council of Jewish Women concentrates its efforts on humanitarian issues and social assistance, according to its basic credo: "For all mankind, without distinction of race, color and creed."[35] A recent example was demonstrated during the cruel events in the Balkans. Without neglecting Israel and the problems of Jews, the ICJW, like many Jewish organizations, has shown that it is possible to combine the specific and the universal; it is possible to preserve its own identity while still identifying with the persecuted of all creeds and nations.

Notes

1. The first edition of *Der Judenstaat* was published in Vienna in 1896 and translated to seven languages (in English it was titled *The Jewish State*).

2. For the sake of convenience, the name "International Council of Jewish Women" or "ICJW" (which came into use only in 1949) will be used in this paper to refer to the organization since its inception at the beginning of the century.

3. ICJW report, May 1999.

4. ICJW Archives, Hebrew University of Jerusalem, Givat Ram, 1960 Convention.

5. The First Zionist Congress, which convened in Basle in 1897, raised controversy among diaspora leaders.

6. "Non-Zionist" is a term used to indicate a Jew who does not support political Zionism (the idea of a Jewish State for all the Jewish people) but who is ready to support a Jewish settlement in *Erez Israel* as a humanitarian action. "Non-Zionist" is different from "anti-Zionist."

7. *Become Visible: Women in European History,* ed. R. Bridenthal and C. Koonz (Boston: Houghton Mifflin, 1977), 337.

8. Hannah Greenebaum Solomon, *A Sheaf of Leaves* (Chicago: Privately printed, 1911), 126.

9. *American Jewish Yearbook,* 16 (1914–1915), 200.

10. Marion Kaplan, *The Jewish Feminist Movement in Germany: The Campaigns of the Jüdischer Frauenbund 1914-1938* (London: Greenwood Press, 1979), 48–49.

11. Ibid. 77.

12. Ibid. 87.

13. Rosa Sonnenschein, "The National Council of Jewish Women and Our Dream of Nationality," *American Jewess,* October 1896, 28–32.

14. Rebekah Kohut, *My Portion* (New York: Albert & Charles Boni, 1927), 218–221.

15. *Papers of the Jewish Women's Congress Held at Chicago: September 4, 5, 6, and 7, 1893* (Philadelphia: Jewish Publication Society of America, 1894).

16. NCJW Collection, Library of Congress, Box 102.

17. Rebekah Kohut, *More Yesterday* (New York: Block, 1950), 125–128.

18. Ibid.

19. *JCB News Bulletin,* London, 7 May 1923, 3.

20. Ibid., 7, 8, 10, 12, 14, 16 May 1923.

21. Ibid.

22. Ibid., 16 May 1923, 2.

23. Hannah Greenebaum Solomon, *Fabric of my Life* (New York: Bloch, 1946), 200.

24. *JTA Bulletin,* 6 June 1929, 23.

25. Ibid., 8 June 1929, 6.

26. Mildred G. Welt, "The National Council of Jewish Women," *American Jewish Yearbook,* 46 (1944–1945), 59.

27. *Council Woman,* September–October 1945.

28. File "History," ICJW Archives (Arch/I).

29. Ibid., Correspondence, 1947–1949.

30. Ibid.

31. Ibid. (The way this invitation was issued provoked controversy among the ICJW leaders).

32. Ibid.; Minutes of the 1949 Meeting

33. Nelly Las, *Jewish Women in a Changing World—A History of the International Council of Jewish Women (1901-1995)* (Jerusalem: Avraham Harman Institute of Contemporary Jewry, 1996), 53–54.

34. Minutes of the 1957 ICJW convention, ICJW Archives (Arch./5).

35. Ibid.

Chapter 9

Hadassah can be viewed as a barometer of the rise and success of Zionism in the American Jewish setting. Imbued since its inception in 1912 with the twin ideals of promoting Jewish life in Palestine and harnessing American Jewish idealism to the larger Zionist project of building a better society, Hadassah in many ways prefigured the Copernican shift in American Judaism away from pre-Zionist conceptions that held strong in the nineteenth and early twentieth centuries—for example, the anti-intentionalist and traditionalist impulse of Orthodoxy and the anti-nationalist universalism of Reform Judaism—and toward a new Jewish consciousness that placed a premium on the notion of rebuilding the Jewish national home in Palestine.

Curiously enough, although the story of Hadassah has been told many times by different authors, there is to date no full-length scholarly study of this central American Jewish and Zionist institution. In the chapter that follows, Mira Katzburg-Yungman delineates a broad outline of Hadassah's scope and activity, focusing mostly on the pre-state period. First, the essay traces the ideological composition and membership profile of Hadassah's constituents. Second, it assesses the range of Hadassah's activities in the Yishuv and emphasizes the links between Hadassah and various Palestinian Jewish agencies and institutions. Finally, it compares Hadassah's activity in the early years of statehood to that of other American Jewish and Zionist groups. In summing up, Katzburg-Yungman posits that Hadassah's vitality and success stemmed from its multifaceted agenda and synthesis of American Jewish and Zionist idealism. In other words, she argues, because Hadassah went far beyond what were then considered to be, strictly speaking, women's issues and concerns, it plugged an important gap in the Zionist spectrum and offered middle-class American Jewish women opportunities for social and political engagement that were otherwise strikingly infrequent. In time, as Hadassah swelled to become the largest Zionist membership organization in the United States, it assumed a key position and ultimately played a crucial role in the success of the Zionist enterprise in Palestine and later the State of Israel.

Women and Zionist Activity in *Erez Israel*: The Case of Hadassah, 1913–1958

Mira Katzburg-Yungman

Introduction

Hadassah is the finest expression, par excellence, of how Zionist women in America organized themselves. Since the 1920s, it has also been the largest U.S. Zionist organization. Hadassah has a lengthy history of activity in Palestine and later Israel, going back to 1913—about a year after it was founded in New York by Henrietta Szold—and continuing to this very day, with the exception of a short period during the First World War. This activity, outstanding for its scope, continuity, stability and diversity, encompasses efforts in the spheres of health and medical services, and for the welfare of children and youth through support of Youth Aliyah, vocational training, and more. This article attempts to ascertain what enabled Hadassah to continue its activity over such a long period of time, during different historical periods and despite changing conditions. It traces Hadassah's progress through the end of Israel's first decade, a juncture that marked the end of its role as the founder of modern health services in *Erez Israel* and a significant shift in its activity as a result of the transition to statehood.[1]

Hadassah in *Erez Israel* from the American Jewish Perspective

An analysis of Hadassah's activity in *Erez Israel* leads to the conclusion that its efforts were firmly rooted in Jewish tradition, in general, in the American Jewish philanthropic tradition in particular, and also in the traditional role of women in Jewish society.

From the perspective of Jewish tradition, Hadassah's medical undertakings were the embodiment of three central *mizvot* [religious command-

This article is based on the author's forthcoming book, *American Women Zionists: Hadassah in Historical Perspective*, to be published by the Littman Library of Jewish Civilization in 2005.

ments] with which women were traditionally involved: *zedakah* [charity], *gemilut hasadim* [deeds of loving-kindness], and *bikur holim* [lit. visiting the sick, but in practice caring for the ill]. In traditional Jewish society, women were not obligated to pray like men, did not study Talmud and other parts of the Jewish law, nor did they participate in the management of communal affairs. They were limited to raising their children and performing acts of charity, thus enabling them to fulfill certain commandments. Even after secularization became common in much of Jewish society, women continued to be active in these fields, which had now become the responsibility of modern social welfare organizations.[2] Hadassah's health and medical services were also intimately connected to professions that in turn-of-the-century America were identified as women's professions: nursing, and especially public health.[3]

These conditions produced a felicitous combination of undertakings with which a wide spectrum of American Jewish women could identify, and which enabled their husbands to willingly contribute financial support for the philanthropic Zionist objectives that Hadassah aimed to achieve. The establishment and support of hospitals, Hadassah's central undertaking in *Erez Israel,* stemmed from a widely accepted historical tradition among American Jews. Many Jewish hospitals were established across the United States—a philanthropic endeavor of the highest order for American Jewry—even before the Civil War. It was also quite common for wealthy American Jews to bequest sums to hospitals in their wills.[4]

What further characterizes Hadassah's activities in *Erez Israel* and the State of Israel is the traditional Jewish emphasis on providing relief and succor to Jews outside the United States. "Rescue work, the secular counterpart of the traditional Jewish commandment of *pidyon shevuyim*" [ransoming of captives],[5] was a central theme in Hadassah's ideology and the basis of its practical work: medical and health services, support of Youth Aliyah, and—in a wider sense—vocational training and education.[6] The centrality of rescue work in the ideology and practice of Hadassah was expressed in the organization's choice of its name: Hadassah, the Hebrew for Esther, was the young woman who saved the Jews, as chronicled in the book of Esther (2:7). The rescue factor was most overtly manifested when Hadassah assumed responsibility for Youth Aliyah, which it described as a singular, humanitarian effort, dedicated to the rescue of children and youth, to their rehabilitation and reeducation. From this point of view, Hadassah was one of several modern-day Jewish rescue organizations for which there was wide consensus and support within the American Jewish community. Indeed, Hadassah received more widespread support—both from American Jewish women and from

American Jewry in general—then did other women's organizations, which turned to more limited sectors of American Jewish women.

Fundamental Ideas of Hadassah

The Primary Objective

Hadassah's primary objective is to ensure the continuity of the Jewish people and Judaism.[7] From this point of view, Hadassah does not differ from the mainstream of American Zionism as personified in the Zionist Organization of America (ZOA), one of whose primary obligations is to ensure Jewish survival in the United States. That obligation has two facets: in the physical realm, to safeguard the day-to-day existence of individual Jews;[8] in the spiritual realm, to ensure the continuity of Judaism as a culture. This double obligation was expressed in the organizational aims drafted at Hadassah's very inception: "In *Erez Israel*: to promote Jewish institutions, in America: to foster Zionist ideals."[9] These objectives, differing both in essence and in their geographical application, have been the basis for Hadassah's undertakings through its lengthy history in the two arenas of its activity: in *Erez Israel* (the physical realm) and in America (the spiritual realm). Thus Hadassah's highest purpose is a general objective acceptable, to a very great degree, to the entire American Jewish community, enabling the movement to turn to American Jewry in its widest sense and not only to narrow sectors within it.

Aspiring to a Mass Zionist Movement

One of Hadassah's basic principles was that it should be a mass Zionist movement for American Jewish women, i.e., that every American Jewish woman should be counted among its members. That Hadassah was to be a popular, mass movement, and not an elitist one, was a matter of ideological principle, not organizational tactics.[10] In this, Hadassah was directly influenced by the outlook of Louis D. Brandeis, who believed that every American Jew should be a Zionist, and that American Zionism must become a mass movement. The movement's members, he believed, were its major asset and power base. The basis for fund-raising on behalf of *Erez Israel*, he asserted, was that the movement's members "provided muscle with which to persuade governments" and "money for Palestinian colonies." For Brandeis, the Zionist movement was a financial and political means to achieve Zionist objectives.[11]

Brandeis's outlook became an integral and basic element of Hadassah's ideology. Its leaders, too, believed that it must not be a movement for the elite, for in that case it would not be able to gain wide public support.[12] In order to enable every Jewish woman to feel at home in Hadassah, no member, whether an old-timer or a newcomer, should be faced with demands that she would be unable to fulfill. On the contrary, every effort must be made to meet the members' needs.[13] Like Brandeis, Hadassah's leaders thought that in numbers they would find the strength, including the political power, necessary to fulfill their organization's objectives.[14]

Thus, the target of creating a popular, mass movement of and for Jewish women shaped the policy and the steps adopted by Hadassah. This was reflected in the daily activity of its officers and in their efforts to make all levels of the movement aware of the fact that a broad membership was vital for its continued existence.[15] Much energy was expended on increasing membership: in the 1940s and 1950s officers at the local level were under constant pressure to recruit new members, and the National Board had recourse to sundry tactics for that same purpose. Most outstanding of these measures during the period in which the State of Israel was established was the decision adopted at the Annual Convention in 1949 to inaugurate "Life Membership." A life member did not pay annual fees; rather she made a onetime payment. Life membership fees did not always come out of the member's own pocket: Hadassah expected that its members would acquire life memberships for their daughters on their wedding day and for their newborn granddaughters.[16]

An Apolitical Movement

Hadassah's aim to become a mass movement naturally led to a second principle: it would be apolitical—unaffiliated and unidentified with any political party, whether in the United States or in *Erez Israel*. To this formulation one should add the traditional consensus in the West that political involvement is unsuitable for women. Indeed, the largest women's organizations, among non-Jews as well, are involved mainly in humanitarian efforts.[17]

Hadassah scrupulously avoided any identification with political parties. Though during the first years of the State of Israel there was much affinity between Hadassah and the Progressive Party, Hadassah purposely and openly avoided turning this into a formal relationship. It did deviate from this policy on one occasion, on the internal Zionist front: when the World Confederation of General Zionists was established in 1946 and Hadassah joined its ranks. In fact, some Hadassah leaders were among its

founders, including Rose Halprin, who played a central role in the confederation.[18]

The implications of Hadassah's relationship to the World Confederation of General Zionists become clear when that movement is compared
with WIZO—the Women's International Zionist Organization. WIZO,
which saw itself as an absolutely apolitical movement, strictly avoided
any relationship with political parties, even on the internal Zionist front.
As a result, from the early 1930s to the late 1950s, it played no organizational role in the administrative organs of the Jewish Agency and had no
representatives on the institutions of the World Zionist Organization.
This despite the fact that in many parts of the world, as one observer
noted, WIZO was "the element that holds the Zionist movement together, without which it would collapse entirely."[19] Since WIZO was absolutely without political ties, its roles in the Zionist movement were in
no proportion to the number of its members. The middle course steered
by Hadassah, on the other hand, enabled it to be represented in institutions of the World Zionist Organization as befitted its membership.[20] In
the United States Hadassah could pose as an apolitical movement, thus
attracting to its ranks many women who would not otherwise have joined
a politically aligned organization, while becoming a powerful element in
the international Zionist arena through its affiliation with the World
Confederation.

Zionist Missions on the Basis of Gender and their Development

In a recent study of Hadassah, Mary McCune argues that from the
organization's inception in 1912 and throughout the 1920s, Hadassah's
first leaders developed a set of Zionist ideas that took into account gender
differences, as well as prevailing attitudes to women and "social feminism" in the Zionist arena. Women were generally considered to be more
practical than men and well suited to carry out projects in the fields of
health, medicine, and child care. Men, on the other hand, were regarded
as better qualified to deal with political and ideological issues. A key argument proposed by McCune is that women possessed unique capabil-
ities and special fields of interest that they contributed to the Zionist
cause in these areas no less than the contribution made to Zionism by
men in other—more "masculine"—spheres. This division of labor was
promoted by Hadassah and the wider American Zionist movement until
the mid-1920s.[21]

The idea of unique and different roles for men and women appealed to
many Jewish women in this era. McCune also points out that such con-

cepts enabled Hadassah to attract non-Zionist women as well to its ranks. Furthermore, Hadassah's leadership vigorously promoted its medical activity in *Erez Israel* as a unique contribution of American women to the Zionist cause.[22]

In time, Hadassah's role within the Zionist movement came to be taken for granted. Meanwhile, the notion of unique and different roles for men and women was put aside. By the late 1940s and 1950s, no trace of the ideas discussed above or of feminist ideology could be found in the movement's literature. In fact, feminist aims and objectives are entirely absent from Hadassah's constitutions, the major documents that present its ideology since its inception.[23] Even the *Hadassah Handbook,* another central text, rarely touches upon the advancement of women or women's issues.[24] Hadassah's leadership did not view the members as an object for social change; instead it presented them with challenges having direct bearing on Hadassah's objectives: fund-raising, recruitment of new members, and efforts in the field of Jewish education. Indeed, throughout the 1940s and 1950s, the *Hadassah Newsletter* and *Hadassah Headlines,* the major organs through which the leadership roused the members to action, made no effort to encourage a feminist identity or feminist ideals that challenged the status quo. In short, Hadassah's leaders were apprehensive lest such concepts undermine the organization's overriding aim of becoming a mass movement for American Jewish women.[25]

This process was not limited to the realm of ideology alone; it was also characteristic of Hadassah's efforts in *Erez Israel*. As is well known, Hadassah's first actions in that country were directly connected with the welfare of women. On the basis of a decision taken by the young organization's founders to assume responsibility for a medical project for the welfare of women and children, early in 1913—less than a year after it was founded—Hadassah hired the services of two public health nurses, Rose Kaplan of New York and Rachel Landy of Cleveland. They were sent to *Erez Israel* to establish a network of health clinics for women and children. Funding was supplied by Nathan Straus, who had contributed greatly to public health projects in the United States and was especially renowned for his efforts to further milk pasteurization. Straus and his wife, Lina, even accompanied the two nurses on their journey from the United States to *Erez Israel*.[26]

Henrietta Szold, the driving force behind this initiative, intended to establish a network of local clinics that would provide the necessary services for a healthy Jewish community: health services in schools, prophylactic measures to counter tuberculosis, baby and child care, and training for preventive medicine in general. Szold's model was the famous clinic in

New York established by the renowned social worker Lilian D. Wald, a regional clinic that in itself followed the example of such institutions in England. Wald's clinic was situated in New York's Lower East Side, an area densely populated by Jewish immigrants, and it became a model for similar health centers throughout the world.[27] Szold urged nurses Kaplan and Landy to visit the Wald clinic and study its procedures before they sailed for *Erez Israel*.[28]

Upon their arrival in March 1913, the nurses established a "settlement house" among the poorer residents of the Meah Shearim quarter in Jerusalem.[29] This was in line with the policy of the Settlement House movement, which made a point of locating its institutions in poor neighborhoods in order to combat the social and physical conditions that encouraged disease.[30] The nurses lived in a house that served as both a clinic and their home. Not long after their arrival, they were visited by Jane Addams, the well-known American social reformer and a leader of the Settlement House movement.[31] This event is indicative of Hadassah's relationship to that movement—an important movement during the Progressive period in American history, and one that was almost entirely female in composition—and its leadership, and also of its involvement in the type of activity that was identified with women's movements in the early years of the twentieth century. The First World War, however, put an abrupt end to the nurses' efforts on behalf of women in *Erez Israel,* and they were forced to return to the United States.[32]

The war also completely changed Hadassah's role in the World Zionist Organization and, more specifically, the character of its activity in *Erez Israel*.[33] In the wake of the war, Hadassah began to develop health services for the entire population in *Erez Israel* but was soon forced to quit its countrywide activity. Immediately after the war, Hadassah resumed its efforts. It established hospitals throughout the land, founded a nursing school, was active in preventive medicine and in caring for new immigrants.[34] Hadassah was a central actor in most fields of health and medical services from the final months of the First World War through the British Mandate period. In the 1930s, however, the nature of Hadassah's activities in *Erez Israel* was once more transformed. It adopted a policy of devolution, gradually transferring its health and medical institutions outside Jerusalem to the Jewish municipalities and to Kupat Holim, the health division of the Histadrut.[35] Two objectives lay behind this policy: to encourage the Yishuv to provide its own services and to enable Hadassah to undertake new projects.[36] This led to another policy change: Hadassah would now place its emphasis on developing research and university medical services rather than concentrating on developing health services for the general public, as in the previous decade. This decision also had geographical implications: from now on Hadassah's major thrust would be in Jerusalem, centered for the most part on the Rothschild Hospital, though other services were provided in other parts of the city. Hadassah's health services throughout the country were reduced compared with the 1920s. It assumed direct responsibility for the hospital, which in 1939, in cooperation with the Hebrew University, had become a university hospital known as the Meir Rothschild Hadassah–University Hospital.[37]

In 1949 Hadassah devolved all of its public health institutions—those which, like the one it had founded in 1913, were established primarily for women—to the newly established State of Israel. Exceptions in this regard were agencies in Jerusalem and the "Jerusalem Corridor," which Hadassah continued to control in order to serve the research and teaching functions of the School of Medicine founded in 1949 and the older School of Nursing. Since then, Hadassah's efforts in Israel have focused on medical education and its hospital in Jerusalem.[38]

What emerges from this cursory survey is that efforts related to the welfare of women, the basis of Hadassah's first project in the country, gradually diminished over time. In fact, they had already assumed secondary importance during the final months of the First World War, when Hadassah became a medical organization of the first order in *Erez Israel*. It is as such that it firmly took root in the country.

The Nature of Hadassah's Activity in Erez Israel

One of the major sources that contributed to Hadassah's strength was the manner in which it conducted its enterprises in *Erez Israel*. Five fundamental concepts combined to shape its unique Zionist vision:

Developing Health Services. Hadassah regarded its contribution of *binyan haarez* [building the homeland] as focusing on the creation of health services, medical education and research on the basis of the finest American professional knowledge. It considered health services to include inpatient care, health education, social services, and preventive medicine. This Zionist concept posited that every member of Hadassah was a partner in the effort to develop such services and thus personally engaged in *binyan haarez*.[39]

Modernization of *Erez Israel*. Henrietta Szold, founder and spiritual mentor of Hadassah, defined the motive for Hadassah's activities as "the aim of a group of [Jewish] women in America to express their devotion to the Zionist idea by participating practically in the modernization of Palestine."[40] This aim became a guiding tenet in Hadassah's activity in the Yishuv and Israel. The Hadassah leadership equated modernization with the adoption of accepted American professional perspectives and methods, and it derived its modus operandi from this belief. It introduced basic and advanced training in the United States for the highest administrative level of its enterprises in *Erez Israel*, placed an emphasis on the most innovative American methods and instruments, and recruited American experts to provide training, supervision, and evaluation. However, its projects in *Erez Israel* were developed by local teams.

Pioneering. Hadassah always undertook "to anticipate tomorrow's needs and try to meet them."[41] Toward this end, it introduced new services that the Yishuv or Israel needed, but for which financial or human resources were lacking. A corollary of this concept was that in order to establish new pioneering enterprises, Hadassah would transfer its pilot ventures to the Yishuv (or Israel) as soon as the Yishuv was able to maintain them.[42]

Education. Considering itself an agent of progress in the Yishuv and Israel, Hadassah also regarded itself as an educational force.[43]

American Models. Hadassah believed in introducing American models that would be emulated in the development of local enterprises. This concept rested on the assumption that Hadassah could impart American standards, techniques, and skills to the Yishuv but could not, by itself, sustain the country's entire network of medical and social institutions. This distinction led to the idea of creating model institutions: Hadassah would establish an initial model on the basis of American expertise and techniques. In time, Hadassah's hospitals, clinics, mother-and-child health centers, vocational schools, and vocational training enterprises became models for similar undertakings.[44]

Health and Medicine

Until the late 1920s, the Rothschild Hospital, Hadassah's hospital in Jerusalem and the center of its activity in *Erez Israel,* was directed by American doctors. Problems of communication, exacerbated by differences in language and mentality, arose between the Americans and elements in the Yishuv, particularly the workers' organizations. There were three American directors of the Rothschild Hospital in the 1920s, and there was a severe confrontation between the last of them—Dr. Ephraim

Bluestone—and the workers' organizations, due to misunderstandings or differences in mentality.[45] However, in 1929 Henrietta Szold, then director of the Health Committee of the Yishuv, appointed Dr. Hayim Yassky, a young Russian Jewish ophthalmologist trained in Odessa and now a resident of *Erez Israel,* as the hospital's first non-American director. His appointment was a decisive step toward achieving the hospital's independence from the Hadassah National Board.[46]

Yassky's appointment also set the pattern for Hadassah's activity in *Erez Israel* and its country wide standing in general. From this point on, the directors of Hadassah's institutions would be residents of the country, well versed in its daily life. This assured that the enterprises would be operated in a manner fully compatible with conditions in *Erez Israel* and the needs of its populace. Employment of local personnel was applied to all Hadassah undertakings in *Erez Israel*. In time, financial responsibility for many of Hadassah's enterprises was transferred to Yishuv organs, enabling Hadassah to expand its activities to an extent that would have been impossible on the basis of its budget alone. Taken together, these factors—meeting local interests, widespread efforts encompassing a broad spectrum of activities, and specialization in fields that were necessary to everyday life in *Erez Israel*—transformed Hadassah into an integral part of the Yishuv. When the State of Israel was established, Hadassah, a vital element in the development of specific social and health services in the prestate period, became a factor to be reckoned with. A few examples of its undertakings are in order.

One of Hadassah's paramount contributions to Israel was the establishment of the country's first medical school in 1949. The school was a joint venture of Hadassah and the Hebrew University of Jerusalem. The Hadassah–Hebrew University Medical School was established after a lengthy process when the two institutions concluded an agreement in 1936.[47] It was patterned after American medical schools, a model that was later emulated by the medical schools of Tel Aviv University (1961) and Ben-Gurion University in the Negev (1972).

Hadassah took an important step toward the creation of the medical school in 1945, when it created an advisory agency, the Medical Reference Board, in the United States. The purpose of the board was to assist in the establishment of the school by providing professional advice. Its members were prominent Jewish physicians, including some of the best minds in the United States—medical administrators and public health experts—all of whom served the board as volunteers.[48] The Medical Reference Board gave advice on the educational philosophy to be adopted by the medical school—an issue that was discussed by the bodies involved with establishing the school as early as in 1942.[49] The board members also drafted a curriculum for the future medical school, based on curricula of the medical schools at several leading American universities—Harvard, Columbia, and Johns Hopkins.[50] In early 1947, the committee charged with choosing the medical school's teaching method decided on a model similar to that conventional in American medical schools.[51] This decision was facilitated by the Medical Reference Board, under the influence of Hadassah, and by Dr. Hayim Yassky, director of the Rothschild Hospital, all of whom considered American medical practice to be the epitome of modern science they wished to see take root in *Erez Israel*. They made this decision even though most of the doctors at the Rothschild Hospital had been trained in central Europe and one could not take for granted that they would accept the American methods and practices.[52]

Another contribution of Hadassah to the medical school was a corollary of the decision to follow the American pattern of medical education—in-service training in the United States for the teaching staff. In 1946 the senior members of the Rothschild Hospital medical staff were sent to the United States, where they received research and teaching fellowships and participated in clinical programs at several leading American medical schools.[53] (The fellowship program has since become a regular feature of Hadassah's training initiative.)

After the medical school was established, Hadassah contributed in two ways to putting it on a firm basis: by purchasing medical implements and by providing training grants for senior staff and students—an important matter, because most of the students were recent immigrants.[54] The funds for these grants originated in donations from Hadassah leaders and members of their families. It should be noted that the grants were not limited to doctors only; they were also made available to medical administrators, nutritionists, and other specialists as well. A similar policy was followed by Hadassah's other projects in the country.[55] Hadassah's mode of operation, then, can be summed up in the following manner: American models, local administration, and training in the United States to provide an *Erez Israel*–based health service network for the residents of Palestine and, later, Israel.

Educational and Welfare Projects for Children and Youth

Another field in which Hadassah contributed significantly to the fledgling State of Israel was its activity on behalf of children and youth. This, too, was an outgrowth of Hadassah's essence as a women's organization, and it aptly expressed the feminine aspect of its activity.

Care for children and youth was the common denominator of a series of enterprises that Hadassah supported. Hadassah was founded at a time when social service professions were child-centered and progressive education methods proliferated.[56] These provided inspiration for some of Hadassah's projects. Many leaders of Hadassah had been teachers or educators before becoming active in the organization, and they attempted, in various ways, to apply their ardent interest in education to the Yishuv as well. This endeavor included Hadassah's activity in Youth Aliyah, of which it had become the main patron in 1935, one year after the agency was established.[57] Hadassah did not limit its involvement to the financial sphere but also aspired to influence the educational efforts of Youth Aliyah. In the early years of statehood, Hadassah attempted to modify Youth Aliyah's conception of how to care for and relate to youngsters as individuals. Believing in professionalism—one of its key tenets—Hadassah called in American experts in the relevant fields of education, vocational training, and individualized care for children and youth. In the years 1948–1956, the Hadassah National Board dispatched a series of American experts, all prominent in their fields, to visit the Youth Aliyah enterprises and offer suggestions that might improve their work.[58] Some of these proposals, such as sending members of the Youth Aliyah administrative team to the United States for advanced training, upgrading Youth Aliyah's educational equipment, and adding diagnostic experts to the organization's personnel, were later implemented.[59] As in the case of the medical school, here, too, there were two major traits that characterized Hadassah's efforts in *Erez Israel:* (a) responsibility for the operation of these undertakings was taken up by local administrators and personnel, many of whom were sent to the United States for advanced training; (b) American experts were recruited for evaluation and advice.

Hadassah's other projects for children and youth—Hadassah Youth Services—covered a broad spectrum: playgrounds, nutrition programs, vocational training centers, a coordination and research institute, and so on. All these projects were the first of their kind in *Erez Israel,* and they embodied Hadassah's pioneering idea. All were operated by local personnel, and responsibility for them was gradually transferred to the State of Israel, in line with Hadassah's policy of devolution. The movement's education principle was especially pronounced in these enterprises. Several of the latter, such as the playgrounds, were designed to serve as models for emulation throughout the country.

A good example of how Hadassah created and operated its projects in *Erez Israel* is that of the Alice Seligsberg Vocational School for Girls, established in Jerusalem in 1942. It was founded on American patterns and ideas that were radical at the time: to provide disadvantaged girls with both general and vocational education.[60] In 1944–1945 Hadassah also established workshops for boys in response to one of the Yishuv's severest social problems: youngsters who dropped out before finishing public school. In subsequent years, the Hadassah leadership, guided by another attitude to the welfare of youth, established and maintained vocational training enterprises.[61] These ventures reflected Hadassah's concept of modernizing the country and addressed the Yishuv's industrial needs. For example, Hadassah established two vocational schools in 1949 (again, the first of their kind in the fledgling country): one for hotel staff and the other a fashion institute, both patterned after American models. The former was established along the lines of the hotel management school at the City University of New York (in Brooklyn).[62] To get it underway, Hadassah brought in two experts from the New York school for a brief stay. They arrived laden with the latest equipment needed for such a school, that would train Israelis—who, in Hadassah's view, lacked all knowledge in hotel management—to engage in this profession, the basis for the development of the tourism industry. The fashion institute was created to stimulate the domestic textile industry.[63]

Another contribution to vocational training, established in Jerusalem in 1942, was the Hadassah Vocational Referral Institute (later: Vocational Guidance). It developed diagnostic methods tailored to the country's needs and attempted to promote the field of vocational guidance in various ways.[64]

The scope and diversity of Hadassah's activity in this period is remarkable: medical and paramedical services and professional training, welfare services for children and youth, vocational courses and schools, and much more. For several reasons, such a range of enterprises proved to be an organizational advantage. First of all, it enabled Hadassah to establish a firm presence in *Erez Israel* and play a pivotal role in the development of the state. Second, by presenting a wide range of humanitarian endeavors to choose from, Hadassah enabled many American Jewish women, coming from diverse backgrounds, to find interest and satisfaction in active membership, on both the local and the leadership levels.

A Comparison of Hadassah and Other Zionist Organizations

The implications of what has been described above for an understanding of the source of Hadassah's strength will become clear if we compare Hadassah to other American Zionist organizations active on behalf of Israel during the period just prior to and immediately after the establishment of the Jewish state.

The Zionist Organization of America

From late 1948, the Zionist Organization of America (ZOA) was in the midst of a deep crisis, evident in two major phenomena: a steep decline in membership and a search for new, meaningful fields of activity. Four years after the establishment of Israel, ZOA membership had dwindled from 225,000 in 1948 to 95,000 in 1953. The most likely cause was the disappearance of its central challenge—the political effort to establish a Jewish state. Many of the ZOA's members were businessmen, very much engrossed in their private enterprises. After the establishment of Israel— and despite its need of massive political and financial support—the ZOA lacked a raison d'être sufficiently attractive to sustain a large-scale membership base.[65]

The establishment of Israel also stripped the ZOA of its two major traditional roles: political-diplomatic efforts and fund-raising. Diplomatic activity was now the responsibility of the new state, while the raising of funds for the absorption of the masses of new immigrants encouraged other Jewish organizations to enter the fray, thus diminishing the unique role previously played by the ZOA and others in the pre-state period. This was especially true in the case of the United Jewish Appeal, which raised enormous sums for Israel after 1948.[66]

Here we come to the central difference between Hadassah and the ZOA. Unlike Hadassah, which had firmly taken root in Israel through its health and welfare projects and had become a dominant, even vital, player in some areas, the ZOA was not active in any field of endeavor in the new state. Thus, while the ZOA was relinquishing a major portion of its traditional activities, Hadassah, as we have noted above, found itself obligated to choose between the fields in which it would continue to act and those in which it would shift responsibility to the government of the new state. In other words, whereas the ZOA faced the loss of its central challenge, Hadassah undertook new challenges in Israel, a fact that influenced its ongoing activity in the United States as well.

The ZOA leadership considered strategies for addressing its organizational crisis and sought new fields of endeavor both in the United States and in Israel. Already at the 1949 ZOA Convention, Emanuel Neumann proposed a range of new activities and projects for implementation in Israel.[67] In the end, only two were carried out. The first was the ZOA

House in Tel Aviv, which, it was hoped, would bridge the gap between Israel and American Zionists. It was established along the lines of an American community center, to enrich the cultural life of Tel Aviv. The other project was the Kfar Silver Agricultural School, near Ashkelon.[68]

In America, the ZOA adopted new initiatives in three fields: economic enterprises, public relations, and education. The 1953 Convention resolved to establish an economic department that would encourage private undertakings and investments in Israel. A year later, at the 1954 convention, resolutions were adopted calling for increased public relations and fund-raising on behalf of Israel.[69] As for the third field of activity—Jewish education in the United States—the ZOA was aware of the need to enhance its efforts in this area, which had been neglected in the pre-state years due to more pressing matters. Many American Jewish youth were ignorant of their Jewish heritage and culture, and knew no Hebrew. The 1952 Convention established a department for Hebrew language and culture that created various frameworks for the study of Hebrew and supported a Hebrew radio program.[70]

Despite all these economic and cultural efforts, by the late 1950s the ZOA "had been rendered nearly impotent, a pale shadow of its once powerful self, with few members, little status, and no purpose."[71] What led to the disintegration of the ZOA, whereas Hadassah—to use the Hebrew phrase—went "from strength to strength"?

Hadassah, too, was actively involved in the political efforts for the establishment of a Jewish state. Its senior leaders played various roles in this process, alongside ZOA leaders Abba Hillel Silver and Emanuel Neumann. Moreover, from 1946 on, great efforts were expended within the ranks of Hadassah to prepare its members for Zionist political action.[72] In the sphere of internal Zionist politics, the history of Hadassah—especially from the early 1930s onwards—is marked with examples of energetic political activity within the Zionist movement. Indeed, during the years 1948–1951 Hadassah was deeply involved in political activity and bitter ideological controversies within the World Zionist Organization. Represented by Rose Halperin, its national president, Hadassah vigorously championed its organizational agenda as well as the goals of American Zionism and Zionism in general.[73]

However, Hadassah's diversified political activity was always only a part—and never the major focus—of the organization's overall vision. By directing its energy and organizational resources toward many fields of activity, it struck firm roots in the soil of *Erez Israel*. Since it provided vital services that were implemented by local inhabitants who became full partners, the continuation of such projects was ensured even after historical conditions changed. It was these projects and the manner in which they were implemented that freed Hadassah—in contradistinction to the ZOA—from dependence on special political circumstances and periods of crisis in Jewish history as motivating forces.[74]

Other American Women's Zionist Organizations

Since Hadassah's unique status on the American Zionist scene was a result of its being a women's organization, a comparison with its sister Zionist movements—Pioneer Women, WIZO, and Mizrachi Women—is called for. What gave Hadassah the advantage over the others?

One answer is that the other organizations concentrated on activities for the welfare of women in Israel, whereas Hadassah's projects were intended for the population at large. The major objective of American Pioneer Women was to raise funds for and lend support to Moezet Hapoalot [the Women Workers's Council, which since 1975 has been known as Naamat—a Hebrew acronym for Working and Volunteer Women]. This organization is in the forefront of the struggle for equal rights for women in Israel. Its undertakings include day nurseries and kindergartens, vocational training centers, educational and cultural frameworks exclusively for women, and more.[75] It can be termed, therefore, a militant women's organization intent upon enhancing the welfare of women and advancing their unique interests. American Mizrachi Women, too, supports a network of day care nurseries, social services, educational courses, and schools for girls.[76]

A comparison of Hadassah and WIZO is most instructive. WIZO has defined itself as an organization of Jewish women with the objective of participating actively in the upbuilding and consolidation of the State of Israel. This is to be achieved by establishing and operating institutions and projects in Israel in the following fields: (a) education and training of youth and women in agriculture, home economics and various other crafts and professions; (b) projects for the welfare of youth; (c) training and helping new immigrant women so as to facilitate their absorption into Israeli society. By contrast, the target population of Hadassah's enterprises is Israeli society as a whole, rather than exclusively women and children.[77]

It was Hadassah's focus on services for the public at large, rather than for women alone, that influenced support for its projects and enhanced its strength. The struggle for universal, humanitarian objectives resonated with the mainstream of American and American Jewish philanthropies, and was compatible generally with the American tradition of mission. Such compatibility accounts for Hadassah's great drawing power, which in turn explains its advantage over the other American Zionist women's organizations and WIZO. Another advantage enjoyed by Hadassah was that it appealed to the American Jewish public at large, while other organizations drew their strength from discrete sectors of the American Jewish community.

Indeed, the two other American Jewish women's organizations also focused on services for children and youth, and all three of them supported Youth Aliyah. Furthermore, all three of them stressed philanthropic endeavors in two arenas: practical aid in Israel and Jewish education in the United States. Yet, there were also significant differences between them. In 1952 Mizrachi Women defined itself in the following manner: "Maintains schools and nurseries in Israel in an environment of traditional Judaism; conducts cultural activities for the purpose of disseminating Zionist ideals and strengthening traditional Judaism in America."[78] Whereas Hadassah supported general Zionist ideals common to the majority of American Jews, and aspired to be a broad, popular Zionist movement, Mizrachi Women adhered to ideals and concepts that appealed primarily to Orthodox Jews. Furthermore, Mizrachi Women was (and has remained) part of the World Mizrahi movement and as such linked itself to a political party in Israel, thus narrowing even further its potential base of popular support. Pioneer Women, too, by its very nature, appealed to a limited sector among American Jews because of its relationship to the Labor Zionist party in Israel, known as Mapai. By its own definition, Pioneer Women's major objective was "to build Israel along cooperative lines."[79] Thus, only persons with an outlook that blended socialism and Zionism would tend to lend it their support. In sum, Hadassah appealed to a wider target audience than any other national women's Zionist organization in the United States. Perhaps the most interesting comparison is that which can be made between Hadassah and the National Council of Jewish Women (NCJW), a non-Zionist organization that, as such, could presumably attract all American Jewish women. However, the NCJW was an elitist organization, most of whose members—even in the decades under discussion—came from families of German Jewish extraction and were influenced by Reform Judaism's ambivalent attitude to Zionism.[80] The majority of American Jewish women in the late 1940s and early 1950s, however, derived from eastern European ancestry and belonged to the Conservative movement, which was largely pro-Zionist. In short, they did not fit the profile of the NCJW membership.

Conclusions

A combination of factors facilitated the continuity of Hadassah's activity in *Erez Israel* and the State of Israel over a lengthy period of several decades. Some of these factors stemmed from the character of Hadassah as a women's organization and its Zionist orientation; others flowed from its modus operandi and activity in *Erez Israel*. These factors were Hadassah's adoption of the continuity of the Jewish people as a prime objective; aspiring to be a broad-based popular Zionist movement without any specific political orientation; and the character and diversity of its undertakings in *Erez Israel,* enterprises that resonated with mainstream American Jewish beliefs and attitudes. Taken together, such factors enabled Hadassah to emerge as a countrywide organization with hundreds of thousands of members and public support for projects in the American Jewish community as well as specific medical and social initiatives in *Erez Israel*.

Widespread support of Hadassah in the United States was also the result of a paradox. We refer here to the organization's outstanding success in *Erez Israel* precisely because it did *not* concentrate women's issues alone. Quickly abandoning a central objective it had adopted at its inception, Hadassah was transformed into a movement that organized women for Zionist efforts, rather than an organization of women on behalf of other women. In sum, as this essay argues, Hadassah would not have attained its size, strength and vitality had it limited itself in this way, as did the other American Zionist women's organizations.

Yet another important factor that contributed to the continuity of Hadassah's projects in *Erez Israel* was the manner in which they were run, that is, operated and administered by local persons for whom they were also a source of livelihood and professional standing.

To the list above should be added one final, basic factor: as a result of Hadassah's success in developing medical and youth services during the Mandate period, the organization played a vital role in the state's formative years. In sum, Hadassah contributed to the welfare of the Yishuv and the State of Israel in a manner unparalleled by any other American Zionist organization.

Notes

1. A comprehensive study of Hadassah has yet to be written. However, a not inconsiderable number of studies are devoted to certain facets or periods of

Hadassah's organizational history and to the history of health and medicine in *Erez Israel,* and thus shed light on Hadassah's history. Following is a select list of the major works. Hadassah has been the subject of three Ph.D. dissertations: D. Miller, "The Story of Hadassah, 1912–1935" (Ph.D. dissertation, New York University, 1965) [hereafter: Miller, "Hadassah"]; Mira Katzburg-Yungman, "Hadassah: Ideology and Practice, 1948–1956," [Hebrew] (Ph.D. dissertation, The Hebrew University of Jerusalem, 1997) [hereafter: Katzburg-Yungman, "Hadassah"]; and Carol Kutcher, "The Early Years of Hadassah, 1912–1921" (Ph.D. dissertation, Brandeis University, 1976) [hereafter: Kutcher, "Early Years"].

See also the major studies on American Zionism: Melvin I. Urofsky, *American Zionism from Herzl to the Holocaust* (Garden City, N.Y.: Anchor, 1976) [hereafter: Urofsky, *American Zionism*]; idem, *We are One—American Jewry and Israel* (Garden City, N.Y.: Anchor, 1978) [hereafter: Urofsky, *We Are One*]; Naomi Wiener Cohen, *American Jews and the Zionist Idea* (New York: Ktav, 1975) [hereafter Cohen, *Zionist Idea*]; Samuel Halperin, *The Political World of American Zionism* (Detroit: Wayne State University Press, 1961) [hereafter: Halperin, *Political World*]; Yonathan Shapiro, *Leadership of the American Zionist Organization, 1897–1930* (Urbana: University of Illinois Press, 1971) [hereafter: Shapiro, *Leadership*]; Aron Berman, *Nazism, the Jews and American Zionism, 1933–1948* (Detroit: Wayne State University Press, 1990) [hereafter: Berman, *Nazism*]. Each of these contains a short discussion of Hadassah. See also the popular work commissioned by Hadassah that concentrates on its projects in Erez Israel: Marlin Levin, *Balm in Gilead: The Story of Hadassah* (New York: Schocken, 1976) [hereafter: Levin, *Balm*]. For a recent study dealing with gender issues concerning Hadassah see Mary McCune, "Social Workers in the *Muskeljudentum*: 'Hadassah Ladies,' 'Manly Men' and the Significance of Gender in the American Zionist Movement, 1912–1928," *American Jewish History* 86, no. 2 (June 1998), 135–165 [hereafter: McCune, "Gender"]. See also Joyce Antler, *The Journey Home: Jewish Women and the American Century* (New York and London: Free Press, 1997) [hereafter: Antler, *Journey*].

There are several biographies of Henrietta Szold that provide some information on Hadassah until her death in 1945. The most important is Joan Dash, *Summoned to Jerusalem: The Life of Henrietta Szold* (New York: Harper and Row, 1979) [hereafter: Dash, *Summoned*].

Some studies dealing with the history of health and medical services in *Erez Israel* add to our information on Hadassah's activities in that country. The most important are Doron Niederland, "Influence of German-Jewish Immigrant Doctors on Medicine in *Erez Israel, 1933–1948*" [Hebrew], *Cathedra* 30 (December 1983), 111–160 [hereafter Niederland, "Influence"]; idem and Zohar Kaplan, "The Establishment of the Hebrew University–Hadassah Medical School in Jerusalem" [Hebrew], *Cathedra* 48 (June 1988), 145–163 [hereafter: Niederland and Kaplan, Medical School]; Shifra Shvarts, *Kupat Holim Haklalit—The General Sick Fund, 1911–1937* [Hebrew] (Sde Boker: Ben-Gurion Research Center, 1997) [hereafter: Shvarts, *Kupat Holim*].

2. "Bikkur Holim" [Hebrew], *Encyclopaedia Talmudica*, IV 158; Marion A. Kaplan, *The Making of the German Jewish Middle Class: Women, Family and Identity* (Oxford: Oxford University Press, 1991), 193–194.

3. William L. O'Neill, *Feminism in America: A History* (New Brunswick, N.J., and Oxford: Transaction Publishers, 1988), 142; Sheila M. Rothman, *Woman's Proper Place: A History of Changing Ideals and Practices, 1870 to the Present* (New York: Basic Books, 1978), 154–156 [hereafter: Rothman, *Proper Place*].

4. Alfred J. Kutzik, "The Social Basis of American Jewish Philanthropy" (Ph.D. dissertation, Brandeis University, 1967), 280–285, 290, 308–309.

5. Henry L. Feingold, "Rescue and Secular Perception: American Jewry and the Holocaust" [Hebrew], in *National Jewish Solidarity in the Modern Period,* ed. B. Pinkus and I. Troen (Sde Boker: Ben-Gurion Research Center, 1988), 161 [hereafter: Feingold, "Rescue"].

6. For American Jewish rescue organizations see Ilan Troen, "Organizing the Rescue of Jews in the Modern Period" [Hebrew], in *National Jewish Solidarity in the Modern Period,* ed. B. Pinkus and I. Troen, 7, 10–11. For the commandment of ransoming captives and its secular manifestation, see Feingold, "Rescue," 161. See also Natan Efrati, "Captives, Ransoming of," *Encyclopaedia Judaica,* V. (Jerusalem, 1971), 154–155.

7. Hannah L. Goldberg, *Hadassah Handbook* (New York: National Education Committee of Hadassah, 1946–1950), 53 [hereafter: *Hadassah Handbook*].

8. Ibid.

9. *The Jewish Communal Register of New York City, 1917-1918* (New York: Kehillah of New York City, 1918), 1361. Page one of the first organizational constitution of Hadassah (1914), which lists its objectives, has been lost and is not in the Hadassah Archives in New York [hereafter: HA] nor in the Central Zionist Archives in Jerusalem [hereafter: CZA]. We quote the organization's objectives as they appeared in the *Maccabaean* of 14 July 1914, 160, as quoted by Miller, "Hadassah," 51.

10. Hadassah National Board Minutes, January 1949, 8, HA.

11. Quoted by Urofsky, *American Zionism,* 145. Brandeis's conviction that every American Jew should become a Zionist is most clearly expressed in his address "Every Jew a Zionist," reprinted in *Brandeis on Zionism: A Collection of Addresses and Statements by Louis D. Brandeis* (Washington, D.C.: Zionist Organization of America, 1942), 76–79 [hereafter: *Brandeis on Zionism*]. For his emphasis on the great need of "members" see Urofsky, *American Zionism;* idem, "Zionism—an American Experience," *American Jewish Historical Quarterly* 53, no. 3 (March 1974), 228; Shapiro, *Leadership,* 78.

12. See, e.g., what Rose Halprin said at the session of the Zionist General Council in Jerusalem (5–15 May 1949), *Reports and Addresses, Debates, Decisions* [Hebrew] (Jerusalem: Zionist Executive, [n. d.]), 88 [hereafter: Zionist Executive, 1949].

13. Hadassah National Board Minutes, 10 January 1951, 8, HA.

14. *Proceedings [of] the 35th annual Convention of Hadassah, San Francisco, November 13-16, 1949* ([n. p., n.d.]), 103, HA [hereafter: *1949 Annual Convention*].

15. Ibid.; *Report Rendered to the 33rd Annual Convention of Hadassah, Atlantic City, N.J., October 24-28, 1947,* 5, HA; interview with Sarah Mishkin, New York, 21 June 1991.

16. *1949 Annual Convention,* 103.

17. On women's organizations engaged in humanitarian activities see Berit As, "On Female Culture: An Attempt to Formulate a Theory on Women's Solidarity and Action, *Acta Sociologica* 8 (1974), 142–161.

18. Linda Alcalay, "The Origins and Development of the World Confederation of General Zionists" (M.A. thesis, The Hebrew University of Jerusalem, 1978), 12.

19. See Rebecca Sieff's statement: *The Twenty-third Zionist Congress, 1956, Stenographic Record* [Hebrew] (Jerusalem, 1957), 319–320; see also "Resolution Adopted by the Zionist General Council at its Session Held in Jerusalem and Tel Aviv, August 22–September 3, 1948," quoted in *The Zionist Organization and the Jewish Agency, Reports of the Executives Submitted to the Twenty-third Zionist Congress at Jerusalem, August 1951* (Jerusalem, 1951), 108; ibid., 97.

20. For details concerning Hadassah's representation in the World Zionist Organization see *Twenty-fourth Zionist Congress, 24 April–7 May 1956, Stenographic Record* [Hebrew] (Jerusalem, 1957), xv–xix (list of delegates by faction) and 6–9 (list of officers).

21. McCune, "Gender," 137, 141, 149.

22. Ibid. 150.

23. Folder: Hadassah Constitutions, HA.

24. *Hadassah Handbook.*

25. *Hadassah Newsletter,* 1945–1956; *Hadassah Headlines,* 1947–1956.

26. Antler, *Journey,* 105; Dash, *Summoned,* 112; Shvarts, *Kupat Holim,* 94; M. Waserman, "For Mother and Child: Hadassah in the Holy Land, 1913–1993," *Bulletin of the New York Academy of Medicine* 70 (3) (Winter 1993) 253.

27. Antler, *Journey,* 105; On the Wald clinic see George Rosen, *A History of Public Health* (New York: MD Publications, 1958), 380–381.

28. Antler, *Journey,* 105.

29. "Report of the Proceedings of the First Annual Convention of the Daughters of Zion of America, Rochester, New York, June 29–30," 3, HA; Dash, *Summoned,* 109; Miller, "Hadassah," 87.

30. Antler, *Journey,* 105.

31. Dash, *Summoned,* 112; Antler, *Journey,* 105.

32. Dash, *Summoned,* 11.

33. McCune, "Gender," 146.

34. *Twenty Years of Medical Service to Palestine, 1918-1938: Report Issued to Commemorate the Opening of the Hadassah University Medical Center, May 9, 1939, 20 Iyar 5699* [Hebrew] (Jerusalem, 1939), 17–19 [hereafter: *Twenty Years*].

35. Niederland, "Influence," 144.

36. *Twenty Years,* 24.

37. Niederland, "Influence," 144.

38. A general memorandum sent by Hayim Shalom Halevi (deputy administrative director of the Rothschild Hospital) to mayors and heads of local municipal councils; circular by Dr. Kalman Mann to city and local councils, 16 May 1952; list of twenty-four preventive medicine clinics in the Jerusalem Corridor operated by Hadassah on the day on which the agreement devolving its services elsewhere was signed; Kalman Mann to Chaim Shiba, director general of the Ministry of Health, 7 July 1972; agreement between the directors of the Hadassah Medical Organization, the Clerical Workers Union, the Nurses Union, and

the Hadassah Employees Union, all in Hebrew and all found in the Israel State Archives [hereafter: ISA], 2/1/4/4245 c. For the statement that Hadassah kept its medical services in Jerusalem and the Jerusalem Corridor in order to train its medical students and nurses, see Kalman J. Mann, "The Hadassah Medical Organization Program in the State of Israel," in *The Hadassah Medical Organization: An American Contribution to Medical Pioneering and Progress in Israel*, ed. Joseph Hirsh (New York: Hadassah, 1965), 8.

39. *Hadassah in Erez Israel, 1918-1928: Opening Address by Henrietta Szold at the Inauguration Ceremony of the Nathan and Lina Straus Health Center, on 20 Nissan 5689 [1929]* [Hebrew] (Jerusalem, 1929), 13 [in CZA library, call no. 7250; hereafter: Szold, *Opening Address*]. See also *Proceedings [of] the 33rd Annual Convention of Hadassah, Atlantic City, N.J., October 24-27, 1947*, 82, 87, HA [hereafter: *1947 Convention*]; interview with Dr. Kalman J. Mann, Jerusalem, 28 July 1992.

40. Szold, *Opening Address, 13.*

41. *Proceedings of the 38th Annual Convention of Hadassah, Detroit, Michigan, October 26-29, 1952,* 219, HA.

42. *Twenty Years,* 24.

43. For a very explicit statement of this objective see Julia A. Dushkin, *Hadassah's Child Welfare Program in Palestine* (New York: Hadassah, The Women's Zionist Organization of America, 1942), 3 [hereafter: Dushkin, *Child Welfare*].

44. *Hadassah Handbook,* 58, 68; see also Dushkin, *Child Welfare,* 8-13.

45. Shvarts, *Kupat Holim,* 110-126.

46. Dash, *Summoned,* 208; Levin, *Balm,* 51; Shvarts, *Kupat Holim,* 51.

47. Niederland and Kaplan, "Medical School," 145-146.

48. Ibid., 146.

49. Ibid., 156.

50. Moshe Prywes, *Prisoner of Hope* [Hebrew] (Tel Aviv: Zmora-Bitan, 1992), 260.

51. Record of the Meeting of the Council of the Para-Faculty of Medicine, 9 February 1947 [Hebrew], Hebrew University Archives, Jerusalem [hereafter: HUA]; Niederland and Kaplan, "Medical School," 156.

52. Niederland and Kaplan, "Medical School," 156.

53. Dr. Hayim Yassky at the meeting of the council of the Para-Faculty of Medicine, 8 December 1946 [Hebrew], HUA; Hadassah National Board Minutes, 3 November 1948, 6, HA; interview with Prof. Andre De Vries, Tel Aviv, 1992; Hadassah Biennial Report, 1949-1951, 23-24, HA; Hadassah National Board Minutes, 14 May 1954, 4, HA.

54. Hadassah National Board Minutes, 20 July 1950, 4, HA.

55. Hadassah Biennial Report, 1949-1951, 23-24, HA.

56. Rothman, *Proper Place,* 98.

57. Berman, *Nazism,* 35; Levin, *Balm,* 124; Miller, "Hadassah," 318.

58. Akiva W. Deutsch, "The Development of Social Work as a Profession in the Jewish Community in *Erez Israel* [Hebrew] (Ph.D. dissertation, The Hebrew University of Jerusalem, 1970), 213; Alexander M. Dushkin, "Educational Achievements and Problems of Youth Aliyah in *Erez Israel*: Report Submitted to Hadassah, 1947," 1-15; "Report by Louis Sobel on a Visit to Israel in Connection with Youth Aliya, July 1953"; Hayim Grossbard, "Report to the National Board

[of Hadassah] on My Experience with Youth Aliyah in Israel, August 1954–September 1955," 4–5, all in "Youth Aliyah," Henrietta Szold Documentation Center, file 620.8 H 37.

59. Katzburg-Yungman, "Hadassah," 175, 177–178.

60. Memorandum on the Alice Seligsberg School, [n. d.], ISA GL 1719/241/1.

61. Hadassah Biennial Report, 1949–1951, 36; Annual Report to Hadassah, 1953–1954, 33, HA.

62. Hadassah Interim Progress Reports, Convention 1950 (Hadassah Youth Services), 3–4, HA [hereafter: Hadassah Youth Services].

63. Ibid.

64. Zeev Sardi, *The First 45 Years: The Inception and Development of the Hadassah Vocational Guidance Institute* (Jerusalem: Hadassah Vocational Guidance Institute, 1989), 6–11, 12–15; Hadassah Youth Services, 2; "Reap in Joy: Annual Report to Hadassah," 1952, 25, HA; Eliezer Erenstein, *Studies in Vocational Training: The Hadassah Vocational Training Projects* [Hebrew] (Jerusalem, 1960), viii.

65. For membership statistics in 1948 see in Halperin, *Political World*, 327; for 1953 see *Proceedings [of the] 56th Annual Convention of the Zionist Organization of America, August 26-30, 1953, New York,* 35, in CZA, call no. F38/348 [hereafter: *1953 ZOA Convention*].

66. Urofsky, *We Are One*, 299–301.

67. For Neumann's proposal see "The Convention in Review: A Day by Day Summary," *New Palestine*, 14 June 1949, 2.

68. On the ZOA House see "Monosson in Israel for Cornerstone Laying of ZOA House in Tel Aviv," *New Palestine*, 27 October 1949, 2. On Kfar Silver see "Kfar Silver to Include College of Agriculture," *American Zionist*, 20 February 1953, 2; "Kfar Silver Gets New Water System, Dorms," ibid., December 1954, 13; "Opening of Kfar Silver," ibid., October 1955, 15; "Kfar Silver Now Has 100 Students," ibid., December 1956, 17.

69. For the decision to establish an economic department and other decisions relating to economics, see *1953 ZOA Convention*, 36; for decisions taken at the 1954 convention see: "ZOA Convention Sets New Standards for Israel Work," *American Zionist*, July 1954, 1.

70. Resolutions 3–12: "Zionist Educational Seminaries"; "Yiddish Circles"; "Hebrew Terminology"; "Hebrew Publications"; "Jewish Culture"; "The American Zionist"; "Dos Yiddishe Folk"; "Zionist Book of the Month Club"; "Anthology of Jewish Philosophy"; "Radio and Television," *Proceedings [of the] Annual Convention of the Zionist Organization of America, New York, June 12-16, 1952,* 422–428, in CZA, call no. F38/348.

71. Urofsky, *We Are One*, 279.

72. Ibid., 88–89, 91, 170; for the efforts within Hadassah see Katzburg-Yungman, "Hadassah," 5–13.

73. A few examples of these efforts: In the 1930s, Hadassah firmly defended its interest against the ZOA leadership in order to gain sole responsibility for Youth Aliyah activities in the United States; see Berman, *Nazism*, 35–36. For other examples see Mark A. Raider, *The Emergence of American Zionism* (New York and London: New York University Press, 1998), 117–118; Urofsky, *We Are One*, 117; for the years 1948-1951 see Katzburg-Yungman, "Hadassah," 78–126.

74. For the full range of Hadassah's activities as reflected in its Report for 1947 see Katzburg-Yungman, "Hadassah," 15–16.

75. C. B. Sherman, "Naamat," *New Encyclopedia of Zionism and Israel* (Madison, 1994), 973–974.

76. Y. Goldshlag and B. Mindel, "Mizrachi," ibid., 945.

77. Hannah Herzog and Ofra Greenberg, *Voluntary Women's Organization in a Society in the Making* [Herbew] (Tel Aviv: Tel Aviv University, Institute of Social Research, 1978), 52.

78. *American Jewish Yearbook* 53 (1952), 465.

79. Ibid., 465–466.

80. Faith Rogow, *Gone to Another Meeting: The National Council of Jewish Women, 1893-1993* (Tuscaloosa and London: University of Alabama Press), 268.

PART III

Aliyah, Social Identities, and Political Change

The ultimate expression of Zionist commitment was neither organizational membership nor philanthropy, even though these elements were crucial to the strength of the Zionist enterprise as a whole. Rather, it was the personal imperative of actually immigrating to Palestine and helping to create the Jewish state by one's physical presence. American Zionist organizations typically were (and continue to be) ambivalent about stating that immigration to the Land of Israel—a revolutionary act of "self-realization" called *aliyah* in Hebrew—is compulsory or even desirable. Perhaps realizing that this goal was extraordinarily difficult to achieve, most American Zionist groups downplayed the notion of *aliyah* in order not to feel inadequate and avoid the stigma of failure. Instead, they elevated the notion of America as a *goldene medineh* [Yiddish for "golden land"] that enabled American Jews to help build Palestine's new Jewish society-in-the-making from afar.

In fact, with respect to American Jewish women married and with children, *aliyah* was not really an option unless the entire family immigrated. Thus, even if certain women wanted to emigrate, they were often prevented from doing so because of other obligations. It is not surprising, therefore, that those women who did emigrate were either single, widowed, or married to ardent Zionists. In general, American Zionist women rarely considered actual immigration to Palestine as a personal requirement or even a possibility. Those who did emigrate were seen as heroines or, just as often, incomprehensible. In short, in the first half of the twentieth century a pattern of organizational and political activity emerged that provided American Jewish women with access to the world of Zionism, Palestine, and later Israel—though only a minority ever seriously contemplated *aliyah.* Rather, as the essays in part II demonstrated, this pattern was shaped by partnerships among women who deliberately opted to live on two different continents.

In the period between World Wars I and II there was a swift increase in the pace and scope of Zionist activity in the United States. The unprecedented threats directed at European and Palestinian Jewry produced increasing pressure among American Jews to alleviate the plight of distressed Jewish communities abroad. This awareness of Jewish suffering gradually led to a consensus that crystallized around the Zionist campaign for Jewish statehood. Meanwhile, American Zionist women's activity assumed new and dramatic proportions. Leaving partisan divisions behind, American Zionist women coalesced into a loosely integrated array of individuals and groups that promoted three essential activities: (1) refugee relief activity, (2) large-scale Jewish immigration to Mandatory Palestine, and (3) postwar Jewish reconstruction based on the Zionist blueprint of Jewish sovereignty in the Middle East. The threefold plan of relief, immigration, and construction blended the concerns of those who focused on the plight of Jews, those who wanted to expand the Jewish population in the emerging state, and those who wished to focus on quality of life within Palestine.

World War II and the news of the Holocaust provoked intense social and political activity among American Zionist women, much of which was frustrated by American political intransigence and inflexible laws that hindered citizens from providing military and financial aid abroad. Some scholars believe that Zionist women's activity in the United States during this period was merely philanthropic and not ideologically driven, a kind of guilt-relief in the face of not being able to do much to save the Jews of Europe. The situation was, in fact, more complex. For American Jewry at that time was not yet fully united behind Zionism. Zionism was still viewed by some as antithetical to American Jews' appreciation of the benefits of life in America. Indeed, such key groups as the American Reform movement and the Jewish Labor Committee remained vocally anti-Zionist well into the 1930s and 1940s. By contrast, Zionist women's groups like Hadassah, the Mizrachi Women's Organization, Pioneer Women, and others played a pivotal role in mobilizing Jewish political activism among Yiddish- and English-speaking American Jewish women during the war. At the same time, the leaders of these women's organizations faced the uphill battle of asserting their views in the rough-and-tumble world of Zionist politics, an arena dominated by powerful elitist men. At some point in their experience, many American Zionist women decided that although such organizational struggles were important, they actually depleted the energies of the very people who could make a positive contribution to Palestine if they settled there.

The essays in part III emphasize the variety of experiences of American Zionist women who undertook *aliyah* in the years leading up to the establishment of the State of Israel in 1948. Joseph B. Glass investigates the consequences for a broad spectrum of American Jewish women who immigrated to Palestine and the impact of their choices on the Yishuv and Zionist settlement patterns. Peri Rosenfeld traces the life of Sara Bodek Paltiel (1909–1993), a founder of Kibbutz Kfar Blum and professional nurse, who played an instrumental role in public health enterprises in the Yishuv and later Israel. Sara Kadosh examines the life and activity of another unusual figure, Rose Viteles (1892–1959), who aided the Haganah without making her role public. Shulamit Reinharz explores the path of Irma (Rama) Lindheim (1886–1978), an extraordinary upper-class political activist who continuously remade herself as she attempted to further the cause of Jewish nation building. Marie Syrkin, the subject of an essay in part I of this volume, examines Israel's future prime minister Golda Meir (1898–1978), who began her Zionist career as a young member of the American Labor Zionist movement. Finally, noted Israeli historian Anita Shapira examines an aspect of Golda Meir that is usually neglected—her synthesis of "femininity" and "feminism"—a central factor in her style of political leadership and how she came to be identified in the public eye. All these women were idealistic, believing that they could change the world and themselves, and they were dissatisfied with their lives in the United States. Each had internalized Zionism, not only as a solution to the existential dilemma of the Jewish people in general, but as a solution to the problems of their own life.

The turbulent decade that spanned World War II, the Holocaust, and the birth of the Jewish state gave rise to a broad American women's Zionist movement with its own characteristics. Such figures as Tamar de Sola Pool (1890–1981), Rose Luria Halprin (1896–1978), Rose Gell Jacobs (1888–1975), and Marie Syrkin (1899–1989) formulated an American Zionist women's philosophy that blended Jewish nationalism with American customs and ideals. The challenge for American Zionist women, they reasoned, was to balance organizational independence and interdependence. They wanted to maintain a separate identity with control over their own funds and agenda, while at the same time they wanted to remain part of a larger American and worldwide Zionist movement. They recognized that their success would depend on what they actually accomplished in gaining members and producing projects on the ground in Palestine. Their motto became, in effect, "Zionist efficiency!" Simultaneously, the shock of the Holocaust confirmed their devotion to American society while strengthening their belief in the necessity of the Jewish state. The Holocaust made them recognize how much responsibility they actually had, for if *American* Jews with their wealth and freedom could not come to the aid of world Jewry, then who would? And if not now, when? In the United States, they had imbibed the supreme American value of pursuing freedom and happiness, even if that meant leaving the Golden Land for the Promised Land.

Chapter 10

The concept of *aliyah*—Hebrew for "ascendance" and the term used to describe the ideological imperative of Jewish immigration to the Land of Israel—is a central tenet of Zionism. From its inception, the Zionist movement placed a premium on the notions of *aliyah* and developing a critical mass of Jewish population in Palestine.

Estimates for the start of the nineteenth century indicate that only about 7,000 Jews lived in Palestine, about 2.4% of the whole population, mostly concentrated in the four Holy Cities: Jerusalem, Tiberias, Safed, and Hebron. At the end of the century the number of Jews had grown to about 43,000, about 8.1% of the total population. Well over 90% of these Jews lived in the cities. Some 5,000 Jews lived in Jaffa, for example, half of the total population of the city. Furthermore, by 1890 Jews were already a majority (60%) of the population of Jerusalem, and their proportion was due to grow even more in the following years. Before World War I, the Jews in Jerusalem comprised half of the Jewish population of the country, although these were mostly Orthodox Jews who had little to do with the developing Zionist movement.

In the wake of widespread pogroms in the Pale of Settlement in 1881–1882, scattered groups of Palestine-minded students united in tsarist Russia to found the Bilu movement, an organization dedicated to creating exemplary rural colonies in the Land of Israel. The Bilu pioneers derived their name from the book of Isaiah 11:5: "*Bet Yaakov lekhu venelkhah*" [House of Jacob, come let us rise up]. Although the movement failed to generate mass migration to Palestine, it did lay much of the ideological groundwork for ensuing generations of Zionist pioneers.

The emerging trends in East European *aliyah* during the fin de siècle were very much the product of youthful idealism and generational discord. Faced with dismal prospects for a secure and meaningful future in eastern Europe, thousands of young Russian and Polish Jewish activists gravitated to the Zionist enterprise. To be sure, the number of East European Jews who voted with their feet for the Americas vastly outnumbered those who immigrated to Palestine—some 2.5 million East European Jewish immigrants arrived in the United States between 1881 and 1924. But the Yiddish-speaking newcomers to the United States brought with them a cultural-ideological predisposition that helped to sow the seeds of *aliyah* from the Golden Land to the Promised Land.

A noteworthy example in this regard was the Russian youth leader Eliezer Yoffe (1881–1941), who immigrated in 1904 to the United States in order to conduct Zionist propaganda work among East European Jewish immigrants. His persistent efforts led to the unification of several small groups of would-be American *haluzim* [pioneers], and in 1905 he founded the Hehaluz-Zion Circle, the first American Zionist pioneering youth group. The Hehaluz members viewed themselves as heirs to the tradition of the Bilu pioneers, and they believed that only a revolution in their personal lives would lead to the creation of a Jewish state.

As Jaffe and other activists quickly discovered, however, unlike East European Zionism, which emerged in the final years of imperial Russia's repressive tsarist regime, American Zionism arose in an atmosphere of unprecedented religious and political freedom. Indeed, the American scene was temperamentally and structurally different than that of Europe or Palestine. The hybrid character of American Jewry was perhaps nowhere more visible than in the Yiddish-speaking Jewish immigrant milieu of the late nineteenth and early twentieth centuries, where there was generally no apparent conflict between belonging to a trade union, sending one's child to a Talmud Torah, and identifying as a card-carrying Zionist.

The salient factor in the emergence of American Zionism, as was true of Zionism worldwide, was the swift development and increasing centrality of the Yishuv in modern Jewish affairs. In the 1920s and 1930s, the Jewish community of Palestine grew rapidly and developed new social, political, and economic structures. There were 85,200 Jews in Palestine in 1922 (11.1% of the total population) and 175,100 in 1931(17% of the total population). Due mainly to significant increases in the 1930s, the number of Jews reached 630,000 in 1947, close to one-third of the total population. In 1946, over three-quarters of the Jewish population lived in cities. With over 180,000 inhabitants, Tel Aviv had become the major Jewish center of the country. The creation of a new Jewish society in Palestine had an impact on American Jewish life that is difficult to overstress.

Estimates of the number of American *olim* [Jewish immigrants] in the pre-state period vary from about 8,000 to 13,000; even the higher estimate amounts to no more than 3% of all Jewish arrivals in the country between 1880 and 1948. Historians generally agree, however, that American Jewish settlers and *haluzim,* despite their numerical insignificance, played an important—in some instances, even disproportionate—role in a variety of Zionist colonization and settlement projects. Moshe Davis, the dean of America–Holy Land studies, conducted extensive research on this topic and once compiled a list of pre-state settlements in the Land of Israel founded by American Jews, including over forty rural colonies, collective settlements, villages, and towns.

Against this backdrop, the following chapter by Joseph Glass focuses on the immigration and settlement patterns of American Jewish women in pre-state Palestine. Glass scrutinizes a variety of personal, religious, economic, and ideological factors that influenced the decision-making processes of American *olot* [female Jewish immigrants]. He also pays close attention to the distinctive character of several Zionist projects that attracted *olot* and the ways in which their experience, viewed as an aggregate, differed from and was akin to that of other segments of the Jewish immigrant population.

Settling the Old-New Homeland: The Decisions of American Jewish Women during the Interwar Years

Joseph B. Glass

For the five thousand or so American* Jewish women who settled in Palestine between the two world wars, there was the question of where to settle in their old-new homeland. For those women with the opportunity to choose their new place of residence, the selection of a specific settlement took into consideration a number of factors: economics, religious beliefs, ideology, and personal preferences.

To date, no study dealing with the period has isolated the migration process or location decisions of women. During this period in the United States, women had great freedom in determining their place of residence and destiny as a result of the achievements of the women's suffrage movement and economic advances. This study examines the question of women and migration through a case study of American Jewish women and their moves to British Mandatory Palestine.

To understand this process, the end result or the spatial distribution of American Jewish women in Palestine is first detailed. This is followed by a series of examples of location decisions made by American Jewish women when settling in Palestine, which provide a deeper understanding of the different categories of factors behind the decision-making processes. The discussion also provides insight into the perceptions of Palestine held by American Jewish women in the interwar years and their expectations about life in Palestine.

Spatial Distribution

Prior to any discussion of the spatial distribution of American Jewish women in Palestine, it is necessary to estimate the actual number of

---

*Due to the limited number of examples available, the stories of a number of Canadian women have been included in this discussion in order to expand upon it.

American Jewish women who immigrated to Palestine between the two world wars. Statistical records detailing Jewish immigration to Palestine do not differentiate between women and men according to nationality, and so the number of American *olot* [female Jewish immigrants] can only be estimated. Information on the number of American Jewish immigrants is inconclusive. The Jewish Agency for Palestine figures point to a total of 6,379 American Jewish immigrants to Palestine for the period from 1920 to 1939. The government of Palestine immigration authorities reached a substantially higher figure of 8,438 for the years 1922 to 1939. The 1931 census of Palestine, in fact, suggests that the government immigration figures are incorrect and attempts to adjust the defects in the migration records. Using the suggested adjustments, American immigration from 1922 to 1939 would have been 9,654.[1] A safe estimate for American *aliyah* for the period of study would be 9,000—slightly above government figures to include those who did not register as immigrants.

With approximately nine thousand American Jews settling in Palestine, the question arises as to how many were women. The 1931 census estimates that 55 percent of the Americans residing in Palestine were female (see table 1). Using this ratio, some five thousand American women of all ages settled in Palestine between the two world wars. However, it should be stated almost categorically that the children among them (one-third of the female population) did not have a voice in the decision-making process, although quite often their perceived needs were factored into their parents' decision.

The spatial distribution of American Jews in Palestine is detailed in two censuses (see table 2), one conducted during World War I and the

TABLE 1. Age-Gender Structure of the American Jewish Nationals in Palestine, 1931

Age	Numbers			%		
	Male	Female	Total	Male	Female	Total
0–10	154	185	339	6.78	8.14	14.91
10–20	209	223	432	9.19	9.81	19.01
20–45	266	464	730	11.70	20.41	32.12
>45	392	380	772	17.25	16.72	33.96
Totals	1,021	1,252	2,273	44.92	55.08	100.00

Source: Eric Mills, *Census of Palestine 1931*, vol. 2 (Alexandria, Egypt: Whitehead Morris, 1933), 266–268.

TABLE 2. Rural-Urban Distribution and Distribution among Selected Urban Centers of American Jewish Citizens (Women and Men)

	1916–1918 Census		1931 Census	
	Number	%	Number	%
Urban	627	84.7	1,718	77.3
Rural	113	15.3	504	22.7
Totals	740	100.0	2,222	100.0
Jaffa	71	9.6	7	0.3
Tel Aviv	*	*	702	31.6
Haifa	1	0.01	94	4.2
Jerusalem	546	73.8	851	38.3

Sources: Palestine Office of the Zionist Organization, *Census of the Jews of Erez Israel* [Hebrew] vol. 1 (Jaffa, 1918), 20, 23, 31, 43, 47, 110; Palestine Office of the Zionist Organization, *Census of the Jews of Erez Israel* [Hebrew], vol. 2 (Jaffa, 1918), 5, 14, 22, 36, 71, 110–111; Mills, *Census of Palestine 1931,* vol. 2, 266–268.

* The information for Tel Aviv was probably included in the figures for Jaffa. Tel Aviv was founded as a neighborhood of Jaffa in 1909.

other in 1931. (To obtain the number of females, the figures below should be divided by two.) The first is the *Census of the Jews of Erez Israel,* conducted in Judea between spring 1916 (Adar 5676) and spring 1918 (Adar 5678) in the midst of the war. By the time of this census, some American citizens had fled the country as refugees or had been forced to migrate; others had starved or perished from various plagues. Listed are only 693 American Jewish nationals in Judea of whom the majority, 546, resided in Jerusalem; the remainder lived in the *moshavot* [plantation villages], including 71 American exiles from Jaffa.[2] Between the summer of 1917 (Av 5677) and the summer of 1919 (Tammuz 5779) the census was extended to northern Palestine (Samaria and the Galilee). The American Jewish population there totaled only 47. This figure does not reflect the actual number of Americans who resided in this area before the war. When the United States entered the war in 1917, some of its nationals were expelled from Turkish territory or forced to relocate to other Turkish-controlled areas. Overall, the 740 Americans enumerated throughout Palestine during the war are significantly fewer than the over 1,000 American citizens and protégés listed in 1896, and there are discrepancies between census figures and the number of Americans listed in the consular registries for other dates.[3]

Despite the limitations of the census, two generalities may be observed about the spatial distribution of American Jews around the time of World War I. Approximately three-quarters of the American Jewish population resided in Jerusalem. This expresses the dominant location decision of American Jewish immigrants in the late Ottoman period, which was to settle in the Holy City for religious reasons. The second generality points to the small proportion of Americans engaged in agricultural pursuits. They were found mainly in the *moshavot* of Judea; there was also a noteworthy concentration of Americans, 17 in number, in the American-founded colony of Poriyah in the Galilee.

During the British Mandate period there was a significant change in the distribution of American Jewish citizens in the cities of Palestine. Jerusalem continued into the beginning of the 1930s to have the largest concentration of American Jews, but its proportion of American Jews dropped from 73.8 percent during World War I to 38.3 percent in 1931. Through the 1930s, the number of American Jews residing in Jerusalem dropped from 851 in 1931 to 824 in 1939, reflecting the changing motivation of American Jews for their immigration to Palestine and the high mortality rate of American Jews residing in Jerusalem. A large part of American Jewish immigrants to Jerusalem were elderly and Orthodox.[4]

In both Tel Aviv and Haifa there was a significant increase in the number of American Jews settling in these cities. Tel Aviv and Jaffa had 702 American Jewish citizens in 1931 as compared with 7 during World War I. Their numbers appear to have increased during the 1930s; however, no census was conducted that confirms this assumption. Haifa's American population increased almost threefold, from 94 in 1931 to 272 in 1938.[5] Both Haifa and Tel Aviv were magnets for American Jewish immigrants offering both economic opportunities and the amenities of life they sought.

The distribution of American Jews also changed in the rural sector during the interwar period. During World War I, only 15 percent of the American Jews in Palestine lived in rural settlements. By 1931 their proportion had increased to 23 percent. This was the result of the attraction of American families to both the *moshavot* and the *kibuzim*. In the 1930s the actual number of American Jews in rural settlements increased from 504 in 1931 to 848 in 1941–1942. A significant part of this growth came from some two hundred young American women and men who joined *kibuzim* during this decade.[6]

The changing spatial distribution of American Jewish women in Palestine echoes the shifts in the motivations for migration and the location decisions of American Jews generally. The rate of migration of Orthodox

Jewish women was stagnant or in decline over the British Mandate period. The years following World War I represented an era of great expectations. The Balfour Declaration outlined the promise of a Jewish homeland. The excitement of the era prompted many American Jewish women to participate in the building of the Yishuv. American Jewish women lent a hand in various fields of activity, most notably in health care. A second direction was the return to the soil. American Jewish families purchased agricultural tracts throughout Palestine, and some even settled their land. The years of the Great Depression and the accompanying economic difficulties served as an impetus for increased emigration from the United States, with the cities of Palestine serving as magnets for American Jewish immigrant women. Palestine was enjoying a small economic boom during the 1930s, and it offered American Jewish women various opportunities. Some younger American women sought alternative lifestyles to escape what appeared to be a failed American capitalism. They embraced socialist Zionist ideology and joined the ranks of the *haluzot* [pioneers] in the 1930s. The different motivations and waves of immigration are also reflected in the location decisions of American Jewish women in Palestine.

Location Decisions

In some instances, American Jews decided on the location of their new residence and their occupation before their immigration to Palestine, while in other cases they made a decision only after reaching Palestine. Location decisions were a dynamic process. The encounter with a new environment and its population often led to changes in an earlier decision. Often, it was recommended that an individual visit Palestine first in order to make a clear choice. Some American immigrants, however, chose their future place of residence before departing for Palestine. They may have purchased a tract of land and even contracted for the construction of a new home, or else had made arrangements to rent a house, apartment, or room. Land-purchasing agents and organizations, American or Palestinian, sold tracts of land in urban and rural settings. The immigrant's decision was thus based on information presented by these agents.

Four categories—economic, personal, religious, and ideological—exemplify the decision-making process of American Jewish immigrants but also serve to highlight the multifaceted decisions made by American Jewish women when choosing their new homes in Palestine.

Economic Considerations

The selection of a place of residence often reflected economic considerations. Americans needed to earn a livelihood in Palestine. For many, job opportunity, salary, and educational opportunity[7] outweighed aesthetic preferences and ideological considerations. Some women were assigned positions in Palestine, thus determining where they would live.

Henrietta Szold, the founder of Hadassah, was sent to Jerusalem in 1919 for two years to represent American Zionist interests and to administer Hadassah activities in Palestine. She explained to Alice L. Seligsberg: "The first purpose to be served by my going is that the American [Zionist] Organization may have a direct representative on the Executive Committee on the [American Zionist Medical] Unit, someone in whose mind and time the Unit will have the first and if need be the only place."[8] She arrived in Jerusalem in 1920 and would live out the rest of her life in the city administering Hadassah projects and establishing Youth Aliyah. (fig. 1).

Irma Lindheim, a former president of Hadassah, explained why she settled in Tel Aviv in 1933.

We moved into our new home in Tel Aviv. If it seemed treachery to Jerusalem, my work lay in Tel Aviv, so here it had to be. Second to Jerusalem in choice of cities would have been Haifa, now beginning to build up the slopes of beautiful Mount Carmel, a promontory rising directly from the sea. But, whether Tel Aviv was or was not the best-loved city, it was the hub of the new Palestine, the heart of its driving life; sooner or later everyone and everything was drawn to Tel Aviv, whether for business or pleasure, for organization or cultural purposes. The important factor in choosing it as our home now was that it was the focal point of the federated activities of the Histadrut [General Federation of Jewish Workers in the Land of Israel], and the center of gravity of the surging new wave of immigration.[9]

That same year Lindheim, after a decision to radically change her life, left the city and joined Kibbutz Mishmar Haemek, at first on a trial basis and later as a full member.

The city of Haifa afforded a special opportunity for some of the American Jewish women coming to Palestine. The establishment of the modern port of Palestine at Haifa and the subsequent development of industries in the vicinity created a need for workers of all types. Many of the companies required efficient and competent English-speaking secretaries. For qualified American women of the Depression era, Palestine offered an opportunity to earn a good salary and to see the world.

FIGURE 1. Henrietta Szold (left) and Dr. Judah Magnes (c. 1940). Courtesy of the Hebrew University Photograph Archive.

American businessmen with American methods and connections, naturally want American-trained secretaries who can write literate English and not the stylistic atrocities of the average Palestinian secretary who inevitably claims "perfect knowledge" of at least four or five languages. Efficient girl secretaries from any number of American cities form a distinct class in Palestine, for many a young tourist has seen the opportunity to come and work for a year or two—and the news spreads to others. The Imperial Chemicals Industries and the Iraq Petroleum Company alone have harbored many American girls, a goodly percentage of whom marry Palestinians—of many origins, to be sure—and stay in the country.[10]

Such was the case for Irma Lindheim's daughter, Babs. She became the secretary to the head of British Imperial Chemicals in Haifa. With her relatively high salary, she lived comfortably in Haifa.[11]

Tel Aviv provided increasing employment and business opportunities for American Jewish women as the city rapidly grew in population and economic importance during the British Mandate period. The Jewish population of the Tel Aviv municipal area increased from 15,185 in 1922 to 140,700 in 1941, an increase of 826.6 percent, while Haifa and Jerusalem grew 364.4 and 125.5 percent, respectively, over the same period. Tel Aviv also became the country's industrial center, with the largest number of industrial enterprises and workers and a cultural center of the Yishuv.[12] Thus, it was quite natural that Mrs. Sternberg hoped to reestablish herself in Tel Aviv. "Mrs. Sternberg had won a place for herself in New York as an advertiser. She would inaugurate a large-scale advertising business in Tel Aviv. She would show Palestine the value of high-powered advertising whether Palestine wanted it or not."[13]

Personal Preferences

Women were drawn to certain locales for reasons connected to family and personal obligations, the social environment, and available amenities. Writer and journalist Dorothy Ruth Kahn related the trials of an extended family's search for the right place to live. At the head of this clan was Bill who, among his various endeavors in America, had been a cattle dealer. He thought this group of twenty would remain in Jerusalem for a month while he searched for land appropriate for raising cattle. In the interim, his niece married a Polish *oleh* [new immigrant], and Bill's nephew received a job offer for an engineering position in Tel Aviv. Bill's mother-in-law wanted to remain in Jerusalem's Mea Shearim neighborhood with other elderly women whose companionship she found enjoyable. She found "it was pleasant to sit in the synagogue gallery and chat a bit behind her prayer book between 'amens.'" Bill's sister felt obligated to attend to her rheumatic mother in Jerusalem. The sister also had a job offer at an exclusive tearoom in Jerusalem. The owners of the establishment liked American workers. The group thus began to dwindle. Land, Bill learned, was expensive and not within their means. In the end, Bill and his wife remained in Jerusalem so as to be near their mothers, and the couple opened a restaurant. In this story, the two elderly women, who were most probably eastern European immigrants to the United States, selected Jerusalem primarily in order to be in the society of other Orthodox eastern European women including those who had sojourned in America. Bill's wife and sister sensed daughterly responsibilities toward their respective mothers and chose to live in the same city in order to care for their mothers.[14]

In the 1930s, many middle-class American wives and widows preferred to live in Tel Aviv and Haifa since these large cities possessed the infrastructure necessary to develop comforts they had grown accustomed to in the United States. The lack of services matching American standards was of great concern to certain American Jewish women. Some women made do with the lower domestic standards in Palestine. For example, in the early 1920s Jessie Sampter managed to deal with the trials of cooking and keeping house by relating to them as an adventure like camping in the Adirondacks.[15] For others the low standards of Palestine were a real concern. In the early 1930s, Mrs. Sternberg expressed her worries while en route to Palestine. "She heard that there was no steam heat in winter and no hot water on tap. The food was of a poor grade and good maids were difficult to secure."[16] The situation was not as bleak as Mrs. Sternberg feared. True, at the end of World War I there was no public service power plant. In the mid-1920s, only a few homes had electricity (6,500 consumers in 1926). But the situation changed rapidly in the 1930s, particularly in the large cities, and in 1942 there were over 96,000 consumers of electricity, seventy-eight times the number in 1926. The standards of construction also improved in the large cities during the 1930s. Some luxury homes, particularly in Jerusalem with its cooler winter temperatures, even had central heating.[17]

Sulamith Schwartz (Nardi) in a 1937 article detailed some of the available amenities and the lifestyle some Americans found in the cities:

Americans continue to lead an almost American existence in apartment houses which as often as possible have running hot water, a pretense at central heating, and built-in closets. They possess those greatest of Palestinian luxuries, electric refrigerators and radios, and send their children to private rather than public schools. On Thanksgiving Day you may see the American flag float out of more than one apartment window and canned cranberries carefully served on many a table. There are even spiritual and cultural imports: Americans have brought to Tel Aviv—name and all—something that grew up on the sidewalks of the East Side and Brooklyn, the punctiliously Orthodox Young Israel society.[18]

Many cities also had a critical mass of Americans who developed certain self-help services and organizations. A network of American Jewish women made many even newer American immigrants feel more comfortable in their new homes.

Religious Considerations

Some American women selected the cities of Jerusalem, Safed, or Tiberias as their place of settlement due to their sacredness, concentration of Orthodox Jews, and religious services. One example detailed above showed the desire of an elderly Orthodox American woman to find the companionship of other such women. Such concentrations of the Orthodox population allowed for the observance of Jewish religious commandments and traditions. Synagogues, *mikvaot* [ritual baths], social and philanthropic groups for Orthodox women, and other facilities were more abundant in these locations. American Orthodox women readily found financial and spiritual support in these cities. Kollel America Tiffereth Yerushalaim supported 179 American women in Jerusalem, Safed, and Tiberias: 134 were married, 5 divorced, 19 widowed, 1 was an *agunah* [single but not divorced], 2 were orphans, and 18 were of unknown status.[19]

The members of the Zelig family from Philadelphia immigrated to Palestine at the insistence of the mother, Haya Sarah. This devout Orthodox woman, after the tragic death of her daughter, became more observant and was convinced that life should be lived in the Holy Land. She also feared that if her other children remained in America, they would stray from Orthodox practice and assimilate. She forced the four youngest of her six remaining children and her husband to immigrate to Palestine in 1934. At first, Kfar Irvri, the Mizrahi Hazair settlement also known as Neve Yaakov, provided a suitable religious environment. After her husband and the two older of the four children returned to America, she moved to the area of the Orthodox neighborhood of Mea Shearim in Jerusalem and volunteered her time cooking for students at the Neturei Karta *yeshivah*.[20] She found her place in an Orthodox Jewish environment and took an active role in its perpetuation.

Within the category of religious motivation, two subgroups of American Jewish immigrant women predominated. The first group clung to traditional Orthodoxy (similar to that of eastern Europe) and selected the

Holy Cities for their settlement. A second group identified with modern American Orthodoxy. American Jewish women from the ranks of the latter did not limit their location decisions to the Holy Cities. They could be found settling in other places such as Tel Aviv, where the Young Israel society was established, or in agricultural settlements like Kfar Ivri and religious *kibuzim*.[21]

Ideological Considerations

The settlement of Palestine during the British Mandate was influenced by the ideological schism between pioneering Zionism and other schools of thought on the Zionist spectrum. Researcher Erik Cohen has shown that the pragmatism of the pioneering ideology emphasized the rejuvenation and restructuring of Jewish society in Palestine in contrast to the diaspora. *Haluzim* were proponents of a return to the soil and the development of the rural sector. For them, the city was perceived as the embodiment of social evils and the deterioration of a healthy society.[22] Among the American Jewish immigrants to Palestine, the anti-urban view was held by only a small minority usually affiliated with the pioneering movements. Most American Jewish immigrants had previously resided in urban centers of the United States, and on the whole, they did not grapple with the question of the negation of the city. Members of one group, the Orthodox population, most of whom were associated with Kollel America Tiffereth Yerushalaim, not only accepted the city but were opposed ideologically to the concept of pioneering rural settlement. In 1927, 84 percent of American Jews resided in U.S. cities numbering 100,000 or more, and 9 percent in urban centers of 25,000 to 100,000.[23] Indeed, before their arrival in Palestine, many American Jewish immigrants searched for a city in Palestine in which to settle. They perceived the city as the focus of industrial and commercial development—essential sectors for the growth of a healthy economy. Cities could also provide a variety of cultural activities and hence seemed a natural location in which to live.

In the rural environment, a direct correlation can be found between American Jewish immigrant ideology and different forms of agricultural settlement: *moshavah, kibbutz, moshav,* and *moshav shitufi*. Each settlement possessed distinct economic and social structures and lifestyles.

In the *moshavah* [plantation village], there were very few limitations to the private farmers' activities. They were the proprietors of the land and made their own decisions concerning production, marketing, and labor. The *moshavah* was based on self-reliance and individualism. There was no contractual obligation for cooperation or mutual assistance unless the farmers themselves decided to join a cooperative. The size and development of each farmer's holding depended on the amount of land the farmer was able to purchase and the capital he wanted to invest. The first *moshavah*, Petah Tikvah, was founded in 1878. This attempt failed, but in 1882 First Aliyah settlers established Rishon Lezion, Zikhron Yaakov, and Rosh Pinah. Petah Tikvah was reestablished in 1882. Additional *moshavot* [pl.] were founded in the years following, and by 1904 there were twenty-eight Jewish farming communities in Palestine.

American Jewish immigrant families joined different *moshavot*. No individual American Jewish woman appears to have bought a farm and operated it. Wives sometime decided together with their husbands to settle in a *moshavah*. Occasionally, unmarried women did choose to live in a home in a *moshavah*. For example, Jessie Sampter moved to Rehovot in 1924. Her decision reflected her feelings that it would be best for her adopted daughter, Tamar Sheleg, to grow up in the midst of orchards, groves, vineyards, and rolling hills. Rehovot had a large Yemenite colony whose women Sampter helped educate. In addition, she had friends and acquaintances in Rehovot, including another American named Boris Katzman. Sampter dabbled in farming and gardening, and raised chickens and a milk cow.[24] She later left Rehovot and joined Kibbutz Givat Brenner.

Prior to World War I, American Jewish immigrant families could be found in following *moshavot*: Petah Tikvah, Rishon Lezion, Yavniel, Rehovot, Menahemiah, Beit Gan, Gederah, Zikhron Yaakov, Hederah, Ein Ganim, Shefyah, Kfar Tavor, Merhaviyah, and Ekron. The largest concentration was in Petah Tikvah, with an American population of fifty-eight. American-initiated *moshavot* were developed prior to World War I and were part of the *ahuzah* settlement plan. The plan proposed the transfer of capital to Palestine for the establishment of agricultural colonies and the settlement of groups of Jews from the diaspora to Palestine; it also provided employment for Jewish laborers in Palestine. To this end, groups of approximately fifty families were formed. They pooled their resources, collecting regular installments from each family until a sufficient sum had accumulated in order to purchase a tract of land in Palestine. The group employed Jewish workers to prepare the land, plant fruit-bearing trees, and maintain them. After six or seven years, when the plantations bore sufficient fruit to provide an income for its owners, the land would be parceled and transferred to the individual owners waiting to immigrate, settle on their land, and take over its maintenance. Between 1908 and the outbreak of World War I, at least sixteen *ahuzah* societies were established in American cities. However, only two *ahuzah* societies succeeded in establishing settlements prior to World War I—Hoachoozo [*sic*] of St. Louis founded Poriyah in 1910, and the Chicago Ahuza [*sic*] founded Sarona (also known as Ramah) in 1913. The *Census of the Jews of Erez Israel* (1917) lists a population of 68 persons in Poriyah, of which 25 percent or 17 individuals (4 adults and 13 children) had come from America. There was only one American at Sarona.[25]

Following World War I, New York Achouza Aleph [*sic*] established two colonies in Palestine: Raananah in 1922 and Gan Yavneh in 1932. Middle-class American Jews, mainly from New York, joined these settlements. The American Zion Commonwealth (AMZIC) was established in 1914 to aid in the settlement of Jews in Palestine and to secure for its members and their descendants rights, interests, and privileges in lands occupied by the AMZIC. It founded the agricultural settlements of Balfouriyah and Herzliyah and the town of Afulah. Several American couples made the decision to join these American-initiated colonies. Many subscribed to the New York *ahuzah* and the AMZIC in the United States. American Zion Commonwealth records indicate that a number of women purchased agricultural land through the agency—twenty-two in the urban sections of Herzliyah and two in the agricultural zone of Herzliyah. Although insignificant numerically, this figure highlights the decision of some women to settle on the land. The purchasers received information about the properties they would receive in Palestine and left the United States with great expectations. In 1926, in the AMZIC settlements of Balfouriyah and Herzliyah, Americans comprised 11.6 and 12.8 percent of the population respectively as compared with a countrywide national average of 1.3 percent of the Jewish population. Often, however, the realities of the settlements, with their rudimentary infrastructure and the difficulties of housekeeping, resulted in American Jewish immigrant families leaving the farm for the city.[26]

Another form of settlement American women joined was the *kibbutz*. The first *kibbutz* was established at Degania in 1910. The basic concepts underlying this development were to create economic equality and equality between the sexes. Members of Zionist groups in America with socialist orientations (Poalei Zion, Habonim, Hashomer Hazair, and Hashomer Hadati) were likely to join *kibuzim* in Palestine. During the 1920s there was no organized settlement of American Jews on *kibuzim*. Individuals or small groups contacted existing *kibuzim* and applied to join them. By the 1930s, with the growth of the socialist Zionist organizations in the United States, groups from the Hashomer Hazair and Habonim were organized and joined in the founding of new *kibuzim* in Palestine (Ein Hashofet in 1937, Kfar Menahem in 1939, Kfar Blum in 1943, and Hazor in 1943).

An example of the selection of a specific cooperative settlement by Americans was described by Jessie Sampter in 1930: "I am expecting almost any moment a young American couple with their baby who were supposed to arrive at Haifa yesterday on the *Mauritania*. They are *haluzim,* means they intend to go on the land here, and I have arranged for them to enter a cooperative group [Kvuzat Schiller] near Rehovot—they chose it on account of the good climate for their baby."[27]

Goldie (Golda) Meyerson had hoped to settle on Kibbutz Merhaviyah. As a member of Poalei Zion, the *kibbutz* was the type of settlement that best fit her ideological tenets. Of the twenty existing *kibuzim* in 1921, Golda hoped to join Merhaviyah, located in the Jezreel Valley, since she knew an American who had gone there. Upon reaching Palestine in July 1921, she applied to join Merhaviyah and received a reply that this request would only be considered in September. When September came around, the members of Merhaviyah rejected Golda's application. Golda explained: "Not only because we were Americans, but because we were a married couple. The thirty-two men were all bachelors and they wanted single girls." Furthermore the single women, eight in number at Merhaviyah, objected to Golda's membership since they believed that American women were inferior to their eastern European counterparts. They held that American women were too soft for physical labor. Golda succeeded in convincing them to allow her and her husband to stay on the *kibbutz* for a month-long trail period. After their probation period, they were accepted as members of the *kibbutz.* Golda and her husband had proven that they could endure the hardships of *kibbutz* life. But she also later quipped that "the scales were tipped in our favor by the phonograph" which they had brought from America![28]

The example of Golda Meir reflects the policy of the Young Poalei Zion Alliance, which was "to go to Palestine and assimilate into the Yishuv. Going in groups was permissible but perpetuating a special American identity was not."[29] Thus, Americans were integrated into various *kibuzim,* including Naan, Merhaviyah, Degania Bet, Ginossar, Afikim, Ramat David, and Givat Brenner.

The largest group of American *haluzim* came from the ranks of the Hashomer Hazair movement. The ideology of the latter stressed the necessity of establishing newcomers in collective settlements. The settlement process of American members of Hashomer Hazair was divided into three phases. The first was the absorption, training, and acclimation of the group in an established *kibbutz.* The second phase was the consolidation period on a small tract of land near an existing settlement. This transition usually occurred near colonies in the coastal plain that could provide temporary employment for the *kvuzah* members in orchards and other jobs. The final phase was the group's permanent settlement on Jewish National Fund land. The decision as to where such groups ultimately settled depended upon a number of factors, the most important being the availability of land.

To illustrate the trials of finding a permanent site for the settlement of American *haluzim,* consider the example of the American group that settled at Ein Hashofet.[30] In 1931 a group of six American Hashomer Hazair members reached Palestine. This was the beginning of Kibbutz Aleph. Too few in number and too inexperienced to establish a *kibbutz* of their own, the Hashomer Hazair Executive in Warsaw discussed the possibilities of affiliated *kibuzim* absorbing, training, and helping in the acclimation of the American group. Mishmar Haemek, Karkur, and Merhaviyah were considered. Originally, the first two were ruled out as they were already engaged in the absorption of other groups. Merhaviyah was deemed most appropriate, having had experience in absorbing new pioneers. The successful absorption of this group was considered crucial to the future of the movement in America.[31]

The following year, the number of Americans at Mishmar Haemek increased to seventeen. Proposals were forwarded to allow this group to remain in the vicinity. In 1933 their number grew to thirty. The American Hashomer Hazair movement attempted to force the hand of various bodies to speed the permanent settlement of its *haluzim.* Its leaders proposed that an amount raised above the yearly income of the Jewish National Fund be used for this purpose. They hoped to promote increased donations to the JNF by using the slogan "Land for American *Haluzim*" in their fund-raising efforts. These extra funds would be used to purchase a ten-thousand-*dunam* strip of land between Mishmar Haemek and the archaeological site of Megido. The attraction of the site was its potential for general and diversified farming, which suited the training of the American *haluzim.* Furthermore, they believed the area to be appropriate for the application of American methods and machinery.[32]

In 1934 the American *haluzim* left Mishmar Haemek for a fifteen-*dunam* tract of Jewish National Fund land near Hederah. This was the second phase—independence. Together with a group from Poland, they worked as hired labor in the *moshavah* of Hederah while they awaited their turn for land to be allocated for permanent settlement. This transitional period served the additional purpose of consolidating the group. Over the years, the number of Americans increased to fifty-three. While the members of this group were in Hederah, American Yiddish journalist Avraham Revusky held intimate talks with them. He was

FIGURE 2. Founders of Kibbutz Ein Hashofet (1938). Courtesy of Central Zionist Archives Photograph Collection.

"strongly impressed by the idealistic spirit of these young men and women, nearly all high school graduates or college students, who came to participate personally in the building of a new country under the still-trying conditions of Palestine."[33] They remained at Hederah until July 1937, when the first members established themselves at the settlement site of Juara in the Samaritan Mountains, later known as Ein Hashofet[34] (fig. 2). The settlement's name, Hebrew for "spring of the judge," was chosen to honor the American Zionist leader Louis D. Brandeis, the first Jew appointed to the U.S. Supreme Court. He retained strong connections with the American settlers and personally provided them with financial assistance. By 1943 the *kibbutz* population reached 299, with 4,500 *dunams* of land. In *kibuzim* with American settlers, the proportion of Americans was generally higher than the countrywide average. For instance, Ein Hashofet included fifty-two Americans, approximately 17 percent of its population, while thirty-two Americans resided at Kfar Menahem, or approximately 13 percent, with another fourteen joining after World War II.[35]

The third form of settlement was the *moshav ovdim* [workers' settlement]. The first two *moshavim* [pl.], Nahalal and Kfar Yehezkiel, were established in 1921. American Jews settled individually in a number of *moshavim*.

A number of American Jewish women joined the *moshav* of Avihayil. This *moshav* was established by a group of Jewish legionnaires and their families in 1933. Its name, Avihayil (*avi,* "father," and "*hayil,* "soldier"), reflected its population. Men from the United States who had volunteered in the British army and fought together to liberate Palestine from four hundred years of Turkish rule hoped to settle the land. For over a decade, these men and their wives undertook to obtain land, and only at the end of August 1932 were they allotted land by the Jewish National Fund in Emek Hefer. The plan allocated land for one hundred settlers. However, problems in financing required a gradual development of the colony: twenty families settled by November 1933, another thirty were expected within a year and a half, and the rest four years later.[36]

In 1936 the population of Avihayil reached 280. Not all the members resided in the settlement. According to a list from April 1936, there were fifty-three families (fourteen of them North American) *on* the land at Avihayil and twenty-six families (seven of them North American) residing *outside* the settlement. Some of the American families found that life on an agricultural settlement did not suit them and used their property in Avihayil as a weekend retreat.[37] The lack of a shared commitment to agriculture stemmed from the fact that the colony was not founded on the basis of mutual interests. The common denominator was, in fact, that the men had served together in 1918 in the Thirty-eighth, Thirty-ninth, and Fortieth battalions of the British Royal Fusiliers. When they volunteered they had a common ideal—moral and spiritual—but not shared material interests. There were great differences in the economic, personal, and social standing of those who organized the cooperative agricultural endeavor and founded Avihayil. Once their initial purpose was achieved and began to bear fruit, individuals became preoccupied with their private affairs.[38]

The Herut Plan was also an American scheme for middle-class settlement in Palestine developed for and marketed to the American Jewish public.

Yakhin, the Agricultural Concentrating Cooperative Association of the Histadrut and the directorate of the Jewish National Fund recently reached an agreement whereby the settling of 200 families on a large new tract of land in Vadi Havarit [Emek Hefer] was entrusted to Yakhin. Yakhin has taken upon itself the task of organizing in different countries two hundred working and middle-class families who can in a period of five to six years set aside the sums necessary for the cultivation of the orange groves. According to the plan, by the time orange groves mature, the families will be in a position to settle in Palestine and be assured of a living.[39]

Three settlement groups were organized under this scheme—Herut Alef (later Zofit) in 1931, Herut Bet (later Beit Herut) in 1932, and Herut Gimel in 1933. Fifty-nine North American Jewish families actually signed contracts for these three settlements. Herut Alef and Herut Bet both had American members. Herut Gimel was designed specifically for North Americans but was not developed. In all, five or six American families resided in Zofit.[40] The second group had different ideas as to the structure of their colony. In 1933 Herut Bet members met in Chelsea, Michigan, to discuss the future of their settlement, which was planned to be a *moshav*. A majority of members supported the idea of transforming the settlement into a *moshav shitufi* [agricultural parnership], but a minority group prevented this change. A year later, a second conference at Cleveland approved the plan to change the settlement into a *moshav shitufi*, with two variations: families could construct houses according to their own means, and two *dunams* adjacent to the houses could be worked privately. In relative terms, this was quite early for a discussion of this type of settlement; the first *moshav shitufi* was founded at Kfar Hitim in the Lower Galilee in 1936.[41]

A number of the children of Herut Bet members were sent to Palestine to train in agriculture. In 1939, along with some older members, they assumed responsibility for developing and administering the settlement for others in America. Before World War II, only six American families settled in the colony. Following the war, their number increased to seventeen families. More Americans joined after Israel's War of Independence in 1947–1948. The settlement was renamed Beit Herut.[42]

Reality of Palestine

The location decisions of American Jewish immigrants often changed following their encounter with Palestine. Quite often women who had selected a specific settlement or a type of settlement were unable to realize their decisions. The realities of Palestine and organizations responsible for Jewish settlement often dictated a change in location decisions.

Goldie Hoffman (Yosef) from Montreal, Canada reached Palestine in 1921. She settled in Jerusalem but would have preferred to join the newly settled cooperative of Kfar Giladi in the northern Galilee. She turned to the Zionist Commission (the official body of the Yishuv) requesting permission to join the settlers. She was told that she did not have the right to do so as did *haluzot* from eastern Europe. The reason given was that she would take away this opportunity from an unskilled *haluzah* and that eastern European women were hard workers in the fields and at paving roads. Instead it was suggested that she would fit better in the British Mandate administration. At that time, there were few young women in the country that knew English. In fact, she received fifteen job offers in the span of a week and ultimately decided to work for the attorney general of Mandatory Palestine, Norman Bentwich.[43]

The reality of country life was too difficult for many American Jewish families. The isolation of some colonies and the difficult standard of living made the rural environment unbearable for some. In the colony of Gan Hasharon, which was founded by a group of Jews from the area of Saskatoon, Canada, the wives of two of the founders did not want to adjust to country life.

Sam [Sussman] had created Gan Hasharon and his brother Dave had followed close behind. Both families lived in Tel Aviv and had weekend cottages on the farm. In the city, they basked in the prestige of being growers, on the farm they strutted their city-dweller stuff, the women especially flaunting town airs and impressing us country yokels. . . . The men loved Gan Hasharon and tried by every subtlety to get their women to favor the idea of making their homes there.[44]

The difficulties that American Jewish women faced in Palestine often resulted in a reassessment of their original location decisions. The shifts in location were in all directions: rural to urban, urban to rural, and interurban. Movement also occurred across ideological lines. For a significant number, Palestine did not become their home. An estimated one in three American Jewish women returned to the United States.

Conclusion

The decisions American Jewish women made in selecting their places of residence in Palestine did not differ greatly from the decisions made by most immigrant groups to Palestine and other countries. The primary concern was economic, that is, where one could earn a livelihood to support a family or where job opportunities were available. A second common consideration was the desire to find a place with the highest quality of life—amenities, climate, or environment. Some immigrants weighed economic considerations against those of quality of life. A third consideration related to the population of a settlement. Many Jewish immigrant women wanted to live near family, friends, and relatives already settled in Palestine. The first settlers often spearheaded the relocation of family and friends. In such instances, they also facilitated the acclimation and social absorption of newcomers. A concentration of immigrants frequently served as a magnet for later immigrants from the same country of origin. Such concentrations often allowed for the development of familiar services and social organizations.

Some American Jewish women fit into a different category of immigrants. They were religiously motivated, and their location decisions reflected geographic preferences within a sacred space. Four cities in Palestine—Jerusalem, Safed, Tiberias, and Hebron—were considered holy according to Jewish tradition. Jerusalem was deemed to be the holiest of the four. Thus, Orthodox American Jewish women were found predominantly in Jerusalem but also in Safed and Tiberias.

American Jewish women's location decisions also differed from those of the general immigrant population. Ideological location decisions were not common. Two ideologies (which overlap to a certain degree) stood out—the return to the soil and *haluziut* [pioneering]. The biblical undertones and the sense of a new nationalism resonated with many American Jewish immigrant women. These women and their families settled in the *moshavot* and *moshavim;* quite often they selected settlements that were organized by Americans or for Americans. This allowed them to be together with other Americans including friends and relatives. The motivation of *haluziut* impelled followers of the Zionist pioneer ideologies to join communes in Palestine. The *haluzot* resided on small tracts near established settlements during the consolidation phase of their own group. In the end, *haluzot* settled the land on the *kibbutz* they joined or established.

There appear to be few differences in the location decisions made by American Jewish immigrant women and men. One difference was the stated willingness of men (former members of the Jewish Legion) to settle the borders of Palestine. They viewed themselves a part of a defensive line that would stand up against and possibly prevent Arab attacks. In general, women did not express such strong military considerations, but it should be noted that American *haluzot* did perceive their role in the defense of the Yishuv and demarcation of Jewish territory through the establishment in the 1930s and 1940s of "tower and stockade" settlements. Thee American women accepted the duty of defending their *kibuzim* (fig. 3); however, military considerations as such did not weigh heavily in their decisions to choose a place of residence.

American Jewish immigrant women between the two world wars attempted to find their place in Palestine. Their location decisions reflect the varied considerations of what lifestyle they wanted and the role they would play in the development of the old-new homeland. The American Jewish women who adjusted or adapted to life in Palestine played active

FIGURE 3. *Haluzot* participating in military training exercises, Kibbutz Ein Hashofet (December 1937). Courtesy of Central Zionist Archives Photograph Collection.

roles in the development of their adopted home. Some American Jewish women reached positions of leadership in the Yishuv—Golda Meir in the Histadrut and Henrietta Szold in the Jewish Agency for Palestine. Others assumed significant positions in various sectors of the Yishuv, most notably in the field of health care. American Jewish women also stood out in their contribution to volunteerism in Palestine.[45] However, not all American *olot* found their place in Palestine. There often existed a gap between their expectations and the reality of the Palestine that could not be bridged. American Jewish women who did find their place in Palestine experienced great personal satisfaction and contributed in different ways to the building of a new Jewish homeland in the Land of Israel.

Notes

1. Eric Mills, *Census of Palestine 1931*, vol. 1 (Alexandria, Egypt: Whitehead Morris, 1933), 64–65. The calculation used was (1922–1931 × 1.23) + (1932–1939 × 1.1).

2. Palestine Office of the Zionist Organization, *Census of the Jews of Erez Israel* [Hebrew], vol. I (Jaffa, 1918), 20, 23, 31, 43, 47, 110.

3. Palestine Office of the Zionist Organization, *Census of the Jews of Erez Israel* [Hebrew], vol. 2 (Jaffa, 1918), 5, 14, 22, 36, 71, 110-111; Ruth Kark, *American Consuls in the Holy Land, 1832-1914* (Jerusalem and Detroit: Magnes Press and Wayne State University Press, 1994), 199-204. For example, the American consular agency at Haifa recorded ten American citizens in 1913 as compared with the two Americans listed in the World War I census.

4. David Gurevich, *The Jewish Population of Jerusalem: A Demographic and Sociological Study of the Jewish Population and Its Component Communities, Based on the Jerusalem Jewish Census, September, 1939* (Jerusalem: Department of Statistics of the Jewish Agency for Palestine, 1940), 27-31.

5. O. Eisenberg, *Census of the Jewish Population in Haifa, 1938* [Hebrew] (Haifa: 1940), table 9, 20-21.

6. David Gurevich and A. Gretz, *Statistical Handbook of Jewish Palestine, 1947* (Jerusalem: Jewish Agency for Palestine, 1947), 58-59.

7. For an example of a location decision related to educational opportunities see chapter 11 on Sara Bodek Paltiel, by Peri Rosenfeld, in this collection. Sara Bodek Paltiel decided to be a nurse, and Palestine was the only place she believed that she could engage in this profession and also be *shomer shabbat* [Sabbath observant]. She reached Jerusalem in 1932 and studied at the Hadassah Nursing School from 1933-1936. She was the first American graduate of the school.

8. Letter to Alice L. Seligsberg, New York, 30 November 1919, in *Henrietta Szold: Life and Letters,* ed. Marvin Lowenthal (New York: Viking Press, 1942), 116.

9. Irma L. Lindheim, *Parallel Quest: A Search of a Person and a People* (New York: Thomas Yoseloff, 1962), 360.

10. Sulamith Schwartz, "Americans in Palestine," *Jewish Frontier* vol. IV, no. 2 (February 1937), 12.

11. Lindheim, *Parallel Quest,* 384.

12. Office of Statistics, *Statistical Abstract of Palestine, 1942* (Jerusalem: Government Printing Press, 1942), 10; A. Revusky, *Jews in Palestine* (London: P. S. King and Son, 1935), 64–66, 172-177.

13. Dorothy Ruth Kahn, *Spring Up, O Well* (London: Jonathan Cape, 1936), 82.

14. Ibid., 207-212.

15. Jessie Sampter, Jerusalem, to Elvie, Edgar, and Little Jessie, n.p., 3 January 1921, Central Zionist Archives, Jerusalem (CZA), A219/21.

16. Kahn, *Spring Up,* 83-84.

17. Robert R. Nathan, Oscar Gass, and Daniel Creamer, *Palestine: Problem and Promise: An Economic Survey* (Washington, D.C.: Public Affairs Press, 1946), 177-183, 242-253.

18. Schwartz, "Americans in Palestine," 11.

19. Calculations based on questionnaires to *kollel* members in the late 1920s.

Yad Yizhak Ben Zvi Archives (YYBZA), Jerusalem, RG 4/2 Kollel America Tiffer-eth Yerushalaim; Rachel Weinberg, Jerusalem, to the American Consul, Jerusa-lem, 17 December 1923, Jerusalem Municipal Archives (JMA), Jerusalem, Shuch-man Archives, 2581/5.

20. The mother and four (Yosef, Moshe, Avraham, and Eliezer) of her seven children arrived in Palestine in February 1934, and they were later joined by the father, David Zeev. In the end, only the mother and Avraham remained perma-nently in Palestine. Avraham Zelig, interview by author, Tel Aviv, 16 September 1998.

21. Bessie Gotsfeld, the founder of Mizrachi Women, is an example of an Or-thodox American Jewish woman who settled in Tel Aviv. Her location decision of 1935 was based on her desire to be near her mother-in-law, who resided in the city. For further biographical details see chapter 4 on Bessie Gotsfeld, by Baila Round Shargel, in this volume.

22. Erik Cohen, "The City in the Zionist Ideology," *Jerusalem Urban Studies* 1 (Jerusalem, 1970), 2–9.

23. Harry S. Linfield, *The Jews in the United States, 1927: A Study of Their Number and Distribution* (New York: American Jewish Committee, 1929), 14.

24. Bertha Badat-Straus, *White Fire, The Life and Works, Jessie Sampter* (New York: Reconstructionist Press, 1956), 92–93.

25. Palestine Office of the Zionist Organization, *Census,* vol. 1, 20, 23, 31, 43, 47; vol. 2, 5, 14, 22, 36, 53, 65.

26. Constitution of the American Zion Commonwealth Inc., CZA Z4/762. Irit Amit, "American Jewry and the Settlement of Palestine: Zion Commonwealth, Inc.," in *The Land That Became Israel: Studies in Historical Geography,* ed. Ruth Kark (Jerusalem: Magnes Press; New Haven, Conn.: Yale University Press, 1990), 253.

27. Jessie E. Sampter, Rehovot, to Edgar Jr., n.p., 11 March 1930; see also 10 April 1930, CZA A219/2/2.

28. Marie Syrkin, ed., *Golda Meir Speaks Out* (London: Weidenfeld and Nic-olson, 1973), 38–42; Ralph G. Martin, *Golda: A Biography* (New York: Ivy Books, 1988) 100, 110, 117–118.

29. Saadia Gelb, "Poale Zion and Habonim Settlements," in *Pioneers from America: 75 Years of Hehaluz, 1905-1980,* ed. Sima Altman et al. (Tel Aviv: Bo-grei Hechalutz America, 1981), 65–67.

30. For an example of a woman who joined Kibbutz Kfar Blum see chapter 11 by Peri Rosenfeld, in this volume.

31. Y. Hazan, Shomer Hazair World Executive, Warsaw to Shomer Hazair Executive, Mishmar Haemek [Hebrew], 8 April 1931, Givat Havivah Archives (GHA), Givat Havivah, Israel, RG H1.2, box 4, file 2; *Hashomer Hazair Bulle-tin,* November 1931, 5, GHA RG T-1, box 1, file 5; Morris, *Pioneers from the West* (Jerusalem Youth and Hechalutz Dept., World Zionist Organization, 1953), 26–27.

32. Minutes of the Palestine Executive of the Jewish Agency Meeting, 3 July 1932, CZA S100/13B; "Memorandum on the project of supplying land for the settlement of the first American Kvutzah of Hashomer Hatzair Organization in Palestine," 2 March 1933, CZA KKL5/4931.

33. Revusky, *Jews in Palestine,* 270.

34. Morris, *Pioneers from the West,* 27–29; see the file "Kibbutz American-Banir at Hadera, 1934–1938," CZA S9/465, for details of conditions at the Hederah camp.

35. List of American *haluzim* at Ein Hashofet and Kfar Menahem, c. 1947, GHA RG T-1, box 26, file 3; Edwin Samuel, *Handbook of the Jewish Communal Villages in Palestine* (Jerusalem: Zionist Organization Youth Department, 1945), 73–75. The 1943 populations were Ein Hashofet, 299; Kfar Menahem, 245; and Kfar Blum, 157. Joshua Liebner, "Our First *Kibbutz:* Ein Hashofet," *Youth and Nation* 16, no. 8 (August 1948), 17–20.

36. L. Bawly to Emanuel Neumann, 30 September 1932, CZA S17/150; Letter to Julius Simon, n.p., 26 November 1933, CZA KKL 5/6876.

37. List of settlers on the settlement (Avihayil), 29 April 1936, CZA S15/1972; David Gurevich and A. Gerz, *Jewish Agricultural Settlement in Palestine (General Survey and Statistical Abstracts)* (Jerusalem: Department of Statistics of the Jewish Agency for Palestine, 1938), 5.

38. Asher Sapir, Tel Aviv, to the Registrar of Cooperative Organizations of the Palestinian Government, Jerusalem, 22 July 1938, CZA S15/1978a.

39. "An Extensive Colonization Scheme in Palestine," New York, 27 February 1933, CZA S17/161.

40. Emanuel Liebes, *History of Moshav Beit Herut* (Beit Herut: Private publication, 1994), 3.

41. Ibid.; Efraim Orni and Elisha Efrat, *Geography of Israel* (Jerusalem: Israel Program for Scientific Translations, 1966), 240. A *moshav shitufi* is a type of cooperative smallholders' settlement representing an intermediate form between the *kibbutz* and the *moshav.* It is based on a collective economy and ownership, combining the mechanical and technological advantages of large-scale enterprises with individual living.

42. Liebes, *History of Moshav Beit Herut,* 3, 36–38.

43. Goldie Joseph, *A City and a Mother* [Hebrew] (Jerusalem: Rubin Mass, 1979), 18.

44. Molly Lyons Bar-David, *My Promised Land* (New York: G. P. Putman's Sons, 1953), 40–41.

45. See chapter 12 by Sara Kadosh, on Rose Viteles, in this volume.

Chapter 11

When the Great Depression reached its peak in the 1930s, the Jewish population of the United States was estimated at approximately 4,228,000 people. The entire American Zionist movement consisted of about 64,000 individuals, or a little more than 1.5 percent of the total. Economic hardship was a primary reason for the movement's small size; most American Jews simply could not afford to pay dues to a membership organization. Indeed, in 1929 the Brookings Institute estimated that an average American family required $2,000 a year to survive. At the time, economists calculated that nearly 60 percent of Americans earned less than this amount. By 1932, when the Depression reached a high point, the average American family's income had plummeted to $1,348, or "barely enough to survive."[1]

The situation of American Zionism in the Depression mirrored that of even the strongest American Jewish organizations. For example, the membership of the powerful International Ladies' Garment Workers' Union was reduced from 70,000 in 1928 to 14,000 in the years immediately following the stock market crash. Likewise, membership in the Order of Bnai Brith fell from nearly 100,000 to 30,000 in this period. Even the affluent Union of American Hebrew Congregations (UAHC) dropped from more than 61,000 dues-paying families and individuals in 1930 to roughly 52,000 in 1934. Were it not for the UAHC's policy of retaining families and synagogues unable to pay membership dues, these figures would surely have been lower. In sum, American Jews, despite their relatively high levels of education and white-collar occupations, suffered financial devastation no less than other American ethnic groups.

The acute social, economic, and political crises of the 1930s shocked young American Zionists. Those on the political left viewed the crash of the stock market and the onset of the Great Depression in socialist terms: as the end of one era and the dawn of another. Meanwhile, the Arab riots of August 1929, in which hundreds of Jews in Palestine were wounded or killed, also had a profound impact on Jewish idealists. A Habonim youth leader of the period later recalled:

1. James West Davidson et al., *Nation of Nations: A Narrative History of the American Republic*, vol. 2 (New York: McGraw-Hill Publishing Company, 1990), 948.

We had been under the emotional stress of two traumatic experiences in 1929. . . . Jewishly we were upset by the Palestine riots, during which the Arabs went on · a rampage. . . . On the general scene we were profoundly shaken by the . . . stock market crash and the subsequent Depression. It is difficult to conceive what a sense of helplessness engulfed the country after the crash. Not only the headlines of tycoons turned paupers, news of millionaire suicides, confusing government statements, wild predictions and premonitions by economists, but gnawing doubts about the very foundation of our society upset every American. Those of us who were then in the [Labor Zionist youth movement] had the answers. We knew that Zionism would solve the Jewish problem; socialism the problem of society as a whole.[2]

In the chapter that follows, Peri Rosenfeld traces the life of another Labor Zionist activist, Sara Bodek Paltiel (1909–1993), an American Jewish woman whose remarkable career path was shaped in the 1920s and 1930s. A product of the East European Jewish immigrant milieu, Paltiel was a first-generation American who hailed from a moderately traditional but nevertheless acculturated household in New York City. Possessed of considerable energy, ambition, and courage, she pursued a dual track in American higher education at the Jewish Theological Seminary and Hunter College. Her increasingly secular and strong Zionist sympathies prompted her immigration to Palestine in 1932, where she enrolled in the Hadassah School of Nursing in Jerusalem and later became the institution's first American graduate. Throughout the 1930s, she gravitated to the *kibbutz* movement, with its stress on pioneering, redeeming the land through collective Jewish labor, and pushing back the frontier. Eventually, she joined a *garin* [settlement group] that founded Kibbutz Kfar Blum in the Upper Galilee. In reading Rosenfeld's narrative, one is repeatedly struck by the tireless determination with which Paltiel sought to blend her commitment to nursing with a *kibbutz* lifestyle. As a founder of Kfar Blum and a health care professional whose pioneering medical work radiated from Kiryat Shemonah to the northernmost corners of the country, she seems to have discovered through her Zionism not only psychological wholeness and ideological clarity but a vehicle for improving Jewish life and curing humanity's ills—*dunam* by *dunam,* person by person, starting with herself.

2. Saadia Gelb, "The Founding of Habonim," in *Arise and Build: The Story of American Habonim,* ed. David Breslau (New York: Ichud Habonim Labor Zionist Youth, 1961), 9.

Em Leemahot: The Public Health Contributions of Sara Bodek Paltiel to the Yishuv and Israel, 1932–1993

Peri Rosenfeld

Introduction

I grew up with the legend of my aunt Sara, who left home as a young woman to make a life for herself and start a *kibbutz*. The eldest of ten children, she was the first of five sisters to leave New York City for Palestine/Israel. She was a socialist who left everything behind, especially her Orthodox upbringing. She did not speak to her parents for forty years. She was among the founders of Kfar Blum, a *kibbutz* way up north, far from the "beaten path" of tourists and even most Israelis. When she left America, she believed she was renouncing her citizenship. (Many years later, her Israeli children found out that, not only was Sara still American, but they too were American citizens.)

I first met Aunt Sara in 1970, when she was sixty, and was struck by her rugged appearance and strong opinions. Although she obviously aged over time, her essence remained consistent. She wore plain dresses, with her hair pulled back pragmatically. Her small frame was hunched from years of bending over, but there was a twinkle of brilliance in her eye and optimism so palpable it filled the room. This was someone to admire, I thought. She was inspirational, a role model for the existing Zionist and budding feminist in me.

I visited Sara several times in Israel, though our last few encounters were most significant because we finally knew each other well enough to really talk. She liked to talk about Israel, its history and its future. She loved the Galilee passionately. She resented the funds sent to the West Bank settlements and *haredi* [ultra-Orthodox] *yeshivah* students. Though she eschewed Orthodoxy, she was a religious person. She believed her home was the land of the Bible, destined for the Jewish people. Its topography and agricultural seasons were sacred and worthy of respect. She believed *"blee avar ein atid"*—without history there is no future. Yet, as well as I thought I knew her, I was unaware of Sara's contribution to the development of nursing and health care. She was pleased that I was involved in nursing, and she was clearly proud to be a nurse, yet she never elaborated about her work. Through this research I learned that her greatest contributions were, in fact, in this area.[1]

Sara's Youth on New York's Lower East Side

Sara Bodek was born 1909 in New York City to Annie Koenigsberg and Harry Bodek. She was the oldest of ten children: eight girls and two boys. (fig. 1). The Bodek family was Orthodox and Zionist—not necessarily in the contemporary political sense but in the sense that Zion was a primary concern in their lives. Their prayers were direct to Jerusalem, their charitable dollars were sent to Zion, and their dreams were focused upon actually "returning" to Zion.

Sara was brought up with feelings of passion and commitment to Zion. For example, among Sara's personal papers was a photocopy of an article written in Hebrew (date unknown) titled: *Derekh yisrael* [The Road to Israel], which describes how the road from Safed to Meron was completed in 1928 with funding from Yisroel Koenigsberg, Annie's father. (The road has since been replaced with a modern highway.)

While the word was not used, the Bodeks were "feminists" in the sense that they educated their daughters and expected them to achieve something in addition to families. All the Bodek daughters went to Hebrew schools in addition to public schools, and each was expected to engage in some sort of career. In the days when Jewish education was almost nonexistent for girls, Sara and her sisters attended the Jewish Theological Seminary, a Conservative institution and the only one in New York City that accepted girls. Later, the sisters attended Herzliyah, the first traditional Jewish school for girls in New York City. Others in the community did not share the Bodek family's progressive attitudes toward girls. For example, Sara's cousin Rachel remarked, "My father had learned an important lesson from Harry (Bodek). Harry had let his daughters keep the money they earned. Look how Sara used hers! From this experience, my father insisted on keeping our earnings and doling out weekly allowances!"

There is little information about Sara's early years growing up on the Lower East Side. The sisters closest to her in age (Pninah and Hudie) have passed away, and the others were too young to recall much detail. The youngest sister, Reva, was five years old when Sara left home. What little information exists of Sara's early years comes from her application to the Hadassah School of Nursing in Jerusalem. In her papers Sara described

FIGURE 1. The Bodek family (c. 1930). Sara is seated at the far right in the front row. Courtesy of Bodek family.

her family as "traditional," and she attended Hunter College in addition to the Jewish Theological Seminary. Her first job was bookkeeper in her father's fur business. She accompanied him on business trips, including one to Europe.

I asked all my sources the same set of questions: Why did Sara emigrate to Palestine? What motivated her to make such a gutsy move? Were there any particular role models or sources of inspiration for her decision? The responses I received were as telling about the informer as they were about Sara. I was told that she was escaping the responsibilities of being the eldest of ten, rebelling against the strict Orthodoxy, or simply wanting to start a career. In her own mind, according to an interview in 1972, after she had been in Palestine forty years, Sara recalled wanting to be a nurse from a very early age. Her mother, Annie, had been sick as a child and required surgery to remove an obstruction from her throat. The resulting scar engendered much discussion in the household about the wonders of American health care and the gratitude the family shared for the sympathetic doctor and nurse who saved baby Annie. Sara told an interviewer in 1972, "Having heard this story often in my childhood, I grew up with a great appreciation and admiration for the nursing profession. After finishing school, nursing school was the logical step for me. The main obstacle was violation of the *Shabbat* [Sabbath], which the work entailed. . . . Going to Israel was the logical solution. I could study nursing in a Jewish environment only in Israel."

Sara's husband, Shmulik, believed there were other reasons for her choice, particularly her desire to escape the responsibilities of being the eldest in a large, traditional family—though Palestine in 1932 seems quite a radical escape. Sara's granddaughter, however, interpreted events somewhat differently. She wrote in her *shoreshim* [roots] scrapbook: "My grandmother didn't like her religious home and because of this she left home in 1932 and immigrated to Jerusalem."

In any event, Sara's decision was cataclysmic. One of Sara's sisters recalls that the days prior to her departure "the house was like on Yom Kippur [Day of Atonement]—my father refused to eat and simply sat on his rocking chair in silence." The entire community was aware of this momentous, almost scandalous, event, recalls a cousin. A twenty-two-year-old Orthodox girl was going to Palestine, alone. Her future was far from clear, and communication would, at best, be sporadic. Harry traveled to Palestine in 1936 to persuade Sara to come home but returned to New York alone. It is not clear whether they ever spoke to each other again.

Sara's Pioneering Life in Palestine

In reviewing her life, Sara's eldest son, Naaman (now fifty-six) outlined his mother's pioneering experiences in four phases: (1) nursing school in Jerusalem (1933–1936); (2) early years with the Anglo-Balti *garin* [settlement group] roving among Afikim, Kineret, and Binyaminah (1937–1943); (3) securing permanent land in Naame/Kfar Blum (1944–1954); (4) Kiryat Shemonah (1954–1975). After her retirement, Sara continued working in the Kfar Blum guesthouse and was active in sensitizing the *kibbutz* to the needs of its aging members. She, once again, was "ahead of her time" in advising the *kibbutz* leadership to prepare for the future of its aging population. The remainder of this paper will explore Sara's life using Naaman's categories.

Hadassah School of Nursing in Jerusalem (1933–1936)

Upon her arrival to Jerusalem in 1932, Sara Bodek intended to study nursing at the Hadassah Nursing School. She had submitted an application from New York with a letter of recommendation from Dr. Hayim

Yassky (medical director of the Hadassah Medical Organization and martyr in the ambush of the convoy headed for Mt. Scopus in 1948). She was one of twenty applicants admitted out of a pool of two hundred. Sara had missed the first day of nursing school and had to wait until the next semester to start her studies. In the interim, she took a position as assistant to Dr. Kliger, a renowned bacteriologist at Hebrew University. It was in Dr. Kliger's clinic that she learned about treatments for typhus, trachoma, and other contagious diseases common in Palestine. After completing her basic nursing training, Sara completed an additional year in midwifery and public health while working part-time in the Old City as a "woman in green" visiting nurse. Her classmate Rahel Zalel remembers that Sara began of talking of joining a *kibbutz* while in nursing school and she realized that she would need training in midwifery and public health to prepare for this transition.

According to her nursing school records, Sara Bodek's grades were good, with evidence of particular strengths in interpersonal skills. Sara's instructors considered her stubborn and spirited. One of the more mature members of the class and the only American in the school, Sara was regarded as well qualified and a promising nursing professional. Sara graduated in

FIGURE 2. Hadassah School of Nursing (Class of 1936). Sara is third from left in top row. Henrietta Szold is seated in first row. Courtesy of the Hadassah Archives.

1936, the year that the Hadassah School of Nursing was renamed for Henrietta Szold in honor of Miss Szold's seventy-fifth birthday. Sara Bodek was the first American to graduate from the School of Nursing since its establishment in 1918. Upon the completion of her schooling, Sara was eager to leave Jerusalem for a more rural location in the Yishuv. (fig. 2)

Joining the Anglo-Balti Garin/Binyaminah (1937-1943)

In 1932 Sara had met two girls, Ada and Sara, who were on her ship to Palestine. They were en route to Kibbutz Afikim. Five years later, in 1937, bent on starting her life as a *kibbutznik*, Sara joined her friends in Afikim. The *kibbutz* was lucky to have her, as it was in the midst of a typhus epidemic. Soon after, Kibbutz Kineret asked to "borrow" Sara since it desperately needed a nurse while its medic recovered from an injury. At Kineret, Sara met up with the Anglo-Balti *garin,* and, though offered membership at Afikim, she joined the *garin* because, in her own words, "the reality of a new *kibbutz garin* charmed me." Looking for a new challenge, Sara became the first American to join the Anglo-Balti group. Another first. Esther Peeh, a member of the Anglo-Balti *garin,* remarked: "Sara was not a typical American. Many years later when my husband and I were *shlihim* [emissaries] in the U.S. [1948–1949], we visited the Bodek family and they too were not typical Americans. More Jewish, more personal. The family was Zionist; she came [to Palestine] when there was no influx of Americans yet."

It was then that Shmulik Plotnik came on the scene. In 1939, while he was swimming in Lake Kineret, a scorpion bit Shmulik and Sara "saved" him. Several years younger than she, Shmulik was smitten by the determined and capable Sara. As one contemporary, Yehudit Avni, recalled: "he followed her around—it was really quite funny. He wore her down. . . ."

They then became a "couple." Given the isolated location of Binyaminah, where the Anglo-Balti *garin* was living, it would be months perhaps years before a rabbi or official would wander through town to officiate at a wedding ceremony. As Yehudit, Sara's peer, explained: "In those days you didn't get married. We called it *"nikhnasim laheder"* [going into a room]. . . . Everybody got married eventually. At the beginning it wasn't so important to get officially married."

In October 1943, only months before Naaman was born, Sara and Shmulik were officially married along with four other couples. They adopted the last name "Paltiel," which they felt sounded more Israeli than Plotnick or Bodek. Sara reminisces in her granddaughter's *shoreshim* scrapbook: "At the wedding ceremonies in those days, when money was scarce, there was only one ring, and so the weddings would be run as if on a conveyor belt. The rabbi (a rare commodity) would complete the ceremony for one couple, the ring would be transferred to the second couple, etc. until he married all five couples."

The *garin* had been sent by the Jewish National Fund to Binyaminah in 1938/1939 to get experience in agricultural activities in preparation for obtaining its own parcel of land (fig. 3). Binyaminah, located in central Israel at the southern edge of Mt. Carmel, was a new town with few buildings and little organized infrastructure. The "Anglo-Baltis" lived in tents. Living conditions were difficult, to say the least. Aside from the physical hardships of no water, plumbing, or electricity, the crowding and lack of privacy were constant sources of friction among the members of the group. In an article written in 1944, Sara recalls: "Cheery souls, take warning! This is going to be a very sad story. . . . [In Binyaminah] tents were pitched and *haverim* [members] were parceled out 3 to a tent . . . the first winter saw tents torn to shreds, tents falling on the heads of sleeping *haverim*, tents blown away and tents copiously leaking. Or immediately upon entering the gate the eye was confronted with the feet of Moshe (6 ft 1 inch tall) sticking out of the rent in the tent wall. Oh that never satisfied itch to tickle those sleeping feet!"

In the same article Sara goes on to explain that as the number of married couples and children grew, the housing problems became more acute. Though *zrifim* [shacks] were cobbled together, the conditions became unsafe for children. All sorts of modifications were tried, such as the introduction of the "psychological partition"—a burlap screen stretching across a three-by-four-meter room. Two singles live in the door half while the married couple live in the window half, which means having to cross the bachelors' room to get to their quarters. . . . Since it (the burlap screen) comes to about ½ meter from the ceiling, it is hardly sound or light proof and can scarcely be said to ensure privacy—hence the term 'psychological.'"

Finally, "We were saved by the advent of [the northern town of] Metulah," she explains in her characteristic optimism. "About 20 people went to work in the hotel . . . and in Binyaminah it was possible to breathe again."

At first, Sara was the *metapelet* [child care provider] for the three children present in the *kibbutz*—by the time Naaman, her firstborn, came along in 1943, there were over forty. "I was the first child care worker in Binyaminah, and conditions were obviously very primitive. In order to bathe the children I dragged containers of hot water from the kitchen. I still have marks on my legs that remained from wounds caused by those

FIGURE 3. Binyaminah (c. 1938). Courtesy of Kibbutz Kfar Blum Archives.

containers. . . . Stories too numerous to mention. What didn't we do then! I even played the violin to entertain the children at birthday parties" (fig. 4).

Her contemporary, Esther Peeh, summed up Sara's accomplishments in Binyaminah: "She was not only the nurse; she was everything . . . she was responsible to fetch the doctor (if possible), she took care of the babies, and she was the only one with the education. She took care of pregnant women and accompanied them to the hospital. There were no cars at that time, so they would *tramp* [hitchhike]! In addition to that, she worked anywhere and everywhere else."

Among the stories recalled both in interviews and in written materials, Sara is portrayed as a competent, determined, and very idealistic nurse. Esther Peeh recalled: "She had a mind of her own. . . . She knew how to cope in every emergency. . . . I'm sure there were things she didn't know, but she gave us the feeling that she could handle anything."

But, her fervent idealism was not always appreciated. As one *vatikah* [female veteran] recalls: "Some thought it was difficult to approach her. Sara thought it a pity that one person should be full-time with the children when there was so much to be done, so she would get the children up and feed them and then go to work in the fields! I worked at the machines [as a shoemaker] and I would look up and see my Moshe climbing

FIGURE 4. Sara caring for children in Binyaminah (c. 1940). Courtesy of Kibbutz Kfar Blum Archives.

onto the railroad tracks! I was angry—but she treated her own children the same way. Sara was hard and stoic."

Sara was innovative and creative in meeting the challenges she encountered. In a memorial booklet distributed at her funeral, her contemporaries recall her ingenuity: with no refrigeration, she kept baby formula from spoiling by putting bottles in clay pots and hanging them in the wind to stay cool. She would clean and sterilize old shoe polish cans to store medicines. A pair of twins was born prematurely, and Sara wrapped them in tinfoil to keep them warm on the trip to the hospital.

Collective child-rearing was the practice in *kibuzim* at that time, and Sara was a fervent believer, even when it fell out of favor in the 1960s. Parents spent a short period of time with their children (usually around teatime), and the children slept in separate quarters. Parents did *toronuyot* [rotations] at night. Sara's husband, Shmulik, admits that they disagreed about this. He called Sara a "*frum* [orthodox] *kibbutznik*. She believed in communal living. As religion was the basis for her family, the *kibbutz* was the basis of her life." In the 1960s, when the next generation discontinued communal child-rearing, Sara vocally opposed the change. In Binyaminah, the Anglo-Balti *garin* was faced with a new challenge: competing with Arabs for agricultural jobs. Jewish land-owners routinely hired local Arab workers and were not especially open to hiring Jewish workers, who were considered more assertive and expensive than the Arabs. Tensions flared, culminating in the *mil-hamah levodah ivrit* [war for Jewish labor]. Sometimes the fighting be-came serious, and Sara would treat the wounds caused by sticks, stones, and broken glass.

Naame/Kfar Blum (1944-1954)

For the "Anglo Baltis," this fighting took an ironic turn: several of the young men were "exiled" to Metulah, a remote outpost in northern Pal-estine, under the Golan Heights, as "punishment" for instigating trouble. They found work in a hotel there. *Kibbutz* legend has it that they gazed into the Huleh Valley, fell in love with the land, and requested that their *kibbutz* be established there. While most of the women and children re-mained in Binyaminah, a smaller group occupied a nearby hillock to begin preparations for the ultimate move to Naame, the Arab name for what was later called Kfar Blum. Sara was in this first group. Her nursing skills were sorely needed, and she was the only health care professional in the area. A contemporary recalls: "She was called Dr. Bodek since she alone was responsible for the day-to-day health of the *kibbutz* members and actual doctor's visits were very infrequent." Sara and Shmulik named their first child Naaman, born in 1943, to pay homage to the land that became their home.

The closest physician was in Kfar Giladi (about fifteen miles away), and the only means of communication was signaling with flashlights at night using Morse code. Sara told her granddaughter: "Signaling in-volved many curious incidents—once the signaler returned with a mes-sage that Satan was clean [because of a Hebrew spelling mistake, the word for urine—*sheten*—came out Satan]."

In 1942 Sara wrote a piece for *"Bekibuzeinu"* [In Our Kibbutz]—a column in the international newsletter of the Habonim movement, *Hamekasher* [The Link]. In the article "Health Problems in Naame: The Water System," she relates how the community of Naame obtained fresh water from the Jordan River. This required a half-hour walk to the river for "daily ablutions" and multiple trips each day by donkey (if the don-key was willing and the tins not leaking) for water for the kitchen and laundry. Drinking water was strained through a double thickness of cloth and chlorinated. It tasted "vile" but was acceptable.

Until one day, "When the problem of our garbage disposal became serious, and several of the boys were detailed to dig a pit for the purpose. Imagine their feeling when, at the end of a day's work, at the depth of something under two meters, the soil began to feel moist. By the time we got back from our wash in the Jordan [River] about an hour later, some real water had already begun to seep through. Thus our garbage pit became our well." For another six months water was drawn from the well until pumps were installed. Showers came next. Though water for the kitchen was still brought in tins on a yoke balanced on the shoulders. The water was still strained and chlorinated but as Sara concludes, "Blessed is the well."

In a second article written in 1942, Sara describes the malaria problems in Naame. The Huleh Valley was a perfect location for the breeding of malarial mosquitoes, and while the members of Naame worked to "reclaim," that is, drain, the Huleh Valley, serious attention was paid to prevention and treatment of the disease, including daily doses of quinine, which sat on the table alongside the salt and pepper shakers. It was necessary to build double doors on each house, to stay indoors in the evenings, and to cover one's legs and arms with citronella if venturing out at night. Despite all these precautions, it was difficult to stem the spread of malaria among the *kibbutz* members. In her article, Sara explains why:

"Now I ask you, who can withstand the romance of cool breezes from Lebanon, and wan moonlight over [Mount] Hermon, when a small 3 by 4 room containing four beds, a paraffin lamp and a vague flitty odor awaits one indoors . . . and who will not forgive the *haver* who had just a little more work to finish and can't leave a half hour's work undone! Or the poor overworked *haver* who doesn't even feel when he dozed off between shower and *aruhat erev* [dinner]."

In short, the malarial mosquito had plenty of opportunities to infect the settlers at Naame. One hundred percent of the *kibbutz* members suffered from the disease. Moreover, it was common to suffer many bouts of malaria. Sara's husband, Shmulik, for example, had 9 bouts with the disease—and was considered lucky. Once stricken with malaria, it was difficult to convince members to wait until they were fully recovered before returning to their duties. Frequently, members returned to work before they had recuperated fully, increasing the chances of relapse.

Rahel Avni, a contemporary of Sara, explained: "We all had malaria. From Binyaminah, the men were sent here to get the land [in Naame]. My husband had malaria all the time. I had it in my eighth month [of pregnancy]. There were two kinds: *terzah*—recurrent [i.e. symptoms would return periodically] and *tropikah*—one-shot deal. I had both." Esther Peeh recalls that when she and her husband were *shlihim* in England, her husband got sick. In the hospital he told the MDs, "I know it's malaria," and all the other physicians came running to see a case of malaria.

Despite all this, Sara's optimism and determination in eradicating malaria from their midst is noteworthy. Evoking the mythological image of Saint George slaying the fiery dragon, Sara writes: "We shall push back the frontier of malaria, and make Naame a place to live in and live in well. Though we are now separated from half our *kibbutz* and our children, we shall, and in the near future, bring them here, to live with us. If we cannot exterminate malaria in all of the Huleh, we shall at least, for the time being, make our settlement a malaria-proof island in a sea of mosquitoes, little by little, gaining ground, until the authorities beyond our immediate influence will have to take notice and be moved to do their part in the eradication of malaria forever."

In 1944 land was given to the Anglo-Balti *kibbutz* in Naame. The group had wanted to call its *kibbutz* "Lavi," but the name was already taken, so the members chose the name "Kfar Blum" after Leon Blum, the French prime minister who was Jewish, socialist, and sympathetic to Zionism. "We thought we'd get something out of it," one *vatik* recalls. Another local village abandoned by the Arabs, called Halsa, was designated as a development town and named Kiryat Shemonah, in memory of Yosef Trumpledor and his seven colleagues killed by Arabs in nearby Tel Hai in 1920.

The local Arabs did not welcome the new settlers. Roads were sabotaged and caravans were ambushed. Travelers on the road from Rosh Pinah and Metulah were continually vandalized. Members were forced to travel slowly, making them easy targets for snipers. Steel plates were affixed to cars and trucks. On one occasion the road from Kfar Blum to the main road was destroyed, and the *kibbutz* was under "siege" for six weeks. At this time Sara found herself in a health care crisis she could not control. Saadia Gelb, a contemporary, recalls: "Sometimes she had to assume medical functions beyond her nursing training. . . . The tragedy took place when one of our finest members was fixing a telephone pole when he was shot in the back. He was taken to our dispensary and Sara took care of him. Had we had medical facilities as we have now, he might have been saved. She stopped the blood but we lost him. She never forgave herself, though no one blamed her. She ate herself up alive because of the tragedy."

Sara set up the infirmary in Kfar Blum, as she had done in Binyaminah, and had a hand in all aspects of life related to hygiene, sanitation, nutrition, disease prevention, and treatment. She cared for everyone, from newborns to the elderly. For many years, she was the sole health care practitioner on the settlement.

Sara wrote a piece in the Habonim newsletter *Hamekasher* about the events at Biryah in 1946. The confrontation at Biryah became a symbol of the Yishuv's struggle with the British to secure a Jewish state. Biryah was a hill in the Galilee with biblical significance for the pioneers. Occupied by several hundred young people representing the varied *kibuzim,* Biryah's purpose was to demonstrate unity against the British, who forbade the Jews from securing this land. Sara staffed the first-aid tent at Biryah and recounts the events:

In a meeting with the local council the answer to the [British] army was that we would not leave the place. However, there was to be no active resistance of any kind. . . . Passive resistance was the slogan. . . . Hardly had the orders been given when soldiers by the hundreds broke through the walls, armed to the teeth, bayonets drawn, completely prepared for the worst kind of battle. A live cordon of soldiers with tommy-guns pointed surrounded the modest camp, and started dragging us off one by one. They were there in thousands to our few score.

What prevented the incident of Biryah from becoming a full-sized conflagration, so to speak, was that our non-resistance was a surprise for them, and they were at a loss to deal with it. . . . I was able to catch snatches of their remarks. For the most part, they roundly cursed the Jews who didn't even give them the opportunity for a good fight for their trouble. Here they were all primed for battle and bathos! . . . From the military lorries, we saw the tents being demolished and all our belongings being piled up pell-mell in one big heap. It's very hard to describe our feelings. I saw men, old timers at defense, their lips bitten through to bleeding with the terrific effort at self-control. After all, it's against the most primitive instinct of every living thing not to strike back in self-defense. But it was orders! From the lorries burst peals of song. Perhaps it was the pent-up feelings that had failed to find natural expression. But certainly it was our answer to the [British] army. Though you take us by force, our spirit is not broken.

Sara explains that after the British army had carted her group away, a second group ascended the hill at dusk and began signaling in Hebrew! In the final analysis, Sara notes with modesty: "It was slightly unpleasant being looked upon as a hero, when one's inner feelings were something quite different. . . . The important thing is, Biryah is ours!" I assume Sara knew that Biryah is precisely on the road from Meron to Safed, on the road called *"Derekh Yisrael,"* financed by her grandfather some twenty years earlier!

Halsa/Kiryat Shemona: 1954–1972

In her own estimation, Sara's greatest source of satisfaction was her work with new immigrants in the abandoned Arab village, Halsa, later known as Kiryat Shemonah. After independence, thousands of immigrants from northern Africa poured into the fledgling state. Many were sent by government authorities to remote parts of the country for *klitah* [absorption]. Halsa was known as a *maabarah,* a temporary settlement of people living in tents and sheds. Named after the legendary Yosef Trumpledor and his seven comrades, in 1954 the population of Kiryat Shemonah was 3,300; in five years the population tripled to 10,000. The new Sephardic immigrants, from Tunisia, Morocco, Yemen, and other undeveloped countries in the Arab world, brought customs and beliefs quite different from those of the earlier Ashkenazi pioneers from the West, now settled in the relative comforts of *kibuzim.*

The surrounding *kibuzim* were called upon by the Jewish Agency to assist in the absorption process and to provide work for the new immigrants. Sara was recruited to help the inhabitants in the *maabarah* adjust to their new lives.

The challenges were cultural as well as economic (fig. 5). Even the most elementary and fundamental health care services were missing. Sanitary conditions were meager, with little or no running water, electricity, or proper sewage. As Saadia Gelb, head of the regional council, explained: "It's a saga of no end of trouble, no end of problems, no end to the difficulties, but the health aspect was almost immediately taken care of by volunteer nurses. . . . It was such a difficult problem that without those nurses it would've been impossible because the people kept coming and the Jewish Agency had one principle—'get them off the boats and out into the world.'"

Sara immersed herself in this initiative. Having no means of transportation of her own, she was known to wake up early to catch a ride to town with the fruit trucks, or *"tramp"* with motorcyclists, or even arrive on donkey! She became intimately involved in the lives of the new *olim* [immigrants], visiting them in their homes and providing emotional as well as physical support. She was responsible for setting up the Lying-in Center, an obstetrics center for labor and delivery. The majority of the *olim* had never given birth anywhere but home, and Sara created a homey environment that brought the mothers to the center. She followed up with the mothers and infants by establishing a *Tipat Halav* [Drop of Milk] maternal-child health services program in Kiryat Shemonah. Her focus was always on preventive health care and education, rather than on treatment.

In a 1967 article entitled "My Work at the Health Center in Kiryat Shemonah," Sara recalls: "The maternity ward at the health center treats giving birth as a family event and not as an illness. Only in the case of complications or illness is the woman sent to hospital to give birth. The

FIGURE 5. Sephardic immigrant women waiting in line for health care services in Kiryat Shemonah (c. 1950). Courtesy of Kibbutz Kfar Blum Archives.

center has 'rooming-in' [mother and baby together] which is seen as revolutionary in the era of modern obstetrics. Visitors from Israel and abroad are impressed at such 'modernity' in this out of the way corner [i.e., Kiryat Shemonah]. Thanks to these innovations—family care, out-of-hospital birthing center, mother and child rooming—in, we have developed a reputation and our center has been written about in professional journals in many countries and languages."

In all this, Sara's manner was sensitive and professional. One colleague summarized the conditions: "Much of her time was taken up training the mothers about taking care of their children. And that brought up conflict because they had different ways. For example, some mothers came with the old-fashioned way of chewing up the food before giving it to their children. . . . Mothers would give their infants hot dogs . . . many cultures use a lot of frying. There were the Moroccans and Indians with their sharp curries and spicy foods, and the Tunisians with their breads made on stones. . . . In all this Sara had the advantage of having come from America, so she knew a bit about human relations. Her distinguishing contribution was that she was not high-handed and very patient."

Over time, Sara touched the lives of most people in Kiryat Shemonah. Her daughter Anat recalls: "[When] the *kibuzim* were asked to help [with the immigration of the 1950s], she was still a real *haluzah* [pioneer] and without hesitation she used all her knowledge and experience for twenty years to care for all the people, from babies to the elderly. They called her *em leemahot* or *em hakiryah*—the mother of mothers, or the mother of the village. They came to her with their emotional and physical problems. She went by hitching, in the mud and dust. For many years she hitched on the road, though in later years they came for her. . . . Her reputation was great; she had visitors until the last day of her life from people throughout the Upper Galilee."

In an article published on Independence Day 1966, Sara ponders the meaning of independence. She exhorts the *kibuzim* to reach out to the new immigrants where they live. "This is a national duty and requires that assistance be offered on a professional and personal level." She is critical of the *kibbutz* members who, she believes, have not taken enough initiative in helping to make connections with the people in the nearby immigrant encampments.

Indeed, many in Kiryat Shemonah identified Kibbutz Kfar Blum specifically and exclusively with Sara Bodek. In 1972 the Israeli Ministry of Health recognized Sara's accomplishments. She was given the Nurse of the Year award for her "original and humane approach" in providing health care to new immigrants.

In a newspaper interview, Sara explained: "Many times I asked myself how I was able to communicate and relate to those women in those conditions—in spite of the lack of a common language and background. But I think that the stories of my mother and grandmother from my early childhood stayed with me—stories they told me about their first years in America, about the awesome difficulties of starting a new life with no means, no language, about the struggle and the ambition, to do everything so that the children would have a better life . . . because of this I was able to understand these women and find a common language with them. . . . Today I take great pleasure at seeing the sons and daughters who were born in those tin shacks. . . . My desire to help those in need to begin their lives in new and difficult conditions, is a thread that follows through my whole life. . . . Maybe it is fitting to end with the words which the secretary general of the *kibbutz* movement Yizhak Ben-Aharon said at the award ceremony: 'those who did not work in order to receive a prize—receive the prize.'"

Back at Kfar Blum: 1977–1993

Toward the end of the 1970s, Sara retired from her public role as a nurse. Because of her impeccable English and warm sociability, she was assigned to work in the guesthouse at Kfar Blum. She also continued her interest in health care and social activism. Always ahead of her time, Sara raised the *kibbutz*'s awareness of geriatric issues, specifically the need to plan for the health and social needs of the aging *vatikim.* In a piece for the *kibbutz* newsletter titled "Middle Age and After," she suggests that for members of the *kibbutz* the concept of "retirement" is not suitable, since work is the only valued role in the community. No one wants to be idle, she notes, and "the *kibbutz* must prepare itself to take advantage of what is useful from the range of age groups."

Sara's health began to deteriorate in 1991, and she required daily dialysis for her failing kidney. The *kibbutz* installed a special bathroom for Sara who, as a nurse, performed her own dialyses. Because her health needs made extraordinary demands on her time and energy, she slowly resigned herself to a life of disability. In the memorial booklet prepared after her death, her friend Esther Peeh summarized the last years of Sara's life: "Sara was at the end and people asked 'why does God make her go through this, let her go, why does she have to suffer?' . . . She [underwent many treatments] with strength and never complained. . . . During my visits with her we didn't talk about her illness, and each time Sara aroused in me a feeling of amazement and awe, for she undoubtedly knew what was going on and yet outwardly she didn't talk about it. . . ."

In December 1993, Sara's struggle was over. Two of her sisters had come to visit, and by the time they returned to Jerusalem the message of her death was waiting (fig. 6).

Sara's son Naaman noted: "Summarize my mother's life? She was a pioneer. Pioneering was the most fundamental part of her life. She kept seeking out new experiences: leaving her family for Palestine, leaving Jerusalem to join Afikim, leaving Afikim to start a new *kibbutz*, and then leaving *kibbutz* (workwise) to help in a development town. . . . My mother was naive, she believed that the world operated on idealism."

FIGURE 6. Sara Bodek Paltiel (1993). Courtesy of Kibbutz Kfar Blum Archives.

Naaman added: "Sara educated her children and grandchildren to a belief in and love of mankind." Sara emerges as an extremely determined and idealistic individualist. Shmulik noted that while Sara had a fervent commitment to communal living and the *kibbutz* way of life, she was an "individualistic personality" in that she believed that the individual is an agent of change and each individual is responsible to make that change happen. Clearly her life is a testament to this philosophy. Her writings were always upbeat, optimistic, forward thinking, and passionate. She never shirked her responsibility—she sought challenges. Her contemporary Esther Peeh noted: "She was always there to fight for social justice whenever it seemed to her that it was being trampled on."

Her niece Carmel called Sara "a minimalist"—Sara lived within her narrow definition of the world, which focused on her commitment to Zionism and the *kibbutz* movement. In reviewing her life, one is struck by the singular track she followed. At every fork in the road of life, Sara chose the less traveled roads. Confident in her beliefs and armed with her nursing skills, she chose to stay behind the scenes and actively worked to transform her idealism into reality. Sara's impressive and enduring contributions are particularly noteworthy because she always seemed ahead of the trends. For example, she was both the first American to graduate from the Hadassah School of Nursing and the first American to join the Anglo-Balti *garin*. She reflects the altruism and ingenuity of the nurses during the pre-state era of the Yishuv, helping to build the world-class health care system that exists in Israel today.

Primary Sources (English)

Bodek, Sara. "Health Problems in Naame: I. The Water System," *Hamekasher,* August 1942.
———. "Health Problems in Naame: II. Malaria," *Hamekasher,* December 1942.
———. "Housing Conditions in Kibbutz Anglo-Balti," *Hamekasher,* January 1944.
———. "In the First Aid Tent at Biryah," *Hamekasher,* April 1946.

Note

1. The opportunity to conduct a biographical study of Sara had always been a dream of mine, and I am grateful to the Hadassah-Brandeis Institute for giving my dream life. In starting this project I knew of several obvious sources about Sara: the surviving siblings in New York and Israel, Sara's husband and children still living on the *kibbutz* in the shadow of the Golan Heights, and possibly other veteran *kibbutzniks* who helped develop Kfar Blum. I recalled from one of my visits an archive on the *kibbutz,* which held clippings and photos of the *kibbutz*'s history

and contemporary place in Israeli society. I was extremely lucky to learn that these and other valuable sources were available to me. I also uncovered primary documents written by Sara, which can only be described as God-sent. Sources included:

- Interviews with Sara's three surviving siblings, husband, three children, other relatives, three *kibbutz* veterans *(vatikim)*, one friend from nursing school.
- Hadassah School of Nursing application and nursing education documents and interview with Judith Steiner-Freud, former dean.
- Kfar Blum Archive: Articles written by Sara in English and Hebrew, pictures, obituaries, grandchildren's *shoreshim* [roots] scrapbooks.
- Hadassah Archive: Photos, early nursing descriptions, background materials on notable Zionist personalities such as Henrietta Szold (founder of Hadassah) and Dr. Hayim Yassky (Medical Director of the Hadassah Medical Organization).
- Personal papers including marriage license, certificates of memberships (esp. marksmanship), awards, and official government letters.

Chapter 12

The Haganah—Hebrew for "Defense"—was the dominant Zionist para-military organization responsible for protecting the Yishuv in the decades preceding the creation of the State of Israel in 1948. The Haganah's origins can be traced to Hashomer [The Watchguard], a self-defense group estab-lished in 1907 by a small group of socialist Zionist pioneers who hired themselves out to guard Jewish settlements and colonies throughout rural Palestine. Following World War I, a spirited public debate arose in the Yishuv concerning the value of perpetuating the Jewish Legion, a Jewish battalion organized under the auspices of the British military, including a few divisions that were stationed in or near Palestine. The debate, which hinged on the issue of militarism, was largely resolved in 1920 when a conference of the Labor Zionist party Ahdut Haavodah [Unity of Labor] determined to create the Haganah as a popular militia, whose primary aim was the protection of Jewish life and property. The following year, with the establishment of the Histadrut [General Federation of Jewish Workers in the Land of Israel], an umbrella organization of the Palestine workers movement, control of the Haganah was placed in the hands of the Labor Zionist leadership cohort grouped around David Ben-Gurion (1886–1973), Yizhak Ben-Zvi (1884–1963), and Berl Kaznelson (1887–1944).

Meanwhile, in the spring of 1920 Arab riots in Jerusalem prompted the right-wing Revisionist Zionist leader Vladimir (Zeev) Jabotinsky (1880–1940) to mobilize a separate Jewish paramilitary body known as the Irgun Haganah [Defense Organization]. The Irgun Haganah reflected Jabotin-sky's militant posture and dual political objectives. On the one hand, he advocated an aggressive Zionist military policy, including preemptive strikes and reprisals against hostile Arab groups. On the other, he sought to increase pressure on Great Britain to modify its vague commitment to a "Jewish national home" in Palestine, originally articulated in the Balfour Declaration of 1917, and demanded instead an explicit commitment to Jewish statehood to be realized, in part, by the deployment of a regular-ized Jewish military force working with the British.

While a consensus existed in the Yishuv and the Zionist movement concerning the need for Jewish self-defense units and for a shift in overall British policy, there was sharp disagreement over Jabotinsky's near-term military and political objectives. Indeed, the ascendant Palestine labor movement viewed the Haganah's defense tasks as closely linked to the Zionist movement's overall colonization and settlement efforts, and it soon rallied to make the Haganah a general self-defense corps under the control of the World Zionist Organization and the Jewish Agency. The competing Revisionist and Labor Zionist views gave rise to two distinct paramilitary groups. In the 1930s and 1940s, the Haganah proved central to the military preparedness and mobilization of the Jewish state-in-the-making. The Irgun, on the other hand, continued to operate at the margins of the Zionist consensus and unilaterally implemented its own militaristic agenda, including terrorist strikes aimed at Arab and British targets.

Against this backdrop, Rose Viteles (1892–1959), an American Jewish immigrant to Palestine, played a remarkable and secret role as the Haganah's de facto treasurer from 1934 to 1940 and later as a central figure in the Haganah's defense of Jerusalem during the War of Independence. Only a handful of Viteles' friends and associates were ever aware that the unassuming Viteles, a member of Jerusalem's elite who mixed socially with British, American, and Zionist officials, led a "double life." As Sara Kadosh relates in the following chapter, Viteles assumed a key position in the Haganah starting in the 1930s when she became responsible for managing the funds of its swiftly growing operations. She brought to her position considerable financial acumen and social contacts, which she used both to strengthen the Haganah and to promote other Yishuv organizations including the Histadrut Nashim Ivriyot [Federation of Jewish Women], the Palestine-based council of Hadassah, and the Vaad Arzi Lemaan Hehayal Hayehudi [Jewish Soldiers Welfare Committee]. In 1946 she served as the first representative of the Joint Distribution Committee, an American-sponsored international Jewish welfare organization, in the British detention camps of Cyprus.

The chapter that follows underscores the close ties between the American Jewish experience and the Zionist enterprise. "What was most remarkable about Rose Viteles," argues Kadosh, "was her transformation from an assimiliated American Jewish woman to an activist in the Yishuv's inner circles." Moreover, as Kadosh implies here, strikingly little research has been conducted on the role of American Jews in the development of the Haganah. Her study breaks new ground and is an important contribution to the history of this significant and neglected aspect of American Jewish and Zionist history.

Rose Viteles: The Double Life of an American Woman in Palestine

Sara Kadosh

One of the unsung heroines of the Haganah was the American woman Rose Viteles (1892–1959). A member of the Haganah committee in Jerusalem during the 1930s, she founded the first Magen David Adom [Red Shield of David first aid society] in the city and raised funds for the purchase of arms. During the Arab uprising against the Jewish population from 1936 to 1939, she supplied daily meals to thousands of Haganah volunteers. From 1934 to 1940, she served as de facto treasurer of the Haganah in Jerusalem, increasing its income twentyfold.[1]

Few of Rose Viteles' friends and acquaintances knew of her involvement in the Haganah, for Rose led a double life. To most observers, she was part of Jerusalem's upper-middle-class society. The wife of Harry Viteles, manager of the Central Bank of Cooperative Institutions and Middle East representative of the American Jewish Joint Distribution Committee (JDC), Rose Viteles mixed socially with British government officials, American consular personnel, doctors, lawyers, and leaders of the Yishuv. Together with other women of similar background and social status, she was active in the Histadrut Nashim Ivriyot [Federation of Hebrew Women] (HNI) and in the Palestine Council of Hadassah.

At the same time, however, she was deeply involved in the Haganah, a semilegal organization whose members were subject to arrest or harassment by the British authorities of the Mandatory government in Palestine. She subsequently aided the Yishuv's defense efforts through the *Kofer Hayishuv* [Redemption Fund], a countrywide voluntary Jewish taxation system, and during World War II was a director of the Vaad Arzi Lemaan Hehayal Hayehudi [the Jewish Soldiers Welfare Committee]. In 1946 she became the first JDC representative in the British detention camps in Cyprus. During Israel's War of Independence, she again served the Haganah in the defense of Jerusalem.

What was most remarkable about Rose Viteles, however, was her transformation from an assimilated American Jewish woman to an activist in the Yishuv's inner circles. When she arrived in Palestine in 1926, she had little knowledge of Judaism and no Zionist background whatsoever. Yet within a short time, she came to identify completely with the Yishuv, and was one of its "prominent and outstanding" personalities.[2]

This study will explore how an assimilated American Jewish woman became a central figure in the Haganah. It will also examine the impact of her accomplishments on the fields of education and social service, as a contribution of American Jewish women who settled in Palestine's urban centers, and in the development of the Yishuv.

Little in Rose Viteles' background would seem to have prepared her for her double life in Jerusalem. Born in New York City in 1892 and raised in Cincinnati, Ohio, she came from a family with minimal Jewish awareness. Her mother, originally from Lemberg (Lvov), was the only one of seven sisters to marry a Jew. Her father, Jacob Rassell, who had immigrated to the United States from Minsk, had rebelled against his *yeshivah* education. As she describes in memoirs: "My mother observed some of the traditions, such as lighting candles on Friday night . . . and she tried to keep a *kosher* home. We could not be observant because my father was a freethinker, a member of the IWW [Industrial Workers of the World]. My two younger brothers did not attend religious school and were not *bar mizvah*. We never had a *seder* [Passover service] at home and we celebrated Jewish holidays in a very perfunctory way. . . . I . . . did not know an *alef* from a *bet*," she recalled.[3]

Her Jewish consciousness was stimulated to some extent by her involvement in Jewish social work. At the age of twenty she volunteered to work with teenagers at the local Jewish settlement house and later became executive secretary of the Big Brother Movement in Cincinnati. After her marriage to Harry Viteles in 1919, she moved to Philadelphia, where she worked for the Jewish Children's Bureau and the Orphans Guardian Society.[4]

However, her real introduction to Jewish life came through her husband, who had a much stronger Jewish background than she did. When Harry Viteles traveled throughout Europe on behalf of the JDC, Rose accompanied him; in 1923 she had her first encounter with Orthodox Jewish life in a *shtetl* [village] in eastern Europe.

In 1925 Harry Viteles wrote to his wife, who was then in Philadelphia with their infant daughter, asking her to join him in Palestine, where he had been appointed general manager of the Central Bank of Cooperative Institutions.[5] He warned her that life in Jerusalem was primitive by American standards. There was no electricity, a shortage of water, no refrigeration, and no pasteurized milk for children. Undaunted, Rose Viteles sailed for Palestine in April 1926 with her two-year-old daughter. She promptly fell in love with the country, especially with Jerusalem, which she considered the most beautiful of the world's capitals she had visited. To the amazement of friends, she coped easily with the lack of conveniences, describing them with humor and understatement in her memoirs. Her major problem was learning to speak Hebrew. But while she never completely mastered the language, her lack of fluency did not impede her integration into the life of the city.[6] She lived in Jerusalem from 1926 to 1957, when, already seriously ill, she returned to the United States for an extended visit with her family. She died in the United States in 1959.[7]

Rose Viteles arrived in Jerusalem during a period of urban development for the Yishuv, a period known as the Fourth Aliyah. During the 1920s, the Jewish population of the city doubled, reaching seventy thousand by 1935. With the establishment of the British Mandatory government, the Hebrew University of Jerusalem, and Hadassah Hospital, Jerusalem became a city of government officials, professors, and medical personnel as well as the seat of the Yishuv's institutions. In 1928 the city began to receive electricity, and in 1935 the water supply was improved. During the 1930s, Jewish immigrants from Germany built and populated the new garden suburb of Rehaviyah.[8]

With the growth of the city, there emerged a middle-class cultural and social life—described vividly by Rose Viteles in her memoirs—in which the Viteles family were central participants. They attended Friday night dinners at the home of Miss Annie Landau, principal of the Evelina de Rothschild Girl's School, Friday evening tea at the home of Menahem Ussishkin, head of the Jewish National Fund, Saturday morning *kidush* at the home of Chief Rabbi Herzog, and Sunday tea at the home of the British manager of Barclays Bank. Like others in their circle, they, too, had a particular afternoon when they were at home for tea and available to visitors. And every year, they organized a Thanksgiving dinner for the Americans living in Jerusalem, including personalities such as Dr. Judah L. Magnes, Henrietta Szold, and the American consul and his staff.[9]

Shortly after her arrival in Jerusalem, Rose Viteles was invited to join the HNI, an organization made up largely of immigrant women (mostly non-American) who provided social services to needy families. She subsequently served on their Baby Home Committee (a home for abandoned children), was chair of the Day Nursery, and directed the sale of handicrafts made by Yemenite women. Perhaps her main contribution, however, was in the area of fund-raising. Although she had no prior experience in this field, she successfully organized dances, bazaars, tag days, and, for several years, was treasurer of the HNI. The skills she developed during this time, especially in the area of fund-raising, were later applied in her work in the Haganah.[10]

In 1931 Rose Viteles became a member of the Palestine Council of Hadassah, which had been established in 1930 to supervise Hadassah's non-medical activities in Palestine. The council consisted of about a dozen women, most of them American. Esther Reifenberg and Miriam Granott, however, were of Russian origin. Some of the women held jobs (e.g., Lotta Levensohn was a journalist), but most were nonworking wives of prominent Jerusalemites, such as Ethel Agronsky (Agron), whose husband, Gershon, published the *Palestine Post*.[11]

The Palestine Council of Hadassah was responsible for several projects, which the women took turns directing. Rose Viteles' first project for the council (1933–1938) was to head the clothing and supplies committee, which distributed clothing and linens, sent by Hadassah, to hospitals, orphanages, and other institutions in Palestine. This project of the council was carried out in cooperation with the HNI. The project took on added importance in the 1940s, during the term of Rose Viteles' successor, Esther Reifenberg, when supplies were distributed to three additional groups: illegal immigrants who arrived in Palestine, Jews expelled from the Old City of Jerusalem in 1948, and new immigrants who arrived in Israel during the early years of the state.[12]

Rose Viteles' second Hadassah project was the administration of playgrounds financed by the Bertha Guggenheimer fund.[13] The playgrounds, a novel concept in the Yishuv, included not only play areas but also facilities for arts and crafts and other recreational activities. By 1944, the project had expanded from three playgrounds to thirty-five and included an overnight summer camp, a day camp, and clubs for underprivileged teenagers; by 1950, there were nearly fifty playgrounds. These programs were eventually taken over by the Israeli Ministry of Education.[14]

The Palestine Council's major project was the school luncheon program, which had been established in the 1920s to provide needy schoolchildren with a daily hot cooked meal. In 1944 the program encompassed twenty-seven thousand children and included instruction in nutrition and food preparation. It was supported by both the Vaad Leumi [the Elected Assembly of the Yishuv] and the British Mandatory authorities. The British even appointed a committee, including Rose Viteles, to supervise the expansion of the program to Arab schools. When the Israeli government took over the school luncheon program in 1951, it was providing daily meals to eighty thousand children.[15]

Rose Viteles' most significant contribution through Hadassah, however, was in the area of vocational education. In 1941, with a grant from

Hadassah, she organized the Alice Seligsberg High School for Girls, the first four-year girls' vocational high school in the Yishuv.[16] Rose Viteles subsequently helped establish the Stephen S. Wise Fine Mechanics Workshop for boys, the Julian W. Mack Printing School for Boys, part-time vocational programs for boys and girls, and a vocational guidance service. These programs, known collectively as the Brandeis Vocational Center, became an integral part of the educational system of the State of Israel.[17]

In 1941 Rose Viteles joined the Hadassah Emergency Committee (HEC), which had been established in 1940 to facilitate the distribution of funds to Hadassah programs in Palestine during World War II. She served on the committee first as Hadassah's representative to Youth Aliyah, then from 1941–1954, as chair of Hadassah's vocational education programs in Israel.

After the establishment of the HEC, the Palestine Council of Hadassah was renamed the Hadassah Youth Services Committee. Rose Viteles chaired this committee in the late 1940s as successor to Ethel Agronsky. In 1945 the HEC was renamed the Hadassah Council in Palestine and, in 1948, it became the Hadassah Council in Israel. Rose Viteles' last project as a member of the council was to supervise the distribution of surplus foods sent to Israel in the mid-1950s by the American government.[18]

Rose Viteles' accomplishments and the activities of the Palestine Council of Hadassah illustrate the contributions of the middle-class American Jewish woman in urban Palestine to the development of the Yishuv. The members of the Palestine Council introduced or helped popularize concepts that were unfamiliar to the Yishuv—such as school luncheons or playgrounds. The projects they sponsored improved the quality of life for thousands of poor families, assisted the Yishuv in times of crisis, and had a lasting influence on Israeli society. Their activities demonstrate the impact that a handful of dedicated volunteers had on the development of the Yishuv and the future State of Israel. Their contributions, however, have remained relatively unknown, possibly because, as Hannah Herzog points out, the "feminine" areas they dealt with were "not regarded in the historiography of the Yishuv as a pioneering endeavor worthy of mention . . ."[19]

Rose Viteles' accomplishments in the fields of social service and education were in themselves impressive. What made her unique, however, was the way in which she differed from many of her colleagues in Hadassah. Not only was she willing to become deeply involved in the Haganah, a semilegal organization; she came to understand the mentality of the Yishuv in a way that not every American woman was able to do. Recalling how Henrietta Szold had admonished her and her friends in connection with the HNI Baby Home ("Young women, you have no right to open an institution which you know you cannot maintain"), Rose Viteles commented wryly, " . . . I often wondered if the rapid development of Israel could have taken place if this principle had been followed."[20] She felt comfortable not only with Americans but also with non-American members of the Yishuv. She became close friends with Yaakov Patt, commander of the Haganah in Jerusalem, for example, and she was able to adapt the skills she acquired in the women's organizations to the Haganah and the other committees on which she served.[21]

Rose Viteles became involved in the Haganah almost by accident, as a result of her work in the Vaad Hakehillah [Community Council of Jerusalem]. In 1933 Henrietta Szold had organized the Vaad Hakehillah's first Social Service Bureau, and in 1934 Rose Viteles was serving as a member of the bureau's volunteer supervisory committee. Her office in the Vaad Hakehillah adjoined a room with the innocuous title "Social Assistance," which, unbeknownst to her, served as Haganah headquarters and which received a steady stream of young men and women visitors.[22]

One day she asked the man in charge, Yaakov Patt, to explain the function of his office.[23] Patt, who until then had kept his distance from the American woman with her poor Hebrew and foreign mannerisms, but who nevertheless had been favorably impressed by her work in the Community Council, pledged her to secrecy. He described the activities of the Haganah and asked for her help. Rose Viteles agreed to help, but only after Patt had assured her that the Haganah was not anti-Arab, did not preach hatred, and existed for defense purposes only.[24]

The first project Patt outlined was to raise funds for a Magen David Adom. There already existed a Magen David Adom in Haifa and Tel Aviv, but Patt wanted the Magen David Adom in Jerusalem to be an arm of the Haganah, so that in addition to its medical functions it could serve as a cover for Haganah activities. Within a few months, Rose Viteles had raised the funds, organized a committee of doctors, and arranged for the acquisition of an ambulance. When the Arab riots broke out in Jerusalem in the spring of 1936, the Magen David Adom was already functioning.[25]

Rose Viteles' position in the Haganah was as a member of the local committee, whose task was to raise funds for Haganah activities. Such committees existed during the 1920s and 1930s in Tel Aviv, Haifa, and Jerusalem. Their members were considered part of the local Haganah command, met regularly with Haganah officers, and even discussed operational plans. Members of the Jerusalem committee included Rahel Yanait Ben-Zvi, Selig Weizmann, Shaul Gordon, and another American, Charles Passman.[26]

When Rose Viteles joined the committee in 1934, the Haganah in Jerusalem was in the throes of a serious crisis. In 1931 the Jerusalem Haganah had split into two factions, with the majority of the officers taking most of the weapons and ammunition and setting up a rival faction, known as Irgun B. Yaakov Patt had been sent by Ben-Gurion to Jerusalem to rebuild the fractured Haganah organization in the city. Although Patt embarked on a vigorous recruitment and training program to replenish the losses in manpower, he did not have the funds to purchase new weapons. The total income of the Jerusalem Haganah was only 40£P (Palestine pounds) per month (about $160).[27]

Rose Viteles managed to convince a hesitant Yaakov Patt that she could raise funds discreetly, without compromising the secrecy of the organization. "It took six months for Yaakov and his committee to accept my offer to organize a closed campaign with the help of one paid worker who would solicit subscriptions . . . from a screened list of individuals and institutions. . . ."[28] Within a short time, she had increased the income of the Haganah to £P500 per month, and eventually to £P1000 per month. With these funds, Patt was able to purchase arms, which were used for the defense of Jerusalem during the Arab uprising. Rose Viteles organized the expense accounts in the Haganah office and became, in effect, the treasurer of the organization.[29]

During the Arab uprising of 1936, Rose Viteles used her connections with Hadassah to assist the Haganah. She arranged for the school luncheon program, located in the Strauss Health Center, to prepare three meals a day for thousands of Haganah volunteers on duty in Jerusalem. When hundreds of Jewish refugees arrived from Hebron and from the Old City of Jerusalem, she arranged for them to receive meals from the Strauss Health Center as well. When the Yemenite Jewish community in the Arab village of Silwan appealed to the Haganah for supplies of food, she arranged for the supplies to be delivered by one of her Hadassah colleagues.[30]

In addition to her more official functions in the Haganah, Rose Viteles served as friend and confidante to the young men and women volunteers, despite the fact that she spoke poor Hebrew and was twice their age. She granted them small loans, secured jobs for them, provided blankets, bedding, and warm coats to those on duty, and invited officers and ordinary Haganah members to her home. "We all esteemed her highly," wrote Yaakov Patt, "and if the Haganah had awarded medals, she certainly would have received one."[31]

Rose Viteles' success as treasurer of the Haganah from 1934 to 1940 led to additional positions of responsibility. In 1938 she was asked to join the Kofer Hayishuv, which was established by the Vaad Leumi to raise funds in a systematic manner for the defense of the Yishuv. Drawing on her experience in the Haganah, she solicited contributions from wealthy individuals in Jerusalem, negotiated with businesses for the payment of taxes, and directed a staff of volunteers, Haganah soldiers and paid collectors.[32]

During World War II, she assisted the Yishuv's defense efforts through the Jewish Soldiers Welfare Committee, which was established by the Jewish Agency and the Vaad Leumi in October 1940 to aid Jewish volunteers from the Yishuv who enlisted in the British army. As a member of the committee's Jerusalem branch, she specialized in fund-raising and in dealing with the problems of soldiers' families. In October 1941, she was invited by Moshe Shertok (later Sharett) to join the National Presidium of the committee, and in December 1941 was appointed to the Executive of the newly established Central Committee to Aid the Families of Soldiers, a special committee set up to ease the economic and social problems of soldiers' families. (Jewish soldiers from Palestine were paid less than their British counterparts, even though many were the sole supporters of their parents, wives, and children.) To solve these problems, and thereby encourage more volunteers to enlist, the Central Committee promoted the employment of soldiers' wives, provided day care and long-term care centers for their children, urged the Histadrut to offer the women jobs, and arranged for some vocational training. The Central Committee also arranged discounts for food, clothing, and medical and educational services for soldiers' families and, in severe cases, provided loans and direct financial aid. During the course of the war, five to six thousand families per year were assisted by the Central Committee and its local branches.[33]

The most dramatic period of Rose Viteles' service to the Yishuv, apart from her work in the Haganah, came in August 1946, when she was appointed the JDC's first representative on Cyprus. Three thousand detainees were already crowded in camps on the island, with insufficient food, poor medical care, and a lack of basic necessities, as a result of the British government's decision to deport illegal immigrants trying to reach Palestine. The JDC sent Rose Viteles to Cyprus with a team of doctors, nurses, teachers and social workers, in the hope that, as an American citizen with close ties to British officials and a background in social work, she would be able to negotiate effectively with British army officers. The man who appointed her, Charles Passman, the JDC's Middle East representative and a personal friend, had also been her colleague in the Haganah. During her three-month stay on Cyprus, she obtained supplementary food for the camps; organized a parcel service; arranged for shipments of clothing, religious supplies, medical equipment, and books; dealt with problems of religious observance—she arranged for the first *mikvah* [ritual bath] to be built and for the first burial—and helped set up special facilities for babies and children. In December 1946, she was replaced by Morris Laub, a JDC professional, who remained on Cyprus until 1949.[34]

During Israel's War of Independence, Rose Viteles was once again involved in the Haganah. From the end of May 1948, she helped provide emergency financial assistance to the families of soldiers who had been suddenly drafted, through the Haganah's newly established Paymaster's service.[35] Although the committee of volunteers on which she served consisted of four individuals, most of the work was done by the two women—Rose Viteles and a young social worker, Ora Goitein—with the assistance of a paid staff.[36]

Viteles and Goitein reviewed the soldiers' applications, interviewed the men, and recommended the sums their families were to receive. The work was extremely dangerous, because the women had to walk daily to the Paymaster's Office or to the Jewish Agency building at a time when that part of the city suffered frequent shelling and mortar attacks. Although the women tried to do part of the work at home to minimize the risk, Viteles narrowly missed being killed when a shell fell outside Ora Goitein's residence seconds after she had entered the building.

Despite the dangers and the rigors of the siege—the shortages of food, water, and fuel, and the constant shelling—Rose Viteles refused to leave the city or to cease her Haganah work, insisting that the urgent requests of the soldiers be dealt with immediately. "Ora and I organized the work . . . so that needy families of the men on duty received help promptly. . . . We could not afford to postpone consideration for even one day without inflicting unnecessary hardship on the applicants. . . . Nobody was refused a hearing, irrespective of the time of day or the nature of the complaint."[37]

As in 1936, Rose Viteles placed Hadassah institutions at the service of the Haganah. Students of the Alice Seligsberg High School served meals daily in the school cafeteria to hundreds of Haganah soldiers, while the boys in the Fine Mechanics workshops repaired guns and other military equipment. When the Brandeis Vocational Center was bombed after the Arabs discovered that weapons were being repaired there, the workshops were moved to another location. Hadassah also distributed ten thousand packages of clothing to needy schoolchildren throughout the city.[38]

In describing Hadassah's role in the defense of Jerusalem, Rose Viteles later wrote, ". . . Hadassah's tenacity, Hadassah's refusal to consider Jerusalem a lost cause, played a major part in the survival of the city." Of her own experience she wrote movingly, "Though we suffered greatly during the siege of Jerusalem, we . . . shall never cease to be thankful that we had a part in saving the holy city. . . . we never . . . doubted that if we held on, we would win. We would suffer great losses, . . . but we would not let our city die."[39]

Rose Viteles identified with and was intensely devoted to the Yishuv, its hopes and aspirations. What was the source of this identification, and what motivated her to dedicate herself to the Yishuv's every need?

Rose Viteles had a strong desire to be of service to the community. She believed that women who were economically secure had an obligation to devote themselves to volunteer work. "I think that one should try to be helpful to others . . . ," she wrote in her memoirs. "As the need arose and I had the time, why should I not try to help? I never . . . gave any consideration to questions of prestige or . . . status. . . . I had only one child, a reasonable husband, and sufficient help at home. Why should I not have responded to the call of others?"[40]

But beyond a desire to be of service, Rose Viteles developed a genuine love for *Erez Israel,* a love that is evident from the great pride with which she described the accomplishments of the Yishuv and the State of Israel. She shared her husband's enthusiasm for the country's economic development and glowingly described the *moshavim* and *kibuzim* they visited. Although not an overt political activist, she joined a delegation of women headed by Rahel Yanait Ben-Zvi, who visited officials of the Mandatory government in May 1939 to protest the issuance of the White Paper limiting Jewish immigration.[41] In March 1948, when discussing the difficulties of traveling to Mt. Scopus, she argued that, if the Yishuv had not yet given up any roads, Hadassah should not be the first to do so.[42] When, after the siege of Jerusalem, she wrote, "we would not let our city die," it was apparent that Jerusalem was not just the place in which she lived; it was the city to which she belonged.

Rose Viteles was a pioneer in many areas. She pioneered the advancement of vocational education for girls in the Yishuv, an area to which she attached great importance. According to her daughter, it was she who convinced Henrietta Szold to advocate Hadassah's entry into the field of education for women.[43] She succeeded during the 1930s in providing the Haganah in Jerusalem with a secure financial base, and was the only woman to deal with financial matters in the Haganah and the Kofer Hayishuv. She contributed to the defense of Jerusalem and to the welfare of the Haganah's soldiers, through her own efforts and by enlisting the aid of Hadassah colleagues. She established the Jerusalem branch of the Magen

David Adom. Yet she never received any awards for her work, and her contributions have never been adequately recognized. She was the unsung heroine, the unknown soldier. Her memoirs, which present a rich and fascinating portrayal of life in the Yisuv and which, in themselves, constitute a valuable historical document, have been largely forgotten.

This study is an examination of one woman's contribution to the Yishuv and to the State of Israel. It is an attempt to bring Rose Viteles' accomplishments to public attention and to secure for this modest and unassuming woman the recognition she so richly deserves.

Notes

I would like to thank Mrs. Helen Viteles Rikoon, the daughter of Rose Viteles, Mrs. Esther Reifenberg, and Mrs. Ora Goitein for kindly granting me interviews and sharing with me their memories of Rose Viteles. My thanks as well to Dr. Menahem Weinstein for sharing with me his manuscript on the Cyprus camps. I would also like to thank the staffs of the Central Zionist Archives, the Haganah Archives, and the Jewish National and University Library for their kind assistance.

1. For a review of Rose Viteles' life, see Rose R. Viteles, *An American in Israel 1926-1957* (Jerusalem, 1960), 56ff., and "Rose Viteles," *Hadassah Newsletter* (September 1959), 16. For her role in the Haganah, see also *Darko shel adam: Kovez lezikhro shel Yaakov Patt* (Herzliyah, 1958), 117–119, 216.

2. "Rose Viteles," 16. The article quotes a eulogy delivered by Miriam Granott.

3. Viteles, *An American in Israel,* 1.

4. Ibid., 2.

5. The Central Bank of Cooperative Institutions was established in 1922 by the JDC, the Jewish Colonization Association (ICA), and the Palestine Development Council. It provided loans for the development of cooperative institutions (such as *kibuzim* and *moshavim*) in Palestine. In 1926 the Central Bank became a subsidiary of the Palestine Economic Corporation (PEC), an American company financed by JDC as well as by private investors. The company is known today as the PEC Israel Economic Corporation.

6. Telephone interviews with Helen Rikoon, Rose Viteles' daughter, March 1, 1999, and June 25, 2000. Mrs. Rikoon currently lives in New Rochelle, N.Y. According to Mrs. Rikoon, Rose Viteles also did not speak Yiddish.

7. Telephone interview with Helen Rikoon, March 1, 1999.

8. Viteles, *An American in Israel,* 10. Rehaviyah, where the Viteles family lived, received electricity in 1928, the rest of the city a few years later. See also B. Z. Dinur et al., eds., *Sefer toldot hahaganah,* vol 2, part 1 (Tel Aviv, 1959), 482.

9. Viteles, *An American in Israel,* 14–16. See also Hortense Levy, "How They Live in Palestine," *Hadassah Newsletter* (November–December 1932), 11.

10. Viteles, *An American in Israel,* 36–38. See also Hannah Herzog, "The Fringes of the Margin: Women's Organizations in the Civic Sector of the Yishuv" in *Pioneers and Homemakers: Jewish Women in Pre-State Israel,* ed. Deborah S. Bernstein (New York, 1992), 283–304.

11. See Viteles, *An American in Israel,* 3–51. Also Lotta Levensohn, "The Palestine Council of Hadassah," *Hadassah Newsletter* (January–February 1933), 6–7 and Lotta Levensohn, "The Palestine Council of Hadassah," *Hadassah Newsletter* (February 1937), 20–21; interview with Esther Reifenberg, December 15, 1998; interview with Ora Goitein, June 7, 1999. Goitein was another non-American who became active in the Palestine Council. She also completed the first course for social workers established by Henrietta Szold and worked as a volunteer social worker in the Jerusalem Jewish Community Council.

12. See Levensohn, "The Palestine Council." The council was made up of three committees that had previously operated independently—clothing, school luncheons and playgrounds. It also established committees for publicity and for tourists. Rose Viteles headed the tourists committee in 1932. On the clothing and supplies committee, see excerpt of interview with Esther Reifenberg, in *A Tapestry of Hadassah Memories,* ed. Miriam Freund Rosenthal (Pittsboro, N.C.: Town House Press, 1994), 248–249.

13. Viteles, *An American in Israel,* 44–45. The first playground in the Yishuv was established in the Old City in 1925 through the generosity of Bertha Guggenheimer. Additional playgrounds were subsequently established and maintained by means of a bequest left by Bertha Guggenheimer. Trustees of the Guggenheimer Fund were Irma Lindheim, Stephen S. Wise, and Julian Mack. See Zippora Shahori-Rubin and Shifra Shurz, "*Migrashei hamishakim shel Guggenheimer-Hadassah: Hamatnasim shel shnot haesrim,*" *Cathedra* (January 1998), 75–98.

14. See Marlin Levin, *Balm in Gilead: The Story of Hadassah* (Jerusalem, 1973), 117–119; Hadassah National Board Minutes October 18, 1936, Central Zionist Archives (CZA) F32/146; *Hadassah Newsletter* (November 1941 and September–October 1943); Rose Viteles, "Serving Tomorrow's Yishuv," and Miriam Furst, "Recreation Report," *Hadassah Newsletter* (December 1944), "Child Welfare," *Hadassah Newsletter* (November 1942). According to Shahori-Rubin and Shurz, *Migrashei hamishakim shel Guggenheimer-Hadassah,* 96, many playgrounds closed during the War of Independence. The number of playgrounds fell from forty in 1947 to twenty-four in 1948.

15. Rose Viteles, Ethel Agronsky, and Dr. Sarah Bavli, the nutritionist who supervised the school luncheon program, were on the government's Social Service Advisory Committee. See *Hadassah Newsletter* (September–October 1943); Viteles, "Serving Tomorrow's Yishuv"; Ethel Agronsky, "A Heritage for Palestine's Children," *Hadassah Newsletter* (November 1945). See also Zippora Shahori-Rubin, "*Hakafeteria: Mifal hahazanah shel Hadassah,*" *Cathedra* (August 1999), 135–172.

16. The Alice Seligsberg High School opened in September 1942. It was the first vocational high school for girls in Palestine to receive full academic recognition. Its graduates received high school diplomas from the Vaad Leumi and could be admitted to institutions of higher learning. Other vocational schools for girls in Palestine offered only two-year programs (such as Beit Zeirot Mizrahi) or three-year programs (such as the WIZO schools in Nahalat Yizhak and in Haifa). See Viteles, *An American in Israel,* 46–51; Eliezer Rieger, *Hahinukh hamikzoi bayishuv haivri beerez yisrael* (Jerusalem, 1948), 96–105; *Hadassakh Newsletter* (November 1946), 20.

17. *Hadassah Newsletter* (September–October 1943). To gain practice in sewing, students at the Seligsberg High School repaired clothes donated for the

Teheran children, a group of child Holocaust survivors who arrived in Palestine in February 1943 from Teheran.

18. The HEC was chaired by Dr. Judah L. Magnes. Other members of the committee were Henrietta Szold, Julius Simon, Dr. Hayim Yassky, director of the Hadassah Hospital, Dr. Judah Bromberg, administrator of the Hospital, and Ethel Agronsky, who headed the Hadassah Youth Services Committee. The HEC and its successor, the Hadassah Council in Israel, supervised all Hadassah projects in Israel, including the activities of the Youth Services and Vocational Education Services committees. After Dr. Magnes' death in 1948, Ethel Agronsky became chairman of the Hadassah Council. See Minutes of Hadassah Summer Executive Committee meetings, July 9, 1941, August 13, 1941, and Minutes of the Youth Aliyah meeting in Palestine, May 25, 1941, CZA F32/139. Also Minutes of Hadassah Emergency Committee, May 29, 1945, CZA F32/146. Also Lilli Jerusalem, "HEC The Imprint of the Hadassah Personality," *Hadassah Newsletter* (June–July, 1945). See also Rose Viteles, "The Future of Jerusalem," *Hadassah Newsletter* (June 1949), 10.

On surplus foods see Minutes of Hadassah Council meetings, CZA F32/20; Viteles, *An American in Israel,* 53–54; "Rose Viteles." During her stay in the United States, when she became a member of the National Board of Hadassah (1957–1959), Rose Viteles served as liaison chair for the Surplus Foods Project.

19. Herzog, "The Fringes of the Margin," 302.

20. Viteles, *An American in Israel,* 37. Rose Viteles visited Henrietta Szold together with Anna Ticho and another woman from the HNI committee.

21. Telephone interview with Helen Rikoon, March 1, 1999.

22. See Viteles, *An American in Israel,* 38–40, 56–60. Also *Darko shel adam,* 117–119. On the development of social services, see Herzog, "The Fringes of the Margin," 23–95.

23. Viteles, *An American in Israel,* 56.

24. Interview with Yaakov Patt, Haganah Archives (HA) (84–63).

25. See Interviews with Hadassah Berlinski, HA (196.43), and Zvi Mitterstein, HA (33.11). The Magen David Adom enabled women soldiers in the Haganah to move about freely.

26. Dinur et al., *Sefer toldot hahaganah,* vol. 2, part 1, 273, 564–565; interviews with Yehoshua Aluf, HA (138.8) and (4.13), and Yaakov Yanai, HA (20.44); Meir Pail, *Mihahaganah lizva haganah yisrael* (Tel Aviv, 1979), 26.

27. Viteles, *An American in Israel,* 58; *Darko shel adam,* 88ff: interview with Yehoshua Aluf, HA (138.8). In 1938 most of the members of Irgun B returned to the Haganah. Those who did not return formed the Irgun Zvai Leumi. Viteles had long supported the reunification of the Haganah with Irgun B.

28. Viteles, *An American in Israel,* 58.

29. See *Darko shel adam,* 116–117; Dinur et al., *Sefer toldot hahaganah,* vol. 2, part 1, 565.

30. The Hadassah colleague was Esther Reifenberg. See Viteles, *An American in Israel,* 58–59; interview with Yaakov Patt, HA (84.65); Rose Luria Halprin, "Hadassah at Attention," *Hadassah Newsletter* (October 1936), 10; interview with Esther Reifenberg; Minutes, national board meetings, May 20, 1936, and September 9, 1936, CZA F32/146.

31. *Darko shel adam,* 119.

32. Viteles, *An American in Israel,* 62; Protocols, meetings of local committee

of Kofer Hayishuv, 24.1.40, 6.2.40, 5.8.40, CZA J8/136. For a general description of the Kofer Hayishuv see Dinur et al., *Sefer toldot hahaganah (1973)*, vol. 3, part 1, 204; vol. 2 (1963), 1003. See also Mordechai Berger, ed., *Kofer hayishuv* (Jerusalem, 1964).

33. Viteles, *An American in Israel*, 62–63. While Viteles would have preferred that women with young children remain at home, the men on the committee insisted that going out to work would help the soldiers' wives forget their loneliness. The committee's position was that the women should work unless the cost of child care would exceed their income. See Moshe Shertok to Rose Viteles, 28.10.41, CZA J10/31; Review of activities of the Central Committee to aid the Families of Soldiers, 1942–1945, CZA J10/30; Protocols of meetings of the Central Committee, CZA J10/36. Also Circular #9/42, and Protocol of local committee in Jerusalem, 5.11.40, CZA J10/5; Survey of the activities of the Local Committee for Jewish Soldiers in Jerusalem, September 1940–August 1941, Protocols of meetings, CZA J10/21. Dinur et al., *Sefer toldot hahaganah*, vol. 3, part 1, 204 ff 673ff, 723, 1273.

See also "Report on Residential Center for the Children of Soldiers at Kfar Yehezkel," 9.9.42, CZA J10/5. The mothers visited the children once every two weeks. See also Minutes of Presidium of Jewish Soldiers Welfare Committee, 7.7.41, 22.7.41, joint meeting Jewish Agency and Hadassah, 4.11.41, Protocols of Presidium, CZA J10/43. See also Mordechai Berger, *Magbit hahitgayesut vehahazalah* (Jerusalem, 1970), and Emmanuel Harussi, *Sefer hamagbit: Magbit hahitgayesut vehahazalah* (Jerusalem, 1950).

The Central Committee received most of its funding from the Mobilization Fund established in 1942. It also received partial support form Hadassah and from the Jewish Agency.

34. Viteles, *An American in Israel*, 68–73, Nahum Bogner, *Iy Hageirush: Makhanot hamaapilim bekafrisin, 1946-1948* (Tel Aviv: Tel Aviv University and Am Oved, 1991); Morris Laub, *Last Barrier to Freedom: Internment of Jewish Holocaust Survivors on Cyprus 1946-49* (Berkeley, 1985); Menahem Weinstein, manuscript in preparation on the Torah Vaavodah movement in the Cyprus Camps, chapter titled "Religious Life in the Cyprus Camps." See also Passman to Viteles, 23.9.46, 24.9.46, 3.10.46, American Jewish Joint Distribution Committee (hereafter AJJDC Archives), Jerusalem, Cyprus collection, box 3, file 8; Passman to AJDC Paris, 30.9.46 and 10.11.46, Schwartz to JDC New York, 27.9.46, AJJDC Archives, Jerusalem, Geneva collection, Box 14A, file C34.0134. Also Levin, *Balm in Gilead,* 226 ff.

35. Viteles, *An American in Israel*, 80–81; interview with Ora Goitein. See also Yizhak Levi (Levizah), *Tisha kabin: Yerushalayim bikravot hamilhamot* (Tel Aviv, 1986), Netanel Lorch, *The Edge of the Sword: Israel's War of Independence 1947-49* (Jerusalem, 1968); and Rahel Yanait Ben-Zvi et al. eds., *Hahaganah biyerushalayim: Eduyot vezikhronot mipi haverim* (Jerusalem, 1973), vol. 2.

36. According to Ora Goitein, the two men on the committee were Judge Levenstein and Michael Simon. Goitein herself was asked to join the committee by the wife of David Shaltiel, commander of the Haganah in Jerusalem, apparently because Rose Viteles needed a Hebrew-speaking assistant. Goitein, who was also fluent in English, had worked as a social worker in the Vaad Hakehillah, was active in Hadassah, and already knew Rose Viteles. It is not clear who appointed Viteles to the committee.

37. Viteles, *An American in Israel,* 80. Viteles' description of the work differs somewhat from that of Ora Goitein. Mrs. Goitein remembers that the women dealt mainly with the families of the soldiers, who were referred to them by the Vaad Hakehillah.

38. Viteles, *An American in Israel,* 74–81. Girls from the Seligsberg High School also prepared meals for the Haganah soldiers on Mt. Scopus. The school luncheon kitchen in the Old City provided meals to the Haganah soldiers there. See Dinur et al., *Sefer toldot hahaganah,* vol. 3, part 1 1392, 1459; Rose Viteles, "Heroic Story of Trade School Girls," *Hadassah Newsletter* (October 1948); Rose Viteles, "The Future of Jerusalem"; and Rose Viteles, "Hadassah Carries on Inside Jerusalem's Besieged Old City," *Hadassah Newsletter* (February 1948).

39. Levin, *Balm in Gilead,* 243; Viteles, "The Future of Jerusalem."

40. Viteles, *An American in Israel,* 35.

41. See Ben-Zvi et al., *Hahaganah biyerushalayim,* vol. 1, 196. See also Ethel Agronsky, "Nine Years of Youth Services," *Hadassah Newsletter* (November, 1945). During 1936–1939, Hadassah joined with other women's organizations in Palestine—WIZO, Council of Working Women—to form the Council of Jewish Women's Organizations, to protest against attacks on the Jewish community and against political decisions adversely affecting the community. The council also tried to provide hostels for Jewish women soldiers during the war. "Youth Services" referred to the activities of the Palestine Council of Hadassah, which was renamed the Hadassah Youth Services Committee.

42. Levin, *Balm in Gilead,* 243.

43. Telephone interview with Helen Rikoon, March 1, 1999.

Chapter 13

Irma "Rama" (Levy) Lindheim (1886–1978) was a remarkable and complex figure that stood at the center of the Jewish public arena during the turbulent era that witnessed the rise of Zionism and the birth of the State of Israel. Born in New York City to a highly assimilated wealthy German Jewish family, with roots in the United States stretching back to the start of the nineteenth century, she early on exhibited considerable intellectual acumen and a talent for independent action. A maverick by nature, she eventually rejected the prevailing sensibility of the German Jewish milieu and gravitated to feminist political activism. She studied social work at Columbia University—a decade later, in 1922, she became the first woman to enroll in the new Jewish Institute of Religion, established by Rabbi Stephen S. Wise (1874–1949)—and she also defied her parents' wishes by marrying a young attorney named Norvin R. Lindheim in 1907.

Lindheim's first significant encounter with Zionism came in the midst of World War I. Spurred by the Balfour Declaration of 1917, she became an ardent and articulate Zionist activist, and she quickly caught the attention of Henrietta Szold (1860–1945), the founder of Hadassah, Judge Julian W. Mack (1866–1943), a prominent Zionist Organization of America leader, Menahem Ussishkin (1863–1941), an East European Zionist official, and other highly placed Zionist figures. Inducted into the Zionist movement's organizational work in the early 1920s, she traveled to Palestine, where she came into contact with three of the Palestine labor movement's most significant personalities: Manya (Wilbusheviz) Shohat (1880–1961), Rahel Yanait Ben-Zvi (1886–1979), and Yizhak Ben-Zvi (1884–1963), later the second president of the State of Israel. She was deeply influenced by Shohat and the Ben-Zvis and developed close personal relationships with them that lasted the rest of their lives. Indeed, although Lindheim rose to become national president of Hadassah in the late 1920s, she gradually and increasingly swam against the current of Hadassah's centrist orientation, eventually becoming an outspoken supporter of the Histadrut and advocate of Hashomer Hazair's brand of socialist Zionism. At the age of forty-seven, she immigrated to Palestine and joined Kibbutz Mishmar Haemek of the Kibbutz Arzi movement, located in the Jezreel Valley.

That Lindheim elected to pursue a radical path of her own made her, voluntarily, an outsider at a time when most middle-class American Jews placed a premium on the notions of "belonging" and "normalizing Jewish life." Her radicalism contrasted strikingly with the worldview of most American Jews, including the moderate Hadassah leadership, and her feminist activism challenged the male-dominated hierarchy of American Judaism and American Zionism in the 1930s and 1940s. In later years, she became a tireless proponent of Zionist youth activity and women's education as well as a persistent critic of American Jewish life and Israeli society. Viewed against this backdrop, it is, perhaps, possible to understand why Lindheim was virtually obliterated from the pantheon of American Jewish and Zionist leaders. She became something of a historical "unperson" even in her own lifetime and, until very recently, a sorely neglected figure rarely, if ever, mentioned in academic studies of Zionism and the American Jewish experience.

In the following chapter, Shulamit Reinharz breaks new ground by offering the first systematic treatment and assessment of Lindheim. "As an activist, she was wedded first to Hadassah, then to Hashomer Hazair and Mishmar Haemek," asserts Reinharz, "but always to Judaism and Zionism." Though Lindheim's trajectory certainly deviated from the American Jewish mainstream, her life merits close scrutiny, not only because of her profile as an extraordinary and important leader, but also as a case study of the symbiotic relationship between emergent American Jewish feminism and the Zionist enterprise.

Irma "Rama" Lindheim: An Independent American Zionist Woman

Shulamit Reinharz

An American Zionist Woman

Irma Levy Lindheim (1886–1978) is one of scores of nearly forgotten female American Zionist activists.[1] Her service as third national president of Hadassah (following Henrietta Szold and Alice Seligsberg) and her radically unconventional path of Zionist and Jewish commitment—including study in the 1920s in the rabbinical program at the Jewish Institute of Religion; a lifelong, intimate friendship with socialist Zionist pioneer Manya Shohat; membership in Kibbutz Mishmar Haemek; and authorship of two books—have not yet earned her a place in history.

Irma Lindheim lived in two worlds—the United States, the land of her birth, and Israel, the land of her people. For most of the second half of her life she was a member of a *kibbutz,* but she never relinquished American citizenship. Until her death at the age of ninety-two, she was a restless, determined woman, constantly traveling, always exploring new ideas and ways of solving problems. She was an articulate, forceful speaker and writer, inspiring some and irritating others. Never afraid to speak her mind, she stated in print that Henry Kissinger could "go to hell" (and described Yizhak Rabin as uncharismatic but effective).

If Irma Lindheim is remembered at all, it is for her term as national president of Hadassah. But learning about Irma teaches us that linking a historical figure with an organization may hide her conflict with that organization. Irma, a committed socialist Zionist, was always critical of Hadassah for its apolitical posture.[2] In this regard, history may have proved her wrong: Hadassah's apolitical self-definition helped it grow, in contrast with the Federation of American Zionists, Mizrachi, and Poalei Zion, which predated it[3] and never reached its numbers. The political, educational, and philanthropic activity of women formed the axis of Irma's career. Manya Shohat, nurturing Irma's love of Israel and the way of the *kibbutz,* taught her that it was a society that could reshape women's lives—a world where women "could bear children and assure them the best of care and yet be free to be people—intelligent, respected participants in the affairs of their community and nation."[4] Irma tried valiantly but unsuccessfully as she aged to motivate American Jewish mothers and grandmothers to educate their children privately in Jewish knowledge.

Irma belonged to a generation influenced by American Christian middle-class women reformers like Jane Addams (1860–1935), who declared that she created Hull House in Chicago not to save poor immigrants but to save herself.[5] Similarly, Irma believed "that Palestine has something to give . . . to America and American Jews, and that it is not only America and American Jews who can contribute to Palestine."[6] Like Jane Addams, Irma believed that collective living brings out the best in humanity. And finally, like Jane Addams, Irma had moments of transformation. Following her husband Norvin's sudden death while she was on a grueling Zionist speaking tour in 1928, she described one such moment to her heroine, Henrietta Szold:

Perhaps after all there is no purpose, perhaps even there is no God. I was shaken to my very depths, and life looked ugly and my spirit was heavy. . . . Then two weeks ago I passed through another one of those profound experiences which have left so definite a mark upon the actions of my life. I saw life unroll before me. The "I" which was weak and subject to all the weaknesses that flesh is heir to, was bending under the burden of the great task which had been imposed upon me. Why was I the one to carry this terrible weight and responsibility; why should I be asked to give up home and family and the rest that a very tired body craved? Dear, dear Miss Szold, perhaps without your example I would not have found the answer—a great peace entered into me with the light of understanding which came in the contemplation of your life. . . . I seemed flooded with light and again I saw the "Purpose" and again I experienced the conviction of the great life force which gives strength as it flows through you to others. It was a moment of rededication for me. Palestine is the symbol of the life force to me, the force which in its difficult upward struggle is allowing man to evolve, and again my faith in Palestine was re-established. From that moment any tiredness dropped away. There was no more conflict. Home, family, my future life, fitted into a scheme of which Palestine, the symbol, became the objective.[7]

An Early Independent Spirit

Born in New York City on December 9, 1886, into an extremely wealthy German Jewish assimilated family with roots dating back several generations in the American South, Irma discovered Zionism only at age thirty-one. Her father, Robert Levy, was an importer; her mother, Mathilda

Morgenstern, dedicated herself to her husband and three daughters, Amy, Edna, and Irma. Irma's mother and grandmother felt spiritually attached to Judaism but lacked any Jewish education. The family celebrated no Jewish holidays and had Christmas trees in their home. More attached to class than to religion, the family disdained eastern European Jews.

As a young woman, Irma displayed an independent spirit. She defied her father's insistence on selecting her husband and in 1907 married attorney Norvin R. Lindheim. They set up a magnificent home next to the Woolworth mansion on Long Island[8] and had five children: Norvin Jr. (1908), Hortense [Babs] (1912), Donald (1914), Richard (1917), and Stephen (1919), named for Rabbi Stephen S. Wise. Irma became independently wealthy upon her father's death in 1914, while also enjoying Norvin's law-practice income.

Norvin Lindheim, however, was having legal problems. Because his firm dealt with German companies and he did not serve in the U.S. military during World War I, his loyalty was questioned, a suspicion fueled at the time by antisemitism. In 1920 Norvin was charged with conspiring to defraud the U.S. government. His lengthy trial was followed by a guilty verdict and a prison term that lasted until 1924. Norvin appealed the verdict, but he was finally declared innocent only in 1928, shortly after his death at age forty-seven. During these years, Norvin Lindheim became deeply engaged in American Zionist politics.

In contrast to her husband, Irma enlisted in 1917, though her fourth child, Richard, was only five weeks old. Driving her Cadillac, she was one of the few Jewish women officers in the Motor Corps, earning the rank of first lieutenant. Challenged that same year by an Ethical Culture teacher to learn something about her Jewishness, she visited her husband's cousin Hortense Guggenheimer Moses in Baltimore, where for the first time she met American Zionists (Baltimore physician Harry Friedenwald) and Palestinian Jews (Dr. Ben-Zion Mossensohn, principal of a Tel Aviv school). In her own words, she was "attacked by the virus of Zionism," and after just six months began lecturing for "the cause." Even more remarkably, she was later attacked by socialism.

Moved by the Balfour Declaration of 1917, Irma also began to bring Judaism home, first by replacing Christmas with Hanukah. Her Zionism did not stem from her Judaism, but the other way around. For the rest of her life, Irma's interest in Judaism would continue to grow, as would her conviction that family life was the key to the transmission of Jewish knowledge.

Henrietta Szold, then head of the cultural division of the American Zionist organization, recognized Irma's leadership potential, as did others.

With their backing Irma accepted the challenge to chair New York's un-philanthropic Seventh Zionist District. She used her inheritance to purchase a brownstone in which to create a cultural center, whose opening was attended by Justice Louis D. Brandeis. The center quickly established an Intercollegiate Zionist Organization, offered lessons for children and lectures for adults, and saw its membership and donations soar. However, Irma's efforts were considered part of the American or Brandeisian Zionist approach, which was opposed by the European approach, represented symbolically by Chaim Weizmann and Louis Lipsky. The Brandeis/Weizmann split at the 1921 Zionist convention in Cleveland resulted in the defeat of the American group—and the closure of Irma's center. Henrietta Szold, Irma's mentor, had already left for Palestine.

The personal outcome of this thwarting of Irma's first Zionist project was the redirection of her energies in 1922 to her own intellectual development, and more particularly to serious Jewish study. Disgusted by the Lipsky faction, she was attracted to the rebellious, free-thinking Zionist rabbi Stephen S. Wise, who just that year had founded the nontraditional Jewish Institute of Religion (JIR), with Norvin as a member of the Board of Trustees. In this she was following in the path of Henrietta Szold, who had studied at the Jewish Theological Seminary from 1903 to 1906, and she also bore a resemblance to Elsie Clews Parsons, a rebellious, wealthy non-Jewish New York woman twelve years Irma's senior who defied social conventions to seek intellectual challenges.[9]

Irma was creating a life of her own, because of and despite her husband's trial and imprisonment and her large family. Sending the children off to Glen Cove, Long Island, she lived in New York City for three and a half years with her husband, pouring herself into the study of Bible, Talmud, and Hebrew grammar at Wise's Jewish Institute of Religion and also studying child development with Professor John Dewey at Columbia University's Teachers College.

Women's presence in the founding class of the JIR compelled the faculty to take a stand on whether they would be considered special auditors or regular rabbinical candidates. After a protracted discussion, the faculty ultimately accepted the position that the JIR had been founded "to train, in liberal spirit, men and women for the Jewish ministry, research, and community service."[10] As a psychologically and financially independent woman, aware of all the ways in which she was defying traditional womanhood, Irma hoped through her studies to pave the way for other women to function as congregational rabbis, even though she herself did not aspire to that role.

Encountering Palestine and Manya

Irma first traveled to Palestine with Hortense Guggenheimer in 1925, in order to regain her strength after her husband's release from prison. In addition to attending the opening of the Hebrew University, she toured the country on horseback in an adventure organized by her future life-long friend, Manya Shohat.[11] Accompanied by a Jewish male guide, she dressed as a Bedouin Arab to disguise her gender and nationality. Irma's enthusiastic letters home were published three years later in *The Immortal Adventure* (1928), with an introduction by Stephen S. Wise.

Manya arranged this journey for Irma, because she was

the first woman who expressed the desire to do what I myself did . . . years ago: to ride the length and breadth of Palestine from Dan to Beersheva on horseback to visit Arab as well as Jew.[12]

Irma saw in Manya an example of the free-spirited, fully focused, physically strong, and proud Jewish woman she could become, and of a wife who could live independently of her husband. Manya saw in Irma a (wealthy) potential (female) ally in many unconventional dreams, including the recognition of the existence and rights of Palestine's Arabs. Manya's lessons were not lost on Irma:

Between the two separate worlds in which Jew and Arab lived, [Manya] made clear the necessity to build bridges over what seemed unbridgeable gaps. . . . As a first step toward an understanding of this, she had me meet Arabs as people—not problems.[13]

Teaming up at Kibbutz Kfar Giladi, where Manya was a member, the two visited friendly neighboring Arab villages. Manya taught Irma to view Arabs and Jews as equals, and invited her to help forge a national policy, despite leadership opposition, that would "permit both Jews and Arabs to build Palestine in a spirit of cooperation, without fear of domination of one over the other."[14] Manya's views strengthened Irma's pride in the health services Hadassah provided for Arabs, and in Judah L. Magnes's policy of opening the Hebrew University to Arab students.

On this first trip, Manya also introduced Irma to *kibbutz* life, which immediately intrigued her as a society in which men and women might become equals. In Kfar Giladi, Manya's daughter Anna gave Irma a new name, Rama, by which she was thereafter known in Palestine. Manya introduced Rama to other Yishuv leaders. She arranged for Rama to explore the Negev with Rahel Yanait and Yizhak Ben Zvi, who, in turn, urged her to raise money for its purchase, Manya's major project at the time—an idea reinforced by another new lifelong friend, Zionist leader Menahem Ussishkin. And, like so many travelers, Rama learned about the need for health services at first hand when she was treated for malaria in the Safed Hadassah Hospital.

Upon her return to the United States, Irma plunged again into Zionism as her primary focus. From then on she devoted her life to fund-raising and organizing, abandoning her studies for what she believed to be the greater cause. At this point, Zionism superseded Judaism, and Zionism needed volunteers and money, both of which she knew how to mobilize. In one meeting, she set the example by donating her diamond tiara to finance a children's hospital ward. Sari Berger and Nadia Stein, emissaries from Palestine, helped her train women volunteers for the Women's Jewish National Fund (JNF) Council, later integrated into Hadassah. When she was asked to become president of Hadassah the following year, Irma nearly declined because of her devotion to the JNF. But Szold reminded her that Hadassah had accepted "the fundamental undertaking of the Jewish National Fund" in 1925, and that she had gone into Hadassah as national chairman of the National Fund Council.[15]

During this same period, Norvin Lindheim, Irma's husband, was also heavily involved in American Zionist politics and met Manya in Palestine on a separate trip. Manya hoped to involve Norvin in joint projects with Rama and members of the Yishuv. Strangely, however, Irma never mentions Norvin's Zionist activity in her books and letters, even though by the end of 1925 Norvin had joined Judge Julian W. Mack, Rabbi Stephen S. Wise, Samuel Rosensohn and Robert Szold in the governing bodies of the Zionist Organization of America (ZOA) and the United Palestine Appeal (UPA).[16] Although Norvin's activities paralleled Irma's success, it is possible that she preferred to see herself as independently capable.

Characteristically, the ZOA and the World Zionist Organization (WZO) were embroiled in battles about whether Zionism was a movement of labor or of capital, of Americans or of Europeans, of efficient action or of ideological passion. While the political maneuvering in which her husband was deeply involved unfolded, Irma launched a speaking tour and was asked to succeed Henrietta Szold as a national president of Hadassah (1926), a position that also conferred on her the role of national vice president of the ZOA. Irma preferred that Szold remain president, so that she could work in the ranks. But after being persuaded by the Hadassah board, Irma wrote to Henrietta Szold, asking if she was "willing to trust your life work in my hands." Irma had reservations because of her husband's poor health, her hope for further study, and her passion for the "land" itself, as opposed to Hadassah's welfare and health projects. But Szold telegraphed from Jerusalem, declaring her relief "that the task had fallen upon shoulders that can bear it with dignity and into hands trained to execute it deftly and nobly."[17] Irma could not let Henrietta Szold down.

Irma's moving acceptance speech, couched in the language of servitude, actually expressed her pleasure in becoming a forceful, almost rabbinic, leader of women:

I have a deep and abiding love for my home and my children, and it means that I have made up my mind to be away from my children a great deal. It means that I will act from now on as your servant. I am yours to command. I have accepted for the last nine years the objective of Palestine as my goal and as the directing force in all the activities of my life. I have been the director of those activities; from now on I serve you. . . . Palestine can not be a side issue in our lives. It means that from our rising up in the morning until our lying down at night, we will have to dedicate ourselves to this service. It is not a new thing to you women. You do it year in and year out and it is wonderful to think that no matter how often you do it, no matter how often you are called upon to redouble your efforts, you always answer the call.[18]

At that time, Hadassah faced possible absorption into the ZOA by detractors such as ZOA leader Louis Lipsky, who resented his lack of control over Hadassah's money and leaders. A well-run group that abided by the "100% clause" (all money except dues goes to Palestine), Hadassah, like Irma, fought to preserve its autonomy. In her new role, Irma presented the case for Palestine in speeches throughout the country and reveled in her victory over men such as Lipsky, who had tried to block her nomination in favor of more acquiescent women.

This was a glorious period for Hadassah. From 1921 to 1930, including the period of Irma's presidency, membership increased from ten thousand to thirty-five thousand. Composed of American-born, largely college-educated women, Hadassah did not require its members to adhere to a particular brand of Zionism or even to sign the Basle Program. Rather, its mission was to build health services and welfare institutions in Palestine. As president in 1927, Irma Lindheim understood that health services were a noncontroversial hook that could draw American women into Zionist activism:

Henrietta Szold applied the scientific method in organizing Hadassah and guided it through fifteen years of its development. She reduced the general Zionist idea to a particular part of its program and then proceeded to develop bit by bit the instrument with which to construct this part.[19]

Some historians have taken a negative view of this instrumental approach. Yonathan Shapiro, for one, notes that Hadassah had become a purely charitable organization, and the leaders were afraid to involve themselves in problems outside the narrow field of philanthropy for fear of antagonizing their following.[20]

But Shapiro concedes that the leaders of Hadassah knew what appealed to American Jewish women. They built

an organization that was a neat counterpart to American charitable organizations which were increasingly appealing to middle-class women. It was the perfect organization for the emerging Jewish gilded ghetto in the United States. The goal of Hadassah was charity, as was that of its counterparts; the leaders were middle-class and college-educated, as in the non-Jewish American organization; and the activities and gatherings looked exactly like the gatherings of the Christian women's associations across the street. To this was added the Palestinian element, which gave justification and rationalization for the independent existence of an exclusively Jewish organization.[21]

At the same time, however, Irma fought against Hadassah's attitude of working for Palestine but not for *aliyah*. She rejected Hadassah's defense that its activity was required in the diaspora. By contrast, she tried to present Palestine as Hadassah's basic principle. When she later came on *aliyah* herself, David Ben–Gurion appealed to Hadassah and other Jewish women's movements throughout the world to imitate Szold and Lindheim, symbols of a real connection with the Land of Israel.[22] In 1927 Irma was reelected president of Hadassah and served as its delegate to the World Zionist Congress in Basle. At the congress's conclusion she flew to Palestine, apparently the first woman to do so. In this she defied Manya, who had urged her to delay her trip:

Do not come now, Rama. Preserve your energy and your fiery spirit to bring us hope of new creative work. Let your longing for Palestine give you this strength to fight our cause. . . . Come rather next spring, when, as I fondly hope, you will already meet the first *kvuzah* [rural commune] at work in the Negev.[23]

Even Manya did not control her.

In Palestine, Manya told Irma that "the only salvation of Zionism" was a "scheme for new and systematic agricultural colonization"[24] that required purchasing the Negev. To implement the project, Manya suggested that

an American committee . . . be formed at the same time and along the same lines as the Palestine committee, with which it would work in close contact. I propose as its first members: Miss Henrietta Szold and Mr. and Mrs. Lindheim, who shall have the right to coopt others.[25]

Manya also suggested enlisting Junior Hadassah for purchasing and developing the Negev. Now Manya wanted Irma to stay abroad and raise funds to pay for the items listed in Manya's carefully calculated budget.

The *New York Times* reported on October 17, 1927, that

Mrs. Irma L. Lindheim, president of Hadassah, returned yesterday on the Red Star liner *Belgenland* after attending the World Zionist Congress at Basel, Switzerland, and making a tour of Palestine where she inspected the infant welfare centers and the hospitals under the supervision of Hadassah in the Holy Land.

The announcement depicts Irma as an official engaged in noncontroversial, feminine activities rather than in defiant, bold adventures. At the same time, Manya began a series of regular reports to Irma from Palestine on various subjects, "opening with Hadassah, its present and future." In this first document, a rather shocking review, Manya discussed in gruesome detail the failings of the American physician Dr. Bluestone, then in charge of Hadassah's medical project in Palestine. Manya urged Hadassah in Palestine to merge into the government hospital system and then diverge in a different, unspecified modern direction. She hinted that Henrietta Szold might have left the Hadassah presidency in order to abandon hospital work, had she possessed the courage to inform Hadassah members. In Manya's characteristically dogmatic style, she wrote:

In the future, the Hadassah organization is to take upon itself once more some constructive sphere of work, capable of appealing to and uplifting the spirit of women, as the humanitarian task of bringing medical help and service to Palestine appealed to the American women years ago. I do not propose to discuss at this moment the question as to what form this new activity should take.

But I do know that it is your work, Rama. Perhaps you were called upon to lead the Hadassah organization in order that you might lead it in that direction. . . . [Hospitals] are not the work your nature craves: your constructive and creative spirit needs to work on something healthy and creative to serve the physical and spiritual renaissance of mankind rather than do work which has pity as its foundation.[26]

In her next letter (October 30, 1927), Manya mercilessly criticized the Zionist Executive of the WZO and predicted class warfare. The following day she stated that Rahel Yanait should not raise money in the United States but should try, instead, to awaken people. Next (November 1, 1927), she described the semi-starvation and malaria suffered by members of Kfar Giladi–Tel Hai and the fact that many of them had had to leave. Workers were being abandoned, and Rama should help! A subsequent letter informed Rama of the political conflicts between the Histadrut [General Federation of Jewish Workers in the Land of Israel] and the

Palestine Zionist Executive.[27] Thus, as president of Hadassah, Irma had a constant stream of provocative suggestions from a woman in the Palestinian field—Manya Shohat.

Death and Departure

On January 30, 1928, a large reception was held in Irma's honor in New York. Arabs had been rioting in Palestine, and Irma voiced the unpopular opinion that peace could be attained only if friendly cooperation between Jews and Arabs were developed. Shortly thereafter, free but unpardoned, Norvin Lindheim died while Irma was on a speaking tour "covering 25 cities in 30 days from New York to Texas and back." In the same letter to Henrietta Szold in which she described her inner transformation, she wrote:

In Nashville yesterday thru some divine providence I called up Norvin at ten o'clock. He was so happy and eager when he heard my voice. At one o'clock, I was called back to the telephone to hear from Norvin Junior, that his Dad had been stricken with apoplexy at twelve and had gone out instantaneously.[28]

Irma returned to the podium and gave her speech.

For the first time in the history of Nashville the leading Jews had consented to attend a meeting to listen to the story of Palestine. I was somehow endowed with the strength to go from the telephone to the table and there in a few words I conveyed to them that Palestine was worthy of every sacrifice that could be offered towards the achievement of its upbuilding.[29]

Two months later, the *New York Times* reported that Irma, as president of Hadassah, had recently been criticized for voicing her personal views of the ZOA. But at a special day-long meeting, she received a vote of confidence. Clearly, she was willing to do the political work that the "apolitical" Hadassah required.

Soon grief caught up with her, however, and Irma decided to spend the next year abroad, away from everything, an "enforced exile."[30] The practice of putting Hadassah before her family would have to stop. After a long series of miscommunications, she got word from Hadassah that she had been reelected, but though she wired back that she would accept, she actually meant that she would not. From Europe she traveled to Palestine, with hopes of restoring her health, peace of mind, and peaceful coexistence between Arabs and Jews. *Aliyah* was becoming the logical conclusion—but not quite yet. A two-week return to the United States to settle her affairs, "sell her place, lock stock and barrel, and move her family, all but young Norvin, to Europe"[31] closed a chapter and seemingly severed her connections with Hadassah in favor of Palestine.

Irma organized a farewell lunch at the City Club in New York. Many friends, including former Hadassah president Alice Seligsberg, reprimanded her for being a quitter. Irma countered that retaining the presidency "would so destroy my energies as to make them impotent, perhaps for all time, for the cause of Palestine."[32] She finally found inner repose in Munich by studying music, practicing the cello for hours every day.[33] As a wealthy woman, she had a way out when both the United States and Palestine demanded too much of her.

Irma returned to the United States for what was to have been a brief visit but became a lengthy stay following the 1929 stock market crash. The only part of her fortune saved, ironically, was the money she had invested in Palestine. Capitalism was looking quite shaky. All the time, Manya was sending her letters about collectives, cooperatives, and the merits of Labor Zionism. In 1930, two years after leaving her two-year presidency of Hadassah, disillusioned by capitalism and firmly committed to Zionism, Irma joined the Labor Zionist party Poalei Zion, upon which the Hadassah National Board demanded her resignation.

The Move to Labor Zionism and Palestine

Irma claimed that Manya had guided her political shift by introducing her to the left-wing socialist Hashomer Hazair youth movement. Once she became a socialist, Irma was increasingly critical of Hadassah, defining herself as further to the left and entitled to political autonomy. Instead of soliciting funds for Hadassah, she now raised funds for Hashomer Hazair with Mordekhai and Ziporah Bentov, members of Kibbutz Mishmar Haemek—an involvement that ultimately led to her joining their *kibbutz*.

Irma admired Hashomer Hazair's *kibbutz* training for young people. Many American Zionists, however, vilified Hashomer Hazair as a communist group that abetted Arab against Jew. Shocked by such charges, Irma returned to Palestine to investigate. An article about her, published when she was much older, described her response to the criticism of Hashomer Hazair:

In those days, Hashomer Hazair published an enthusiastic manifesto in favor of Boleshevik Russia and its Communist regime. Rama Lindheim asked the leaders of Hashomer Hazair: "What comes first with you? Zionism or Communism?" They replied: "Zionism is the goal, whereas the socialist communist idea is the universalist doctrine of the liberation of mankind from the chains of bondage." She also asked them whether, in the *kibbutz,* man's potential could express itself freely despite the collective ideology. Again she received an affirmative reply.[34]

Back in the United States, satisfied with her findings, she resumed a speaking tour, believing that the spirit of Palestine could help Americans during the Depression. She seems not to have cared about the antireligious ideology of Hashomer Hazair. At that time religion was not uppermost in her mind; Zionism, Arabs, and the working class had captured her attention. In 1932, acting on her extraordinary capacity to galvanize others into an organization, she helped establish the League for Labor Palestine. Labor Zionism, once again, meant *aliyah* and socialism. Finally, she was ready to act on both.

Full of hope for new beginnings, Irma moved to Palestine in March 1933 with all her children and her eighty-year-old mother-in-law. Her first endeavor there was to try to create a Histadrut-funded clearinghouse for newcomers, but because of bureaucratic obstacles, the project never got off the ground. Finally, after attending a disillusioning Zionist Congress in Prague, Irma decided to abandon organizational work altogether and join three-year-old Kibbutz Mishmar Haemek. Her children were established in various schools and programs around the country. Ultimately, for various reasons, none of them was to remain in Palestine, and they gradually left to pursue their education in the United States. Irma's second son, Donald, served for a while as a bodyguard to Chaim Weizmann and fought in the Haganah, but he, too, later left for the United States to study agriculture and genetics. He was killed in World War II before he could fulfill his plan to return.

Irma selected Mishmar Haemek for its beauty and respect for individuality and privacy, but she knew that she would have welcoming friends there as well. Although she was a forty-seven-year-old widow and mother of five when she sought membership in the *kibbutz,* she was accepted by unanimous vote and remained a member for the rest of her life, despite her frequent sojourns in the United States and elsewhere for Zionist and political work. This wealthy, assimilated New York Jewish woman activist had finally found her true home in a remote spot that offered sparse food, water, and comforts, but was rich in Zionist and democratic spirit. When Rama joined Mishmar Haemek, she was older by twenty-five years than the other members' average age and ten years older than the oldest founding member. Her membership, though real, nevertheless had a guestlike quality. She worked half days in the kitchen (which she defined as productive labor) and half days on writing, studying Hebrew (which she never mastered), and knitting. Szold visited Irma in Mishmar Hae-mek and admired her choice, but tried to reengage her in organizational activity. Szold reported to a friend:

I met a new group of young immigrants last Monday, sixteen of them, and accom-panied them to Mishmar Haemek, Irma Lindheim's *kvuzah*, ... Mrs. Lindheim's enthusiasm over it is justified. Its members are not above thinking about and car-ing for externals. For instance, families do not live in congregate houses, but in separate one-room huts. That means securing that precious commodity—privacy. Mishmar was selected by all the Hashomer Hazair groups in the country as the fittest place for the central school of the movement.[35]

Remaining committed to Hadassah's practical rather than political stance, Szold wrote to Rama:

A member of Hadassah is free to express herself politically as she chooses, with-out in the least detracting from her Hadassah loyalty, and all these variously political-minded women units can get together for a piece of practical work in Palestine, since they are all Zionists desiring the upbuilding of Palestine.[36]

Szold also stressed the need for education, noting acerbically that "thought among Hadassah members is a consummation devoutly to be wished in the present state of Jewry and of Jewry in Palestine"[37]—an idea Rama had abandoned.

Eighteen months later, Irma visited Poland before sailing to America. She was horrified at the unproductive economic system (Nalewki) thrust upon the Polish Jews but proud of the way Hashomer Hazair had orga-nized the youth. Reporting to Szold on Hashomer education, she wrote:

They made them scouts, they taught them the codes of honor and truth and cour-tesy. There are thirty thousand of them in Poland alone, seventy thousand in the world, a reservoir for the ideals of Palestine, my belief is, the one guarantee of the future of the *kibbutz* as a movement.[38]

The problem of Polish Jewry, as she saw it, was unmitigated poverty rein-forced by antisemitism:

3 million Jews where no Jews are wanted, and even with good will ... [only] 2 mil-lion can find subsistence, and there is no good will. I have received my first baptism in a devastating poverty. I came out an uncompromising revolutionary."[39]

Despite her commitment to the *kibbutz*, Irma remained an indefati-gable activist and seeker. In this period, for example, she asked the Ha-dassah national convention if she could deliver an address titled "The Moral Challenge of Palestine—Can We Meet It?" She persuaded her aunt to establish the Guggenheimer Foundation for Playgrounds in Palestine. She debated with Szold about whether Hadassah should turn its hospital over to the government. She helped establish Kibbutz Ein Hashofet (1937), named for Louis D. Brandeis. That same year, at the thirteenth annual convention in New York of the National Labor Committee for Palestine, she urged American workers "to realize that Palestine was not only the place to give to but also to receive from." Palestine, she believed, offered the only security in a disturbed world:

It is not a physical security, but we know what it means to be secure when comrade helps comrade. This year was the most critical when they tried to take the country away from us. But despite all obstacles, we are mastering the difficulties, and I am glad to say that my four sons have chosen Palestine.[40]

From Palestine, Irma initiated projects intended to motivate Jewish youth in English-speaking countries. Her son Stephen, then also in Palestine, described her lifestyle:

She travels all the time. Every two weeks she comes up to the *kibbutz* for a weekend. The rest of the time she is in Tel Aviv or Jerusalem. This piece of work is having a great success. During Shavuot there is to be a camp in Kfar Vitkin in which the committees from the various towns are to meet.[41]

Since Irma and her children never seemed to be in the same place at the same time, she carried on an intense correspondence with them, at times loving and at times estranged. After living mostly on her own for over a decade, she had become a fiercely independent and forthright woman.

The War Years: Motivating American Jewish Youth

During World War II, the JNF asked Rama to leave Palestine, sail through "the submarine infested Atlantic" and lead the drive in England for five months during the Blitz.[42] Irma accepted wholeheartedly, having learned from Manya and life in Palestine that one has to live fearlessly in order to accomplish anything. She wrote later:

Despite nightly bombs, the Jews came to hear of and to give to Israel, [until] equal status with the Keren Hayesod [Palestine Foundation Fund] had been achieved.[43]

She also petitioned the lord chancellor of England for the cessation of home-destroying searches in Palestine, an initiative for which she earned the praise of Chaim Weizmann.

Irma spent the remainder of the war years in the United States, working simultaneously to advance her brand of Labor Zionism, to shore up the identity of American Jewish youth, and to do her part in the war effort. In 1941 Irma contacted Louis D. Brandeis about encouraging people to join *kibuzim,* agreeing with him that the principles upon which these were founded could help non-Jews as well as Jews.[44] From Mordecai M. Kaplan she received an enthusiastic endorsement for her project of a "land and labor movement for American Jewish youth."[45] She desperately wanted to instill in others the love of land and labor that she had learned, and sometimes she was effective. For example, in 1941 a Hadassah member heard Irma Lindheim and Emanuel Neuman debate at the national convention in Pittsburgh:

Until four in the morning, I listened with awe and the knowledge of how little I knew of political Zionism then. . . . It was that convention that made it possible for me to expand and explore, educating myself first, and then my chapter, and then the lower N.Y. State region, and then the Long Island region. Getting away from all the socialite activities that had previously enveloped many of us.[46]

In 1943 Irma was distressed by the antisemitism she perceived in the United States and by the lack of a Zionist youth movement there. These two related issues formed the crux of the next problem on which she focused intensively:

The other night I took down some of the slogans scrawled obscenely on the walls of the 8th Avenue subway—"sleazy kike ratzies," "kike parasites war," "kikes are red."[47]

In a memo to the National Board of Hadassah, Irma discussed its educational activities for young people. She had been instrumental in establishing a youth commission (Avukah) for Hadassah, but it had failed miserably—fewer youth were involved after three years than at its establishment—because, she asserted, Hadassah leaders denied the existence of antisemitism in the United States and therefore did not want the youth commission to address it. Irma, on the other hand, believed that antisemitism was a problem for all Americans, Jews and non-Jews alike, because it challenged the American principle of equality. She also believed that American Jews must learn to recognize that Zionism was important, not only for

those people over there who need a state, but for them, themselves who need it for self-respect and for a way to combat antisemitism and to have access to the richness of the Jewish heritage and to have faith in a Jewish survival.[48]

The Young Judea youth movement was probably worthwhile, Irma said, but campuses were bereft of a Zionist organization, the communities have a Junior Hadassah that it-self only barely knows the purpose of what it is doing and where it is going, and Masada is almost non-existent.

Hadassah should focus on the "the needs of our youth, not the needs of our organizations."[49] Irma's solution was to set up a farm near New York where young people could learn about Palestine in America and could meanwhile constitute a "Land Army." She got this idea from her success working with the Volunteer Land Corps, groups of people who volunteered to work on farms during the war. Her scheme called for young people from New York to go to the farms on weekends and holi-days, while also providing leadership in the city. From her role as a leader in the corps, Irma had data to show that Jewish youth were interested in farming:

In 1942, of the 2300 applications we had for farm work (Volunteer Land Corps), 80% were Jews, and of the 630 placed in Vermont, over 50% were Jews, most of whom made good and stuck it out on isolated farms for [several] months. At Far-mingdale, of the 200 or so high school and college youth which passed through my hands from Thanksgiving to March, approximately 95% were Jews, and those the finest and most alive young Jews, spiritually and mentally that I have met in America.[50]

The "socially good and specific" appealed to young people, Irma be-lieved; working the land satisfied a deep need in urban American Jewish youth, and it would also bring young people closer to Palestine. It should be accompanied by the other joyful activities she had experienced in the ten years she had lived in Mishmar Haemek: "evenings before an open fire," simple living,

group singing, folk dancing and story telling . . . the joy of discovering new crea-tive gifts of expression as well as new muscles which ache from unaccustomed work but give a new sense of power and satisfaction as dormant muscles are brought into life.[51]

Moreover, revitalization of the body and spirit must lead to a desire to study, and Irma outlined a course for Jews to explore their situation in the United States.

Irma felt that she was the only person who could put the "farm idea" into practice, and she regretted that her unpopularity and her identifica-tion with Labor Zionism might obstruct its realization. She had learned that "*haluziut* [pioneering] makes of Judaism a way of life," not only a set of religious ideas. In the wake of antisemitism, Irma feared, young people would flock to communism, which also held out the promise of racial equality and social-political activism. Knowing that their people were building a new and better world would make Zionism an inspiring alternative. They had to be shown that Zionism is a progressive movement, and that Zionism and Americanism are firmly linked. In Irma's words, "The ideals of the American and the Jew are the same."[52]

As with so many of her organizational activities in the United States, Irma's attempts to realize this vision, too, yielded continual frustration. In March 1943 she had been asked to become executive director of Hadassah's Youth Aliyah work, but by early February 1945 she wrote to her daughter-in-law that

all my plans for youth have fallen through. A cautious directorate have decided on raising money for a reserve before underwriting a plan for the youngsters, so I am . . . left high and dry with my hopes to do something really important again shattered.[53]

Irma was away from Mishmar Haemek from 1940 through 1946, in the United States, England, back again in the United States, and on to Australia and New Zealand, raising money for many causes, including the Weizmann Chemical Institute, Hadassah Medical School, and Youth Aliyah. On Peace Day, 1945, she received the news that her son Donald was dead. Her eldest son, Norvin Jr., had died of illness in the United States six years earlier. Both had died at the age of thirty-one, and both had intended eventually to make Palestine their home.

For Israel and for me, an irreparable loss, and later, with my two other sons at college, leaving me alone in Israel. They had married girls in America who were not prepared to go to Israel.[54]

Her daughter, Hortense, had never been interested. She had married a non-Jewish man and converted to Christianity.

On January 1, 1946, Irma returned to Palestine. The hostile British regime, "still denying to the tortured Jews of Germany the haven longing to receive them,"[55] remained firmly entrenched, and she witnessed the terrorism and counterterrorism of Jews and British soldiers. Subsequently, she began writing long round-robin letters to friends in the United States, England, Australia, and New Zealand, reporting on life in Palestine.

In 1948 Irma was back in the United States, to run for the Queens, New York, congressional seat on Henry Wallace's Progressive Party ticket, which advocated civil rights and world government. Losing the election prompted her return to what was now the newly independent State of Israel. She celebrated her seventieth birthday in Mishmar Haemek in 1956 and was honored by the Hadassah council in Israel at a reception in Jerusalem. Miriam Granott, chair of the council, praised Irma as a thinker, writer, and educator. Julia Dushkin praised her for her drive, as an American Jew, to "greater self-fulfillment by personal participation in the upbuilding of Zion."[56]

A few months later she traveled to the United States, for her granddaughter's wedding and addressed the National Board of Hadassah. She was pained at leaving Israel after the Sinai Campaign.[57] According to the Hadassah National Board minutes of June 19, 1958, Irma again made an appearance. She had just finished writing a book dealing with her forty years of Zionist activity and reached the conclusion that "Hadassah had done more than any other organization officially to create a climate of good relationships with the Arabs living in Israel."[58] Back home once again, Irma helped create Kibbutz Adamit (1958) on the Lebanese border in northern Israel, affiliated with Kibbutz Arzi–Hashomer Hazair.

Irma suffered from various health problems throughout her life but rarely mentioned them. In 1959 she was a patient at the Hadassah Hospital in Jerusalem. Afterward she wrote to Dr. Karpas, pointing out that the quality of care she had experienced was superior to anything she had seen in the United States, "especially in the treatment each individual receives, not only as patient, but as a human being."[59] At age seventy-five, in 1961, she was again hospitalized at Hadassah for six days—and enjoyed it. Writing to Dr. Kalman Mann, director general of the Hadassah Medical Organization, she was relieved that the diagnosis of arteriosclerosis made by her *kibbutz* doctor and another physician had been ruled out. Recovering in Beit Hanasi, the Israeli president's official residence, she wrote:

I only wish I could do something to repay in measure the joy of the days I spent with you. If it were not for the ban Hadassah has put on my speaking for them (because of my association with the Hashomer Hazair!), I would be happy again to raise my voice, and be of assistance in raising some of the funds in the States which I know you are badly in need of. But things being as they are and the utterly senseless attitudes towards the effect of peril of political differences [*sic*] preventing my functioning, I can only voice my deep appreciation to you and your staff.[60]

Irma continued to view living in Israel as one of the greatest privileges in her life and implied a criticism of Hadassah for not educating toward *aliyah.* The group she singled out for praise on that score was the *kibbutz* movement of Hashomer Hazair.

Had the education stressed *aliyah,* we might have seen more personal involvement in Israel itself. If large numbers of young Jews in the *golah* [exile] do not immigrate to Israel or do not take root here properly, the main fault is not theirs but their parents, since the latter did not prepare them for their destination.[61]

Writing Women's Lives

Irma's waning years were a time of intense literary output. She remained an avid correspondent with Henrietta Szold, Manya Shohat, political leaders, and family members, and she wrote diverse articles for Zionist publications, including a lengthy appreciation of Henrietta Szold in 1960, on the one-hundreth anniversary of her birth. Her "eulogy" of Manya Shohat, following her death in 1961, reflects the powerful effect that Manya, her role model and intimate friend, had upon the shaping of her own values:

Manya was my guide . . . throughout my Zionist life: a measuring rod of the good and the bad, the positive as against the negative of the policies guiding the State of Israel and the Zionist movement. The measure of their value she judged by their effectiveness in bringing about the regeneration of the spirit as well as of the body of the Jewish people. The gauge was, as Manya used to say over and again, quoting the words of her brother, Moshe, "whether it was *Zion lemaalah* or *Zion lematah* [the heavenly Zion or the earthly Zion] that was being built."

Manya had taught Irma to abhor

[the] evils of the military rule over the Arab sections of the country, and the shame—and peril to the State of Israel—of thus giving her Arabs the status of second-class citizens. . . . Manya became the symbol to me of all that was best in Palestine, Israel, and the world: the *kibbutz* and its way of life, of which she was the soul and embodiment.

Irma wrote about these colossal figures in Zionist history because she loved them, but also out of concern that they would be forgotten.

There has arisen a generation that "knew not Joseph" and for these the life of no single individual can have more meaning than [Manya's]. . . .
Born of a generation of giants, [Manya] towers above them. . . . Of the many privileges of my life, I rate none more highly than to have had Manya choose me as a friend. No two people could have come from circumstances and backgrounds more diverse and yet no two ever established a contact more immediate, vital and lasting.

Irma spoke of Manya in the highest possible terms:

Life has held great rewards, but none greater than to have known and loved Manya and been loved by her.[62]

In 1962, at age seventy-six, Irma published *Parallel Quest: A Search of a Person and a People,* in which she documented her struggle to express Jewish, Zionist, and American values, ending her story in 1933. Every Hadassah woman, she concluded, experiences conflict as she undertakes to serve her people and her family.[63]

An Educational Plan for Women

A little later, Irma wrote that she "would like to be able again to serve Hadassah"—she wanted to be needed.[64]

What I want most out of life now is to help others discover the road I have found to successfully call a halt to assimilation. . . . I am ready to give this priority over everything.[65]

In the summer of 1963, at age seventy-seven, Irma was again in New York, having lunch with members of the National Board of Hadassah, "full of plans for the future, involving a unique education program which she hoped to work out with Hadassah." She saw the need

for an education program in Israel to make Israelis more aware of the contribution and role of American Jewry in the development of the State of Israel.[66]

In December she was invited to attend Hadassah's midwinter conference, and she used the opportunity to plead that Hadassah make education a high priority. She was struck by the "inroads of assimilation" in America and alarmed by Dr. Judah Shapiro's presentation at the previous convention, focusing on the rising rate of intermarriage among third-generation Jews in the United States. Irma saw the guilt and terror Dr. Shapiro's talk aroused in the Hadassah delegates. Asserting that "need is the dynamic of action," Irma stressed the necessity of starting, as Henrietta Szold had done, with the needs of American Jewish women themselves:

Comparable consideration [should] be given to meeting the needs of the Hadassah women here as have been given to meeting the needs of the Hadassah medical services in Israel.[67]

Their present need was to fight assimilation, and that could be accomplished even if, as she realized, her advocacy of *aliyah* was not realistic. She reminded Hadassah that at the celebration of its fiftieth anniversary in 1962, it had proclaimed a policy of devoting the next fifty years to halting assimilation in the United States And yet nothing had been done. If Hadassah was the "future of our people," it should not jeopardize its own future:

My belief is that only as Hadassah prepares a program to meet this need of its women to do for themselves what Hadassah has guided them to do for others, will Hadassah remain the great constructive force it has been in Jewish life. To ignore the source from which Hadassah has drawn its strength is to endanger its continued effectiveness for both Israel and America.[68]

Feeling that her many years of experience made her an expert, Irma proposed yet another program. As a woman who had written books and articles, she knew how to persuade through writing and speeches. There were many similarly talented Jewish women in America. They could influence the next generations by steady, careful instruction. Irma labeled her solution "the Gramsie Hour," a mode of educating grandmothers to educate their grandchildren in Jewish learning. The grandmothers, as she saw it, were available and could easily be motivated. But Irma's new plan was not really workable and attracted few followers.

In the mid-1960s Irma stayed in the United States, developing numerous programs to counteract assimilation among Jewish children. In March 1965 she presented her program "Operation Jewish Survival: A Preliminary Manual of Guidelines," whose goal was "to equip the Jewish mother or grandmother with the source material, methods and approach to enable her to imbue her child with a sense of Jewish identity." The mother or grandmother would meet with her children in the intimate home atmosphere after school one day a week. Irma suggested a snack, particular books and maps, and ways of making history come alive. Her new focus was Judaism and Zionism, perhaps ultimately Judaism in the service of Zionism. The two had become completely intertwined.

When her program was turned down by Hadassah, Irma gave her ideas to the American Jewish Congress, which implemented them to a certain extent. In September 1965 she handwrote a hundred-page, twenty-two session syllabus outline titled "Experimental School for Parent Education," including clippings of exciting news articles, excerpts of letters, and other materials. Irma feared the lack of response:

Will there be parents to attend the 22 sessions being planned, and—more important—will they study to equip themselves to transmit to their children or grandchildren the meanings and values of their Jewish heritage? I was on the telephone most of the day. The result was discouraging. One of the best of last year's women participating in the pilot project cannot join in the work this year. She wants to, but cannot. She feels obligated to serve the Magen David which meets on our Mondays. . . . Her son-in-law, an avowed atheist, prefers to teach his children himself. . . . The problem of grandparents being allowed to instruct their young ones is a real one.[69]

Irma believed in the wisdom of older women and the special bond between grandchild and grandparent, which the intervening generation might disparage as they tried to steer children in a different direction. Perhaps she was also expressing rebellion against ageism, as she had against antisemitism, anti-Zionism, and sexism throughout her life.

In 1966–1967, the Theodor Herzl Institute in New York announced the School for Jewish Parent Education. Its brochure praised Irma for initiating the school. The administrator tried hard to involve New York Hadassah and to "reach people over the heads of those women's organizations that have been staying aloof." He advertised widely and tried to involve the Conference of Jewish Women's Organizations,[70] all with little success: just eight students enrolled in the first class. Irma's goals might have been admirable, but the techniques were not working. She was beginning to be out of touch with American Jewish women's lives and needs. All the same, the biennial convention of the National Women's Division of the American Jewish Congress, held in April 1967, adopted the following resolution:

We especially encourage our chapters and division leadership to undertake the kind of programs in parent education such as the successful American Jewish Congress–Herzl Institute extension of the original Lindheim parent-education project . . . in order that they may begin to fulfill the unfinished business of educating and informing American Jewish parents about their Jewish heritage, Jewish values, and Jewish culture.[71]

At Peace in Israel during War

Returning to the *kibbutz* on the eve of the Six-Day War, Irma wrote of the "calm assurance awaiting the signal to set into motion the answer to Nasser's oft-repeated threat to annihilate Israel and the Israeli people."[72] She made copies of her letters so as to have a complete record of her thoughts and wrote continuously so as to diminish her family's worries. She still enjoyed working in the *kibbutz* kitchen, because of the sense of efficacy and shared purpose it gave her:

Yesterday we made thousands of cookies to send to our soldiers. . . . I am happy to report that I am still a good worker and love it.

The day the war broke out, Irma went to Afulah to become an official resident of Israel, which apparently she had not previously done. She reports with joy the successes in the war:

All we really want is peace to continue to develop this wonderful little country and the great breed of human beings it has raised.

Even preparations for the possibility of the war reaching her front door did not faze her:

Trenches have been placed before each group of houses which I actually enjoyed using at 4 a.m. after an evening and night of strict black-out.[73]

Her long letters are crammed with political analysis and commentary on radio broadcasts:

Don't believe that miracles have ceased! Our miracle is that we've raised a third generation of youth who, in every way, have repeated the phenomenal character of the pioneers of the Second Aliyah, of the Third, the fighters of the Palmah, of Sinai, and now the people's army of Zahal [the Israel Defense Forces] who in three days, routed the armed might of Egypt, of Jordan and Iraq, and who, today, will undoubtedly turn further attention to Syria.[74]

She reiterates in several letters that there is no hate in Israel for the Arabs. Israelis want to go back to work to bring in the crops. The youth of Israel should be admired by people worldwide. They are

a species of mortals who have not only received the heritage of 4000 years of immortality, but who have shown themselves to be endowed with the genius to ensure its further continuance.[75]

She wanted so much to see American Jewish youth imbued with the same spirit.

After a stay in the United States, she returned to the *kibbutz* in August 1968 and resumed writing letters of political analysis. Acknowledging that the *kibbutz* was building children's shelters against gas attacks and that the military tension was explosive, she was more concerned about the United States, which suffered from

disunity—the upheaval of its youth, against what exists, without vision to guide its rebuilding into something better, stands in stark contrast to the unity of purpose that exists here in our youth as in the adult population, in spite of divergent opinions and differing ways of life.[76]

Her faith in Israel was never shaken.

Whatever happens here, this is where I chose and still choose, to be . . . Israel seems more like an ark to me than ever, in which to ride out the storm of evil threatening to swamp what is good in the world.[77]

Renewed Hope for America and New Beginnings in Israel

A couple of months later, Irma received an encouraging letter from the American Jewish Congress informing her that a group of young women in Philadelphia would try parent education training. This letter, asking Irma "not [to] feel hopeless or even defeated partially in her intensive effort to save a remnant of our people,"[78] gave her a new lease on life. She was irritated by

the terrible indifference of the Jewish leadership in America to an obviously good approach to effect a change for the better in the education of our young Jews. I found myself unable to pull out of the frustration which left me without hope of achieving anything further and was just about ready to sign off when your letter came.[79]

At age eighty-one, Rama "adopted" a young new immigrant from India in the *kibbutz* as her son, perhaps providing solace for the loss of her two sons and the distance from her family in the United States. Irma had a habit of befriending young foreigners in the *kibbutz*: "My room has become a center for the young ones."[80] Eight months later she wrote: "A real love has grown between us and he has really become a son!"[81] Irma reveled in her knowledge that this young man, who came from a wealthy family, was choosing a *kibbutz* life as she had done. She enjoyed providing him with a home when he returned on leaves from the army and was delighted when he told her he wanted to learn more about Jewish history and Israel.

So, I am once more in my favorite role of "teacher" and will have my first opportunity to try my methods out on a 19-year-old.[82]

It is likely that Irma did not exaggerate her knack for developing friendships with young people. A published letter from "Diane," sent from Kibbutz Mishmar Haemek to her family in the United States, testifies to this ability.

I have met Rama, the most fascinating woman I have ever encountered. . . . She is past president of national Hadassah in the United States, was a private student of John Dewey at Columbia University, and the only woman to study for a rabbinical degree at the Jewish Institute of Religion. . . . At the age of 81, Rama vibrates with the spirit of adventure, a zest for life, and a love for people. My roommate, Julie, and I talked with her for two hours—of home, Israel, Judaism, and life. She did most of the talking, and we sat with our mouths agape and our eyes sparkling with fascination.[83]

Irma's educational success seems to have come more from chance encounters on the *kibbutz* than from large-scale, organized programs.

Sustained Values, Sustained Annoyance

In an interview for the daily newspaper *Haarez* [The Land], conducted at age eighty-six in 1973, Rama expressed enthusiasm for the *kibbutz* way of life but criticized Israeli decadence and political interparty factionalism. Wealth and luxury meant nothing to her; people meant everything. She wanted to retain the "old Israel," which was fast disappearing.

My beautiful room with a corner for cooking in the *kibbutz;* my books . . . the desire to read and the inclination to write, life in the *kibbutz,* like life in Israel in general, the radiant happiness of the *kibbutz* children—these are my wealth and happiness.[84]

In her old age, and sometimes in earlier years, Irma was irritated at not being remembered or appreciated for her contribution. In June 1975, for example, she wrote to Marlin Levin, the representative of *Time* magazine in Jerusalem, expressing bitterness at not being included in a book he had written about Hadassah.

I am the Hadassah president whom it was thought unnecessary for you to meet . . . , too "different" to be understood by the hierarchy but elected unanimously by the women of the country to follow Henrietta Szold in the presidency, at this, Hadassah's darkest moment, when a Lipsky takeover was indicated and Hadassah's special projects and autonomous actions could be brought to an end. . . .[85]

The editorial staff . . . succeeded in erasing each and every achievement made by me, even those which laid the foundations on which Hadassah won its complete emancipation from the domination of the ZOA.[86]

Perhaps her bitterness reflected disappointment at the fate of her educational project. She interpreted Hadassah's rejection of her plan as "fear of her influence on their children to go on *aliyah* and *kibbutz*." Moreover, they "waited until I was back in Israel . . . to adopt at the Hadassah convention of 1969 what they called 'operation late start.'" In this instance, Hadassah took her ideas and called them their own.

In an interview published in the *Jewish Ledger* in November 1975, Irma reported not having "pleasant memories of her relationship with the Hadassah leadership, for whom her Zionism of personal realization was premature by decades."[87] That same year, at age eighty-eight, she learned that a Massachusetts chapter had celebrated "Women's Day 1975 by remembering her."[88] Clearly, despite her love-hate relationship with Hadassah, her story inspired young people both in the *kibbutz* and in the United States. Throughout the years, she received telegrams of birthday congratulations from Hadassah in Israel and was feted in various ways.

Irma always valued the *kibbutz* community, in which, she felt, people learned to live together in peace, "a true brotherhood of man as nowhere else on earth."[89] Although she had hoped to remain there to the end, she found that the care she needed was too much of a burden for the *kibbutz*. She spent her last years near relatives in California and died in Berkeley in 1978 at age ninety-two, survived by her children Richard, Stephen, and Babs (Wheatley) and their families.

Irma was not afraid of death. In a letter to her eight-year-old granddaughter, written years earlier and given to her upon Irma's death, Irma wrote,

Death is always hard to accept and the death of one you love is like losing an arm, a leg, or an eye. It leaves you with the feeling that you cannot get along without it. But you can, my darling. I know because I have had to do it so often and I am writing to tell you how.

Remember, my darling, how I always told you that there is a way to keep what you love alive? If you remember them, they just don't die. We loved each other so much that you just can't forget the wonderful times we had together: the walks, the talks, and above all, the love you and I shared for Israel and for our people— the Jews. Every time you think or hear of Israel, Gramsie will be alive for you. As long as you remember, she will never die.[90]

Irma was buried in California, and her ashes were later reinterred at Mishmar Haemek with a delegation of Hadassah leaders present to participate. Representatives of the WZO General Council, the Jewish National Fund, and of several *kibuzim* were present. Among the many memorial essays, one offered by Charlotte Jacobson, a national president of Hadassah, is quite telling:

During the last few months of her life, Mrs. Lindheim was quite ill; she also wanted to be with her children and grandchildren, so she returned to the U.S. Once she arrived in California, she stopped talking and did not utter a word for months. A member of her *kibbutz* happened to be in California and stopped by for a visit. At that point, almost miraculously, she started talking. However, as soon as her Israeli friend left, she again stopped talking and withdrew into her own world.

Irma never saw Hadassah as an organization focused on the single goal of raising funds for medical services in Palestine/Israel. Rather, she saw it as "an instrument—second to none—for Jewish survival in the United States."[91] Nor was she a woman who had her moment of glory in her youth and then faded from the scene. Rather, throughout her long life, she was constantly planning, plotting, and trying to persuade. Always given to poetic expression, Irma connected the death of her husband to the new life she chose:

When my husband died in 1938, in the USA, I got married again—to Palestine, with the ideals of which I had been very much in love ever since 1917.[92]

As an activist, she was wedded first to Hadassah, then to Hashomer Hazair and Mishmar Haemek, but always to Judaism and Zionism. These were her loves; the others were mere organizations. Jewish survival through Palestine was her life's ambition. Hadassah, she wrote, had the potential to "stem the tide of assimilation" and to equip women to answer the "constantly reiterated and all important question: 'Why be a Jew?'"[93] The questions with which she struggled remain unanswered. American Jewish women—Zionist or not—confront them anew in each generation.

Notes

I would like to express my thanks to Mary Lindheim and Dorothy Lindheim for their generous and trusting assistance in providing me with a large set of documents relating to the life of their mother-in-law, Irma Lindheim, and to Susan Lindheim for materials about her grandmother. My thanks also to Deborah Greniman for her diligent and creative editing.

1. A two-hundred-word entry on Irma Lindheim appears in the *Encyclopaedia Judaica*.

2. Memorandum to the National Board of Hadassah from Irma Lindheim (hereafter IL), July 26, 1943, 1 in Irma Lindheim Correspondence, July 26, 1943–August 1, 1963, Hadassah Presidents Correspondence Series, Hadassah Archive (hereafter HA): Record Group no. 7, Special Collections.

3. Naomi W. Cohen, *American Jews and the Zionist Idea* (New York: Ktav, 1975), 7.

4. IL, "Manya," Archive of Kibbutz Mishmar Haemek (hereafter AKMH), 12 (no date, circa 1962).

5. More books and articles have been written about Jane Addams than about any other American woman; see Mary Jo Deegan, *Jane Addams and the Men of the Chicago School, 1892-1918* (New Brunswick, N.J.: Transaction Books, 1988), 4.

6. Memorandum of July 26, 1943 (above, note 2), 2.

7. IL to Henrietta Szold, February 9, 1928, Central Zionist Archives (hereafter CZA), A274/40.

8. Phillip Bernstein, unpublished memorial essay on Henrich Schalit, Lindheim family archive, March 1976. They had many other homes.

9. Desley Deacon, *Elsie Clews Parsons: Inventing Modern Life* (Chicago: University of Chicago Press, 1997).

10. Pamela S. Nadell, "The Women who would be Rabbis," in *Gender and Judaism: The Transformation of Tradition,* ed. Tamar Rudavsky (New York: New York University Press, 1995), 129.

11. On Manya see Shulamit Reinharz, "Toward a Model of Female Political Action: The Case of Manya Shohat, Founder of the First Kibbutz," *Women's Studies International Forum* 7 (1984): 275–287; and idem, "Manya Wilbushewitz Shohat and the Winding Road to Sejera," in *Pioneers and Homemakers in Pre-state Israel,* ed. Deborah Bernstein (Albany, N.Y.: SUNY Press, 1992), 95–118.

12. IL, "Manya" (above, note 4), 11.

13. Ibid., 14.

14. Ibid.

15. Irma Lindheim, "Woman of Valor," CZA, A274/45, 4–5. Fifty years later, a Hadassah volunteer wrote:

> I was president of the West End Group when you became national president. I was very young . . . I shall never forget what you did for me as a new president, how you enlarged our horizons, how you gave us a new outlook on the potentialities of our work. I remember very well the convention at which you introduced JNF as an integral part of our Hadassah program. There is no question of the contribution which you made, not only on this front but on . . . many others (Mrs. Judith Epstein to IL, September 11, 1975, Lindheim family archive).

16. Yonathan Shapiro, *Leadership of the American Zionist Organization, 1897–1930* (Chicago: University of Illinois Press, 1971), 194.

17. CZA A274/40.

18. Speech given by Mrs. Irma Lindheim, extracts, from *Hadassah Newsletter,* August 1926, CZA A274/40.

19. IL, "Hadassah: The Bond for Jewish Womanhood," *New Palestine,* June 24, 1927, 572; quoted in Shapiro, *Leadership* (above, note 16), 204.

20. Shapiro, *Leadership* (above, note 16), 204–206.

21. Ibid.

22. Shimon Samet, "A President Who Chose a Kibbutz, the Festival of Irma (Rama) Lindheim, Age 86," in idem, "Where They Are Today," *Haarez,* July 6, 1973, CZA, A274/1.

23. Manya to IL, April 20, 1927, Beit Hashomer Archive, Kfar Giladi, 4/3.

24. Manya to Miss Szold and Mr. Lindheim, April 22, 1927, Beit Hashomer Archive, Kfar Giladi, 4/3, 3.

25. Ibid., 9.

26. Manya to IL, October 24, 1927, CZA.

27. Manya to IL, CZA.

28. IL to Szold, February 9, 1928 (above, note 7).

29. Ibid.

30. IL to Szold, September 8, 1928, CZA.

31. Ibid.

32. IL to Szold, October 29, 1928, CZA.

33. It is strange that she went to Germany, given the accusations against her husband.

34. Samet, "A President" (above, note 22).

35. Szold to Mrs. Rose Jacobs, February 22, 1935, in *Henrietta Szold: Life and Letters* ed. Marvin Lowenthal (New York: Viking Press, 1942), 278.

36. Szold to IL, March 8, 1934, CZA.

37. Ibid.

38. IL to Szold, September 26, 1934, CZA.

39. Ibid.

40. "Palestine Policy of Britain Scored," *New York Times,* November 29, 1937.

41. Stephen Lindheim to Donald Lindheim, April 23, 1939, Lindheim family archive.

42. IL to "my dear if distant friends of Hadassah," September 10, 1975, CZA A274/2.

43. Ibid.

44. Louis D. Brandeis to IL, April 21, 1941, CZA, A274/7.

45. Mordecai M. Kaplan to IL, May 22, 1941, CZA, A274/7.

46. Dorothy to Bernice, April 13, 1978, Lindheim family archive.

47. IL to her children, July 24, 1943, private archive.

48. Memo to the National Board of Hadassah, July 26, 1943, HA.

49. Ibid.

50. Ibid.

51. Ibid.

52. Ibid.

53. IL to "Mary darling," February 11, 1945, private archive.

54. IL to Hadassah (above, note 42).

55. Ibid.

56. Irma Lindheim Correspondence (above, note 2), January 28, 1957.

57. Ibid., Board notes, March 21, 1957.

58. Ibid., National Board Minutes, June 19, 1958.

59. Ibid., HMO-Medical Center Meeting, November 10, 1959.

60. Ibid., IL to Dr. Kalman Mann, undated (1961).

61. Samet, "A President" (above, note 22).

62. IL, "Manya" (above, note 4), 7, 9, 12, and 18.

63. Irma Lindheim Correspondence (above, note 2), IL to Lola, June 14, 1962, 2.

64. Ibid., IL to Lola, no date (1963?).

65. Ibid.

66. National Board Minutes, August 1, 1963, HA.

67. IL to Hannah Goldberg, December 30, 1963, HA.

68. Ibid.

69. Irma Lindheim, "Experimental School for Parent Education," 1965–1966, Lindheim family archive.

70. Emil Lehman to IL, December 6, 1966, CZA, A274/46.

71. National Women's Division, American Jewish Congress, Resolution of Jewish Affairs adopted at its Biennial Convention, April 4–6, 1967.

72. IL to family, June 5, 1967, AKMH.

73. Ibid.

74. IL to her children, June 8, 1967, AKMH.

75. IL to her children, June 9, 1967, AKMH.

76. IL to her family, Lindheim family archive, October 28, 1968.

77. IL to her family, October 28, 1968, private archive.

78. Julius Schatz to IL, December 13, 1968, CZA AZ74/8.

79. IL to Julius Schatz, American Jewish Congress, December 18, 1968, CZA A274/8.

80. IL to her children and grandchildren, December 20, 1967.

81. IL to her family, October 28, 1968, AKMH.

82. IL to her children and grandchildren, December 20, 1967.

83. "Diane to Dearest Family, December 1967," in *Letters from Israel: The Making of a Nation, 1948-68, ed.* Bill Adler (New York: Coward-McCann, 1968), 153–156.

84. Samet, "A President" (above, note 22).

85. IL to Marlin Levin, June 1975, Lindheim family archive.

86. Ibid.

87. Carl Alpert, "'Terribly Alive' at 89," *Jewish Ledger,* Friday, November 21, 1975, 4.

88. IL to Hadassah (above, note 42).

89. Ibid.

90. IL to Suzi, March 30, 1961, private archive.

91. IL to Lola, June 14, 1962 (above, note 63), 2.

92. Samet, "A President" (above, note 22).

93. IL to Lola, June 14, 1962 (above, note 63), 2.

Chapter 14

No book on the history of American Jewish women and Zionism would be complete without serious consideration of Golda (Goldie Meyerson) Meir (1898–1978), Israel's fourth prime minister, who is one of the two or three best-known female figures in Jewish history. An individual of astonishing political ability and talent, she rose from humble East European Jewish origins in the Pale of Settlement, where her earliest childhood memory was of a pogrom, to become a revered albeit highly controversial political leader on the world stage.

The Mabovich family immigrated to Milwaukee, Wisconsin, from Russia in 1906 when Golda was a child. Raised in the Yiddish-speaking immigrant milieu of early-twentieth-century America, she soon came into contact with the ideologies of socialism and Jewish nationalism. She eventually joined the American Labor Zionist party Poalei Zion [Workers of Zion] in 1915. She emigrated to Palestine in 1921 with a small group of would-be American *haluzim* [Zionist pioneers] in accordance with her belief that the aim of Zionism was to end the errant existence of Jews in the diaspora. In Palestine, she joined Kibbutz Merhaviyah but soon left due to the ill health of her husband, Morris Meyerson.

Rising swiftly through the ranks of the Histadrut to become secretary-general of Moezet Hapoalot [Women Workers' Council] in 1928 and a member of the World Zionist Organization Executive Committee in 1934, she helped found Mapai, the Labor Party, in 1930, where she gained increased respect for her loyalty and ability. Her political role continued to grow in the years leading up to independence; she became head of the Political Department of the Jewish Agency in 1946 and, as such, negotiated with the British regime and King Abdullah of Jordan to try to convince the latter not to participate in the imminent war. During the War of Independence, Meir went to the United States, where she raised considerable funds for the war effort. After Israel was established in 1948, she was appointed the Jewish state's first ambassador to Moscow. She subsequently served as a Knesset member and David Ben-Gurion's (1886–1973) minister of labor and housing from 1949 to 1956. Thereafter, she served as foreign minister for ten years, finally becoming prime minister in 1969. She resigned in 1974 in the midst of humiliation brought on by the nearly calamitous Yom Kippur War even though the investigating commission lauded her handling of the conflict.

The following essay by Marie Syrkin is presented for both its substantive and its historiographic value. Syrkin, a noteworthy Zionist figure who is also the subject of a different chapter in this volume, was a close personal associate and friend of Golda Meir. A vigorous champion of Meir's legacy, Syrkin wrote one of the first full-scale biographies of Israel's preeminent female figure. She sharply dismissed the caricature of "Golda as Israel's Jewish mother, dispensing a sublimated Hebraic chicken soup." Rather, she asserted, "in [Meir's] unflinching demands on herself and her people she was the reverse of the cliché. . . . She was a shrewd tactician and realistic enough to measure how much material reinforcement the spirit needed, she had the power to lead and inspire her people in their hours of victory and adversity."[1]

In the chapter that follows, Syrkin elaborates on this theme by placing Meir in the context of what she refers to as "other Americans." What she really means is the broad spectrum of American Jews who viewed Zionism not only through the prism of *aliyah* [immigration to the Land of Israel] but also as the best strategy for Jewish renewal in a period that witnessed continued existential threats to Jewish life in different quarters of the globe. By comparing Meir to Henrietta Szold (1860–1945), the founder of Hadassah, and Judah L. Magnes (1877–1948), the first chancellor of the Hebrew University of Jerusalem and a leading exponent of Palestinian binationalism, Syrkin lays out divergent political paths that were taken by similarly forceful American Jewish personalities. She also alludes to lesser known American Zionist figures whose impact was striking—the Mapai leader Dov Yosef (1899–1980), Gershon Agronsky (1894–1959), editor of the *Jerusalem Post* and mayor of Jerusalem; the educator Deborah Kallen (1888–1957), and Ben-Zion Ilan (1913–1975), a founder of Kibbutz Afikim in the Jordan Valley and Mapai activist. Weaving together these different strands with the insight and sensitivity of a firsthand observer, Syrkin examines the high-stakes context of the period that gave Meir and other American Zionists the scope and inducement to flourish. To be sure, one can hardly fail to note the sporadically apologetic undertone of Syrkin's piece, particularly her insistence that Meir's detractors misconstrued her attitude to the plight of the Palestinian Arabs. There is,

1. Marie Syrkin, *The State of the Jews* (Washington, D.C.: New Republic Books and Herzl Press, 1980), 167, 168.

however, much to be gleaned from Syrkin's overall assessment of the dynamic interplay between American Judaism and Zionism as well as the profile she draws of Meir as a generational paradigm and role model. These issues, which are at the core of Meir's complex legacy, inform her place in the history of American Zionism.

Golda Meir and Other Americans

Marie Syrkin

Zionism in the United States did not originate with Judah L. Magnes, Stephen S. Wise, and Henrietta Szold, of course. In tracing the story of the relationship of American Jews with the Zionist idea one ought to begin with Mordecai Manuel Noah, the first well-known native-born American Jew. Although best known for his fantastic Ararat project, which was to have become a Jewish state "revived, renewed, and reestablished under the auspices of the United States" on Grand Island, near Buffalo, New York, in 1825, even more significant were his Zionist writings, most notably, his *Discourse of the Restoration of the Jews,* in 1844, which antedate those of Theodor Herzl by fifty years.[1] One also must not overlook Emma Lazarus, whose Zionist writings were partly influenced by the misery of Jews in tsarist Russia, and partly inspired by the writings of non-Jews such as Laurence Oliphant and George Eliot, particularly her first novel, *Daniel Deronda.* As early as 1883, Lazarus wrote, "I am fully persuaded that all suggested solutions other than this [Zionism] of the Jewish problem are but temporary palliatives."[2] If the list were extended to include crackpots, romantics, and geopolitical realists, it would be considerable. In the 1880s and 1890s, the State Department was so plagued by proposals from Zionists that Assistant Secretary Alvey Adee complained that, "Our volumes of Foreign Relations are plentifully supplied with correspondence on the subject from 1884–1898. . . . Every few months we are asked to negotiate [with Turkey] for the cession of Palestine to the Jewish 'nation.' The project is chimerical."[3]

Clearly, my study must be limited to the discussion of Americans who in fact settled in Palestine. Yet even within these confines difficulties appear. Who is an American? The conundrum is posed early. Although Jewish settlements of varying magnitude had existed in Palestine since the dispersion, American Jews only began to be identified about 1870, and for the most part, were naturalized American citizens and their offspring. When they claimed protection from the Turkish government, American

Source: Marie Syrkin, "Golda Meir and Other Americans," in *Like All the Nations? The Life and Legacy of Judah L. Magnes,* ed. William M. Brinner and Moses Rischin (Albany: State University of New York Press, 1987), 113–123, 217–218. Reprinted by permission of David Bodansky.

consuls lamented that these were "spurious Americans" who had been born in Russia or Poland, had spent a few years in the United States and had settled in Palestine with no intention of returning to their country of citizenship. One outraged American consul, Selah Merrill, distinguished himself by his distaste for "Russian Jews" who demanded privileges due Americans: "To call them 'Americans' is an insult to American civilization."[4] His successive estimates indicated that from 150 in 1882, the number of these naturalized American Jews in Jerusalem had risen to 1,000 in 1902. In Jerusalem, in this medley of Orthodox Jews, living mainly on *halukah*,[6] one Polish Jew, Simon Bermann, who immigrated to the United States in 1852 and settled in Palestine in 1870, distinguished himself by his early plans for agricultural cooperatives combined with individual holdings. His book, *The Travels of Simon,* published in 1879, stimulated Jewish immigrants to settle on the land. Though his proposals had no practical result because of the antagonism of the *halukah* rabbis who feared that philanthropic funds might be deflected from their support, Bermann created something of an ideological stir. At any rate, he was dubbed the "American," a designation to which his American style of dress and his eighteen years in the United States presumably entitled him.[7] He can be viewed as a precursor of Eliezer Lippe Yoffe, a Russian Jew who went to the United States in 1904 to study new methods of agriculture and settled in Palestine in 1910. His pamphlet, "The Establishment of the *Moshavei Ovdim*" (1919), emphasized cooperative settlements and individual initiative in cooperative settlements in contrast to the *kibbutz.*[8]

The question as to who can be designated an American has been arbitrarily answered by some writers on the subject who accept a five-year residence in the United State as sufficient. This is as it should be, for it justifiably includes some of the chief ornaments of the American contingent, most notably Golda Meir. If place of birth or length of residence are to be decisive, Henrietta Szold and Judah Magnes are among the few early American Zionists with impeccable credentials. Of the hundreds of American volunteers who joined the Jewish Legion after World War I, an indeterminate number remained in Palestine. Many of them, like Golda Meir, had been brought to the United States in childhood and left in youth.

Born in Kiev in 1898, she came to the United States in 1906 and settled in Palestine in 1921. Her American experience had amounted to fifteen years, but these included the formative years of childhood and early youth. Her education was the American public school where she precociously distinguished herself. Her English, like her Yiddish, the language of the poor first generation immigrants who constituted her world, was always to remain better than her Hebrew. She never looked back on Milwaukee with the nostalgia of Henrietta Szold for the flowers of Baltimore, but she had been shaped as much by free America as by the tsarist oppression that terrified her early childhood. The never-healed trauma of the five-year old cowering in fear before an imminent pogrom had determined her future beliefs, but by a fortunate alchemy she had been able to transform the suffering of Russia and the opportunities of the United States to her purpose. The American pioneer struggle and the country's achieved liberties were all signs of the possible. The reality of the American dream emboldened her Zionist vision. When she signed Israel's Declaration of Independence without truculence, her quiet assurance among the rich and titled owed something not only to her character but to the democracy in which she had grown up. When, at the end of her life, she went back to be honored in the Milwaukee public school from which she had graduated, she acknowledged the American link in her strength. Nor did Zionist pioneers of other nationalities allow her to forget that she was American. On the Mediterranean crossing, her group of twenty young Labor Zionists encountered Lithuanian *haluzim* who were travelling on deck, Mediterranean-style steerage. Golda characteristically persuaded her fellows to give up their luxurious third-class cabins to join the Lithuanians. Despite some protests at Golda's "moralistic" leadership none of the Americans balked. But the sacrifice had been in vain. The Lithuanians spurned the comradely advance: "We don't want Americans."[9] The Lithuanians were well-versed in Hebrew and trained in agriculture; the Yiddish-speaking Americans with no agricultural skills were dismissed as bourgeois and dilettante. The Americans, conscious of their ignorance and their enjoyment of American comforts, humbly accepted the role of a lesser breed.

Even in the early months at Merhaviyah, the *kibbutz* Meir and her husband joined, her American background was suspect. While waiting in Tel Aviv for admission to the *kibbutz,* she had given English lessons; her critics charged that she should have chosen housework instead of a soft intellectual occupation. During the trial period at the *kibbutz* she betrayed a number of American refinements, such as skinning the herring, a *kibbutz* staple, and ironing her dress—she was always compulsively neat. These were potential bourgeois deviations. However, her physical energy, capacity for work and enthusiasm finally defeated the skeptics.[10]

I mention these seemingly insignificant matters because the distinction early made between "spoiled Americans" and other immigrant streams was to persist. Skinning the herring was symptomatic of a future cleavage.

In the case of Golda and her fellow voyagers, the description "spoiled" could only be comparative. Her family never made the transition from poverty to the middle class; her older sister Shana, who with her two young children recklessly joined Golda on the S. S. *Pocahantas* in 1921, had contracted tuberculosis in girlhood as a factory worker. Worse privation was to be endured in Jerusalem after Golda left the *kibbutz* at her husband's insistence. To get a notion of the poverty endured by the young family—her two children were born in Jerusalem—two examples will suffice: for six months she did the washing for a nursery school, heating the water pail by pail and scrubbing clothes on a rough board. And when a neighbor warned the milkman not to extend credit to the destitute Meyerson menage, she caned the meddler in outraged fury: "No one will take milk from my children."[11]

But there was never any danger that her Zionist resolution would weaken. What she wrote shortly after her arrival in Palestine to her brother-in-law, who had stayed behind temporarily in the United States to earn money to send to his wife (Shana showed me the letter when I was writing the biography of Golda), remained valid till her death almost sixty years later:

Those who talk about returning are recent arrivals. . . . I say that as long as those who created the little that is here are here, I cannot leave and you must come. . . . Of course this is not America and one may have to suffer a lot economically. There may even be pogroms again, but if one wants one's own land, and if one wants it with all one's heart, one must be ready for this. . . . Get ready. There is nothing to wait for.[12]

From this simple credo she never wavered.

In the same letter, the twenty-three-year-old woman ventured some political observations: "I am no politician and cannot exactly describe to you the politics of England. But one thing is clear to me. If we will not go away, then England will help us. England will not choose the Arabs instead of us to settle Palestine." These less than prescient words from the woman who would become one of the chief protagonists in Jewish Palestine's struggle against the British twenty-five years later were the measure of her innocence. She had neither personal sophistication nor academic training; her power lay in her limitations and her absolute espousal of two articles of faith: first, that Jews must have equality as a people; and second, that all human beings must have social and economic equality. The synthesis of these beliefs was socialist Zionism, whose banner she had raised in Milwaukee and was never to drop. In time, Golda would become an astute politician although not a geopolitical theorist or intellectual. She would never lose the sometimes alarmingly simple yet wonderfully persuasive force of her elementary convictions. They transformed her into a world leader.

Her career, so rich in drama that it might have been plotted by an overimaginative second-rate Hollywood script writer determined to place his heroine at the center of every world crisis that affected her people and with the temerity to add the familiar family versus career conflict as a tearjerker, is well-known. I will concentrate on that aspect of her activities of greatest contemporary interest: her views on the Arab problem. First, let me dispose of a current canard. As evidence of her egregious lack of sensibility, she has been repeatedly charged with denying the existence of Palestinians. Her actual words were: "There is no Palestinian people; there are Palestinian refugees."[13] In the [present climate], such a distinction is damning; within its historic context it is not at all so. When Golda arrived in Palestine, the only avowed Palestinians were Jewish pioneers. Arab nationalists stridently rejected the designation of "Palestinian" as an attempt to fragment an ideal Arab unitary state. From the Versailles conference until the Partition debate at the United Nations, Arab spokesmen insisted that Palestine was southern Syria and that to confer independent status on this territory, cherished in Jewish history, infringed on the Arab nationalist vision. As late as 1956, Ahmed Shukairy, subsequently head of the Palestine Liberation Organization, argued at the Security Council that "it is common knowledge that Palestine is nothing but southern Syria." Golda took her adversaries at their word.[14]

Only in the 1960s did the Palestine Liberation Organization come forward with the demand that Arab refugees be renamed a homeless Palestinian people. Since that time, the distinction has become archaic. So completely has the new nomenclature triumphed that when some years ago the Herzl Press, of which I was editor, reissued two Zionist classics, one *A Palestine Diary,* written in the 1880s by Hayim Hisin, a Bilu pioneer, the other *The Plough Woman: Memoirs of Pioneer Women of Palestine,* originally published in 1932, fears were expressed that the titles would be misleading. I am happy to say that we stood our ground, perhaps to the confusion of librarians. But Golda saw no reason to comply with a revision of history that she viewed as an astute tactical ploy directed against Israel.

Not that she ever underestimated the force of Arab nationalism or the urgency of the Arab refugee question. Well known are her eloquent demonstrations of Arab responsibility for the plight of the 550,000 refugees who joined the Arab exodus in 1948 and her numerous proposals, when a member of the government, to reach a constructive solution for that plight.[15] In time, she accepted the fact that the changed vocabulary of Arab nationalism represented not merely a semantic trick but a sobering political reality, however spurious in its origin. This did not alter her view of the justice, absolute not relative, of Israel's cause; nor would she make peace with the facile formula that two homeless peoples, the Jews and the Palestinians, were battling for the same land. In weighing the claims of Arab and Jewish nationalism, she put in one scale Jewish need and the compromises already made through the whittling away of the original compromised homeland by the successive amputations of Trans-Jordan, in 1922 and the U.N. partition resolution in 1947; and in the other, the rich gratification of Arab nationalism in twenty-one independent new states with vast territories and rich natural resources.[16]

These arguments are standard Zionist exposition. What gave Meir's rhetoric its extraordinary force was that she had suffered each state of the debate in her own experience and that her attitudes derived directly from that knowledge, not from polemical theorizing. She remembered keenly the young years when she was the Palestinian and recognized as such. She did not have to study British census figures to know that her coming had not displaced a single Arab. The barren fields of Merhaviyah she helped make habitable between bouts of malaria, the dahlias and apricots her daughter would in time send her from the Negev *kibbutz* of Revivim, gave her the assurance to challenge adversaries with the proud declaration that Jewish toil had created more living space for both Arab and Jew. In her capacity as foreign minister and prime minister, she mastered the appropriate diplomatic terminology and learned how to negotiate toughly in the international arena just as she had been a tough labor leader in the Histadrut and a shrewd party politician in Mapai. But the moral core of her conviction, in its pure, some would say simplistic clarity, was what sustained her.

Between such an approach and Judah L. Magnes's early perception of the immediate critical need for Arab-Jewish conciliation, there was no meeting point. No mention is made of Magnes in her long autobiography. Nor do her close associates of the prestate decades in Palestine recall any discussion of Magnes with her. In the 1930s, when she was secretary of the Histadrut, the great labor union of Jewish Palestine, she might well have had dealings with Magnes in his capacity as administrator of a university that employed many workers. Recall, however, that Magnes was away from Palestine in 1946 which was the time of Golda's rise to prominence as a political activist. But there is little doubt as to her disagreement with the Magnes political program. Like Magnes, she opposed partition when it was first proposed by the British Royal Commission in

1937, but she changed in response to the catastrophe of the Holocaust when partition became the official policy of the Jewish Agency. Her views on Brit Shalom or the Ihud are easy to deduce.

Golda's political mentors were David Ben-Gurion and Berl Kaznelson, the spiritual teacher of pioneer Palestine whom she venerated. Both men were involved with Magnes in negotiations with Arab leaders—a process Ben Gurion describes in his book, *My Talks with Arab Leaders* (1973). As early as 1924, at a meeting called by Brit Shalom, Ben-Gurion stated his opposition to a binational state on the grounds that Jewish national independence could be enjoyed only in the tiny area allotted whereas Arabs had vast unpopulated territories for settlement and dominance.[17] However, Ben-Gurion early favored parity, and throughout the 1930s the cooperation of Magnes in arranging meetings with Arab notables was often enlisted. As related by Ben-Gurion, the tortuous discussions form a disheartening record.

Whether there was any realistic possibility of accommodation between the opposing viewpoints of the parties is not within the scope of this essay to assess. Both Ben-Gurion and Kaznelson espoused binational parity in the legislative bodies to prevent domination of one national group by the other. Kaznelson was a passionate advocate of this position, however, with one proviso: Parity would come when Jewish independence had reached full development. A break with Magnes came in 1938 when it was reported to the Jewish Agency that he had negotiated with Nuri Pasha in Beirut on the possibility of a Jewish agreement based on a minority status for Jews in Palestine and a fixed ratio for Jewish residents, supposedly a third, in relation to other inhabitants of Palestine. In answer to this charge, Dr. Magnes wrote to Ben-Gurion that he had advocated a temporary, not a permanent, minority status for Jews, a reply that despite Ben-Gurion's professions of personal esteem for Magnes was not likely to placate the Jewish Agency.[18]

In 1947, during the hearings before the United Nations Commission on Palestine in Jerusalem, the Ihud delegation headed by Magnes, proposed, in contrast to the Jewish Agency's demand for a Jewish state, a United Nations trusteeship and Jewish immigration to Palestine till numerical equality between Jews and Arabs had been achieved. Obviously, Golda, by then head of the political department of the Jewish Agency and totally committed to a Jewish state that even if truncated would be able to authorize the free immigration of the survivors of the Holocaust, would find little to applaud in such a proposal. Unlike the Revisionists who were maximalists in their demand for territory—a Jewish state on both sides of the Jordan River—Golda was a maximalist in her concept of national independence. She was realistic enough to accept territorial compromise as in the partition resolution, but she insisted that within the confines agreed to as a painful but necessary sacrifice, freedom to act in behalf of martyred Jewry should be untrammelled.[19]

That the longed-for Jewish state brought not only national independence that at last opened the gates barred by the British, but also unending hostility baffled and grieved her; but it never shook her faith in the necessity and goodness of what had been achieved. When in the euphoria of Israel's dazzling victory in June 1967 she declared to a huge Madison Square Garden audience gathered to celebrate with a sadness that haunted her hearer, "The last thing that Israelis want is to win wars. We want peace,"[20] she was voicing her deepest disappointment. As her repeated public appeals to Arabs from 1948 on indicate, she was tormented by a sense of lost opportunities, and by the tantalizing awareness of how much Arab-Jewish cooperation might achieve for both peoples in the Middle East. And with maternal intensity, she mourned the waste of young lives in sterile warfare. But this did not weaken her insistence on full national independence and on "secure borders," an insistence that her critics regarded as short-sighted and inflexible, but that her admirers viewed as high-minded and hard-headed. She could, with equal sincerity, reach the ethical nobility of her much-quoted statement, "When peace comes, we will perhaps be able to forgive the Arabs for killing our sons, but it will be harder for us to forgive them for having forced us to kill their sons,"[21] and she could also reply sharply to those who feared that Israel might become militaristic, "I don't want a fine, liberal, anticolonial militaristic, *dead* Jewish state."[22]

In June 1967, in a private conversation, I asked her what would happen to the newly conquered West Bank. Her answer was instantaneous, "What would we do with a million Arabs!" The concerted refusal of the Arabs to negotiate with Israel changed what might have been a temporary occupation into a continuing presence. And there is no denying that with the passage of time and constant Arab belligerence the Israeli mood hardened. However, as prime minister, Golda advocated the "Allon plan," the unofficial program of the Labor party [authored by Yigal Allon], that called for withdrawal from most of the populated West Bank, while opposing a separate Palestinian state.

The idealistic girl matured into an adroit stateswoman, skilled in negotiation, temperate in argument, yet granite in action and desire. Her sometimes despairing outcry, "We wanted to be good farmers, not good soldiers," did not weaken her will for what seemed to her the ultimate good: Jewish national survival in a just society. To the end, she believed that the national and social visions of her youth would be fulfilled despite the failures of which she was bitterly aware. Among these, American Jewry's refusal to settle in Israel in significant numbers rankled keenly. "You are ready to die with us, why don't you live with us?" she asked young American volunteers in one of Israel's wars. That was her wound as well as the wound of Zionism.

Although Golda was the most illustrious of the early American Zionists, others should not be overlooked. First come those who accompanied her on the aptly named S. S. *Pocahantas.* In 1961, forty years after the arrival of the original contingent, Foreign Minister Meir invited her old comrades to a celebration of the anniversary. Of the original nineteen only eight came; some had died, some were ill, one had returned to America. However, children and grandchildren, blond, blue-eyed sabras and dusky Yemenites whose presence testified to the authentic melting pot of Israel, filled Her Excellency's drawing room. To the bewilderment of one American guest, the young folks preferred to sing popular American songs rather than the well-worn pioneer lyrics of their grandparents.

Of those who achieved eminence besides Golda, one ought to name Dov Yosef, a Canadian who enlisted in the Jewish Legion and settled in Jerusalem in 1921; and who would come to be known as Yosef, the provider, for his heroic role as military governor of Jerusalem during the siege of the city in 1948. Another notable recruit of the Jewish Legion to settle in Palestine was Gershon Agronsky, known as Gershon Agron, editor of the *Palestine Post,* later the *Jerusalem Post.* Among those who also ought to be included are the poet Jesse Sampter who settled in Palestine in 1919 and the educator, Deborah Kallen, sister of the distinguished American Jewish philosopher, Horace Meyer Kallen.

Throughout the thirties small organized groups of Hehaluz went to Palestine after receiving agricultural training in preparatory farming communes in the United States. Ein Hashofet and Kfar Blum are among the first *kibuzim* established by Americans.

Various memoirs of the period written by members of Hashomer Hazair or Habonim, describe the particular difficulties of American workers. Ben-Zion Ilan, born Benjamin Applebaum,[23] who in 1931 at age nineteen left the Bronx to spend his life in the *kibbutz* of Afikim, dwelt not only on the physical hardships but on what he calls the "cultural gap," a phrase that would echo in a different context in the future, for few Americans knew Hebrew. There was the further disadvantage of what Ilan called, "the light in darkness," the American passport, a temptation and escape hatch for the socialist pioneer in the Emek (Valley of Jezreel), just as it would be in later years for the middle-class American in

Jerusalem or Tel Aviv, who would cite a favorite horror story about the imbecilities of Israeli bureaucracy. In the 1920s and 1930s, the individual could blame only his personal inability to endure danger, disease, and backbreaking toil.

Unlike later doubts, in these early memoirs, the conviction of the splendor of the ideal embraced shines forth. Strikingly absent are the realistic misgivings of the intellectuals of the Magnes circle. Was this difference due solely to deficiencies in maturity and comprehension? Part of the explanation may lie in the difference between the life of a university scholar and that of a *kibbutznik* draining a swamp in the Huleh valley. Young Benny Applebaum and his comrades were, like Golda, convinced by their daily labor that their activities were socially productive and nationally redemptive. Their lives confirmed their ideology. If Arab marauders from a neighboring village attacked an installation obviously beneficial for the country and all its inhabitants, then as socialists and Zionists these pioneers could deplore blind obstructionism instead of doubting the righteousness of their cause. In that Zionist dawn, Golda and her comrades saw the creation of the homeland within the parameters of their initial concept. It gave them the uncritical assurance to dismiss the shadows and misgivings already perceived on Mount Scopus. It also gave them the spiritual energy to create the state.

Notes

1. See "Noah, Ararat, USA," in Marie Syrkin, *The State of the Jews* (Washington, 1980), 215–21; Jonathan Sarna, *Jacksonian Jew: The Two Worlds of Mordecai M. Noah* (New York, 1981), 61–75, 163.

2. Emma Lazarus, "The Jewish Problem," *The Century Magazine,* 25:4 (February 1883), 610.

3. Frank E. Manuel, *The Realities of American-Palestine Relations* (Washington, 1949), 114.

4. Ibid., 93.

5. Ibid., 94.

6. Funds for the support of the Jewish inhabitants of Palestine from contributions of Jews in the diaspora organized especially after the end of the eighteenth century but begun in the sixteenth century. See "Halukah" in *Encyclopaedia Judaica,* vol. 7, 1207–1215.

7. Manuel, *The Realities of American-Palestine Relations,* 44–46.

8. See Alex Bein, *The Return to the Soil* (Jerusalem, 1952), 223.

9. Marie Syrkin, *Golda Meir: Israel's Leader* (New York, 1969) new rev. ed., 64.

10. The Merhaviyah period is briefly portrayed in Marie Syrkin, ed., *Golda Meir Speaks Out* (London, 1973), 38–42.

11. Syrkin, *Golda Meir: Israel's Leader,* 85.

12. Syrkin, ed., *Golda Meir Speaks Out,* 240–241.

13. *New York Times,* 14 January 1976, "Golda Meir, on the Palestinians," 35.

14. Ibid.

15. Syrkin, ed., *Golda Meir Speaks Out,* 141–143.

16. Ibid., 139–140.

17. David Ben-Gurion, *My Talks with Arab Leaders* (New York, 1973), 22–23.

18. Ibid., 162–182.

19. Syrkin, *Golda Meir: Israel's Leader,* 156–157.

20. Ibid., 343.

21. Syrkin, ed., *Golda Meir Speaks Out,* 242.

22. Ibid.

23. Ben-Zion Ilan (Applebaum), *An American Soldier/Pioneer in Israel,* with an introduction by Golda Meir (New York, 1979).

Chapter 15

Golda (Meyerson) Meir (1898–1978), Israel's fourth prime minister, occupies a place in the pantheon of twentieth-century Zionist leaders unparalleled by any other female figure. In the following chapter, Anita Shapira, the noted historian of the Palestine labor movement and biographer of the socialist Zionist leader Berl Kaznelson (1887–1944), offers a sketch of Meir's complex profile as a political leader who functioned in "primarily a male world that had, at best, an ambivalent attitude toward assertive women with a powerful presence." Brushing aside timeworn assumptions about Meir, who was pejoratively referred to as "the old woman" by detractors and "the castrating woman" by political rivals, Shapira scrutinizes Meir's exceptional ability to navigate the male-dominated landscape of Zionist politics, the Yishuv, and the State of Israel. That Meir did so without resorting to special pleading and, in fact, with strikingly little regard for the status of women in the Zionist movement is a curious aspect of her legacy as a female activist.

Shapira also underscores Meir's distinctive American inheritance—the American ethos that prompted her drive for independent action, the Protestant work ethic that informed and sustained her "social commitment to the welfare of others," the sentimentality and affection she openly displayed in contrast to the machismo of the Israeli *sabra* [native-born Israeli Jew]. Despite serious misgivings about her peripatetic family life, which seem to have dogged every step of her political career, Meir projected a strong, confident female image that blended an unapologetic American Jewish sensibility with socialist Zionist idealism. This unusual combination, asserts Shapira, which served her so well amid the rough-and-tumble of the international political arena, was never fully appreciated by Mapai's inner circle or, at a later stage, a changing Israeli public.

In the final analysis, Shapira's artful sketch of Golda Meir opens up new avenues for exploring the private life and public legacy of this formidable political female figure. Shapira demonstrates that Meir was, in many respects, atypical and unrepresentative of the generation of the Zionist women pioneers who arrived in the Yishuv with the Second and Third *Aliyot*, the waves of Jewish immigration to Palestine during, respectively, 1903/04–1914 and 1919–1923. At the same time, she argues, it is simplistic (as some scholars have contended) to overstress the qualities and talents that enabled Meir to dwarf her male contemporaries. For although she bested most men at their own political game, she ultimately insisted that they accept her on her terms, that is, as an independent woman in a male-dominated world. In short, she embraced her feminine identity to produce an assertive style that melded warmth, sensitivity, and charm with considerable political savvy, directness, and force of personality. To be sure, the last word on Golda Meir—a towering figure in the history of Zionism and the modern Jewish experience—has yet to be written. The following chapter raises intriguing questions and opens up new and fresh possibilities that that will no doubt shape the work of Golda's future biographers.

Golda: Femininity and Feminism

Anita Shapira

When Golda Meir passed away in 1978, millions of people throughout the world mourned her. In her old age, she had become a symbol that spoke to the hearts of many people, including those who did not understand her language, or those who were unfamiliar with her world, and even those who were opposed to positions taken by the State of Israel. Golda captured people's imaginations with a power that is virtually unequaled—as a leader, as a human being, and as a woman. Her errors and failures, which diminished her image in the eyes of the Israeli intelligentsia and of vast sectors of the Israeli public, did not mar her standing as an admired figure. Even after the Yom Kippur War she continued to arouse spontaneous support among a broad range of groups. After resigning from the premiership, she became an important national and international figure, surrounded by affection. Somehow, her charisma continued to attract people's hearts, regardless of her standing. There was something solid in her clumsy, somewhat heavy figure, something that was able to weather the storms of history and engender trust and confidence, precisely because it was so stable, so immutable, so predictable.

The world in which Golda functioned was primarily a male world that had, at best, an ambivalent attitude toward assertive women with a powerful presence. Golda could not be ignored. Did this fact benefit her or did it stand in her way? In this essay I will attempt to examine the manner in which Golda related to the fact that she was a woman, and to the manner in which those who came in contact with her related to her being a woman.

Golda grew up in three different societies, all of which served as wellsprings of her identity: eastern European Jewry, early-twentieth-century immigrant American Jewry, and the Jewish labor movement in Palestine. A child of the Pale of Settlement, Golda's name was associated both with Kiev, the city in which she was born, and with Pinsk, the city in which she was raised. Her memoirs, *My Life,* open with a description of her childhood in Kiev. The first experience she relates is fear before the outburst of a pogrom. Although she herself never experienced a pogrom, this fear was to serve as a formative experience for her. The sense of being part of a weak and vulnerable Jewish minority facing the threat of violence from its powerful gentile neighbors remained with her throughout her life.

In 1973 Golda made the first historic visit by an Israeli prime minister to the Vatican. During that visit, one careless remark by the pope was enough to return her to these childhood experiences. The pope wondered how the Jews—who, of all people, must be capable of compassion after having suffered so much—could treat the Palestinians with force. "Your Holiness," she replied, "do you know what my first memory is? Anticipating a pogrom in Kiev. Allow me to assure you that my people know all there is to know about real 'force' and that we learned all there is to learn about true compassion when we were led to the Nazi gas chambers."

The transformation that had occurred in the Jewish people's situation from the time of Golda's first fear of pogroms in Kiev and her meeting as the head of the Jewish state with the Holy See can serve as a symbol for her life and for her psychological constitution.

The second chapter in Golda's life took place in the United States, between Milwaukee and Denver.

For Golda, the move to the United States was revolutionary. For the first time she was exposed to a non-Jewish environment. She discovered that in spite of fears, hostility, and Jewish ethnic specificity, she was able to conduct a dialogue with this world. Opportunities became available that set her imagination aflame. At school she learned about English-language culture. Her meeting with Morris Meyerson exposed her to realms of music, literature, and art of which she had previously been entirely unaware.

Although she was raised in a traditional Jewish culture that emphasized family discipline, she found sufficient support from the culture around her and from her sister to rebel against her parents, to establish her independence, and to move to Denver to continue her studies. The Golda who stood in the street in front of the synagogue, making one of her first public speeches on behalf of socialist Zionism (and in so doing, disobeying her father), was a young woman who had internalized important American principles and norms.

Later, in the 1920s, she was sent by the women's labor union to organize the Pioneer Women movement in the United States. On this, her first mission to the United States, she discovered her ability to influence people, use her charms on strangers, and excel at public speaking. But the influence of the American ethos went deeper. The Protestant work ethic, which ties success to hard work and perseverance, was an integral part of the norms that molded her life. An individual's responsibility for his or her own fate, and the ability to alter that fate and change the course of one's life by an act of will, were principles she absorbed from the American heritage. In Israel, these principles were transformed into her profound distaste for a culture which held that "I am entitled to. . . ." Along with her social commitment to the welfare of others, she would not stand for laziness or for "parasitic lifestyles." She was intolerant toward those who shunned hard work and diligence. Her lack of empathy for the Black Panthers, for example, a group of young Sephardic Jews who placed the ethnic question on the Israeli agenda in the early 1970s, stemmed from her individualistic, almost puritanical streak that defined them as lazy.

The third major influence came from her encounter with the activists of the Jewish labor movement in Palestine—the Russian pioneers of the Second Aliyah. A cursory glance at the age of the Jewish socialist leadership in Palestine shows that most were born around 1887, approximately a decade before Golda. But philosophically Golda belongs to that political and cultural milieu. During her tenure as prime minister, she was often referred to as "the last of the Bolsheviks"—a reference to a political culture that demanded loyalty to the party and to its members, was hostile toward the media and intolerant of leaks to the press, and demanded disciplined activity.

Golda was never impressed by ostentatious consumerism or technological progress, as was her successor, Shimon Peres. She remained loyal to a view, characteristic of the Second Aliyah, that celebrated simplicity and the suspension of personal gratification. In stark opposition to the American conception, she adopted the view that the state must direct the economy, that the state must guarantee its citizens' physical existence, and that it must care for the weaker strata of society through progressive social legislation.

In the 1950s, during her "seven good years" (as she referred to her tenure as minister of labor), Meir attempted to implement her principles. Unlike Henrietta Szold, who believed in a policy of social aid, Golda preferred a policy of social *security:* social support sounded paternalistic to immigrants of the Second Aliyah—somewhere between charity and soup kitchens. On the other hand, state guarantees of medical services, old-age insurance, health and accident insurance, and maternity leave and grants seemed to her to be a part of the state's duty toward its citizens. In 1954, at a time when some immigrants who arrived in the early fifties were still dwelling in *maabarot* [temporary settlements], Golda was able to pass the social security law in the Knesset. Since then, with improvements over time and experience, her law has been at the center of Israeli social legislation. Of all the positions she held, she was most fond of the ministry of labor. That role gave her the opportunity to fulfill the Second Aliyah socialist program, as the minister responsible for absorption of mass immigration, employment, and housing.

Golda was not a feminist in the sense of struggling actively for women's rights. She did not recognize the need for such a struggle—or at least this is what she claimed. She projected her personal positive experience of finding a place within the political structures of the labor movement and the State of Israel onto society and women at large. "If I can do it," she seemed to say, "then the path is open to any woman." In fact, however, Golda was not a representative example, but rather the exception. Golda's achievements as a woman did not create changes for women in general. Her entire life was marked by precedents she set in terms of women's participation in politics. For example, Ben-Gurion, who wished to include her in his provisional government in 1948, explained that it would be good to have one woman in the Israeli government. This reasoning failed to convince any of his party colleagues to forgo their seats for her sake. In contradistinction to Ben-Gurion's "affirmative action," the religious parties in Tel Aviv blocked her candidacy as the city's mayor, reasoning that a woman should not be in a position of power over men. This reasoning was no longer mentioned in 1969, when she was elected prime minister.

In an intended statement of praise, Ben-Gurion expressed the male character of the world in which Golda operated when he called her "the only man in the government." "He thinks that it's a compliment," Golda responded ironically when she heard the comment. As a woman, she was exposed to double criticism: critiques focused not only on what she did or did not do but also on her appearance. "Golda shoes," the plain shoes she used to wear in the 1950s due to a vein ailment, came to symbolize her alleged lack of sophistication and elegance. When, as foreign minister, she joined the prime minister and the chief of staff at the conference in France that prepared the Sinai Campaign, Ben-Gurion's younger colleagues (Moshe Dayan and Shimon Peres) enjoyed hearing the French participants' derogatory comments about "their secretary's" appearance. As prime minister she inspired a different type of resentment: native-born Israelis thought she, the old-timer, had blocked Yigal Allon's and Moshe Dayan's path to leadership. "The castrating woman" was the term the media used to describe the relationship between her and these two generals. Thus, her power, in contrast to the two men's weakness, inspired not admiration but criticism: they were viewed as creative, Israeli, and modern; she was seen as belonging to the old generation, holding back history's progress. Golda's kitchen—the informal forum in which Labor Party leaders met to formulate positions in preparation for government discussions—took on an almost diabolical image in popular mythology. Golda had transformed the traditional term that indicated women's banishment to housekeeping jobs ("a woman's place is in the kitchen") into a center of "political cooking," a symbol of power. She was in charge of both types of kitchens.

Golda's biographer, Meron Medzini, often adopted a clearly antifeminist view in his evaluation of her career. Her prominence in the party and promotion to senior positions, he explained, resulted from the fact that she had been loyal to party leaders and had climbed the bureaucratic ladder. Anybody unfamiliar with the facts might get the impression that she was an obedient, loyal clerk, who was eventually rewarded for her loyalty.

Medzini referred to the years of her rule as a "maternalistic gerontocracy." Ben-Gurion's nickname, "the old man," expressed fondness and esteem; but for Golda, mention of her age was invariably made in a derogatory sense, as the "grandmother of the state." The only positive reference Medzini made with regard to Golda's femininity was the fact that she never took advantage of being a woman to demand special treatment.

To a large degree, Medzini's attitude toward Golda reflects the attitude of the young intellectuals of the Left, who were hostile to her political positions and felt uncomfortable with her style of leadership. Did their hostility stem solely from substantive political considerations, or did it reflect a certain deeper opposition to a woman having so prominent a position of power?

Golda's attitude toward being a woman is reflected in her autobiography, *My Life*. It is surprising to note the extent to which she internalized the stereotypes prevalent in Jewish society at the time regarding women's roles and conduct. On the one hand, she was comfortable with her femininity. She enjoyed dressing up nicely and receiving compliments for her appearance. In her memoirs, she repeatedly mentions her concern for proper attire at various occasions. She enjoyed projecting the image of a sentimental housewife: she frequently mentioned that her method of concentrating and relaxing was by arranging her kitchen shelves. When she remarked in an interview that she liked cooking chicken soup, she was swamped with requests for the recipe from all over the world. Golda promptly published it. Her tears during moving events practically became her trademark. She cried during the ceremony of the declaration of the State of Israel, she cried when she was elected prime minister, and she cried when she visited the White House. Members of Kibbutz Revivim (where her daughter resides) relate that when a movie was going to be shown at the *kibbutz,* she would ask whether it was a tearjerker. If it was, she would say, "then I'm going." However, it was precisely at the most difficult moments in her life and in the history of the State of Israel, during the Yom Kippur Way, that she did not cry. Moshe Dayan testified to

Golda's astounding self-control and ability to function during the war, at times when he himself and other military heroes lost their resolve and ability to think clearly.

Golda did not consider public display of emotions to be a sign of weakness, even at a time when Israeli machismo was clearly uncomfortable with tears. Her sentimentality was open for all to see. She provided a shoulder to cry on for a soldier at the Western Wall after the Six-Day War, and she was moved to tears by her encounter with Soviet Jews in 1948, and again in 1970. She presented her cheek for Henry Kissinger to kiss at the end of tough and exhausting negotiations, and quipped: "I thought you kiss only men."

The story of her family life, with and without her husband Morris, also serves as material for feminist analysis: Golda met Morris at meetings of young immigrant radicals in her sister's home in Denver. Morris was not a Zionist, but he brought to her the world of music, literature, and art, which intoxicated her. Morris fell in love with the attractive, lively young Golda and was willing to follow her to that desolate land in the Middle East, perhaps secretly hoping that she would soon give up her Zionist dream. Golda dragged Morris with her to Merhaviyah, because she wanted to live on a *kibbutz* and work in agriculture. Quickly, however, she learned that Morris was not cut out for *kibbutz* life. He was not adept at manual labor, he found the physical conditions at Merhaviyah difficult, and he was apparently unable to find a common language with the members of the *kvuzah*. Golda, on the other hand, blossomed at Merhaviyah: She very quickly found her place within the group and indeed reached senior positions. Morris was chronically ill—or at least this is the way she presents the matter—and she accepted his ultimatum to leave Merhaviyah and move to the city. From this point and up until 1928, Golda followed her husband to Jerusalem, remained at home, and gave birth to two children—something she defined as a woman's greatest joy. During these years, she withdrew from all public activity. However, she was so miserable that Berl Kaznelson, who met her by chance in Jerusalem, became alarmed. The breakthrough came in 1928, when she was offered the opportunity to go on a mission for Pioneer Women in the United States. It was at this point that she reached the decision to abandon her husband for the sake of public activity.

In hindsight, the Golda-Morris relationship sounds like a classic story of a young and talented woman who marries a husband who is nice but ineffectual and carries him on her back for years, until she decides that her life has a worth of its own. It is interesting to note the contrasting way in which Golda tells this story. She paints a picture of guilt for which there is no forgiveness. She presents Morris as flawless, far superior to her in every way, a man of *haute culture* to whom she owes an immeasurable debt. The fact that she was miserable in her marriage, that he was unable to provide for her and their children, that he showed no ability to integrate himself into his new life in Palestine, and that he was nevertheless *unwilling to grant her a divorce until the day he died in 1951*—a fact she chooses to mention only in passing—are all secondary in her account, when compared with her great "sin" for deciding to take advantage of the opportunity to embark on the path of public activity that she so desired.

These same feelings of endless guilt surround her relationship with her children. Going away frequently for months and leaving them with Morris or a nanny was an unforgivable sin in her eyes. She presents her children as victims, sacrificed to her own ambitions. When her daughter became ill and Golda was abroad, Morris called her back from the United States, since he was unable to cope. She did not complain. On the contrary, she was racked with guilt for having placed him in such a situation. In the end, she goes to the United States with her two children and is able both to obtain a cure for her daughter and to fulfill her mission. Although she maintained a warm and loving relationship with her children and their families throughout her life, paying a great deal of attention to them and to her grandchildren, her book repeatedly stresses how poorly she treated them. Feelings of guilt for having failed to live up to the expectations of a Jewish woman and mother were fueled by her controlling mother and her sister Shana, the former revolutionary. They complained incessantly that Golda was neglecting her children. Shana and their mother accepted the prevailing stereotypes of motherhood and family, and could not appreciate Golda's success in such atypical roles for the traditional Jewish woman.

Golda's femininity comes through once again in the manner in which she relates to the time she spent on Merhaviyah. She did not agree with the *kibbutz* girls' demands for equality of labor with the *kibbutz* boys. The girls fought against being pigeonholed in the *kibbutz*'s service industries, which were considered less prestigious and less productive than the boys' agricultural jobs. Working in the kitchen was considered degrading. Golda, on the other hand, announced that she did not understand why feeding cows was okay while feeding the *kibbutz* members was not. She enthusiastically began working in the kitchen. It was there that she first displayed a quality that Berl Kaznelson once termed "a talent for life," which related—in a positive sense—to women's nature. The "talent for life," according to Kaznelson, is the opposite of self-neglect, the opposite of "hippie" culture. The talent for life represents the transition from a temporary to a permanent way of life. The talent for life creates conditions that allow for the establishment of a living, working, and positive community over an extended period of time.

Golda displayed this talent by concentrating on details, many of which she considered worthy of mention in her book, many years later. For example, she took pains to cook a hot oatmeal breakfast for the *kibbutz* members. While at first they considered this effort an American quirk, they later learned to appreciate it as an important source of energy. Golda saw to it that the number of cookies baked on the *kibbutz* was doubled, to put a halt to the custom of stealing the few cookies that had been baked. Golda took the trouble to peel the skin off the herring served at supper, so that the *kibbutz* members would stop wiping their dirty hands on their work clothes. The other female members did not approve of these steps. They found that Golda's innovations set dangerous precedents for the quality of the food served in the *kibbutz* dining hall. Golda painstakingly ironed the shirts she received from the communal laundry—another habit that others considered an American idiosyncrasy. Her need to create a clean, pleasant, and aesthetic environment—a sense of home—comes through clearly in her memoirs. These small details appeared to be more important than her achievements in the *kibbutz* economy. In her memoirs, Golda skips over the fact that she was a pioneer of chicken farming in Palestine and that she established the first large-scale, modern chicken coop in the Jezreel Valley. The skinning of herring, on the other hand, is stressed.

According to photographs and testimonies of her contemporaries, she was an attractive and endearing woman, but readers of her memoirs might think that after her separation from Morris, she retired to a convent. This was another matter in which she accepted traditional mores. She had at least two serious relationships with men and eventually sat alongside one of them in government. The other was president at the time that she was prime minister. In the revolutionary atmosphere of pre-state Jewish Palestine, nonmarital relationships were tolerated. Aside from envy directed at her from a number of quarters, these relationships raised no eyebrows. On the level of public imagery, however, Golda remained uncomfortable about exposing these relationships, even years later. Moshe Dayan had many scandalous love affairs that were discussed in the Israeli press in "real time." But what is permissible for a man in public life is not necessarily permissible for a woman, even in socialist Israel.

Zalman Hen, general director of the Ministry of Labor, relates that in March 1954, on the day the social security law Golda had formulated and passed was implemented, and when new mothers began to receive maternity grants, he came to Golda's house to congratulate her. Golda suggested that they sit in the kitchen so she could iron some shirts for her son Menahem. In a very natural manner, she served him tea and biscuits, and prepared a cup of Turkish coffee for herself. Such stories appear repeatedly in testimonies about her. One anecdote tells of an eminent foreign minister of a friendly country who came to visit Golda at home at a time when she was already prime minister. He received the shock of his life when the prime minister herself opened the door for him. After he overcame his initial shock, she asked him what he would like to drink and disappeared from the room. When he asked one of her aides where she was, he was told that she was in the kitchen, preparing the drinks. Finally, she invited him to join her at her kitchen table so that they could converse while she prepared *hors d'oeuvres*.

Such stories, of which a great many exist, show a number of aspects of Golda's personality: first, her great comfort at carrying out women's roles. She never downplayed the fact that she was a woman. Rather, she turned her femininity or femaleness, as she understood it, into a trademark, her central image. She did not play by the rules of the male world: she did not imitate male behavioral norms. Rather she forced men who came into contact with her to accept her as she was—a woman playing as a woman in the men's sphere. The strong contrast between her soft, maternal, "in the kitchen" image and her personal strength and toughness in negotiations became a central political asset for Golda. She transformed supposed feminine weaknesses into advantages. Golda did not adopt the outward conduct of the male world of power politics—either in party affairs or in diplomacy. Golda felt uncomfortable at black-tie events held in the Foreign Ministry. She never learned the language of diplomacy, the art of telling half-truths, the skill of insinuation, or the practice of intellectual sophistication that involves saying one thing and meaning something else. Instead, she raised the banner of a politics of directness, sincerity, and warmth. Her associates were forced to come to terms with her style and to cope with the discourse of supposed female simplicity. This was her way of being assertive: she redefined the rules of the game according to her own style and forced others to accept them. The somewhat embarrassed foreign minister who sat at Golda's kitchen table and drank the coffee she had prepared for him in effect underwent a process of conditioning that prepared the grounds for their subsequent substantive discussion.

Aaron Remez (son of David Remez, first minister of transportation and Golda's longtime lover) described Golda in the following words: "In the personal realm, behind her self-assured appearance, she was very feminine. She was always searching for a sense of support, security and warmth from those around her. She was unable to be alone." The contrast between her feminine vulnerability and the personal strength and rock-like confidence she seemed to convey was one of the reasons why men had difficulty accepting her. On the one hand, she played the male game with great skill and with a strength that dwarfed many men. On the other hand, she maintained her qualities as a woman and rejected the male rules of the game. She wanted to be a woman, a mother, a public figure, and not to forgo any of these. In her generation, this was thought to be an impossible task, perhaps even an unforgivable sin.

Sources Consulted

Golda: Zmihatah shel manihigah, 1921–1956, ed. Meir Avizohar (Tel Aviv: Am Oved and Tel Aviv University, 1994); Yizhak Ilam and Drorah Bet-Or, *Bimehitsatah shel Golda: Sihot im Yizhak Ilam al Golda Meir bitkufah sheben September 1985–Fevruar 1986* (Tel-Aviv: Amutah lehantsahat zikhrah shel Golda Meir, 1987); Meron Medzini, *Hayehudiyah hageah: Golda Meir vehazon yisrael, biografiyah politit* (Jerusalem: Edanim, 1990); Golda Meir, *Hayai* (Tel Aviv: Sifriat Maariv, 1975).

PART IV

Women Report and Remember: Documentary Portraits

Zionism, the modern Jewish national liberation movement, succeeded in creating a sovereign state after World War II by virtue of historical, economic, political, military, and other factors that evolved over time. It also succeeded because a sufficient sector of the international Jewish community supported Zionism as a paramount goal. Without participation by Jews from around the globe, it would have been difficult, if not impossible, for the state to come into being.

In order to understand the emergence and development of Zionism as an idea and a practical enterprise, one must examine the role of Jewry in each country and, within each of those larger groups, the role of women. The latter—women Zionists—have yet to receive systematic scholarly attention, and thus it has been impossible to fully assess the place of women in the history of Zionism and Israel. Studies of Zionist women are few and far between, and studies of Zionist women in societies other than Palestine (later Israel) and the United States have yet to be undertaken at all.

In this section, we put aside the question of the *collective* participation of American Jewish women in the Zionist movement, which was examined in previous chapters. Rather, our focus here is on *individual* experiences and the way individual Jewish women defined their own roles and emergent identities. We do this by presenting a series of documentary portraits culled from letters, personal reflections, and oral histories of American Zionist women recording their experiences.

Today, narrative analysis is being used extensively in the study of social history. The study of narratives elucidates social movements from the perspectives of both leaders and rank-and-file members. Similarly, the emergence of "women's history" has made it clear that both men and women have played substantive roles in shaping social events. Narratives are also useful in deciphering those roles as lived experiences.

The narratives in this concluding section demonstrate that American Jewish women interested in Zionism forged their own paths in order to play substantive roles in Zionist affairs and the Jewish public arena. Had they merely remained members of male-dominated Zionist organizations, they would likely have been second-class citizens or passive participants, relegated to roles not of their own choosing. In building organizations and developing effective political strategies of their own, Zionist women created opportunities—deliberately or not—for individuals to become leaders as well as active participants in a larger movement. Some of the figures noted here, such as Irma "Rama" (Levy) Lindheim (1886–1978) and Golda (Meyerson) Meir (1898–1978), were driven by ideology. Others sought adventure and others still were unclear about what Zionism really entailed until they had arrived in Palestine. Some came to Palestine to escape the restrictions they felt in the United States, while others came to Palestine to continue the traditions they enjoyed in America. Each woman forged a kind of Zionism of her own because she had the freedom to do so. And each woman discovered a Zionism of her own through the praxis in which she was engaged.

As in all social movements, the activities in which these women engaged were linked to a central goal (in this case, creating a haven for Jews) while, at the same time, the activities were intended to lift up the members themselves. This dual process is analogous to African American women's experience of "lifting as we climb." American Zionist women combined taking personal responsibility for Jewish continuity and survival in the Land of Israel with the goal of ensuring the vitality of Jewish life in the diaspora. To this end, Hadassah, the Mizrachi Women's Organization, Pioneer Women, and other women's groups invested considerable resources in American Jewry's sociopolitical and educational infrastructure. These organizations took root and flourished in virtually every American Jewish community in the decades leading up to the creation of the Jewish state in 1948.

The documentary portraits in this section represent the tip of an iceberg that has yet to be rescued from a sea of obscurity. They are "small stories" of great experiences that shaped people's individual lives and, indeed, the life of the Jewish people. The accounts in this section were written by a variety of American Jewish women whose lives became bound up with the Zionist movement. Engee Caller (b. 1918), Ruth Halprin Kas-

love (b. 1923), Judith Korim Hornstein (1908–1996), Irma (Rama) Lindheim, Golda (Meyerson) Meir, Yocheved Herschlag Muffs (b. 1927), Zipporah Porath (b. 1923), and Lois Slott (b. 1926) all offer rare personal reflections on encounters with Zionist figures and leaders in America,
Europe, and Palestine as well as on critical historic and political episodes
in which they participated, including hardscrabble Jewish self-defense efforts in pre-state Palestine. In the aggregate, these women's stories express
a common theme: When faced by overwhelming crises—as was clearly
the case during the Holocaust and immediately following World War II—
American Zionist women intensified their Zionist commitments and efforts. To participate in nation building during turbulent periods required
considerable personal and political courage. It meant working against the
grain of what was expected from a "nice Jewish girl." It meant dealing
with men's work, military danger, political intrigue, and public leadership. In the portraits that follow, the twin projects of developing fully as a
human being and participating in historic events are clearly evident.

It is also worth noting that because of the concrete tasks before them,
American Jewish women took on the challenges in their Zionist work that
American women in general took on only later with the birth of the "second wave of the women's movement." Thus American Zionist women differed from American women in general not only by anticipating some aspects of the feminist movement but also in combining their special
political responsibilities with traditional female roles.

Over time, many American Jewish women and women's organizations
exerted a profound impact on the emerging Jewish state. To omit the individual and collective experiences of women from the historical record inevitably yields a distorted understanding of the nexus between American
Jews, Zionism, and the Land of Israel. It is the editors' hope that the documents in this section will prompt other Zionist veterans to write down
their personal stories and researchers to seek out hitherto neglected primary materials that further illuminate the complex role of American Jewish women in the Zionist enterprise. Feminist research approaches to
women's lives have made it possible to analyze documents such as these
by employing theoretical models that help uncover significant personal
and political dimensions.[1] This area of study is in its infancy, but the
wealth of ideas contained in the documents that follow points to new and
productive research opportunities for the future.

---

1. See, for example, Miriam B. Raider-Roth's introductory essay concerning the voices
and self-reflective understandings of Zionist women pioneers in *The Plough Woman:
Records of the Pioneer Women of Palestine; A Critical Edition*, ed. Mark A. Raider and
Miriam B. Raider-Roth (Hanover, N.H., and London: University Press of New England,
2002), lix–lxxiii.

Chapter 16

Contemplating *Aliyah* to Palestine

Judith Korim Hornstein

(Chelsea, Massachusetts, 1935)

My dear Sara, Yosef and Yael,

. . . Tell me, Sara, how do you like the farmer's life? Unless I am mistaken, you all seem to have taken to it quite well: raising chickens, growing vegetables and so forth. What is the social life like? Do you ever miss the theater, movies, lectures, and concerts? Or do you have all of that there, as well? You will probably laugh at my questions, but these are the questions that I have. . . .

It may be that I don't understand that life at all. I think though that the country life around Dabeik, in Lithuania, was without these pleasantries. They didn't miss it much, because they didn't know about such things. But how can people who have been brought up differently ever live a country life? Can one leave behind all of the things tied up with the city? Or do you have all of those things in the country? Sara, why have you never written about the size of your village, how many people live there, and about the life in general? I imagine you are so busy that such foolishness is far from your mind.

Sara, I know you don't often leave home, but do you ever hear from old acquaintances?. . . Does anyone regret coming?

. . . My dear sister, I had decided to write you a long letter long ago. But, but apart from the fact that I am seldom in the right mood, there is another reason. You seem so busy that you will probably have no time to answer me, and also, we've become a bit estranged, and it might not interest you to write back. Therefore, I am not sure if I should write to you or not. I think Atarah told you that I want to come to Israel. Either you don't take this seriously, because you think that I'm joking, or it doesn't interest you at all, because you haven't let fall a single word about it. Why not?. . . My dear sister, this is a real problem for me, because if I were rich, without a second word I would come as a tourist, and if I could and wanted to stay—good. If not, I'd come back. But my situation is otherwise. I don't know if I have developed an attraction to Israel because I am an idealist or because I am an egotist. I think the former is less pressing. I know that Israel doesn't need all idealists to come to Israel. There are enough volunteers for that already. And perhaps I could do even more for the ideal by remaining outside of the land.

It's more likely that the attraction of immigration has developed out of my own desire, because here it is very difficult to lead a full life. Life remains fairly empty, without anything to fill it up. I think I wrote you once that a person makes a great mistake when they come to a land like America in adulthood . . .

Life here is so unusual. Some certainly experience it differently than I do. Maybe years ago, when immigration to America was greater, it was otherwise.[1] But those years are gone, and today, the few that immigrate come as adults, when it's difficult to adapt to this strange life, and they find themselves estranged and rejected, as I do. When I first arrived, I did not comprehend how complicated this life was. I thought, "I have only to learn a little English and everything will be fine." *Nu*, I've learned a little English, but it means nothing. The greenhorn[2] and the American differ not only in language, but in lifestyle as well.

I joined an organization called Young Judaea,[3] allegedly a Zionist organization, but I couldn't stay in it long, because of differences over party intentions. The group is made up of young, American, intellectual men and women, all students at Harvard. Their purpose is to educate the Jewish youth to be knowledgeable about Judaism, and generally Zionist. However, if [Zeev] Jabotinsky[4] were in Boston it would soon be evident that 95% of them are Revisionists.[5] They know very little all together about Zionism. Firstly, I don't need to be educated on how to be a Jew; I

1. The reference here appears to be to the era of mass emigration from eastern Europe at the turn of the nineteenth and twentieth centuries that brought some 2.5 million Jewish immigrants to the United States between 1881 and 1924.

2. A pejorative term used describe new immigrants.

3. Young Judaea was founded in the early twentieth century as the youth division of Hadassah. It later became a separate Zionist youth organization with branches in most major American urban centers and a national network of summer camps.

4. Vladimir Zeev Jabotinsky (1880–1940), the founder of the right-wing Zionist movement known as Revisionism, was an outstanding Zionist writer, thinker, and orator.

5. Revisionist Zionism, a militant faction of the Zionist movement, founded in 1925 by Vladimir Zeev Jabotinsky (see note 4 above). The Revisionists opposed the leftist orientation of the socialist Labor Zionist parties and the Histadrut as well as the gradualist policies of Chaim Weizmann (see chapter 22, note 14), emphasizing instead a maximalist program of military strength, laissez-faire economic policy, and Jewish sovereignty in the entire Land of Israel.

was one well before I met these educators. Secondly, there can be no real common ground between an American-born intellectual and an actual unionist.[6] I'll tell you about all of the organizations in Boston, so that you can see how little social life is to be found here . . . Young Israel[7] is like Mizrachi; they are linked. Hadassah is made up of American-born Yankees. I have little love for them. Avodah [Labor], a student union—if you aren't in college you can't belong. The Workers' League for Palestine[8]—they are American-born. This would be interesting, for, as little as the American-born and the unionist understand each other, at least this group is a little closer. But the League is an hour and a half away from us, and it's hard for me to go so far when I have to work. I can't belong to Hashomer Hazair either, as it's also over an hour away, and they ask a lot of work of you. You have to give them all of your time, and I can't do this, because when I have to work it's impossible.

In short, in our *shtetl* of 20,000 Jews there are no Jewish organizations in which I can take any interest. In fact, there is only one, the Young Men's and Women's Hebrew Association,[9] and even this one is not very interesting. Their intent is to prevent the Jewish youth from assimilating. It's not for me.

I spent my first year here in Revere, [Massachusetts] by the sea. I didn't speak any English and I didn't want for anything. But a year later we came to Chelsea, a bigger city, and here there are no interesting places at all. I went to Boston and searched here and there for some group to join. A year ago I wanted to organize a union[10] in Chelsea. There are Jewish youth here, but where are they? Eventually, I succeeded, with help from the chairman of the Action Committee of the Zionist Organization of New England, in organizing a Poalei Zion union. The result is that as hard as we try, we can get no great number of young people to participate. Our union currently consists of twenty-two members, young people

6. The term "unionist" is used here to refer to members of the United Zionist Socialist Labor Party Poalei Zion-Zeirei Zion, which was a union of the Poalei Zion and Zeirei Zion parties in the United States, offshoots of Russian socialist Zionist parties transplanted to American soil by Yiddish-speaking immigrants in the early twentieth century.

7. Young Israel, the youth division of the Mizrahi religious Zionist party.

8. Workers' League for Palestine, an American association of working-class Jewish men and women who supported and identified with the Labor Zionist movement in Palestine.

9. Originally founded as a network of literary societies in the 1850s, the Young Men's Hebrew Association swiftly became a locus of Jewish cultural activity in many major American urban centers by the early twentieth century. The rising popularity of the YMHA also prompted the creation of Young Women's Hebrew Associations.

10. The reference is to the possibility of organizing a branch of the Poalei Zion–Zeirei Zion party (see note 6 above).

and adults. We share leadership, and apart from party matters, little of interest goes on, because of a number of other things. You may ask, "What is important to the young people?" Firstly, I don't know myself. Secondly, only the idealistic ones belong to these unions. And it's certain that if something doesn't interest them, they can't take it in. They want to Americanize, dance, and play ball. None of these things are bad, but apart from them there's nothing else. How can Poalei Zion and the like interest them?

In the Boston area, which has over 100,000 Jews, there are two Poalei Zion unions, which together have maybe fifty members—who are more sluggish than energetic. I am referring to the young people. There are a small number of older unionists.[11]

In a word, this life is a mystery no matter how much one learns, and it is impossible to figure out why it's this way and not another. My dear sister, you're getting a strange picture of life in America. I want to draw your attention to the fact that I say all of this about Boston. . . . Boston is considered a city of Yankees, and the Jews also try very hard to be Yankees. It is certainly possible that life is different in other places. And truthfully, I have thought a few times about going elsewhere. America is such a big place, why shouldn't I take advantage of the opportunity? But it was, of course, our fate to come at a time of crisis, and in the five years that we have been in America, the situation has not improved, but just the opposite. . . .

Now I will ask you a few questions. First, I must tell you that I can't come yet. It could still be as long as a whole year, because our dear parents want only one thing: that I should become an American citizen before I go, so that I don't burn my bridges behind me. And I must obey them, even if I don't want to.

Now tell me, if you know, if I come to Israel what can I do, if I can't or don't want to join a *kibbutz*? And if I do go to a *kibbutz*, can I join without first going through the training? What do you think of *kibbutz* life in general? Do you think there is some way that I can prepare myself? I mean for a kind of work, as I don't have a trade. I have spent five years working in a shoe factory, and there I have learned nothing apart from how to stitch shoes. And do you think it is important that I learn Hebrew beforehand, as I have nearly forgotten what I knew? Or do you think I will pick it up in Israel?

---

11. The reference here is to the ideological and philosophical differences as well as the historical experiences that separated the generation of party members who immigrated to the United States before the early 1920s from those who came somewhat later and/or grew up during the interwar years.

I will not come as a *haluzah,* as I would then have to go through training,[12] and I cannot do this, because I have to work in order to save up
enough money . . . Sara, I forgot to mention that through influence I am
getting a certificate,[13] or so I've been told. I'll find out more about that.

My dear, be healthy and strong. Our dear parents and everyone send
you hundreds of heartfelt greetings. A kiss for dear, beautiful Yaelinka.

Yours, Judith

12. In this period, there were several training farms along the eastern seaboard of the
United States, known in Hebrew as *hakhsharot* [agricultural and vocational training camps]
that prepared would-be Zionist pioneers for rural and communal life in Palestine.

13. This reference is to immigration certificates granted by the British Mandatory regime to the Jewish Agency for Palestine in accordance with Article 6 of the *Mandate for Palestine.* The Jewish Agency allocated the immigration certificates to individuals and Zionist
groups on the basis of criteria set by the World Zionist Organization. In general, the British
authorities severely restricted Palestine's Jewish immigration quota. Fueled by the tragic catastrophe of European Jewry during World War II and the Holocaust, the demand for certificates swiftly outpaced supply, causing enormous hardship and suffering as well as considerable political turmoil in the Zionist movement. Against this backdrop, the Zionist
organization instituted the program of clandestine immigration to Palestine known as
Aliyah Bet. See also chapter 21 in this section by Yocheved Herschlag Muffs for a discussion
of immigration certificates.

Chapter 17

From Brooklyn to Palestine in 1939

Engee Caller

(Kibbutz Kfar Blum, 1985)

Coming on *aliyah* was a complicated procedure during the days of the British Mandate. Some of the roads we traveled to get there were legal, some were not.

The most sought-after route for the would-be *oleh* . . . was via a certificate of entry, issued by the British and distributed by the World Zionist Organization [WZO] to potential immigrants around the world. Throughout the 1930s, these certificates steadily decreased in number as Britain sought to appease the increasingly violent Arab opposition to Zionism. In May 1939 the door was practically shut with the issuance of the infamous White Paper, putting a limit of 15,000 per year, or 1,250 a month, on the number of Jews allowed into Palestine. Of course, the plight of European Jewry demanded that the WZO use most of its certificates for rescue.

There were other ways to get in, though. One could enter the country as a "capitalist." A capitalist was someone who could show the British he or she had enough money to avoid becoming an economic burden on the country. Habonim [The Builders] was able to produce several such capitalists. After a member entered Palestine, flashing the appropriate sum in front of the British officials, he or she would return the money to the movement, which would pass it on to another "capitalist" about to enter the country.

People married to Palestine citizens were allowed to enter the country legally as well. Not surprisingly, more than one Palestine citizen married a prospective immigrant only to divorce after several months and then remarry.

Another legal route was available to the children of people who had joined groups intending to take over citrus plantations prepared by the Histadrut citrus cultivation organization. Moshav Beit Herut was founded that way.

Source: Engee Caller, "From Brooklyn to Palestine, 1939," in *Builders and Dreamers: Habonim Labor Zionist Youth in America*, eds. J. J. Goldberg and Elliot King (New York: Herzl Press and Cornwall Books, 1993), 68–70. Reprinted by permission of Herzl Press.

And then there were the methods that did not just bend the rules but broke them completely. After World War II, Habonim members would come and then "get lost." Others bought tickets to travel to Greece by boat and then, with the aid of the Haganah, jumped ship in Haifa. And finally, many members of Habonim participated in the "illegal" immigration organized to bring in the refugees from Europe.[1] Those who were caught and banished to Cyprus often would slip into Palestine later on small fishing boats.

I arrived in Palestine in early March 1939, just before the White Paper, drawn there by three important influences—my home, my school, and Habonim. My parents' house in the Bensonhurst section of Brooklyn was strictly religious and served as a community center for those of our neighbors who had come from the same eastern European *shtetl*. Many times I felt that I still lived in the *shtetl* myself. My first language was Yiddish. I learned to read from the Yiddish papers I brought home for my parents. My education included the Sholem Aleikhem Folkshul,[2] where we spent our afternoons being introduced to a secularist view of Jewish history and Yiddish culture.

I was introduced to Habonim at a Hanukah party in Manhattan where I was taken by my older sister Bella, who was working in the Pioneer Women's office.[3] Watching children my age singing Yiddish and Hebrew songs, dancing the *hora,* performing skits about Jewish history and Palestine, fired my imagination.

At my invitation, a few of my friends from school and *folkshul* met in Bensonhurt for a few Habonim sessions. But the chapter was short-lived, and my *madrikhim* [leaders] suggested I join the Kadimah Club of Young Poalei Zion,[4] which met in Flatbush, quite a distance from my home. I soon established a regular routine: after sharing a traditional *Shabbat* meal with my family, I would hurriedly wash the dishes and then dash off to the Kadimah meeting and all the Habonim activities that followed.

1. The reference here is to the Zionist Organization's clandestine immigration operation of the 1930s and 1940s, known as Aliyah Bet, which brought more than 100,000 European Jewish refugees and Displaced Persons to Palestine in defiance of the British Mandate's restrictive immigration policies.

2. The Sholem Aleikhem Folkshul, a Yiddish-language school that emphasized East European Jewish culture as well as instruction in secular and socialist subject areas, was a locus of Jewish immigrant life in most American urban centers in the first half of the twentieth century.

3. Pioneer Women, an American organization affiliated with Moezet Hapoalot and the Histadrut in Palestine, was founded in 1925. For more information on the Pioneer Women's Organization, see Mark A. Raider's article in this volume.

4. Young Poalei Zion, the youth branch of the American Poalei Zion party (see chapter 16, note 6). For more information see Mark A. Raider, *The Emergence of American Zionism* (New York and London: New York University Press, 1998), ch. 2.

Oddly enough, despite my deep involvement in the movement, I arrived in Palestine without much thought or planning. I entered on a three-month visitor's visa, but after two months at Kibbutz Kfar Giladi, the *kibbutz* decided to legalize my status in the country. A young man, a stranger to me, was asked to accompany me to the chief rabbi of Tiberias and "take me as his wife." Ironically, upon hearing my name, the chief rabbi was overjoyed. He knew my parents well, and now he had the honor of marrying their daughter.

A few weeks after the "wedding," en route to a national *kibbutz* conference near Tel Aviv, my bus was stopped by the border patrol at Rosh Pinah. As usual, the police, on the lookout for illegal immigrants, demanded that the passengers show their identification papers. Since I had neglected to have my papers prepared to reflect my new status, I brazenly showed them my American passport, hoping they would not notice the expired visa. No such luck.

I was yanked off the bus and questioned by the British commanding officer. Fortunately, he accepted my explanation and reprimanded me for not applying for my ID immediately after my marriage. And, since he and his wife were headed for Metulah that very day, he offered to drive me back to Kfar Giladi.

But that presented some problems. Etiquette would demand that I invite them in for tea, perhaps introduce them to my husband. How could I manage that? I had no idea where my husband's tent or cabin was. I mulled on these troubling thoughts as I climbed into their car and headed north.

A few miles from Rosh Pinah, a jeep suddenly came careening towards us and braked just in front of the car. Out bounded the secretary of Kfar Giladi and my "husband." They had been alerted to what was happening by a very effective grapevine.

I introduced the officer and his wife to my husband and thanked them profusely for the lift. After they left, my husband asked, "What would you have done if I had given you a good, resounding husbandly kiss?"

"I would have given you a good resounding slap in the face," I replied, astounded at his audacity. The next day I applied for an ID card.

Years later, when he was ready to marry in earnest, my "husband" and I went to the chief rabbi of Tiberias to get a divorce. The poor rabbi spent hours trying to convince us to make up and give our marriage another chance. He hated to see the daughter of good friends get divorced. And though he saw my parents several times in the years to come, I don't think he was ever told of my fictitious marriage.

Chapter 18

"They Couldn't Imagine an American Girl Would Do the Work"

Golda Meir

(Kibbutz Revivim, 1971)

When, while still in America, I decided to settle in Palestine, I knew that I would go to a collective settlement. I chose Merhaviyah because a friend from Milwaukee was already there. To my astonishment, [Morris] Meyerson[1] and I were not immediately accepted. As we had arrived in July, we were told that no applications could be considered in the middle of the summer. We would have to wait until Rosh Hashanah, when the *kvuzah* [collective] knew who was staying and who was going, so that new members could be accepted in the place of those who were leaving.

Meanwhile, we went to Tel Aviv, then being built. Our group from the United States made a tremendous impression on the Tel Aviv of the time. One day I met a Tel Aviv woman who, upon learning that I had come from the United States, clapped her hands in astonishment: "Thank God, now the redemption is near—at last Jews have come from America (the millionaires). Now it will be all right!"

Shortly before Rosh Hashanah, we applied to Merhaviyah to be accepted as members and again received a negative reply. Only two members supported us; one of them was my friend. One reason for the rejection was that this community of unmarried men and women did not at that time want families. Babies were a luxury the young *kibbutz* could not afford. The greatest opposition came from the "veteran" women, who had been in the country all of eight years; they could not imagine that an American girl would do the hard physical work required.

Source: Golda Meir, "From Milwaukee to Merhaviyah, 1921: 'They Couldn't Imagine an American Girl Would Do the Work,'" in *Builders and Dreamers: Habonim Labor Zionist Youth in America,* eds. J. J. Goldberg and Eliot King (New York: Herzl Press and Cornwall Books, 1993), 42–43. Reprinted by permission of Herzl Press.

  1. Morris Meyerson was Golda Meir's husband. For additional information on their relationship, see Anita Shapira's article in this volume.

Despite the rejection, we were invited to come to Merhaviyah for two or three days so that the members could look us over. I well remember my first day's work. It was the threshing season, and they told me to "sit" on the board of the threshing machine that revolved in the barn and threshed the grain. My efforts at work did not make as great impression on the young men as the phonograph and records we brought with us. It was the first time anyone had arrived with a hornless phonograph, which aroused general admiration. Of course, they would have been happy to accept the phonograph as a dowry without the bride who owned it, but we would not agree to that. They finally accepted us after a third meeting of the whole *kvuzah*. After that, I had been careful not to make any slip expected of an American girl.

I forced myself to eat every kind of food or dish, even if it was hard to look at, let alone swallow. The food generally had a most unpleasant taste because of the oil we bought from the Arabs; it was not refined, kept in leather bags and bitter as gall, but it was the base for all of our dishes.

Every month a different member took her turn in the kitchen. Conditions were so grueling that two weeks before her turn came around, the girl in question would generally become depressed. With plain common sense I decided to take things as they came, including kitchen duty. I never considered work in the kitchen demeaning.

In those days we drank from enamel mugs, which looked fine and shiny so long as they were new, but after a while began to chip and rust and became repulsive. I decided to stop buying these mugs, although we sometimes reached a state when we were left with two or three glasses, from which we drank in turn. For the whole *kvuzah* I bought nothing but glass.

Another "bourgeois" feature I introduced into out *kvuzah* was a white sheet spread as a tablecloth on Friday night, with a vase of wild flowers—that adornment gave us a bad name throughout the Emek [Jezreel Valley]. I also insisted on ironing my dress or blouse carefully. This was also viewed as a "bourgeois" weakness.

The farm was not particularly well developed, and we lived mainly on work for the Jewish National Fund,[2] digging holes for planting trees. The holes naturally had to be dug in a rocky hill and be dug deep enough to hold their shape. After a day's work of this kind, I used to long to wash and have a rest. But I overcame such desires and went to help in the kitchen, though I was so tired that an ordinary fork seemed to weigh a ton. But you get used even to such hard work.

2. The Jewish National Fund, known in Hebrew as the Keren Kayemet Leyisrael, was created in 1901 by the Fifth Zionist Congress for the purpose of purchasing and developing land in Palestine to be held in trust in behalf of the Jewish people.

Chapter 19

Memories of Rose Luria Halprin

Ruth Halprin Kaslove

(Norwalk, Connecticut, 1999)

I am the daughter of Rose Luria Halprin.[1] Mother was, and remained, a brilliant and a beautiful woman throughout her lifetime. She was a great teacher and an ardent Zionist. As a young child and as the oldest of seven children, the first four of whom were girls, Mother was sent by her father to study in a *heder*. She would tell how often she asked questions and was rewarded by having her knuckles rapped for being too eager to question "why?" Her ability to question, to challenge and to voice her opinion no matter how it may have opposed that of other leaders, remained throughout her life. And throughout her life, Mother remained a staunch and committed Zionist.

When I was very young she took me everywhere, before, during and after her first stint as national president of Hadassah—to Palestine and to Basle, Switzerland for the Zionist Congress. However, I never heard her speak to an audience until she was elected president of Hadassah for the second time. By then, I was a member of Hashomer Hazair which, I am sure, caused her grief. I was awed by her strength, articulate voice and phenomenal thought process.

Rosie was an extraordinary thinker, and her opinions were sought out by David Ben-Gurion, Chaim Weizmann, Golda Meir and others who remained staunch friends despite their disagreements. She conveyed her opinions honestly and forthrightly with her peers in the Jewish Agency or the Confederation of General Zionists.[2] Nevertheless her opinions were

1. Rose Luria Halprin (1896–1978) was a prominent American Zionist leader and national president of Hadassah. She served on the American Section of the Jewish Agency Executive and was also an officer of the American Zionist Emergency Council during World War II. For more information on Hadassah, see the chapters by Mary McCune, Esther Carmel-Hakim, and Mira Katzburg-Yungman in this volume.

2. Confederation of General Zionists, a centrist Zionist coalition that espoused neither socialist nor right-wing principles, but rather identified with mainstream Jewish middle-class values. The General Zionists grew to become the dominant political force in American Zionism under Louis D. Brandeis (1856–1941), Stephen S. Wise (1874–1949), Louis Lipsky (1876–1963), Abba Hillel Silver (1893–1963), and Henrietta Szold (1860–1945).

respected if not always agreed with and not always admired in the days before women's liberation. She was a great teacher and a Zionist through and through. She was a leader who played a historic role at a dark moment in time. Most particularly for me and my generation, Rosie was a shining light in a world recuperating from madness.

In 1945, Mother was part of the delegation that carried gruesome evidence of the inhumanity of the Nazi Third Reich to San Francisco where the United Nations was first convened. She, along with Moshe Shertok (later Sharett) and other members of the Executive Committee of the Jewish Agency, carried bars of soap, a wallet, a lampshade and other unspeakable and gruesome evidence to make the world face the inhuman treatment accorded to Jews under Hitler—and to plead the cause for a Jewish homeland in Palestine.

Mother served on the American section of the Jewish Agency for Palestine. She was the only woman to serve on the Agency until long after the State of Israel was established. When the State of Israel was born, the offices at 16 East 66th Street in New York City became the Consulate General of the State of Israel. Part, of the time, Mother served as the Jewish Agency's treasurer. Later, Mother served as chairman of the American section of the Jewish Agency.

I worked at the Jewish Agency, from 1947 through 1951, before Israel's statehood and after it became the official Consulate General office. I was part of the consular staff. By tacit agreement, no one on staff knew I was Rosie's daughter except for Arthur Lourie,[3] Abba Eban,[4] and Teddy Kollek.[5] Teddy Kollek was my "boss." Unfortunately, I was the one who received the telegram informing us that Mickey Marcus,[6] commander of the Jerusalem forces of the Haganah in the War of Independence, had

3. Arthur Lourie (1903–1978), a Zionist diplomat and protégé of Chaim Weizmann (see note 56 in this section), who later served as Israel's ambassador to Canada (1957–1959) and Great Britain (1960–1965).
4. Abba Eban (1915–2002), a premier Israeli statesman and diplomat who was a protégé of Chaim Weizmann (see chapter 22, note 14) and David Ben-Gurion (1886–1973). He rose through the political ranks to become Israel's first ambassador to the United Nations as well as foreign minister and deputy prime minister.
5. Teddy Kollek (b. 1911), a Haganah leader (see "Haganah" in the glossary), who later became an important Israeli public figure and served as the mayor of Jerusalem from 1965 to 1993.
6. David Daniel "Mickey" Marcus (1902–1948), a trained American soldier and lawyer, hailed from New York City. Throughout the 1930s and 1940s, he served in various official capacities in New York City as well as the U.S. military. In 1947, he retired from the army with the rank of colonel and returned to private legal practice. In 1948, at the suggestion of Haganah representatives in the United States, Marcus was called to Palestine to serve as David Ben-Gurion's personal military advisor. In May 1948, he was appointed commander of the Jerusalem front. He was the first officer to attain the rank of brigadier general

been killed by one of the Haganah soldiers because he did not have the night's password.

In the early 1930's, Mother, my father and I moved to Jerusalem where Mother worked closely with Henrietta Szold.[7] Ms. Szold was living at the old Eden Hotel in Jerusalem and, in addition to working with Mother at the Hadassah office on Ben-Yehudah Street, Ms. Szold was a frequent visitor to our home. I often was a visitor to both the office and to Ms. Szold's rooms at the Eden Hotel. Mother's work included both the design for the building of the "new" hospital on Mt. Scopus and, most especially, Hadassah's work with Youth Aliyah, beginning in 1943. On a few occasions, I accompanied Ms. Szold, Mother and Hans Beyth[8] . . . when they went to the port of Haifa to welcome ships with Youth Aliyah youngsters escaping from the Nazis. Rosie spoke German, Hebrew, and French. She told us their stories, and how whenever she spoke to these frightened and lonely youngsters, someone in the group would invariably ask *"Van kompt muti?"* [Yiddish: "When is mother coming?"]. It was, she said, a repetitive refrain, and it was dreadful to hear and to know the answer—never.

In 1936 or 1937, Mother was sent by Ms. Szold to Germany. She traveled by ship to Italy and then, I believe, by train from Naples to Berlin. I learned the following story some forty years later: Mother sat in a compartment when a man boarded the train in Rome saying goodbye to his friends in Italian. When the compartment emptied out, he suddenly said to Mother in German, "You are an American and probably a Jew." When she asked him how he knew, he looked at her luggage and said "from the labels on your luggage." At the time, she was reading Youth Aliyah papers, and he questioned wasn't she afraid to be going into Germany rather than in the opposite direction. She said he was quite clear that this was a very bad time for her to be traveling into Nazi Germany. As an American, Mother had never been afraid before, but she tore up all other notes on Youth Aliyah and Hadassah. Arriving in Berlin, she did not know where to go to find anyone meeting her—when, suddenly a

---

in Israel's fledgling army. On June 11, 1948, he was tragically killed by a sentry in friendly fire incident outside of military headquarters in Abu Ghosh. Mishmar David, a Judean settlement, is named in his memory.

7. Henrietta Szold (1860-1945), the founder of Hadassah and director of the Zionist Organization's Youth Aliyah division, was a major force in American Zionism. For further discussion of Szold, see the chapters in this volume by Allon Gal, Mira Katzburg-Yungman, and Mary McCune.

8. Hans Beyth (1901-1947), a German Zionist youth leader, worked closely with Henrietta Szold as an assistant director of Youth Aliyah. He was killed by Arab attackers in December 1947.

woman appeared surreptitiously carrying a picture of Henrietta Szold. She was the Jewish contact who took her to a small *pension* [hotel], helped her settle in, then told her she would call in the morning and would start the conversation in a special way to identity herself so Mother would know she had legitimate contact. After the woman left the phone rang and Rosie was told that she would find three carnations on the front desk—the card and the flowers were from the Warburg family,[9] but she was to tear the card to shreds.

At the time, Youth Aliyah was a permissible organization under tight scrutiny by the Gestapo. Mother spent a week in Berlin on Youth Aliyah, but she was not taken around by anyone—they told her to travel alone to various Jewish neighborhoods where it was suggested she visit where doors were left open for her. She found children in these apartments who had been gathered to make the trip to Palestine. To find her way back to Berlin, she asked one of the Jewish women returning to Berlin if she could join her—the woman was petrified at the prospect of being seen with an American woman. Needless to say, they went their separate ways.

During that same week, Mother went to an area about three quarters of an hour outside Berlin where some of the children were being trained for their transfer to Palestine. Again, she took public transportation alone because no one wanted to be seen accompanying her. SS officers shared her train compartment. Since she did not have exact direction to the area, she often found herself fearing to ask directions to the Jewish camps. Mother admitted, when she told us the story years later, that the fear generated from going into and returning from these areas was not pleasant. One night when she returned to the *pension,* she found a note on her pillow telling her the Gestapo was closing in on her and it was suggested she leave immediately. She did. Interestingly, the rumor being circulated in Jerusalem while Mother was in Germany was that my parents were getting a divorce! I remember rushing to my father in a panic. He reassured me it was untrue but to allow people to talk and I would find out the truth later. Later turned out to be almost forty years.

Rosie was in Palestine at the Vaad Hapoel [Executive Committee] of the Jewish Agency meeting on April 13, 1948, when the convoy of Hadassah doctors and nurses was ambushed going up to Mt. Scopus. She was then national president of Hadassah for the second time. Upon her return to the United States, she was scheduled to speak in Brooklyn. When she finished telling the story of the convoy, of the deaths of beloved

9. The reference is presumably to Felix (1871–1937) and Frieda (1876–1958) Warburg, prominent non-Zionist leaders and members of the American Jewish elite, who promoted and supported Jewish nation-building efforts in pre-state Palestine.

doctors and nurses, of the destruction of the hospital she had been responsible for helping to build, people threw money from the balcony and from the floor onto the stage. She later told us, "I talked about destruction, and the Hadassah members were saying 'we will build again'—and we did.'"

Mother was truly an *eshet hayil* [woman of valor]—with the brainpower to cut through the verbiage to its essential points, an uncanny ability to speak extemporaneously but directly to the issue, with great insight into issues and using language in a beautiful and meaningful way. She was often told she thought like a man, which made us in the family laugh—since we knew she thought much more succinctly than most men!

To quote my Mother: "Sometimes a monument marks the work and achievement of one who labored long and well in a great and worthy cause. Sometimes a book tells the tale of a life and the deeds that destiny wished it. Sometimes the story is written in the hearts and minds of the generations which witnessed it unfolding." Rosie's life encompassed all three. . . .

Chapter 20

Coming of Age in *Kibbutz*

Irma "Rama" (Levy) Lindheim

(Kibbutz Mishmar Haemek, 1954)

Not everyone can boast of remembering his own birth, [. . .] but I remember [. . .] that important occasion, twenty-one years ago. More than that, I have a prenatal recollection, which extends back far enough to remember a previous birth, more than sixty years ago, when I came to life in a wealthy, German Jewish home in New York City. . . .

That [earlier] event took place at a time when the United States was entering into a new phase of its history. It began to look then as though its period of hard struggle was coming to an end and its golden age was dawning. "Progress" seemed as inevitable as life itself and there seemed to be nothing for America to do but to get richer and richer.

Jews who had emigrated to the United States from Germany after 1848 shared in this prosperity, and a process of assimilation set in which made the rich Jews, in proportion to their riches, melt into the "melting pot" of this, their Promised Land. Toward the Jewish people, as such, the rich Jews of this period felt little or no responsibility and they disassociated themselves entirely from any idea of Jewish race or nationhood. After fulfilling their obligations to provide for the poor amongst them, they felt no further obligations as Jews, save to appear at their "Temples" on Rosh Hashanah and Yom Kippur; and to send their children to "Sunday School."

It was into this completely negative kind of Jewish life that I was born and was raised, and when I was old enough to think for myself I repudiated any affiliation with it. . . . I refused to accept being a Jew merely because I was born one. . . .

But even if, after serious enquiry, I found no positive values in Jewish life, neither was I finding them in the life of America. The pioneer values of America had always been very real to me, and yet I found myself having to raise my children in an atmosphere that gave these values no expression. "Success" was the purpose of the life of America—success interpreted [. . .] as money.

Into this life came the dynamic stream of Zionism . . . No longer was life without purpose; no longer was Jewishness a negative, outworn faith; no longer was the world I lived in a world that had reached completion—everything lay ahead. A world was to be built; a society was to be changed; and in the vanguard of this change and pioneering the way, were Jews—my people.

From then on I chose to be a Jew.

Small wonder then, that as this new life developed within me, that I rejected the passive kind of Zionism . . . help build a home in Palestine for others to live in. Zionism was to me not an organization—but a civilization, a way of life to be lived, and I longed to live it. And for many years . . . I groped for a way to express the new civilization of Zionism in action. . . .

And so it was that, after thirteen years of search, experiment, and gestation, a life was born in Kibbutz Mishmar Haemek that now has reached its maturity.

Consciously and with eyes wide open I was born into the world of *kibbutz*. Nothing seemed hard for me. I was like one in love. *Pishpushim* [flies] invaded my first *zrif* [cabin] and I waged a mighty and successful war against them with FLIT[1]—America's greatest contribution to the new social order of *kibbutz*.

A wooden floor in my *zrif* that resisted my best efforts to scrub it clean—making more *boz* [mud] the more I scrubbed it—finally conquered, and no feeling of triumph could surpass mine when I learned to clean that floor without leaving any mud-puddles behind.

The shower in a corrugated tin hut where the water would stop running just at the moment you were nicely soaped up, didn't bother me in the least—it was fun when the *haverot* [comrades] would come . . . and would douse me with pails of water. And the nightly walks in the pouring rain—two, three, four times when dysentery struck—this was just something else to overcome. And no matter the distance, no matter the cold and wet, no matter anything—this was *hagshamah azmit* [self-fulfillment] and, at long last, I had discovered the kind of world I had been searching for. And in it I was happier than I had ever been.

At this time Mishmar Haemek was not the place that it is today. Then, with the exception of one real building—the children's house—there were only *zrifim* [tents], tarpaper huts and a *dining room*!

It was then that I worked in the kitchen . . . peeling potatoes and I used to sit on a box half in and half out of the building—and half in and half out of the *boz*!

---

1. The reference is to a popular American commercial bug repellent used to kill flies and mosquitoes.

A cake I had learned to bake at this time was very much in demand for people with special diets. (At that time, the budget for food per person was three-and-a-half piastres a day, so only people with special diets got cake!) For this cake I needed raisins, so I asked the *ekonomiyah* [kitchen manager] where I could find the raisins. She did not know—no one knew—so I went in search of them in the no-man's-land of the provisional storeroom.

In this storeroom boxes were piled on top of barrels; sacks were piled on top of boxes; and *pahim* [crates] were piled on top of sacks. And it was on the top of this perilous Everest of a mountain that I was forced to climb in my search, until, after having braved the dangers of an avalanche and a broken neck, I found—hidden in a biscuit tin on the top of the pile—at its very peak—*the raisins*! And the cake was baked.

A triumph! Every obstacle provided me with the joy of overcoming it. Like when I was told to plant garlic in the garden and I planted it, as I thought, according to instructions—fifteen centimeters apart and in a straight line. Only that night did I remember being told that I was to plant the small end of the garlic down—and then the nightmares began! I dreamed that I planted the down side up and that the roots grew up in the air and waved around in the breeze—and that the *kibbutz* would have to do without its garlic because of me. It was only a dream, but when the garlic grew, as it should have—nice and white and plump and fragrant—and the *haverim* [members] said it was the best garlic ever, it was an occasion for me—and another triumph!

Everything was wonderful! Even in the afternoons, at the end of the day's work when the back started to ache and it was a little hard to straighten up after picking beans or weeding carrots. It was *davkah* [in spite of obstacles] then that I made a great discovery! I found that bending down could be exciting for, when I bent down and looked between my legs the colors of the sunset on the mountains took on shades of purple, and rose, and blue such as I had never seen or dreamt of.

With all the work it was the same, especially the tree nursery.[2] It was thrilling and seemed like a miracle to me that trees—big trees such as grew in the forest—should grow from the tiny seeds we planted. And when the seeds would sprout just a few days after we planted them, and I would run my hand over their tender green shoots, then I would get ecstatic, because they felt exactly like a baby's hair.

2. In this period, tree nurseries were often the special purview of Zionist women pioneers, known in Hebrew as *haluzot*. For extensive discussion of the role of tree nurseries in the training and acclimation of Zionist women pioneers in pre-state Israeli society, see *The Plough Women: Records of the Pioneer Women of Palestine. A Critical Edition*, eds. Mark A. Raider and Miriam B. Raider-Roth (Hanover and London: University Press of New England, 2002).

The vineyard was my favorite though. It was intoxicating to work there in the springtime and tie up the new tendrils of the vines so that they should not run wild, but [be] trained in the way that they should go. It was a little hard though not to steal off too much time to look out over the Emek [Jezreel Valley], and to grow ecstatic over Mount Hermon, a cloud that looked like a great, white object suspended from nowhere. . . .

All the work seemed good to me. Picking the apricots and the peaches with their sun-warmed globes of rosy-cheeked gold and the bronzed Santa Rosas. It had the rhythm of a dance—arms raised to pick—lowered—and then raised again. And I used to wonder as I picked, why in California, picking was considered "black" labor and given only to the "foreigners" to do. And why more people had not discovered that work—even the most menial work—could be a creative experience and could bring about self-realization, if it is done with conscious purpose.

To have this in principle as the *haluz* creed was different than experiencing it in practice. In the mornings, when I would write—usually in the forest—I dug deep in my earlier life. I tried to uncover the forces, which had not only been strong enough to uproot me and impel me to change worlds but had created this new kind of *kibbutz* world into which I had been transplanted and where the simplest work could release a flow of creative energy.

Only now, since I have reached "old age" in *kibbutz,* have I been able to analyze and to understand the deep necessity, which made me take the first steps away from my life at Glen Cove, Long Island, and . . . [toward] a *kibbutz* on the slopes of Mt. Ephraim. In the environment of Glen Cove, Zionism was a completely strange and foreign manifestation and yet—without knowing "how" or "why" I had been forced into its stream. And surely not because of any economic necessity, nor any discrimination that I had experienced as a Jew.

What was it then—this force that singled out individuals in families and forced them to act counter to their traditions, their social groupings, and seemingly their best interests—even their closest ties?

At the time it seemed to me that my conversion to Zionism was caused by the workings of an outside force which compelled me from within and from without and went through a period of intense mysticism. Now I know better, and I understand how the contradiction between life as I saw it around me, and life as I wanted it to be, had set up in me a resistance to my environment so strong that the dynamic to change became irresistible.

At thirteen I had been passionately Jewish but the deep emotional desire I had had to dedicate my life to my people was frustrated by the negations of a Jewish life empty of meanings. Later, when I began to bear children and demanded a better world for them to be raised in than I found around me, my drive to action was blocked by the assurance around me that this was the best possible of all worlds.

In a world of individualism I craved for a group to function . . . was filled with fear of the softening effect of our environment of luxury and ease which could unfit my children for the new kind of world that I was convinced was coming. All of these drives together, I can see now, were the deep inner necessities which attracted me into the Zionist movement as steel is attracted to a magnet.

It was a kind of class-consciousness in reverse. As the exploited feel the need to fight and change the conditions which lead to the exploitation of themselves and their children, so I was impelled by necessity to change the pattern of life which threatened the future of myself and my children. In the America of that period no echo of progressive action reached me, and when Zionism came into my life, it came as a great liberating force, which revolutionized me and my world.

But within the Zionist movement I found that, there, also there were contradictions. The thesis was great. At first, in 1917, when I entered the movement, it looked as though Zionism was to be a step in the direction of the millennium. Justice was to be built into the foundations of the Jewish state and Jew and Arab, workers and capitalists, all alike were to benefit by the equality to reign in the Land of Israel. Cooperation was to replace competition; there were to be no exploiters and exploited and no classes. For the Jew had been made to suffer throughout his history and in this—his renaissance—he would establish a rule where none would be discriminated against, and where none would have to suffer.

The rebuilding of the Jewish nation was not to institute just another "nationalism," but was to incorporate into its structure, and to transmute into its laws and social forms, the justice of the prophetic teachings. The Jewish homeland was to be an example to the world, and the law was to go forth from Zion.

It was in these days that the individual Zionist grew big—bigger than he knew how to be. Lifted out of the small provincialism of his life and imbued with the greatness of Zionist purpose, he took on new proportions and as a personality, became enlarged.

No longer was he just a single, insignificant unit struggling alone against the counter current of American life that forced him to swim hard or sink. As a member of the Zionist group, and no longer just an individual, he derived the strength not to struggle any longer against the stream but as a Jew with other Jews, to go with it, and be himself. It was as a member of a group that the Zionist Jew felt himself big and grown to a new stature—as a part of the group's collective strength that he gained the power to speak as a representative of his people and could talk as an equal to governments, and in the council of nations.

But then, into this garden of men I saw a serpent crawl, tempting with his wares. To these newly inspired individualists he displayed the contradictions between the "idealism" of the Zionists and the "realities" of the homeland in Palestine. He showed the attractiveness of the "American way;" the "opportunities" in this newly opened land; the benefits of "private initiative;" of anti-unionism; and anti-socialism; and the need of making the Land of Israel over in the image of America.

And less and less was the *haluz* held up to the eyes of the world as the pattern of the new Jew. And the *kibbutz*, which had been presented proudly as a demonstration of the social justice to be built into the new society, came to be spoken of with condescension as a form, useful in the pioneer stage of the building, but outdated now. . . .

And I examined what had happened to both men and women—leaders in the Zionist organizations of America—when they came to Israel with the intention of settling here, where there was no Zionist movement of which they could be a part—only parties. No longer were they enlarged by the power conveyed to them by their contact with others working towards the same ends as they; and no longer did they feel themselves big— bigger than they knew how to be. Tragically, they felt themselves disconnected from their source of their power, and shrank—shrank to a size smaller than they remembered how to be—and left Israel to seek again the strength of their group affiliation. . . .

At this point I made a discovery. I saw in perspective that *kibbutz*—as a form of collective group living—was destined to be a permanent form of social grouping for the future. I realized now that in the group lay the strength of the individual; and that it was in his contact with the group that the individual became invested with the strength of the collective, and grew to be bigger than he, functioning alone, knew how to be. I discovered that, as electricity requires a direct circuit to conduct its power, so the group, in society, is essential, in order that the energy to create may be conducted to each and every individual, instead of only to the individually gifted ones.

And I saw how in *kibbutz*, this power was conveyed to its members through their work—any kind of work—because each part of the work was a part of the pattern as a whole, and in the consciousness of the bigness of the whole, each derived his satisfactions. . . .

And I asked myself how was it possible that an individual could organize a life for himself and his children where jobs, shelter, education and cultural enjoyment, and security for young and old could be assured in the present and future? How but through the group could men and women feel themselves *effective* parts—no matter how minute the part— the building of a state, or within the state or the world—of being able to mould a society to meet their own needs and beliefs?

And because I made this discovery and found that collective living *could* give the individual the opportunity to develop to his full capacity; that it *could* have people live and work together in peace; and *could* develop a real comradeship between its members, these twenty-one years of life in *kibbutz* have filled me with a great enthusiasm and faith in *kibbutz* and its role in the future. . . .

Chapter 21

Life in a Religious *Kibbutz*

Yocheved Herschlag Muffs

(New York, New York, 1999)

In early July 1947, I set sail on the *Marine Car,* an unreconverted troop ship from World War II. Destination: British [Mandatory] Palestine and to *kibbutz,* where I planned to spend the rest of my life. The ship was headed to Beirut, Haifa, and Alexandria, and the passengers were a mixed multitude.

I was a member of Hashomer Hadati [The Religious Guard], a religious Zionist *kibbutz*[–oriented youth] movement. After a year and a half at [New York University], I quit college and went to the movement's . . . *hakhsharah.* Some of us stayed at the farm for a year and a half, waiting for British visas to get us to Palestine. It was not easy to get to British Mandate Palestine. The British were issuing few immigration certificates and very few temporary visas. A group of us had already started to plan to get to Europe, join with [World War II] Displaced Persons, get on a ship that was bound to be taken over by the British, and be taken to a detention camp in Cypress.

Luckily, in the summer of 1947, the Hebrew University was planning to hold a conference of Hebrew teachers, and, I think, the first world conference of Jewish studies that summer. In order to attend, however, one needed a visa—good for two or three months. But in order to obtain a visa from the British government you had to prove you were indeed a Hebrew teacher. Well, I wasn't, so I called my childhood friend, Miriam Zirin, secretary of the newly created *yeshivah* of Central Queens in Jamaica, New York, where I grew up. "Miriam, help me."

Miriam consulted with her mother, a wonderful woman who said, "to go to *Erez Israel* you can lie." So Miriam typed a letter on official Yeshivah of Central Queens stationery saying that I was the librarian of the *yeshivah,* sent by them to the conference. The day I heard my visa had come through, my friend Rahel and I danced a *hora* in the middle of Grand Central Station.

My parents drove me to the pier on Manhattan's West Side. Those were the days when mighty liners crossed the oceans and traveling by plane was relatively rare. My mother was able to get on board ship with me for a few minutes before we departed (set sail). The facilities: almost all the girls and women were in rooms that held twenty-six double-decker bunks—while the 150 boys/men traveled in the hold. A few cabins had only six bunks that must have been officers' quarters during the war. I will not describe other facilities except to say that the *Marine Car* was not a luxury ship. My mother didn't say anything while we were on board, but when we disembarked we walked a few blocks to a Woolworth 5-and-10, where she bought a little money pouch, put my money in it and said, "Put it in your bra."

We reached Haifa two weeks later, a day after the *Exodus* arrived. The nine *haverim* [comrades] in our *garin* [pioneering settlement group] were steered to a special customs official because it was a little peculiar to come to Jerusalem for two or three months with a dozen pairs of dungarees. Somehow, this particular official asked no questions. Leaving the port we went to Tnuvah,[1] a very simple workers' luncheonette, for a cup of coffee. No sooner had we sat down, when two young men dashed in and ran out the back door. About a minute later, in came two British policemen looking around and asking questions. And like the three monkeys, no one said anything; no one knew anything. Afterwards, we left through the back door of the luncheonette and saw that it opened up to a big yard from which many trucks were leaving to *kibuzim* and other areas, outside Haifa.

It was obvious to us that those two men must have been illegal immigrants—we were only semi-legal—and were being spirited away from the British.

That evening we stayed in Haifa. The room had . . . a *mirpeset* [balcony]. We opened the door to the *mirpeset* to watch the strange sight of British armored cars riding up and down the streets. One of the *haverim* who had come from South Africa and who was accompanying us pulled us back. "It's dangerous," he said. "*Ozer* [stop]—there's a curfew!" And so I learned a brand new Hebrew word.

The following day we went to Kibbutz Ein Hanaziv in the Beit Shean valley. It was a new *kibbutz,* part of [the] Kibbutz Hadati [movement]. There we were met by others from the [United] States who had preceded

1. Tnuvah, a national dairy cooperative established by the Palestine labor movement, operated a network of workers' kitchens and restaurants in the Yishuv's urban centers.

us and by several *haverim* from South Africa. We constituted a *garin* and would be there until we could start our own *kvuzah*. That very first evening we studied rabbinic texts on the question: Is Beit Shean *halakhically* [English variant of the term meaning "lawfully," according to rabbinic code] part of *Erez Israel*? It was exciting to see a reality to the motto of the movement: "*Torah veavodah*."[2] I must admit that I don't remember what the answer was, but I remember learning it, or at least being there.

Shortly after that we went on a *tiyul* [trip], to get to know, see and touch *Erez Israel*. We traveled to Metulah on the northern border, and stopped at Tel Hai where [Yosef] Trumpeldor[3] fell calling out: "*Tov lamut bead hamoledet*."[4] We traveled south to Jerusalem and I was immediately captivated. I even had the sacrilegious thought that if I ever left *kibbutz*— an unthinkable idea—I would like to live in Jerusalem. There I also learned something very important, even before the siege of Jerusalem. You never left the faucet running. Jerusalem had always had a water shortage, and water was always "recycled." For example, first you washed the dishes, then the floor, and then you flushed the toilet, all with the same pail of water. For years afterwards I would go around shutting off faucets.

We went to the *kotel*, the Western Wall [of the Temple mount in Jerusalem]. There was a space ten feet wide for people to congregate, pray, and meditate between the Wall and the houses in front of it. There was no *mehizah* [ritual barrier], no separation of men and women. On one side of the Wall a booth stood with British police who checked identity cards, a new and unpleasant experience for me, and on the other side were the steps to the mosque where the *muezzin* [Muslim clerics] called faithful Muslims to prayer. Images to last a lifetime. It was time to go back to Ein Hanaziv and to work.

Except for a short period when I worked in the clothing room darning socks (I was recovering from the results of some rather primitive sanitary conditions during our *tiyul*), my place in the *kibbutz* was in the kitchen. I

---

2. The Hebrew phrase literally means "A life of Torah and labor." However, *avodah* is also the Hebrew term for "worship," and thus the slogan implicitly refers to the transformation of Jewish life in toto.

3. Yosef Trumpeldor (1880–1920), a Russian socialist Zionist pioneer leader, was killed in March 1920 during an Arab attack on the outpost of Tel Hai in the Upper Galilee. There is a scholarly debate about the veracity of the legendary account of Yosef Trumpeldor's death in battle, which became an important symbol of the Yishuv and the Zionist movement in the pre-state era.

4. This Hebrew phrase means "It is good to die for the homeland." Yosef Hayim Brenner (1881–1921), the important Second Aliyah writer, popularized this apocryphal statement that became a rallying cry of Zionist youth in the early decades of the twentieth century.

was a cook, a "bottle washer," and later in our own *kibbutz,* the kitchen manager. We cooked on Primus stoves. I think they were originally from Sweden. They are about a foot high and use kerosene. If you are cooking for a few hundred people and use pots that are rather big (some of them big enough to put a child into), you needed several Primus stoves to put under each pot. So the metal shop constructed stands to put the pots on and under which we would put two, three stoves.

The dishes—some years ago, Bloomingdales was promoting chi-chi summer picnic dishes. They were enamel-covered tin plates. Those were the dishes that we used, not for picnics, but for all the time. Each table in the *kibbutz* dining hall seated about eight people. We each had a plate, a cup and a tablespoon. And there was one knife for the table. (Years later, I saw a cartoon by Dosh[5] in which he showed the *kibbutz* dining table with a knife chained to the table.)

The meal might consist of sardines and then tomato soup and then chocolate pudding—all eaten with the same spoon and from the same dish.

At the beginning we had potatoes. Then we had dehydrated potatoes (not very good). I think they were from the British. And they went too. Then we had no potatoes. But no one ever starved. No one went hungry. As a matter of fact, all the girls gained weight. There was an institution called *arukhat eser,* ten o'clock tea. They still have it. It consisted of watery tea and bread and jam. The bread was delicious. To make the jam go further, we (the kitchen staff) took a large tin of jam, added flour to it, and then diluted it with water. The jam went a long way. You can see why you didn't lose weight.

Except for a small generator for the refrigerator, there was no electricity in the entire *kibbutz.* The lighting for all over was with kerosene lamps, and in the dining room, there was a bright light called [in Hebrew] a *lux.* The dining room also served as the *beit knesset* [synagogue]. The tables were the *mehizah.* The men sat on one side of the table, the women on the other side. The *davening* [praying], especially on Friday night, was beautiful.

Shortly after we got back from our *tiyul,* we were approached by the Jewish Agency. They needed American passports for . . . whatever. I had no intention of ever returning to the United States, so I gave them my passport. Maybe one day I'll find out who used it. Meanwhile we were busy living, working in the kitchen, doing all kinds of things. I stood guard on the watchtower. (I was okay climbing up the ladder, but was

5. Dosh, the pseudonym of a popular contemporary Israeli satirist and cartoonist Kariel Gardosh (1921–2000).

always afraid climbing down.) I learned how to shoot rifles, how to throw grenades, and how to crawl in trenches. I learned the names of the parts of a rifle in Hebrew before I ever knew what they were in English.

November 29, 1947, was the day the United Nations voted to partition Palestine. Everyone stood around the radio, anxiously listening to the vote. We listened on an illegal band called Kol Hagalil, the Voice of the [Galilee]. The station would identify itself by playing a few bars of the Palmah anthem and then call out, "*Zeh kol hagalil, zeh kol hagalil . . .*" ["This is the voice of the Galilee"]. That evening, we gathered in the dining hall, pushed all the chairs and tables aside and, with great joy and vigor, danced *horas* for hours. At that time, in religious *kibuzim* males and females danced *horas,* other Israeli dances and polkas together. The guard was doubled that night and for good reason.

The war was about to begin. In the following months we were to end up in the trenches in Ein Hanaziv many times. On *Tanit Esther* [the Fast of Esther], the day before Purim,[6] the area was under attack by Palestinian Arabs and forces from Arab countries. We were in the trenches and word came from Tirat Zvi, another religious *kibbutz* two settlements down toward the Jordan River. Because they had a sausage factory, they had a *mashgiah* [supervisor of dietary law], a rabbi. And he said that even though it was a fast day, we were in the middle of a battle, and no one was to fast. By evening the fighting had quieted down, but we were still in the trenches. It was Purim evening when you are supposed to hear the *megillah* [the Scroll of Esther]. So group by group, we crawled into the dining hall. We listened to the *megillah* in silence. Then we left, crawling back to the trenches. Each group had at least ten males—to make a *minyan* [ritual quorum]—plus a number of females.

Note: Bahurim [boys]? Guys? Men? Girls? Women? *Bahurot* [girls]? What to call us—we were all 20, 21, 25, 27. I don't think anyone was older than that.

There were different degrees of being "on alert." There were always *haverim* on guard duty, circling the perimeter of the *kibbutz,* watching from the tower. When the probability of attack was high, we slept with our clothes on. And when the probability was imminent, we slept with our shoes on as well. My assignment during attacks was as a *razah* [a messenger]. And if you are running along in trenches, head bent down, sooner or later your glasses are going to fall off. So I learned a trick—to tie them behind, and they stayed on. Once, running in the trenches to

6. Purim, a Jewish holiday derived from the Book of Esther, celebrates the deliverance of the Jews of Persia from a plot by Haman to kill them.

deliver supplies to one of the outposts, a *haver* called out, "Yocheved, get your fanny down!" I learned fast. Another time, I had to take ammunition and some food to an outpost at the edge of the *kibbutz* that bordered on a government agricultural experimental station. I was given a message to take back: "*Yesh rishrush bapardes*" [Hebrew: "There's a rustling noise in the orchard"]. Well, my Hebrew was improving, but there were words I didn't know. I knew what *yesh* meant—"there is." I knew what *pardes* meant—"grove" or "orchard." I didn't know what *rishrush* meant. But I knew that my responsibility was just to get to the message back. Crawling back, I figured out *rishrush* has to be an onomatopoeia. It sounds like *raash*—noise. It must mean rustling. "There's rustling in the orchard." That indeed was the message and I delivered it.

It wasn't all war, it wasn't all crawling in trenches. Ein Hanaziv means the spring of the *naziv* [column] and right outside of the *kibbutz* was a spring where we swam.[7] It also served as the *mikvah* [bath for ritual immersion]. One day we were swimming, and Galilit, who was originally from Lodz, started to drown. Now when I was fifteen, I earned a junior lifesaving certificate at John Adams High School in Queens, and here I was twenty and my certificate had expired. But I had to do something. So I went to save her—and I did. But I realized later that I saved her the wrong way. The official way, which makes absolute sense, is to dive under the water and grab the drowning person from behind, by the ankles, work your way up, get your arm around the upper part and haul the person in. You don't go head-on, because people who are drowning flay around and strike out—and everybody drowns. Right way, wrong way, I saved her, but for days afterward I was so depressed: what if I hadn't?

For the *kibbutz*, for the Yishuv, there were periods of "normalcy," periods of joy, and periods of anxiety, depression and fear. Early in 1948, Gush Ezion, a bloc of four *kibuzim* including Kfar Ezion, was besieged. The *gush* [bloc] was situated between Bethlehem and Hebron, and, according to the Partition Plan was not to be included in Jewish Palestine. And from Jerusalem, thirty-five young men, mostly students from the Hebrew University, fully backpacked with supplies, started to hike through from Jerusalem to Kfar Ezion. They were discovered and they were killed. Our *haver*, Moshe Avigdor Pearlstein,[8] was one of the thirty-five, the

---

7. In fact, Ein Hanaziv was named after Rabbi Naphtali Zvi Judah Berlin (1817–1893), head of the Volozhin *yeshivah* and a Hibbat Zion leader known by the acronym "Hanaziv."
8. Moshe Avigdor Pearlstein (1925?–1948) was raised in Brooklyn, New York, where he became active in Hashomer Hadati. He studied at the Hebrew University of Jerusalem in 1946–47 and was killed by Arab attackers while en route to Gush Ezion.

"Lamed Hei."[9] A few weeks after Purim, Kfar Ezion and the whole *gush* fell. Many were killed and many, many were taken into captivity. It was a most painful time.

Pesah [Passover] was upon us. Jerusalem was besieged. We gathered in the dining hall to celebrate the holiday, to read the *Hagadah* [Passover service prayer book]. When we got to "*Leshanah habaah beyerushalayim*" [Hebrew: "Next year in Jerusalem"] we banged on the tables, we yelled, we screamed: "*Leshanah habaah beyerushalayim! Leshanah habaah beyerushalayim!*" We banged and we screamed and we yelled, because we couldn't do anything else.

I must tell you that I haven't the vaguest memory about the day the state was declared. For all I know we were in the trenches again. The day, the event, simply did not register.

Shortly afterward, I was sent to a course for *kibbutzniks* on kitchen management in Tel Aviv sponsored by WIZO, the Women's International Zionist Organization.[10] I was the only American, the only "Anglo-Saxon." The others seemed to be obsessed with American movies. "Have you ever been to Hollywood?" "Is this star Jewish, is this actor Jewish?" They were asking the right person! Having been a most zealous member of a socialist *kibbutz* movement, I had turned up my nose at such bourgeois frivolity. In the same vein, I never paid attention to the "Hit Parade" popular songs my sister listened to. But when, one day, Temmy, one of the *haverot* from [New York] began to sing, "When the Deep Purple Falls"—suddenly I knew the words!

Late that spring, when I was at the course in Tel Aviv, Jerusalem was still besieged. No supplies, no weapons, could get in. Water was severely rationed. One evening, I walking along the side streets of Tel Aviv and I saw a convoy of fifteen, twenty—probably more—trucks khaki-painted, loaded high. The next day we read that the "Burma Road," dug from an old goat path leading to Jerusalem, had been opened, and that a convoy of trucks bringing supplies had reached Jerusalem. The very trucks that I saw in Tel Aviv. The siege was broken!

At one point that summer, I was sent down the road to the now Jewish town of Beit Shean. Some of our *haverim* in the army were stationed there, and I was assigned to cook for their unit. As it turned out, I was there just for a few days. After Rosh Hashanah, I had another assignment. We still hadn't gone on our own settlement, so we were helping out in other places. I was asked to go to Biryah Aravit, near Safed.

9. Hebrew letters whose numerical value is thirty-five.
10. WIZO, the Women's International Zionist Organization, was founded in London in 1920. For further information about WIZO and its leadership, see Esther Carmel-Hakim's chapter in this volume.

Formerly an Arab village, it was now a new *kibbutz* group whose members were all from North Africa—primarily Libya—and Turkey. I was to be in charge of the kitchen. On the way from Ein Hanaziv to Safed, I stopped off in Haifa with a friend. Leonard Bernstein,[11] who was in Israel playing for the troops, was giving an all-Beethoven concert in Haifa. So Shoshanah and I went. After the concert, we went backstage and said, "Mr. Bernstein, may we have your autograph?" We thought he would enjoy hearing American voices. And he did.

In Biryah Aravit, aside from myself, there was only one other person who spoke some English. He was from Turkey and spoke eight languages! We all slept in what had been the homes of Arabs. The rooms were painted blue, because that's a good luck color for Muslims. It was the first time I dreamed in Hebrew and that was very exciting.

I was in Biryah Aravit for about two months, and every Friday I would take a 20 minute walk to the bakery in Safed to make yeast cakes for *Shabbat*. I told the baker that my father was a baker. He was delighted and said, "I'll bake for you." So he made the cakes. One time, walking back to the *kibbutz,* I saw a whole convoy of army trucks coming towards Safed. Suddenly I hear someone yelling, "Yocheved!" The *haverim* I had left in Beit Shean were coming to take part in the battle of Meron. Although the *kibbutz* was in little danger, we were still told to be in the trenches. The *bahurot* . . . especially those from Libya, were terrified. But I was from Jamaica, New York. What did I know about being terrified!

In the fall of 1948, our *garin* of Americans and the South Africans joined with those who had been evacuated from the original Kibbutz Kfar Darom, very close to Gaza. They were from Europe, most of them survivors. After a brief period in Kibbutz Yavneh, we moved to the not-yet-finished and soon-to-be Yeshivat Kerem Beyavneh down the road from the *kibbutz*. The army had just vacated the building. It was the beginning of our own community. The living quarters were makeshift. What is today the shower room was my kitchen. The steps leading up to the roof were my shelves and storage space. The boys slept in what would later be the *yeshivah*'s main study hall. Sacks of wheat and flour separated it from the unfinished concrete partitions where the girls and the married couples slept. It was winter, and many nights I would sleep in that open raw concrete building with my head under the covers. We had to walk to Yavneh to shower. Once, after showering, I put on clean clothes, walked out into the rain, and slid in the mud.

11. Leonard Bernstein (1918–1990), an American Jewish composer and conductor who wrote numerous choral and symphonic works but is best known for his Broadway musicals, including *West Side Story* (1957).

Just about that time, Yehiel Friedman, a dear friend who was an army officer, stepped on a land mine and his foot was blown off. Yehiel had been a student of Rabbi [Yosef] Soleveichik[12] at Yeshiva University [in New York City], a soccer player, and a sweet person. Because of his background, the army assigned him to be a *mashgiah,* but he insisted on being in a combat unit. Anyway . . . I went to visit him at Tel Litvinsky, the army hospital. I brought him a cake I had baked. Yehiel must have seen how upset I was and tried to make me feel better. Yocheved, your cake is heavier than the leg I lost!"

The first elections for the Knesset were held in the spring of 1949. Since I had registered to vote while I was up north, I had to go back there to vote. I spent most of the day on busses. I wasn't sure which party I was going to vote for. Originally, I had planned to vote for Hapoel Hamizrahi [the Religious Labor party].[13] But at the last moment they removed the names of women from their list of candidates. And while I had never been concerned about the role of women in religious services, this was different. And I was very bothered by it. I wasn't sure which party I was going to vote for. Finally, the bus arrived and I immediately went to the voting place, only to be told that they had lost my registration. I was gypped out of casting my vote in that very first election!

That spring we went on *hityashvut* [settlement] in our permanent home. We left Kerem Beyavneh and established our own *kibbutz,* the second Kfar Darom. It was between Yavneh and the ocean. "Moving Day" was very impressive. There was a procession with a *sefer Torah* [Torah scroll], *horas,* and Sam Klausner,[14] one of our friends, flew a Piper Cub over us.

Shortly after that I decided to leave the *kibbutz* and Israel. It was a very painful decision . . . I went to the American consulate to get a new passport. "What happened to your old passport?" "I lost it." "When did you lose it?" "About a year ago." "Where?" "In the Beit Shean Valley." "So why didn't you come then?" "There was a war on. It wasn't so easy to get to Tel Aviv." I had to place an ad: "Did anyone find my passport?" in the *Jerusalem* (formerly *Palestine*) *Post.* I got my new passport about two months later.

12. Yosef Dov Soleveichik (1903–1993), an American Talmudic scholar, religious philosopher, and leader of the Mizrachi religious Zionists, was generally regarded as the unchallenged leader of enlightened Orthodoxy in North America.

13. Hapoel Hamizrahi, a non-Marxist religious socialist Zionist party, established several religious *kibuzim* in pre-state Palestine.

14. Sam Klausner (b. 1923) was an American member of Mahal (see chapter 23, note 5) and served as a pilot in Israel's fledgling air force during the War of Independence. He later became a professor of Sociology at the University of Pennsylvania.

I left on the *Kedmah*, an Israeli passenger ship. Before boarding, customs officers checked to make sure no one was taking out forbidden items. The man in front of me was a soap salesman going to Germany. They cut open many of his bars of soap, probably expecting to find diamonds. Well, they took a look at my papers, which stated that I was from Kibbutz Kfar Darom. They knew I would have no contraband, no suspicious items. I boarded without delay. . . .

Chapter 22

"I Became a Zionist on the Top Floor"
Lois Slott

(Bethesda, Maryland, 1999)

I went to work as a stenotypist for the American Section of the Jewish Agency for Palestine in 1947. I was relatively uneducated in the history of my people and in the dynamic forces that were at work then, both inside and outside of the Jewish world. There was no Israel in 1947; the British country was called "Palestine" and the "Palestinians" were the Jewish settlers.

The meetings that I covered were called "executive meetings," very confidential. I was supposed to record them weekly, spend a couple of days transcribing them, and use the rest of the time at the discretion of the executive director. However, this was in the period when the [United Nations] was discussing what to do with the Palestine Mandate. The once-a-week meetings quickly turned into once-a-day, sometimes twice-a-day meetings. At the time, Rabbi Abba Hillel Silver[1] of Cleveland was the chairman of the [Zionist] Executive. He was probably the most overwhelming figure I have ever met personally in my own lifetime. Both physically and through force of personality he towered over all of his colleagues and commanded every situation so completely, that the rest of the body literally paled into insignificance. Either they were with him politically, in which case their brilliance was merely an echo of his own, or they disagreed with him politically, in which case their light was often smothered by his dominating eloquence—no mean feat in an assembly of capable political leaders of large intense organizations.

The schedule of meetings accelerated as the U.N. meetings dealing with the Palestine question accelerated. My stenotype notes became miles and piles of paper that were never transcribed, because before I could sit down at my typewriter and begin, another emergency arose and another meeting was called. . . .

1. Abba Hillel Silver (1893–1963), a prominent American Reform rabbi and Zionist leader, was American Zionism's dominant political figure from 1943 to 1949.

The meetings of the Executive dealt with strategy, tactics, and planning, such as how to reach one delegate or another of those countries that were on the borderline in their support of our cause, or how to present our case to one committee or another, etc. The Executive consisted of the heads of all the major Zionist organizations in America, including Hadassah's president, Rose Halprin.[2]

In addition, there was a back-up team of young men, most of whom were later to become leaders of Israel, but at that time were used as resource men, or what is known in Congress as "staff." I'm referring to Teddy Kollek,[3] Abba Eban,[4] Michael Comay,[5] I.L. Kenen,[6] Yosef Tekoah,[7] Gideon Rafael[8]...

Side by side with the above men and one woman of the political scene, and housed in the same building in the pre-state days for a while, were the "cloak and dagger boys." The Haganah had a team of men here to work with the American fundraisers and with the underworld of gun runners, contact men, etc. The young men coming off the ships, particularly the *Exodus*, would also touch base with us, since they were used very effectively as speakers for the Haganah at their clandestine meetings.

Many of the young men were Jewish idealists, some returning from World War II, who were quite valuable on the ships. I was often lent to this group as secretary for their luncheon meetings, because I had the highest security clearance necessary for their purposes. . . .

Needless to say there were many political confrontations within the Jewish Agency Executive. Rabbi Silver was on the right-wing of the Zionist Organization; most of the members were in the center or on the left and disagreed with him. Rose Halprin, a tough, articulate opponent, who

---

2. On Rose Halprin, see chapter 19, note 1.

3. On Teddy Kollek, see chapter 19, note 5.

4. On Abba Eban, see chapter 19, note 4.

5. Michael Comay (1908–1987), a Zionist diplomat who held many official positions, including Israel's representative to the United Nations in 1960 and ambassador to Great Britain in 1970.

6. Isaiah Leo "Si" Kenen (1905–1988), an influential American Zionist activist and lobbyist, who rose through the ranks of the organized American Jewish community in the 1940s and 1950s to become the Washington representative and registered lobbyist of the American Israel Public Affairs Committee (AIPAC) in 1959. During his tenure at AIPAC, which lasted until 1974, Kenen advised key political figures on Israel and U.S. policy in the Middle East, including Hubert Humphrey, Harry S. Truman, and John F. Kennedy.

7. Yosef Tekoah (1925–1991), a Zionist career diplomat, served as Israel's ambassador to the United Nations and deputy foreign minister in 1970 under Abba Eban (see chapter 19, note 4).

8. Gideon Rafael (1913–1999), a junior member of the Jewish delegation to the United Nations General Assembly in 1947, served as an Israeli career diplomat for thirty years. In 1985 he retired from the Israeli Foreign Ministry.

followed the line most Hadassah women took at the time, for many reasons, whether as centrists or because of tradition, usually disagreed with the ZOA across the board. Even the Israelis disagreed with Silver to a degree. He was independent of them all.

For instance, he was a registered, active, outspoken Republican—at that time unheard of in the New Deal and Fair Deal days of Jewish Democrats—and believed strongly that the Jews should not put all their eggs into the Democratic basket. Being from Cleveland, Ohio, he had considerable leverage with Senator Robert Taft,[9] then leader of the Senate Republicans. Rabbi Silver also felt that the Jews should not be preparing plans to partition the Land of Israel [according] to the various [schemes of the] investigating committees of that period, that the Jews should stand fast for an undivided Palestine—especially since the creation of Transjordan had already divided Palestine once. He also felt that if you came with a Partition Plan already outlined, they could cut you back even more. Your room for bargaining was gone; there would be no room to retreat, since the retreat had already taken place. He was not a likable person, but his silver tongue, convincing oratory and cold logic always won my young mind. However, there was one major argument that I witnessed in which he did not win my heart or my head, but in the long run he won even that one. Golda Meir[10] had come from Palestine for some of the last-minute meetings. At the time the Haganah was doing a valiant job of running illegal immigrants through the British waters, while at the same time, Menahem Begin's[11] Ezel[12]—or Irgun as it was known in America—was destroying the public image of a law-abiding Yishuv—the Jewish community

9. Robert Taft (1889–1953), an influential Republican leader from Ohio, was the son of President William Howard Taft (1857–1930). He served in the U.S. Senate from 1939 to 1953, where he proved to be a dominant political figure. Taft was a traditional conservative. He decried centralizing power in the federal government, cosponsored the Taft-Hartley Act to restrict organized labor, and opposed U.S. involvement in postwar international organizations. He was a "favorite son" candidate at the Republican national convention of 1952 but was defeated by Dwight Eisenhower (1890–1969).

10. On Golda Meir, see the entry in "About the Contributors" in this volume.

11. Menahem Begin (1913–1992) was a Revisionist Zionist youth leader, commander of the Irgun Zvai Leumi (see the following note), right-wing Zionist political leader, and prime minister of Israel from 1977 to 1983.

12. Ezel is the Hebrew acronym of the Irgun Zvai Leumi [National Military Organization] (also known as the "Irgun"), a right-wing paramilitary group that advocated violent Jewish resistance to the British Mandatory regime in the pre-state era. In July 1946, the Ezel blew up the King David Hotel in Jerusalem which was serving as the headquarters of the British military administration. In 1946–1947, the group conducted a series of violent operations including the bombing of the British embassy in Rome, the assassination of the British ambassador Lord Moyne in Cairo, dynamiting British airplane hangers and railway convoys in Palestine, and a raid on a British military officers' club in Tel Aviv that resulted in seventeen deaths.

struggling for positive values. It was the feeling of the Palestine Jews that they had to use all their energies and resources to save the lives of the [Displaced Persons] languishing in the camps, bringing in as many as possible, and also to defend the Jews from Arab terrorist attacks. At the same time, the Irgun was harassing the British army by blowing up the King David Hotel, assassinating British soldiers, and other sensational acts. The Irgun was grabbing headlines in America, and Ben Hecht[13] was raising money for them in the Jewish community here with the promise of saving the D.P.'s. Actually, the Irgun never ran an immigrant boat through the British blockade. Golda's private conversation with Rabbi Silver burned itself into my memory. I never took notes on it as I did the hours and hours of meetings that now escape me, but that one-on-one argument impressed me forever. She begged him to publicly denounce Menahem Begin, to publicly denounce the Irgun and their acts of terror, to cut down the flow of money that was being pumped into this band of Jewish terrorists—a very small minority in Palestine—dollars which should have been going to the legitimate cause, and that he should lend credibility to the fact that the Yishuv, the Haganah, the Palmah, the leaders of the Palestine Jewish community, were responsible, law-abiding citizens, ready for a state of their own in the family of nations. Silver simply refused in any way to go public with this line, thereby forcing the Jews under David Ben-Gurion a little later to openly fight the Irgun themselves. You remember the *Altalena*, which was an American ship purchased by friends of the Irgun. On June 22, 1948, it approached the one-month old State of Israel that was fighting for its life, with 1000 volunteers and $5 million worth of precious arms and munitions. Prime Minister Ben-Gurion called on the ship to turn the arms over to the new army of which the Irgun was ostensibly a part. When the Irgun refused to give the weapons to any but their own soldiers, a short battle ensued and the ship was sunk. It was believed that Begin was arming his separate army, possibly for a showdown with the Haganah, to try to gain political control after the British left. It would have been devastating to the new state. Rabbi Abba Hillel Silver is probably the only voice in America that could have discredited the Irgun and Begin at the time. His refusal was a self-serving, political position for him to take, but I have learned often since then that many idols have clay feet.

13. Ben Hecht (1894–1964), an American Jewish writer and dramatist best known for *The Front Page* (1928), was an active and outspoken advocate of militant Zionism in the United States during the 1940s. Together with Hillel Kook (Peter Bergson) (1915–2001), he launched a right-wing Zionist propaganda campaign in the United States that garnered nation-wide attention at the end of World War II and in the turbulent period preceding the creation of the State of Israel.

The week preceding November 29, 1947, was the most hectic and exciting as the votes were tallied, retallied, and then our lead was observed to be slipping. Although President Truman had been persuaded to support the creation of the Jewish state by Chaim Weizmann,[14] he had many Arabists in the State Department, combined with the oil lobbyists; all were working feverishly to present a trusteeship proposal and to set aside the partition plan. There were many last-minute phone calls and a lot of hasty leg-work done to put things back together again. . . . The U.N. finally approved partition with a vote of 33 for, 13 against, and 10 abstentions. The Russians at the time were pro-Jewish. [Andrei] Gromyko[15] was heard to say that they, the Russians, would do anything to hurt the British. Thus we benefited, because they brought their satellite countries along with them. . .

Truman's instantaneous recognition of the state was an added bonus. . . . The months that followed, after the instant joy and celebrating in the streets of New York and Tel Aviv, were not happy months. . . . [The] arms embargo [against Israel] . . . played a role in developing a complete underground of Jews, both Americans and Israelis, with their headquarters in the Hotel 14 on East 60th Street in whose basement was the Copacabana nightclub. [Rudolph] Sonneborn,[16] a multi-millionaire from Baltimore, organized many clandestine fundraisers to gather money for the desperately needed arms and ammunition. . . . Young men who scurried around the country making the contacts, finding the stuff, came in and out of our lives. Most of them didn't even have last names, and their first names were only nicknames . . . Shapik, Moosik . . . handsome, intense young Israelis. They would come to our parties and then disappear for days, sometimes weeks at a time.

The operation was headed by Teddy Kollek. . . . He was young and blond; he looked like a cross between a Minnesota farmer and a Viennese aristocrat. He spoke English fluently and while he came from a *kibbutz* on the Kinneret, he was originally from Vienna. His father was a Rothschild

14. Chaim Weizmann (1874–1952), the dominant Zionist leader on the world scene for much of the pre-state period, later became the first president of the State of Israel.

15. Andrei Gromyko (1909–1989), a Soviet political leader who served as ambassador to the United States (1943–1946) and the United Nations (1946–1948).

16. Rudolph Goldschmidt Sonneborn (1898–1986), a leading American Jewish industrialist and Zionist philanthropist, recruited a group of several dozen Jewish business leaders and philanthropists (known as the "Sonneborn Institute), who secretly raised considerable funds to purchase weapons, ammunition, machinery, surplus planes and boats, and other supplies for the Yishuv and the Haganah in Palestine in the period immediately preceding Israel's War of Independence. Teddy Kollek (see chapter 19, note 5) served as a main point of contact between Sonneborn and the Yishuv leadership.

banking executive. Teddy had worked for the Haganah in Istanbul during the war smuggling refugees out of the Balkans, and had also done some intelligence assignments for the British. He saw himself as a traffic cop, directing all of the people to and fro; the ships, the hardware, the money, the experts. He loved technicians, because they always went directly to the heart of the matter and got things done; and he liked America so much because it was full of technicians.

. . . I remember when Ben-Gurion himself came [to the United States], just days before the final vote was taken on partition. It was probably the most frustrating experience in my memory, because he addressed the meeting in Yiddish—the common language they all understood, except me. But the fiery little man projected quite an image as I sat and watched him mesmerize his colleagues.

You all remember the story of Mickey Marcus,[17] the American World War II West Point colonel who was bored with his civilian law practice and a bit of an adventurer. He quickly accepted an invitation to Palestine before the state, seeing a chance as an American to contribute more than money. He was credited with whipping the Haganah into an army from a collection of small defensive units. During his tour of duty he was sent back to the States to report on the status of the defense. Once again, I was selected because of my security clearance, to work with this great hero . . . When we received the coded cable months later of his death I felt a personal loss. . . .

The stature of the people who touched my life in those few short years changed me forever. I became a Zionist on the top floor. . . . One of the young cloak and dagger people said, "Here was an opportunity that happened maybe once in a lifetime—maybe not even that often." We could live dangerously and feel highly virtuous about it. We could actually make history. . . . It gave us a feeling of accomplishment that nothing else we did before, that nothing we will do later, will ever equal. . . . For me it meant *aliyah*. I knew that I had to try life in Israel after those exhilarating years.

17. On Mickey Marcus, see chapter 19, note 6.

Chapter 23

Remembering Israel's War of Independence

Zipporah Porath

(Givat Savyon, Israel, 1999)

. . .When Israel marked its 50th anniversary, we old-timers were asked: What was it like to be in *Erez Israel* when the State was born? Hard to remember? Difficult to describe? Fortunately, I don't have that problem. I can tell you exactly what it was like, effortlessly, thanks to letters I wrote to my family during that momentous time.

The letters describe day-to-day life in Jerusalem and capture the thrill and excitement of the historic events as they were happening. My parents preserved these letters, which I found after they had died: they were published in a book, *Letters from Jerusalem, 1947-1948.* . . .

When I wrote the letters in this book, I certainly didn't expect to be rereading them 50 years later. As I was growing up in New York, I never imagined in my wildest reveries that I would see the Zionist dream of a Jewish state materialize in my lifetime or that I personally would take part in helping make the dream come true. I had no way of knowing I would arrive in *Erez Israel* at the right moment in history.

In October 1947, I came to the Hebrew University in Jerusalem for what was supposed to be a carefree year of study. Instead, I got caught up in Israel's War of Independence. It turned out to be a year that changed my whole life.

. . . I should tell you about my family background. We were *meshugineh* [Yiddish for "crazy"] Zionists. My father, Samuel J. Borowsky, was a prominent Zionist leader—one of the founders of Young Judaea.[1] He was also a well-known Hebrew educator, dedicated to promoting the study of Hebrew as a modern language. My mother was a Zionist activist who hailed from Richmond, VA. Growing up during the 1930s and 1940s in a household where Zionism and the revival of Hebrew were the

---

1. On Young Judaea, see chapter 16, note 3.

focus of our lives, it was only natural that I, too, become active in Zionist youth movements. I was a Young Judaea leader, attended the first Brandeis Leadership Camp, headed a [Zionist Organization of America (ZOA)] district and was a member of Plugat Aliyah[2] [Immigration Division]. And that's how I got involved in the trip to Jerusalem.

The ZOA was offering a one-year scholarship to the Hebrew University, including a year's free tuition and a valid student visa to British Mandatory Palestine. My father urged me to submit an essay I had written on "Why a Jewish State?" I was invited for an interview. Nobody was more surprised than I when I won the scholarship.

At the time, I had a terrific job at the National Jewish Welfare Board producing program material for their worldwide network of Jewish community centers, as well as for the [U.S.] Army and Navy Chaplaincy Service. I should also mention that I had a score of boyfriends.

To go or not to go? Every Zionist dreams and talks of going to *Erez Israel* . . . Some day. Soon. But not immediately! What decided the dilemma for me was the chance to find out what being a Zionist meant in *Erez Israel* and not at Zionist meetings in New York.

I left the USA on September 26, 1947 on the *Marine Jumper,* a reconditioned army troop ship. After seventeen days at sea, we finally reached Haifa. The thrill and excitement of arrival were heightened by an awareness of something much deeper, which I sensed from the minute we came ashore, watching the stevedores unloading the ship. They formed a human chain and tossed the heavy baggage from hand to hand, calling out to each other in Hebrew. Strong, rowdy, muscle men, dressed in grubby khaki shorts—a new type of Jew, for me. We headed for Jerusalem the next day, trying to arrive before the 6:00 PM curfew imposed by the British.

My first impressions of Jerusalem, then the seat of British Mandatory Government in Palestine, were very unsettling. The city was rife with barbed wire and barricades, scary searches and arms requisitions, a hotbed of trigger-happy "Tommies."[3] Jerusalem was divided into a British sector, Arab sectors, Jewish sectors, mixed sectors, and inaccessible areas—which included the [Western] Wall at that time.

My first days were filled with fascinating new encounters and getting used to almost everything. My Hebrew was good, but archaic. If I ordered

2. Plugat Aliyah, Hebrew for "Immigration Division," was a framework for American college-age Zionist youth planning to immigrate to Palestine.

3. "Tommies," a term used to denote British soldiers, was derived from "Thomas Atkins," which, like "John Doe" in the American setting, was commonly used on sample British forms.

a meal, I would have no idea what I was eating, except that it was filling, fattening, and foreign. I missed some of the physical comforts of home, simple things like hot water! To take a bath I had to make a wood fire at the bottom of a boiler, literally with the sweat of my brow.

The school year at the campus on Mt. Scopus hadn't yet started, but I was having a great time. We American girls were very popular: there were so few of us! It was exciting to meet *sabras* [native-born Palestinian Jews] and *kibbutzniks*. For me, another new breed of Jew. A whole new way of life.

I had begun writing letters to my family the day I boarded the boat and I wrote almost every day. I felt an obligation to share my experiences with my Zionist family, keenly aware of being an advance guard for them. I kept my letters cheerful, amusing and informative. But a month later they were to take a more serious tone.

On November 29, 1947, the United Nations decided in favor of the Partition Plan, heralding the end of the British Mandate and sanctioning a Jewish state and an Arab state. All hell broke loose. Jewish Jerusalem went wild with joy. History was in the making and I was where it was happening. Like a good reporter, I described what I saw, what I thought, and what I and those around me were feeling.

Jerusalem. Sunday morning. 11:00 AM November 30, 1947
. . . I walked in a semi-daze through the crowds of happy races, through the deafening singing of *"David melekh yisrael, hai hai vekayam"* [Hebrew: "David, King of Israel, lives and rules"], past the British tanks and jeeps piled high with pyramids of flag-waving, cheering children. I dodged motorcycles, wagons, cars and trucks, which were racing madly up and down King George Street, missing each other miraculously . . . ! I pushed my way past crying, kissing tumultuous crowds and exultant shouts of *"mazal tov"* [congratulations]. . . .
Rumor had it that David Ben-Gurion had just arrived from Tel Aviv . . . sure enough, there he was standing on the balcony of the Sokhnut [Jewish Agency] building. He looked slowly and solemnly around him—to the rooftops crammed with people, to the throngs that stood solid in the courtyard below him. He raised his hand. An utter silence waited for his words: *"Ashreinu shezahinu layom hazeh,"* [Hebrew: "Blessed are we who have been privileged to witness this day"]. He concluded with *"Tehi hamedinah haivrit"* [Hebrew: "Long live the Jewish state"] and called for *"Hatikvah"* [The Hope]. A solemn chant rose from all sides. The moment was too big for our feelings. There were few dry eyes and few steady voices. Ben-Gurion tossed his head back proudly, tenderly touched the flag that hung from the railing and charged the air with electricity when he shouted defiantly.

Within days, the Arabs were ambushing buses on the road to Jerusalem and Haifa. By December, it became clear that no one was going to hand us a state on a silver platter. We would have to fight for it. I had no idea what that meant!

Tension started to mount in the city. Mt. Scopus was inaccessible. Studies were abandoned, students and faculty mobilized. It was a grim signal to the American students to pack up and go home or join the forces helping to defend Jerusalem. Some of the students, who were World War II veterans studying on the GI Bill of Rights, opted to stay on. Most Americans left while the going was possible.

I was blithely unaware that my fellow students were leading a double life. Under the very noses of the British, they were training in the Haganah, the army-to-be of the state-to-be. And, my American alarm clock had a lot to do with getting them to clandestine rendezvous on time.

It wasn't long before I, too, joined the Haganah. The induction ceremony, in the basement of the Rehaviyah High School,[4] was in the best cloak and dagger tradition. Confronted with a [Hebrew] Bible and a pistol, I was sworn in, with no idea what I was getting myself into. I graduated from guard duty to gun running, including hand grenades stuffed under my blouse. The British were too polite to do body searches on girls. We also were very useful at eavesdropping on British radio transmissions. I decided to opt for a first aid course. The hardest part was learning human anatomy in Hebrew! How I worried that my patients might expire long before I could tell the doctor what was wrong.

I finished the two-month course on the very day in February of the devastating Ben-Yehudah Street bombing, an explosion which rocked the city and reduced the entire area to rubble, killing over fifty people and wounding over 170. Not waiting for official assignments, I waved my Magen David Adom [Jewish emergency medical unit] arm band and pushed past the cordons to see if I could be helpful. In all the pandemonium it was impossible to find a first aid station, so I set up one of my own. With my lipstick I drew a large Magen David Adom [red Star of David] in a prominent place and before I knew it, I was in business—doing first-aid for the first time. That was the day I became a real member of the Yishuv. I wrote to my parents: "I am becoming like the Jews who live here: every shock and sorrow nurtures them to grim restraint and fierce dedication."

Within a month, Jerusalem was beset by a series of grim tragedies: the bombing of the *Palestine Post* (now the *Jerusalem Post*) building, the Jewish Agency building in the heart of the city, and the attack on the Hadassah Hospital convoy en route to Mt. Scopus. Several of us American girls were sent on a ten-day Haganah training course where we learned to

---

4. The Rehaviyah High School, an elite academic institution in Jerusalem, served as a locus of Haganah activity in the pre-state period and a point of entry into Zionist leadership circles for many of first-generation Palestinian Jews.

clean guns blindfolded, throw rocks instead of hand grenades, and crawl zig-zag across the *wadis* [ravines] of Jerusalem till our bellies ached.

In the city, there was incessant sniping, shooting, shelling, with a terrible toll in casualties. But, surprisingly, life went on as usual, though mail and other services were discontinued. All we talked about was *food* and where to find it. Severe shortages of food, water, fuel and ammunition plagued the population and the prospect of the Holy City being blown to kingdom come was constant and terrifying. The Arabs terrorized the roads, ambushing convoys, confiscating supplies, trying to throttle and isolate Jerusalem and starve us into submission. My fellow students and close friends were among the armed Palmah escorts who protected the convoys, trying to clear the road to Jerusalem. To no avail. Eventually, Jerusalem was completely cut off from the rest of the country.

The siege of Jerusalem lasted almost three months. The last convoy to reach the city—some 200 lorries—arrived miraculously unharmed on the eve of Passover, April 1948. We students were rationed a portion of margarine, *mazot* [Hebrew, plural of *mazah*] a little oil, cheese, some other stuff and *one egg* each. To get the rations we had to risk our lives on a bus ride to the store, located in mid-town, at which we were registered. Six of us drew lots to see who would go. I was the lucky victim who would duck snipers all the way to town and back. The grocer relieved me of the ration coupons and packed up my parcel, gently placing the eggs on top. I guarded them carefully all the way home . . . where I tripped on the doorstep. The eggs went flying but my friends, who were awaiting my return, managed to collect some of the mess. We added a dash of powdered eggs, powdered milk, and lots of love and scrambled up a delicious, muddy *mazah brei* [fried *mazah* dish].

During the siege, I was assigned to set up and run infirmaries and first aid stations on the outskirts of the city. I spent two miserable months in the Arab village Deir Yassin, after it had been taken over by the Haganah. At night, by kerosene lamp, I poured my heart into writing letters, which weren't going anywhere . . .

On May 14, 1948, when David Ben-Gurion who was light years away in Tel Aviv proclaimed to the world the establishment of the State of Israel, we were so completely cut off, we never heard the broadcast. There was no electricity; the battery radio was out of commission. All we heard was a rumor—everything was rumors. . . .

The British pulled out. The war started officially and went wildly into high gear, every side striving to gain control of key strongholds. The terrifying night before a proposed ceasefire, airplanes soared overhead, the air was thick with whining shells, relentless pounding of thundering blasts and ear-splitting explosions. Not a moment's respite. My teeth rattled ever time the infirmary building shook. We had been issued a pamphlet about how to conquer fear. . . . We never expected to survive.

On June 11, 1948, a small jeep convoy, laden with blessed arms, ammunition and food, made it over the hills bypassing Latrun, where the main battle for the road was taking place. It broke the siege and lifted our morale sky high. Later, through heroic efforts, the ancient donkey trail carved out of the mountains was made viable for heavy traffic and became known as the "Burma Road."

Among the *Palmahniks* in the jeep convoy was a friend who offered to take my packet of letters on the return trip. He was headed for Kibbutz Hulda. From there, he would pass it along to a mutual friend who in turn would transfer it to another friend, like a pony express. When and if it would reach Tel Aviv—where there were mail services—it might be stamped and mailed or given to a Mahal[5] overseas volunteer pilot flying to Czechoslovakia to pick up arms and airplanes, which might mail it to my family in America. This offer was as unreliable as life itself, but I accepted. I added a hurried note with a report on other American students so that my mother could call their parents with the first word about their children in many months. Miracle of miracles, the packet of letters arrived.

Incidentally, the rumor that an American West Pointer, Col. David "Mickey" Marcus[6] (alias "Stone"), was directing the operation to open the road to Jerusalem was true but unfortunately he was tragically killed the night before the cease-fire went into effect. A year later, on the first anniversary of his death, Ben-Gurion wanted to honor the memory of Marcus' heroic role in Israel's War of Independence and instructed the Israel Defense Forces to interview those who had served or had contact with Marcus, while their memories of him were still fresh. I was the lucky soldier selected for this assignment.

During the first truce, under the protection of the United Nations, I accompanied a Magen David Adom convoy of wounded fighters out of besieged Jerusalem. Most of the patients were amputees and lurching over the rugged terrain was sheer agony for them. How desperately I tried to be cheerful, sympathetic, and efficient. At some point, suddenly, it dawned upon us that we were actually in the new State of Israel; a wild and joyous moment, filled with relief, pain, pride, and overwhelming

5. Mahal, the Hebrew acronym for *Mitnadvei Huz Laarez* [Overseas Volunteers], an organization of diaspora volunteers, many of whom were World War II veterans, who fought for the Yishuv during the War of Independence.

6. On Mickey Marcus, see chapter 19, note 6.

excitement. The patients banged their crutches and canes on the ambulance and bus doors. The din was deafening, the exultation uncontrollable. Arriving at a converted hospital camp in Kfar Bilu, we were given tea and sandwiches with honest-to-goodness vegetables. After months of food deprivation, the fresh vegetables tasted like everything we had ever dreamed of eating during hunger pangs in Jerusalem.

My pass to paradise expired three days later and the fragile ceasefire ended soon after. Back in Jerusalem, back to war, air raids, fire and hell and nursing. Eventually, an effective ceasefire truce was arranged; the war stood still. I was transferred to the fledgling Israel Air Force (IAF) at [headquarters] in Tel Aviv as a [public relations] officer assigned to foreign journalists. Later, I helped set up IAF nursing services in the Haifa area.

On November 29, 1948 . . . I wrote to my family:

From the roof of the hospital, I watched this morning's parade, a parade of soldiers of the Jewish state. Not partisans or underground fighters. Soldiers standing erect and proud, in rain puddles six inches deep, wearing shabby outfits—winter uniforms still haven't reached us—listening to lofty words of accomplishment and tribute.

I, too, listened but my thoughts wandered—drifted back to last November 29, 1947, Jerusalem, the courtyard of the Sokhnut [Jewish Agency] building, and the spontaneous joy that filled the streets when the United Nations resolution calling for a Jewish state was approved.

And now we march, we form ranks, we listen to speeches, we salute officers: Natan, as they taught him in the Russian army; Bill, as he learned in the [British Royal Air Force]; Yosef, as they do in the Polish army; Uzi (the *sabra*), reluctantly; Moshe, in Turkish style. All of them, saluting the Jewish officer in command, representing Zvah Haganah Leyisrael [Israel Defense Forces]. The same people, who were partisan fighters last year, are soldiers today and civilian citizens of the State of Israel tomorrow. I wondered whether "tomorrow" would be another year or an eternity?

The command rang out "*hofshi*" [dismissed]. The ranks broke to the count of three and everyone dashed to the canteen where they mimicked each other marching, saluting and even drinking tea. Nobody mentioned the words we had heard, nobody referred to the historic importance of the day or the momentous events that had transpired, transforming us into a state with an army. Nobody marveled at the wonder of it all. Were these miracles already being taken for granted?

For me, this pathetic parade was a fulfillment, a consummation. . . . It had taken not one year but two thousand years to materialize. Next year, the parade will probably be more impressive. We'll have smart uniforms, everyone will salute in the same way, stand in straight lines and know all the marching commands. We will have learned so much and probably forgotten so much. . . . A fighting people hasn't time to be sentimental. . . .

But I couldn't help thinking of Moshe, Oded, Zvi, Amnon, Yaakov, Aryeh, Matty, Nahum and a hundred others in Jerusalem, who a year ago danced and sang through the night with me, but didn't live long enough; they fell before the dream came true. The lump in my throat was too big in my mouth. . . .

I can't believe this year. So much has happened, but the most important thing by far is the birth of the state. I've been part of it and it will forever be part of me. I guess that means I am telling you I intend to see this war through and then remain on, whatever happens. This is now my home. . . .

Glossary of Terms

aliyah (pl. *aliyot,* Hebrew for "ascent"): a term used to indicate Jewish immigration to the Land of Israel. The First Aliyah is usually dated 1881–1903; the Second Aliyah, 1903/4–1914; the Third Aliyah, 1919–1923; the Fourth Aliyah, 1924–1928; and the Fifth Aliyah, 1929–1939.

Ashkenazi Jews: the term used to identify Yiddish-speaking Jews of East European ancestry.

dunam: term for one thousand square meters, approximately a quarter of an acre.

Erez Israel (Hebrew), *Erez yisroel* (Yiddish): according to the social, religious, or political context, the term may denote the Land of Israel, Holy Land, or Palestine.

galut: Hebrew for "exile" (*golus* in Yiddish): pejorative term used to describe both spiritual and geographic conditions.

garin: Hebrew for "settlement group," literally "seed."

Hadassah: the centrist American women's Zionist organization established in 1912 by Henrietta Szold (1860–1945).

Haganah: Hebrew for "Defense," the self-defense organization of the Yishuv in the pre-state era and the precursor of the Israel Defense Forces.

hagshamah azmit: Hebrew for "self-fulfillment," the Zionist ideal of realizing one's full potential.

hakhsharah (pl. *hakhsharot*): Hebrew for "training," usually in reference to agricultural and/or manual skills required for life in the Jewish colonies of Palestine, including communal values, conversational Hebrew, and self-defense.

halukah: Hebrew for "distribution"; the traditional system for the distribution of financial contributions from abroad to the Jewish community of Palestine, particularly in Jerusalem.

haluz (pl. *haluzim*): Hebrew for "pioneer," used to describe the Labor Zionist pioneers in Palestine.

haluzah (pl. *haluzot*): Hebrew term for "women pioneers," used to describe the Labor Zionist female pioneers in Palestine.

haluziut: Hebrew for "pioneering."

Hashomer Hazair: Hebrew for the "Young Guard," a worldwide Marxist Zionist youth movement established in Vienna in 1916, that stressed class struggle and pioneering settlement in Palestine; it later gave rise to a left-wing Zionist party in Palestine by the same name as well as a framework of communitarian rural settlements.

Hehaluz: Hebrew for "The Pioneer," an organization that emerged after World War I in Russia and became a nonpolitical body embracing all factions of the Zionist movement dedicated to *aliyah* (see above) and pioneering values.

Histadrut: a shortened form of Histadrut Haklalit Shel Haovdim Haivrim Berez Israel, Hebrew for "General Federation of Jewish Workers in the Land of Israel," the umbrella framework of the Labor Zionist movement in Palestine, established in 1920.

hora: Hebrew term for a vigorous circle dance (mostly of Rumanian origin), very popular among the Zionist pioneers.

Jewish Legion: the military formation of Jewish volunteers in World War I who fought in the British army for the liberation of Palestine from Turkish rule.

Jewish National Fund (JNF): known in Hebrew as Keren Kayemet Leyisrael; founded at the Fifth Zionist Congress in 1901 to further the acquisition of land and development of Jewish colonies in Palestine.

kibbutz (pl. *kibuzim*): Hebrew term for a cooperative rural settlement in Palestine.

kvuzah (pl. *kvuzot*): Hebrew term for a communal rural colony in Palestine.

Labor Zionism: the colonizing movement of socialist Zionist pioneers that created an intricate countrywide network of social, economic, and political institutions which shaped the infrastructure of the Jewish state-in-the-making; comprised of a variety of rival factions, each with a different emphasis on Marxism, Hebraism, Yiddish, etc.

Mapai: an acronym for the Hebrew Mifleget Poalei Erez Israel [Workers' Party of the Land of Israel], established in Palestine in 1930; the party dominated Labor Zionism in the Mandatory and early state periods.

Mizrahi: acronym for the Hebrew phrase *merkaz ruhani,* meaning "spiritual center," and also the Hebrew term for "eastward." It is the name of the Orthodox religious Zionist party that was established in eastern Europe in 1902. The American wing of the party used the spelling "Mizrachi."

Moezet Hapoalot: Hebrew for the "Women Workers' Council," established in 1922 as part of the Histadrut (see above) and the sister organization of Pioneer Women in the United States (see below).

moshav ovdim: Hebrew for "workers' settlement," a rural Jewish colony in Palestine incorporating some cooperative principles.

moshavah (pl. *moshavot*): Hebrew for "plantation village," usually associated with the private landholding Zionist pioneers of the First Aliyah (see *aliyah* above).

Pioneer Women: the Labor Zionist women's organization in the United States, established in 1925; affiliated with Moezet Hapoalot in Palestine (see above).

Poalei Zion: Hebrew for "Workers of Zion," a Marxist Zionist party that originated in Russia in 1901–1903 and subsequently established branches in other countries, including Palestine.

pogroms: Russian term for anti-Jewish riots perpetrated by the Christian population against East European Jews; widespread in Russia between 1881 and 1921 and generally accompanied by destruction, looting of property, murder, and rape.

Sephardi Jews: the term used to identify Jews of Iberian ancestry who speak Judeo-Spanish (i.e., Ladino).

shaliah (f. *shlihah,* pl. *shlihim/shlihot*): Hebrew term for "emissary."

shomer (pl. *shomrim*): Hebrew for "watchman" or "guard."

shtetl (pl. *shtetlkh*): Yiddish for a small town or village in eastern Europe.

World Zionist Congress: the representative body and highest authority in the World Zionist Organization (see below), created by Theodor Herzl (1860–1904), the founder of modern political Zionism. The First Zionist Congress was held in 1897; between 1898 and 1939 the congress convened every one to two years on twenty-one occasions. Only after World War II did the Twenty-second Zionist Congress convene, thereafter meeting every four to six years in the early decades of the Jewish state.

World Zionist Organization: the political organization established by Theodor Herzl and the World Zionist Congress (see above), responsible for coordinating and implementing the political, financial, and development strategies of the Zionist movement in the diaspora and Palestine.

yeshivah (pl. *yeshivot*): the Yiddish term for a school of advanced Talmudic study.

Yishuv: Hebrew term for the Jewish community in Palestine before the creation of the State of Israel in 1948; the "Old Yishuv" refers to the traditional, religiously observant Jewish community established prior to 1881.

Young Judaea: the centrist Zionist youth group affiliated with the Hadassah Women's Zionist Organization, established in 1909.

Youth Aliyah: the program of the World Zionist Organization designed to facilitate the immigration of European Jewish refugee children to Palestine during and after World War II.

A Note on Bibliography

There is a rapidly growing body of scholarly literature concerning American Jewish women, Zionism, and the State of Israel. To date, no effort has been undertaken to compile a comprehensive guide to this emerging field of study. The present bibliographic survey seeks to address this lacuna by tracing the broad outlines of scholarship past and present (in English) that best illustrates the nexus between American Jewish women and the Land of Israel in the nineteenth and twentieth centuries.

First, a few words are in order concerning general resources about women in American Jewish history. For a comprehensive treatment of Jewish women in the United States, including many Zionist leaders and significant women's Zionist organizations, see Paula Hyman and Deborah Dash Moore, eds. *Jewish Women in America: An Historical Encyclopedia,* 2 vols. (New York and London: Routledge, 1997). Additionally, *American Jewish Archives, American Jewish History,* the *Journal of Israeli History* (formerly *Studies in Zionism*), and *Studies in Contemporary Jewry* frequently include articles relevant to the exploration of American Jewish women and Zionism. Another useful resource is the *American Jewish Year Book.*

Second, there is a sizable body of literature on the history of American Jewish women. Some especially useful studies that also refer to Zionism are Charlotte Baum, Paula Hyman, and Sonya Michel, *The Jewish Woman in America* (New York: Schocken, 1976); Susan Glenn, *Daughters of the Shtetl: Life and Labor in the Immigrant Generation* (Ithaca, N.Y.: Cornell University Press, 1990); Jacob Rader Marcus, *The American Jewish Woman: A Documentary History* (New York: Ktav Publishing House, 1981); Faith Rogow, *Gone to Another Meeting: The National Council of Jewish Women, 1893-1993* (Tuscaloosa: University of Alabama Press, 1993); Sydney Stahl Weinberg, *The World of Our Mothers: The Lives of Jewish Immigrant Women* (Chapel Hill: University of North Carolina Press, 1988).

For secondary analyses of American Zionism that include detailed examinations of women see Samuel Halperin, *The Political World of American Zionism,* reprint (Silver Spring, Md.: Information Dynamics, 1985); Marlin Levin, *Balm in Gilead: The Story of Hadassah* (New York: Schocken Books, 1973); Mark A. Raider, *The Emergence of American Zionism* (New York and London: New York University Press, 1998); Melvin I. Urofsky, *American Zionism from Herzl to the Holocaust,* reprint (Lincoln: University of Nebraska Press, 1996). A useful article is Mary McCune, "Social Workers in the *Muskeljudentum:* 'Hadassah Ladies,' 'Manly Men' and the Significance of Gender in the American Zionist Movement, 1912-1928," *American Jewish History* 86 (June 1998): 135-165. See also the *Herzl Year Book,* 8 vols. (New York: Herzl Press, 1958-1978); Raphael Patai, ed., *Encyclopedia of Zionism and Israel,* 2 vols. (McGraw-Hill and Herzl Press, 1971).

368 A Note on Bibliography

Third, the literature on Zionism is obviously too vast to summarize here. A good place to start would be Ben Halpern and Jehuda Reinharz, *Zionism and the Creation of a New Society* (Hanover, N.H., and London: University Press of New England, 2000). Useful touchstones in the field of Zionist history are Shlomo Avineri, *The Making of Modern Zionism: The Intellectual Origins of the Jewish State* (New York: Basic Books, 1981); Abba Eban, *Personal Witness: Israel through My Eyes* (New York: G. P. Putnam's Sons, 1992); Amos Elon, *The Israelis: Founders and Sons* (New York: Penguin, 1983). Hershel Edelheit, *Israel and the Jewish World, 1948–1993: A Chronology* (Westport, Conn.: Greenwood Press, 1995); Arthur Hertzberg, ed., *The Zionist Idea: A Historical Reader and Analysis,* reprint (New York: Atheneum, 1984); Walter Laqueur, *A History of Zionism,* 2nd revised ed. (New York: Schocken Books, 1989); Itamar Rabinovich and Jehuda Reinharz, eds., *Israel in the Middle East: Documents and Readings on Society, Politics and Foreign Relations, 1948–Present* (New York: Oxford University Press, 1984); Jehuda Reinharz and Anita Shapira, eds., *Essential Papers on Zionism* (New York and London: New York University Press, 1996); Shmuel Almog, Jehuda Reinharz, and Anita Shapira, eds., *Zionism and Religion* (Hanover, N.H., and London: University Press of New England, 1998); Gideon Shimoni, *The Zionist Ideology* (Hanover, N.H., and London: University Press of New England, 1995).

By contrast, there is but a handful of book-length secondary analyses specifically related to women, Zionism, and Israel. (Though such studies are at best only tangentially concerned with American Jewish women, they are nonetheless essential as they illustrate the backdrop against which the history of Zionism and American Jewish women unfolds.) Among the most instructive of such studies are Deborah Bernstein, *The Struggle for Equality: Urban Women Workers in Pre-State Israeli Society* (New York: Praeger, 1987); Deborah S. Bernstein, ed., *Pioneers and Homemakers: Jewish Women in Pre-State Israel* (Albany: State University Press of New York, 1992); Lisa Gilad, *Ginger and Salt: Yemeni Jewish Women in an Israeli Town* (Boulder,Colo.: Westview Press, 1989); Leslie Hazleton, *Israeli Women: The Reality Behind the Myths* (New York: Simon and Schuster, 1977); Carol Bosworth Kutscher, "The Early Years of Hadassah, 1912–1921" (Ph.D. diss., Brandeis University, 1976); Beata Lipman, *Israel, the Embattled Land: Jewish and Palestinian Women Talk about Their Lives* (Cambridge, Mass.: Harvard University Press, 1988); Donald H. Miller, "A History of Hadassah, 1912–1935" (Ph.D. diss., New York University, 1968); Natalie Rein, *Daughters of Rachel: Women in Israel* (New York: Penguin Books, 1980); Lionel Tiger and Joseph Shepher, *Women in the Kibbutz* (New York and London: Harcourt Brace Jovanovich, 1975); Barbara Swirsky and Marilyn Safir, eds., *Calling the Equality Bluff: Women in Israel* (New York: Teachers College Press, 1993); Yael Yishai, *Between the Flag and the Banner: Women in Israeli Politics* (Albany: State University of New York Press, 1996); Hanna Zacks Bar-Yishay, "Female Labor Force Participation in a Developing Economy, Pre-State Israel as a Case Study," 2 vols. (Ph.D. diss., University of Minnesota, 1991). Useful articles in this vein include Joan Dash, "Doing Good in Palestine: [Judah L.] Magnes and Henrietta Szold," in *Like All the Nations? The Life and Legacy of Judah L. Magnes,* ed. William M. Brinner and Moses Rischin (Albany: State University of New York Press, 1987), 99–111; Allon Gal, "Hadassah and the American Jewish Political Tradition," in *An Inventory of Promises: Essays in Honor of Moses Rischin,* ed.

Jeffrey S. Gurock and Marc Lee Raphael (Brooklyn, N.Y.: Carlson, 1995); Dafna N. Izraeli, "The Zionist Women's Movement in Palestine, 1911–27: A Socio-logical Analysis," *Signs* (1981): 87–111; Rachel Elboim-Dror, "Gender in Uto-pianism: The Zionist Case," *History Workshop* 37 (1994): 99–117; Nick Man-delkern, "The Story of Pioneer Women," *Pioneer Woman*, parts 1–4 (September 1980-March/April 1981); Ann S. Masnik, "Israel," in *The Jewish Woman: An Annotated Selected Bibliography, 1986-1993*, ed. Ann S. Masnik (New York: Biblio Press., 1996): 103–112; Marianne Sanua, "The Esco Fund Committee: The Story of an American Jewish Foundation," in *America and Zion: Essays and Papers in Memory of Moshe Davis*, ed. Eli Lederhendler and Jonathan D. Sarna (Detroit: Wayne State University Press, 2002), 117–160.

Several broadly construed studies examine women in the context of modern Jewish history and also raise important conceptual and methodological questions that relate to Zionism, Jewish nationalism, and political activism. Among the best are Judith R. Baskin, ed., *Jewish Women in Historical Perspective*, 2nd ed. (De-troit: Wayne State University Press, 1998); Paula Hyman, *Gender and Assimila-tion in Modern Jewish History: The Roles and Representation of Jewish Women* (Seattle: University of Washington Press, 1995); Elizabeth Koltun, ed., *The Jewish Woman: New Perspectives* (New York: Schocken Books, 1976); Naomi Shep-herd, *A Price Below Rubies: Jewish Women as Rebels and Radicals* (Cambridge, Mass.: Harvard University Press, 1993). Some useful monographs are Nelly Las, *Jewish Women in a Changing World: A History of the International Council of Jewish Women, 1899-1995* (Jerusalem: Avraham Harman Institute of Contem-porary Jewry, 1996); Claudia Prestel, "Zionist Rhetoric and Women's Equality, 1897–1933: Myth and Reality," *San Jose Studies* 20 (Fall 1994): 4–28; Susanne A. Shavelson, "Anxieties of Authorship in the Autobiographies of Mary Antin and Aliza Greenblatt," *Prooftexts* 18 (1998): 161–186; Margalit Shilo, "The Double or Multiple Image of the New Hebrew Woman," *Nashim: A Journal of Jewish Women's Studies and Gender Issues* 1 (Winter 1998): 73–94.

There are several useful primary sources and women's memoirs, including Shulamit Aloni, "Israel: Up the Down Escalator," in *Sisterhood Is Global*, ed. Robin Morgan (Garden City, N.Y.: Anchor Press/Doubleday, 1984); E. M. Broner, *A Weave of Women* (New York: Holt, Rinehart and Winston, 1978); Henry M. Christman, ed., *This Is Our Strength: Selected Papers of Golda Meir* (New York: MacMillan, 1962); Kathy E. Ferguson, *Kibbutz Journal: Reflections on Gender, Race, and Militarism in Israel* (Pasadena: Trilogy Books, 1995); Mar-cia Freedman, *Exile in the Promised Land: A Memoir* (Ithaca: Firebrand Books 1990); Miriam Freund-Rosenthal, ed., *A Tapestry of Hadassah Memories* (Pitts-boro, N.C.: Town House Press, 1994); Sylvia Gelber, *No Balm in Gilead* (Ot-tawa: Carleton University Press, 1989); Leon S. Hoffman, *Ideals and Illusions: The Story of an Ivy League Woman in 1920s Israel* (New York: S. P. I. Books, 1992); Melaine Kaye-Kantrowitz, Irena Klepfisz and Esther F. Hyneman, eds., *The Tribe of Dina: A Jewish Women's Anthology* (Boston: Beacon, 1986); Rebe-kah Kohut, *My Portion* (New York: Albert & Charles Boni, 1927); Bette Roth Young, ed., *Emma Lazarus in Her World: Life and Letters* (Philadelphia: Jewish Publication Society, 1995); Irma L. Lindheim, *Parallel Quest* (New York: Thomas Yoseloff, 1962); Golda Meir, *My Life* (New York: Dell, 1975); Mark A. Raider and Miriam B. Raider-Roth, eds., *The Plough Woman: Records of the Pioneer Women of Palestine. A Critical Edition* (Hanover, N.H., and London: University

Press of New England, 2002); Jessie Sampter, "A Confession," in *Self-Fulfillment through Zionism,* ed. Shlomo Bardin (New York: American Zionist Youth Commission, 1943); Marie Syrkin, *The State of the Jews* (Washington, D.C.: New Republic Books/Herzl Press, 1980); Marvin Lowenthal, ed., *Henrietta Szold: Life and Letters* (New York: Viking Press, 1942).

Some useful biographical studies are David Adler, *Our Golda: The Story of Golda* Meir (New York: Viking, 1984); Michael Brown, *The Israeli-American Connection: Its Roots in the Yishuv, 1914-1945* (Detroit: Wayne State University Press, 1997), esp. "Henrietta Szold: Health, Education, and Welfare, American-Style," 133–160, and "Golda Meir: 'Minister of American Affairs,'" pp. 161–196; Margaret Davidson, *The Golda Meir Story* (New York: Charles Scribner's & Sons, 1976); Irving Fineman, *Woman of Valor: The Life of Henrietta Szold, 1860-1915* (New York: Simon and Schuster, 1961); Deborah Hitzeroth, *The Importance of Golda Meir* (San Diego: Lucent Books, 1998); Thea Keren, *Sophie Udin: Portrait of a Pioneer* (Rehovot, Israel: Old City Press, 1984); Harriet Miller, *The Biography of Minette Baum* (Ft. Wayne: Indiana Jewish Historical Society, 1975); Israel Shenker and Mary Shenker, *As Good as Golda* (New York: McCall, 1970); Marie Syrkin, *Golda Meir: Woman With a Cause* (New York: G. P. Putnam's Sons, 1963); Marie Syrkin, *A Land of Our Own: An Oral Biography of Golda Meir* (New York: Putnam's Sons, 1973); Marie Syrkin, "Golda Meir and Other Americans" in *Like All the Nations? The Life and Legacy of Judah L. Magnes,* ed. William M. Brinner and Moses Rischin (Albany: State University of New York Press, 1987), 113–126; Rahel Yanait Ben-Zvi, *Before Golda: Manya Shohat,* trans. Sandra Shurin (New York: Biblio Press, 1989).

About the Contributors

Engee Caller was born in Brooklyn, New York, in 1918. She grew up in a traditional family setting and was deeply influenced as a teenager by the local Sholem Aleikhem Folkshul and the Habonim youth movement. She immigrated to Palestine in 1939, arriving in Palestine under the guise of a tourist visa and subsequently entered a fictitious marriage in order to circumvent the prevailing British restrictions on Jewish immigration to Palestine. She was among the founders of Kibbutz Kfar Blum and served in the Haganah, the Palmah, and later the nascent Israel Defense Forces. In 1945–1947 she was a Histadrut emissary in the United States and in 1951–1957 she served as the personal secretary to various leaders of the Ihud *kibbutz* movement. She also set up and maintained the Kibbutz Kfar Blum archive, a task to which she devoted herself until the age of eighty.

Esther Carmel-Hakim is a Lecturer in the Land of Israel Studies Department at the University of Haifa and a regional high school teacher. Her doctoral dissertation is titled "Women's Agricultural Training in the Yishuv, with the Assistance of Jewish Women's Organizations, 1911–1929." In 2001 she introduced the first course on "Jewish Women in Pre-State Israel, 1882–1948" at Haifa University.

Allon Gal is Professor of Modern Jewish History at Ben-Gurion University of the Negev. His latest article "Louis D. Brandeis and American Zionism," will appear in *The Legal and Zionist Traditions of Brandeis*, ed. Allon Gal (Jerusalem: Israel Academy of Sciences and Humanities, 2004) (Hebrew). He is currently working on a two-volume project titled *World Regional Zionism: Geo-Cultural Dimensions,* to be published in Hebrew and English by the Historical Society of Israel and the Ben-Gurion Research Institute. He is the founder of the Center for the Study of North American Jewry and head of the English-speaking World Division, Ben-Gurion Research Center, Ben-Gurion University.

Joseph B. Glass is the Academic Coordinator of the Halbert Centre for Canadian Studies and Adjunct Lecturer in the Department of Geography and the Rothberg International School of the Hebrew University of Jerusalem. His latest book is *From New Zion to Old Zion: American Jewish Immigration and Settlement in Palestine, 1917–1939* (Detroit: Wayne State University Press, 2002). Together with Ruth Kark, he is working on a second volume in their series dealing with Sephardi entrepreneurs in the Land of Israel. The latter focuses on the activities of a Jerusalem banking family—the Valeros.

Sara Kadosh is Director of the American Jewish Joint Distribution Committee Archives in Jerusalem. Her latest article is "Jewish Refugee Children in Switzerland 1939–1950," published in *Remembering for the Future: The Holocaust in an Age of Genocide,* ed. John K. Roth and Elisabeth Maxwell (London: Palgrave, 2001). She is currently working on a book on this subject.

Ruth Halprin Kaslove lived in Jerusalem when her mother, Rose Luria Halprin (1896–1978), who was a close associate of Henrietta Szold, served as national president of Hadassah. For the past twenty-seven years she has been a member of Hadassah's National Board. She was the first nongovernmental official at the United Nations, representing Hadassah, when the latter was accepted into the U.N. Economic and Social Council.

Mira Katzburg-Yungman is in charge of developing and teaching distance education courses on American Jewry at the Open University of Israel. Her forthcoming book *American Women Zionists: Hadassah in Historical Perspective* will be published in 2005 by the Littman Library of Jewish Civilization. She is the author of several articles on American and English Zionism, as well as editor of *American Jewry, 1914–1950*, a three-volume bilingual anthology of historical documents and essays (forthcoming), and co-editor of *American Jewry, 1881–1914*, a source book on German and East European Jewish migration to the United States (forthcoming).

Carole S. Kessner teaches in the departments of Comparative Studies and English and in the programs in Judaic Studies and Women's Studies at the State University of New York at Stony Brook. She is the recipient of the Marie Syrkin Fellowship and her books include *The "Other" New York Jewish Intellectuals* (New York: New York University Press, 1994).

Judith Korim Hornstein (1908–1996) spent her youth in the *shtetl* of Dabeik, Lithuania, where she was raised in a traditional Jewish setting. In 1930, she immigrated to the United States and found work as a shoe stitcher in Chelsea, Massachusetts. She earned a high school diploma and eventually studied accounting and business management at the Harvard Extension School. In Chelsea, she became active in the Labor Zionist movement and was later selected as a delegate to the Twentieth Zionist Congress (1937). With other delegates, including Golda Meir (see below), she continued on to Palestine, where she met and married Jacob Hornstein, formerly of Rohatyn, Poland. The Hornsteins returned to Chelsea in 1939, where Judith worked as a storekeeper, a dealer of surplus merchandise, and for fifty years co-owned and managed a real estate business. She helped to establish the Horn-Berger Fund for Judaic Studies at Boston University and the Judith and Jack Hornstein Scholarship Fund at the West End House in Allston, Massachusetts.

Nelly Las is a researcher at the Hebrew University of Jerusalem. Her latest book is *Jewish Women in a Changing World: A History of the International Council of Jewish Women, 1899–1995* (Jerusalem: Harman Institute of Contemporary Jewry, Hebrew University of Jerusalem, 1996) (originally published in French by L'Harmattan, Paris, 1996). She is now working on the topic of poverty and social deviance in the Jewish world at the beginning of the twentieth century. Her publications include articles and studies on French Jewry and the Zionist movement.

Emma Lazarus (1849–1887), an American Jewish poet and proto-Zionist advocate, is best known for her sonnet titled "The New Colossus," which is engraved at the base of the Statue of Liberty: "Give me your tired, your poor, your huddled masses yearning to breathe free. . . ." Lazarus was deeply involved in relief and rehabilitation efforts and took a special interest in the plight of East European Jewish immigrants. Much of her writing anticipates the development of American Zionism.

Irma (Rama) Lindheim (1886–1978), an affluent American Jewish fund-raiser and educator of German ancestry, succeeded Henrietta Szold as president of Hadassah in 1926. In 1933 she immigrated to Palestine at the age of forty-seven and joined Kibbutz Mishmar Haemek, where she remained (aside from frequent trips to the United States) to conduct Zionist political activity. Throughout her adult life, Lindheim sustained an activist agenda that dovetailed with both Hadassah and the Labor Zionist movement.

Mary McCune is a Visiting Assistant Professor of History and Women's Studies at the State University of New York at Oswego. Her article "Creating a Place for Women in a Socialist Brotherhood: Class and Gender Politics in the Workmen's Circle, 1892–1930" will appear in a future issue of *Feminist Studies*. She is currently completing a book manuscript tentatively titled "'Charity Work' as Nation-Building: American Jewish Women and the Crises in Europe and Palestine, 1914–1930." She is also active in the Oswego Women's Studies community, participating in a Learning Community and helping students to organize informational panels and a support group for nontraditional students.

Golda (Meyerson) Meir (1898–1978) moved to Milwaukee in 1906 from Russia. In 1915, she joined the Poalei Zion party in the United States, and in 1921 she immigrated to Palestine with her husband, Morris Meyerson. They joined Kibbutz Merhaviyah but soon left due to her husband's ill health. Meir rose through the ranks of the Histadrut, becoming secretary of Moezet Hapoalot in 1928 and a member of the Executive Committee in 1934. She also helped found Mapai (Mifleget Poalei Erez Israel) in 1930, where she swiftly gained respect for her loyalty and ability. Her political role continued to grow in the years leading up to independence. In 1946 she became head of the Jewish Agency's Political Department and negotiated with the British regime and King Abdullah of Jordan to try to convince the latter not to participate in the imminent war. During the War of Independence, Meir went to the United States, where she raised fifty million dollars for the effort, and, after the war, she was appointed Israel's first minister to Moscow. She subsequently entered the Knesset and was selected as David Ben-Gurion's minister of labor and housing. Next, she served ten years as Israel's foreign minister and finally became prime minister in 1969. She resigned in 1974 in the midst of the humiliation brought on by the nearly calamitous Yom Kippur War even though the investigating commission lauded her handling of the conflict. In 1975 she wrote her autobiography, *My Life*.

Yocheved Herschlag Muffs was a member of Hashomer Hadati, the religious Zionist pioneer youth movement in the United States, when she quit college in 1947 and obtained a temporary visa to go to Palestine under the false pretense of traveling to a teachers' conference at the Hebrew University of Jerusalem. Upon her arrival in Palestine, she joined a settlement group at Kibbutz Ein Hanaziv in the Beit Shean Valley. In 1949 she returned to the United States and resumed her college studies, eventually completing her graduate work at New York University. From 1949 to 1959 she worked for the Young Judaea youth group, including five years as national program director. She next worked for the United Synagogue Commission on Jewish Education from 1959 to 1963 and then with the

Anti-Defamation League from 1963 to 1992, where she edited periodicals and books and produced numerous educational materials. She is married to Yochanan Muffs and lives in New York and Jerusalem.

Zipporah Porath is a freelance writer, editor publications consultant, and lecturer who has been living in Israel since the establishment of the state. She is the author of *Letters from Jerusalem 1947–1947* (Jerusalem: Association of Americans and Canadians in Israel, 1987). The AVI CHAI Birthright Bookshelf featured her "On My Mind" piece, "Eyewitness to Israel's Birth," with a review of her book. Her articles and essays have appeared in the *Jerusalem Post, ESRA Magazine, Jewish Life & Family* web magazine, and *JewzNewz.com.* Israel's Ministry of Education recently published a booklet, *Mahal: Overseas Volunteers in Israel's War of Independence,* which she initiated and co-authored in Hebrew and English.

Mark A. Raider is Associate Professor of Modern Jewish History, Chair of the Judaic Studies Department, and Founding Director of the Center for Jewish Studies at the State University of New York at Albany. He is the author of *The Emergence of American Zionism* (New York: New York University Press, 1998) and coeditor of *Abba Hillel Silver and American Zionism* (London: Frank Cass, 1997), with Jonathan D. Sarna and Ronald Zweig, and *The Plough Woman: Records of the Pioneer Women of Palestine. A Critical Edition* (Hanover, N.H., and London: University Press of New England, 2002), with Miriam B. Raider-Roth. He is editor of a new anthology titled *Nahum Goldmann: Statesman without a State,* to be published in 2005.

Shulamit Reinharz is the Jacob Potofsky Professor of Sociology at Brandeis University, the Founding Director of the Women's Studies Research Center (2001) and of The Hadassah-Brandeis Institute (1997). She is the Chief Editor of the Brandeis Series on Jewish Women. Her most recent article is a discussion of the special properties involved in interviewing women and her most recent publication is a study of the ways in which women celebrate Purim in one hundred countries today. Her next project concerns revolutionizing the concept of *bat mizvah.*

Peri Rosenfeld is Senior Research Associate at the New York Academy of Medicine in New York, New York. Her latest article, "From the Lower East Side to the Upper Galilee: The Pioneering Experiences of Sara Paltiel, 1932–1993," was published by *Nursing History Review,* and she is now working on an article on nursing contributions to immigrant and refugee health in Israel during the 1950s. She is also conducting research on the evolution of the Acute Care Nurse Practitioner workforce in America.

Anita Shapira is the Ruben Merenfeld Professor for the Study of Zionism at Tel Aviv University. Her recent publications include *Land and Power: The Zionist Resort to Force, 1881–1948* (Stanford, Calif.: Stanford University Press, 1999) and *"Hirbet Hizah:* Between Remembrance and Forgetting," *Jewish Social Studies* (Fall 2000). She is now working on issues related to Israeli Jewish identity.

Baila Round Shargel is an Adjunct Assistant Professor at Purchase College, State University of New York. Her latest book is *Lost Love: The Untold Story of Henrietta Szold; Unpublished Diary and Letters* (Philadelphia: Jewish Publication Society of America, 1997). She has just completed a new book titled "Love,

Death, and Renunciation: The Last Days of Israel Friedlaender" and is currently working on an extensive study of the life and work of Bessie Gotsfeld.

Lois Slott lived in Israel from 1950–1962. A member of Hadassah since 1955, she has also served as a member of Hadassah's National Board since 1978. Two of her children are members of Kibbutz Ketura in the southern Negev.

Marie Syrkin (1899–1989), an American Zionist polemicist and scholar of literature, was the daughter of Nahman Syrkin (1868–1924), a preeminent Russian Jewish theoretician of socialist Zionism. She played an active and central role in the Labor Zionist movement in the United States. Many of her most important essays appeared in *Jewish Frontier,* of which she was an editor for many years. She also served on the editorial board of *Midstream* and was editor of the Herzl Press. Her books include *Your School, Your Children* (1944), *Blessed Is the Match* (1947), *Nachman Syrkin: Socialist Zionist* (1961), and *Hayim Greenberg Anthology* (1968).

Arthur Zeiger (1916–2002) was a Professor of English Literature at the City College of New York. He earned his Ph.D. from New York University.

Index

Page numbers in italics represent illustrations.